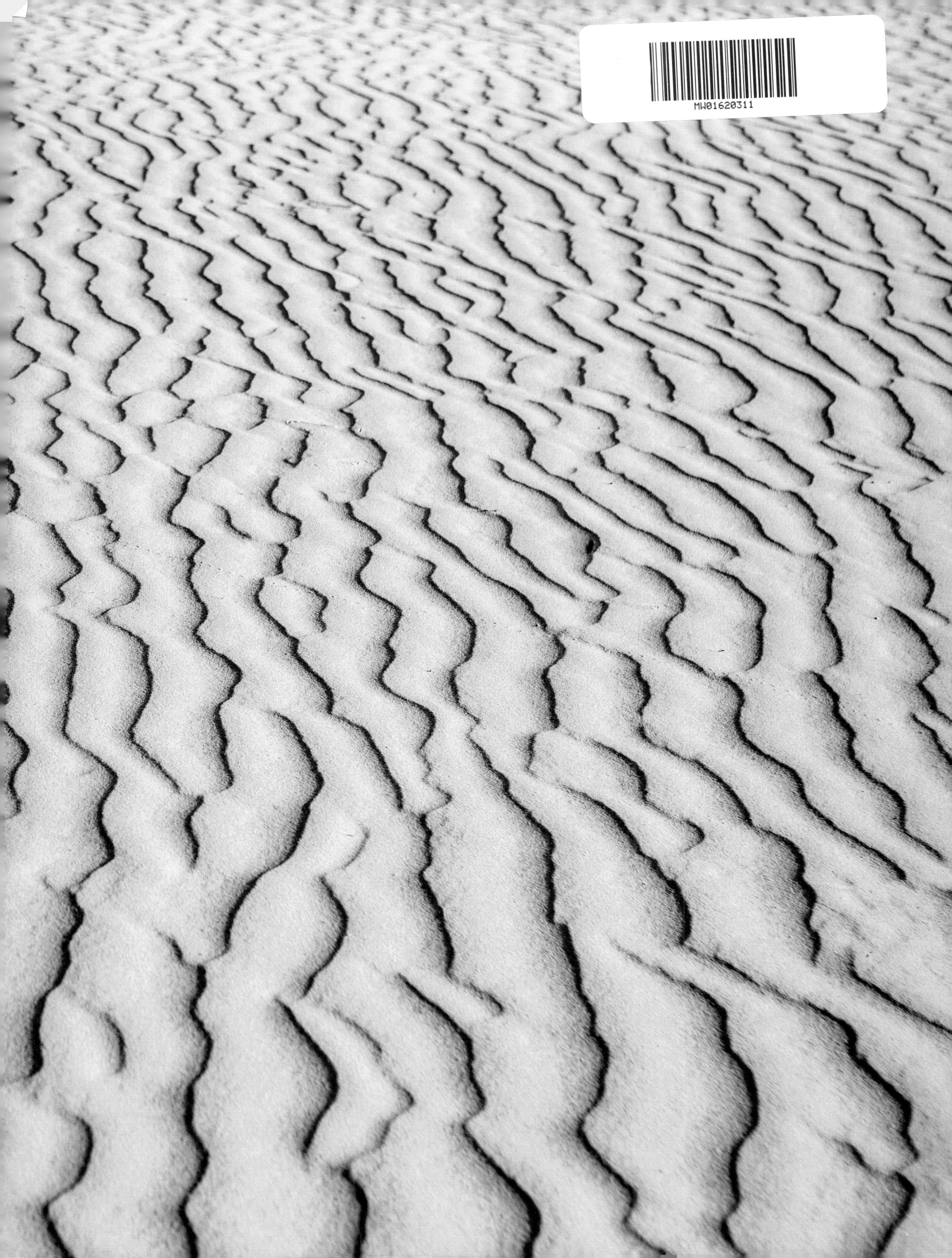
MW01620311

AS FAR AS YOU CAN SEE

Dear Dean Field,
Your vision has inspired us this year,
and a book of beautiful Texas photography
therefore seemed appropriate.
With great appreciation and
affection for you,
Kelly and
Claire

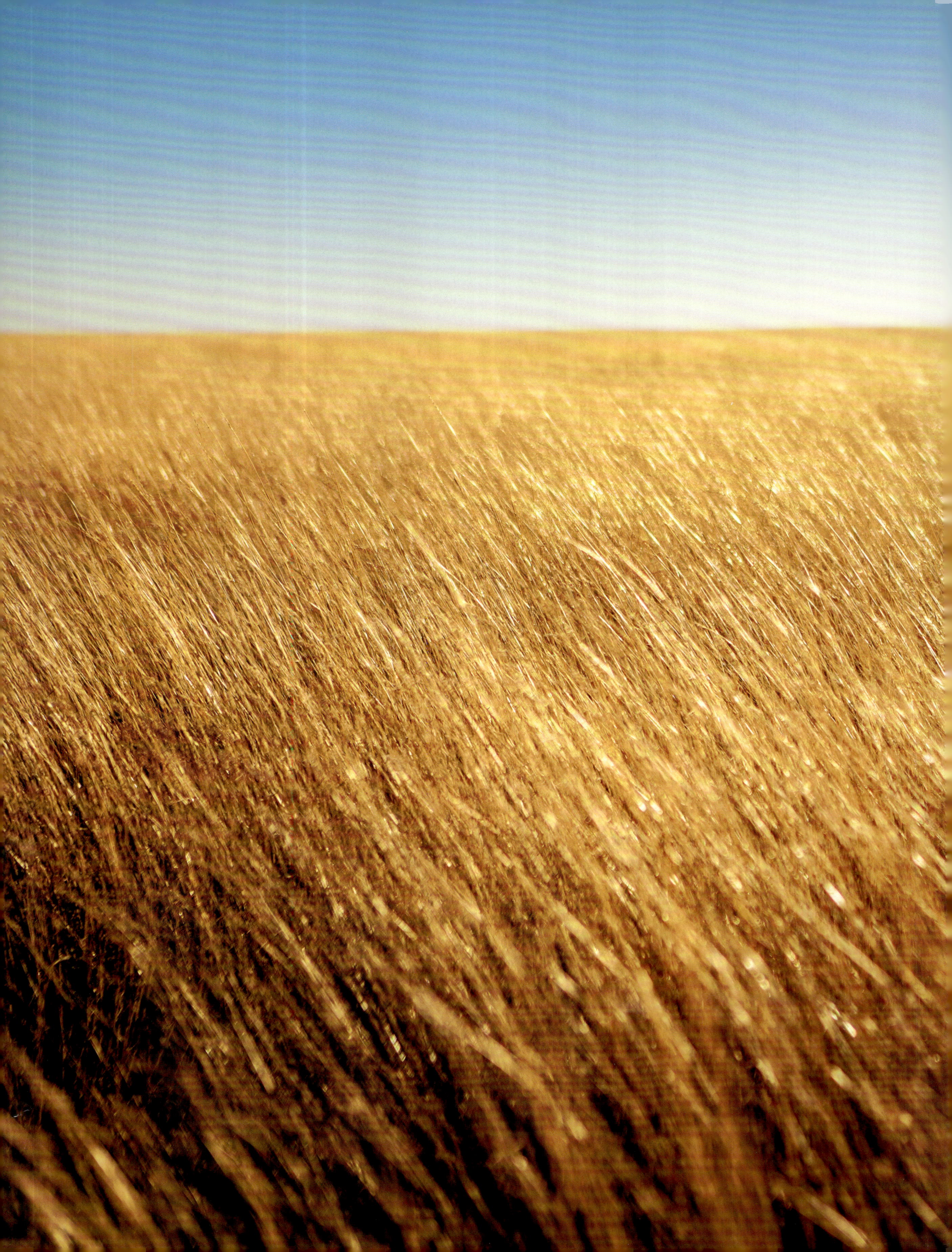

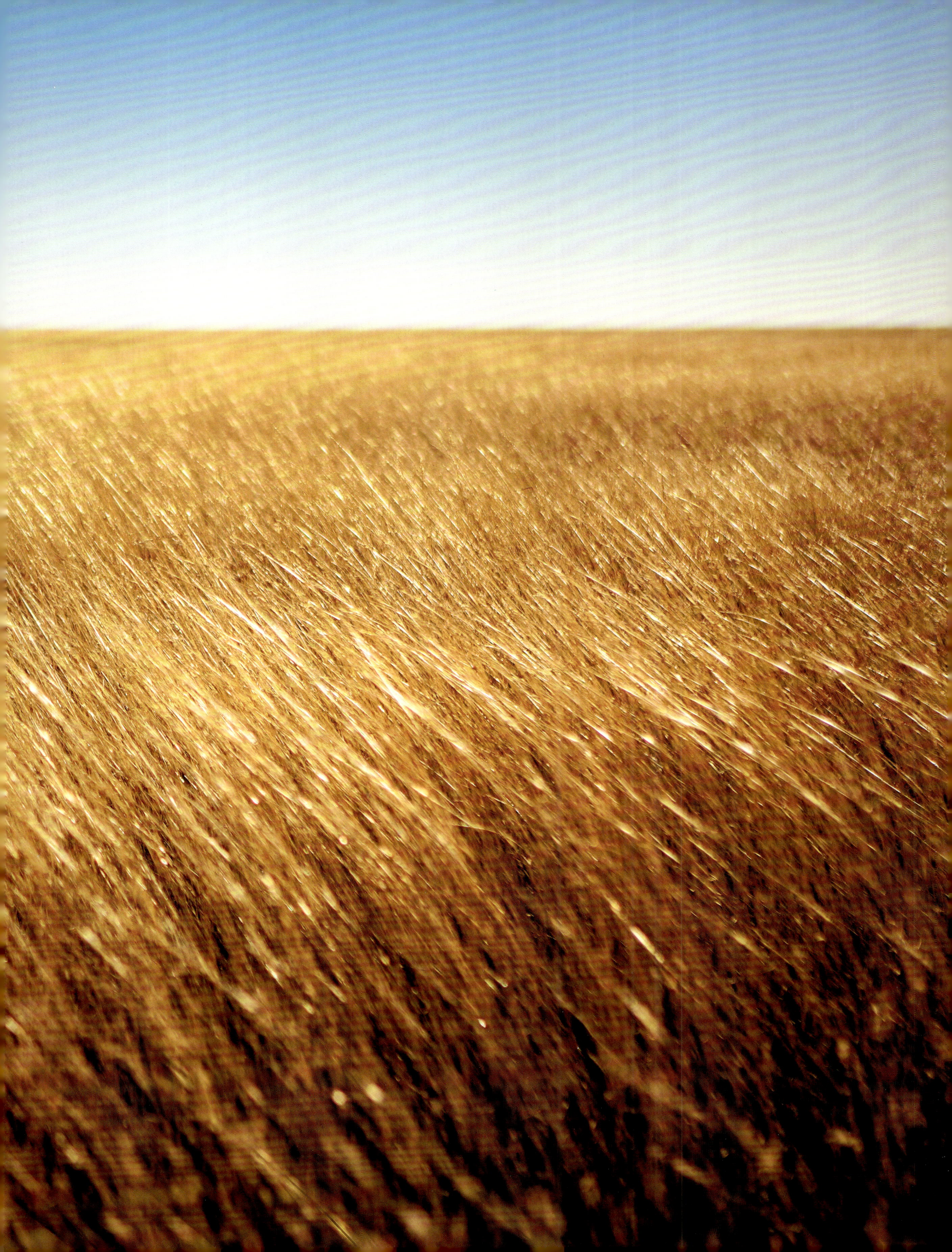

BILL and ALICE WRIGHT PHOTOGRAPHY SERIES

AS FA

YOU CA

RAS
AN SEE

PHOTOGRAPHS by
KENNY BRAUN

FOREWORD
by S. C. GWYNNE

UNIVERSITY of
TEXAS PRESS
AUSTIN

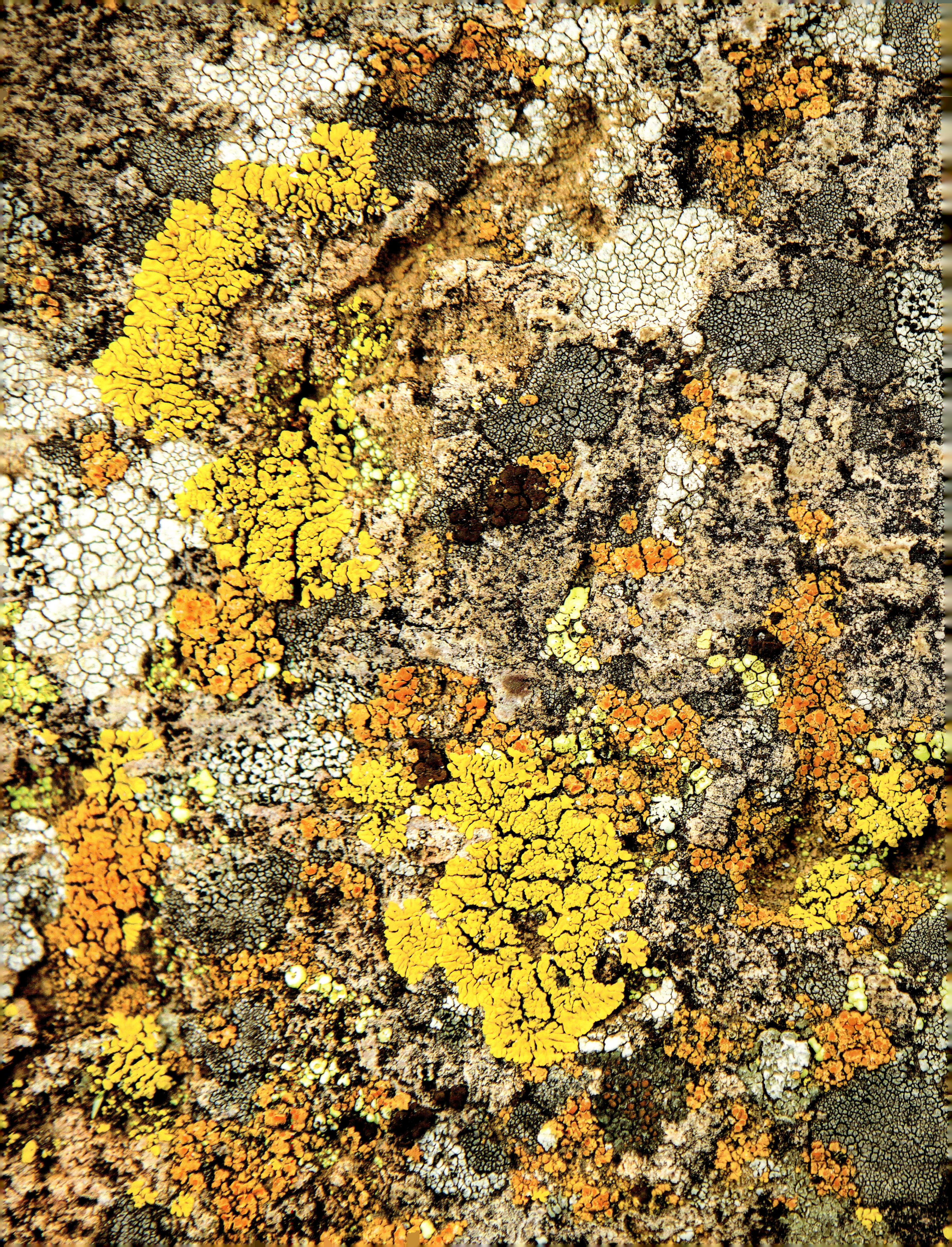

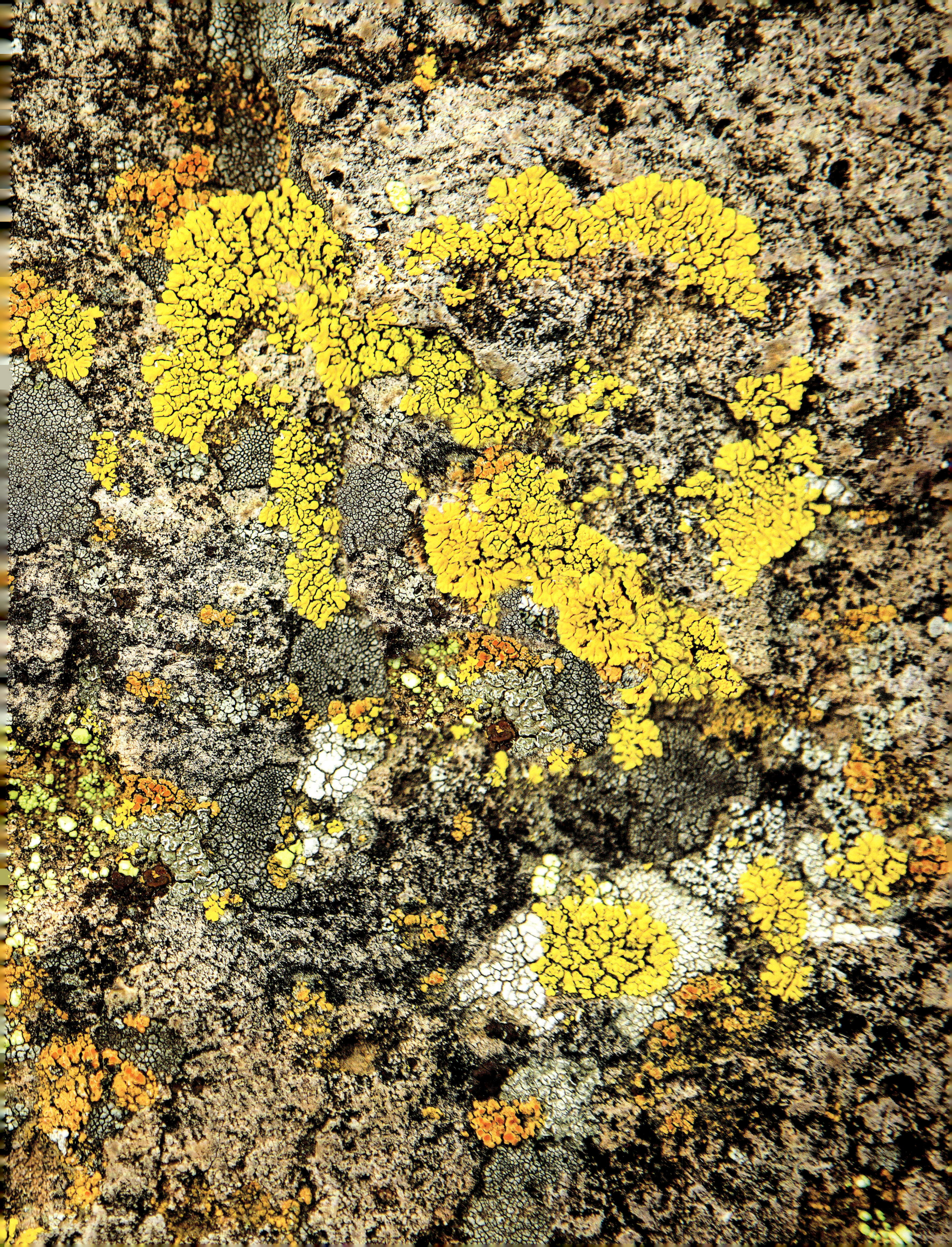

Publication of this work was made possible in part by support from Bill and Alice Wright and a challenge grant from the National Endowment for the Humanities.

Printed in China by Four Colour Print Group, Louisville, Kentucky
First edition, 2018

♾ The paper used in this book meets the minimum requirements of ANSI/NISO Z39.48-1992 (R1997) (Permanence of Paper).

Library of Congress Cataloging-in-Publication Data

Names: Braun, Kenny, 1959–, author, photographer. | Gwynne, S. C. (Samuel C.), 1953–, writer of supplementary textual content.
Title: As far as you can see : picturing Texas / Kenny Braun ; foreword by S. C. Gwynne.
Description: First edition. | Austin : University of Texas Press, 2018.
Identifiers: LCCN 2017043087 | ISBN 978-1-4773-1547-7
Subjects: LCSH: Texas—Pictorial works. | Landscapes—Texas—Pictorial works. | Landscape photography—Texas.
Classification: LCC F387 .B745 2018 | DDC 976.40022/2—dc23
LC record available at https://lccn.loc.gov/2017043087

doi:10.7560/315477

FOR ESTHER AND MC BRAUN, MY PARENTS, WHO PROVIDED THE NATURE AND NURTURE THAT ALLOWED ME TO FIND MY PLACE IN THIS WORLD. I WOULD ALSO LIKE TO THANK MY BEAUTIFUL, CARING, SUPPORTIVE, FUN, ROAD-TRIPPING, AND NATURE-LOVING FAMILY: LORI, CAROLINE, AND JULIET.

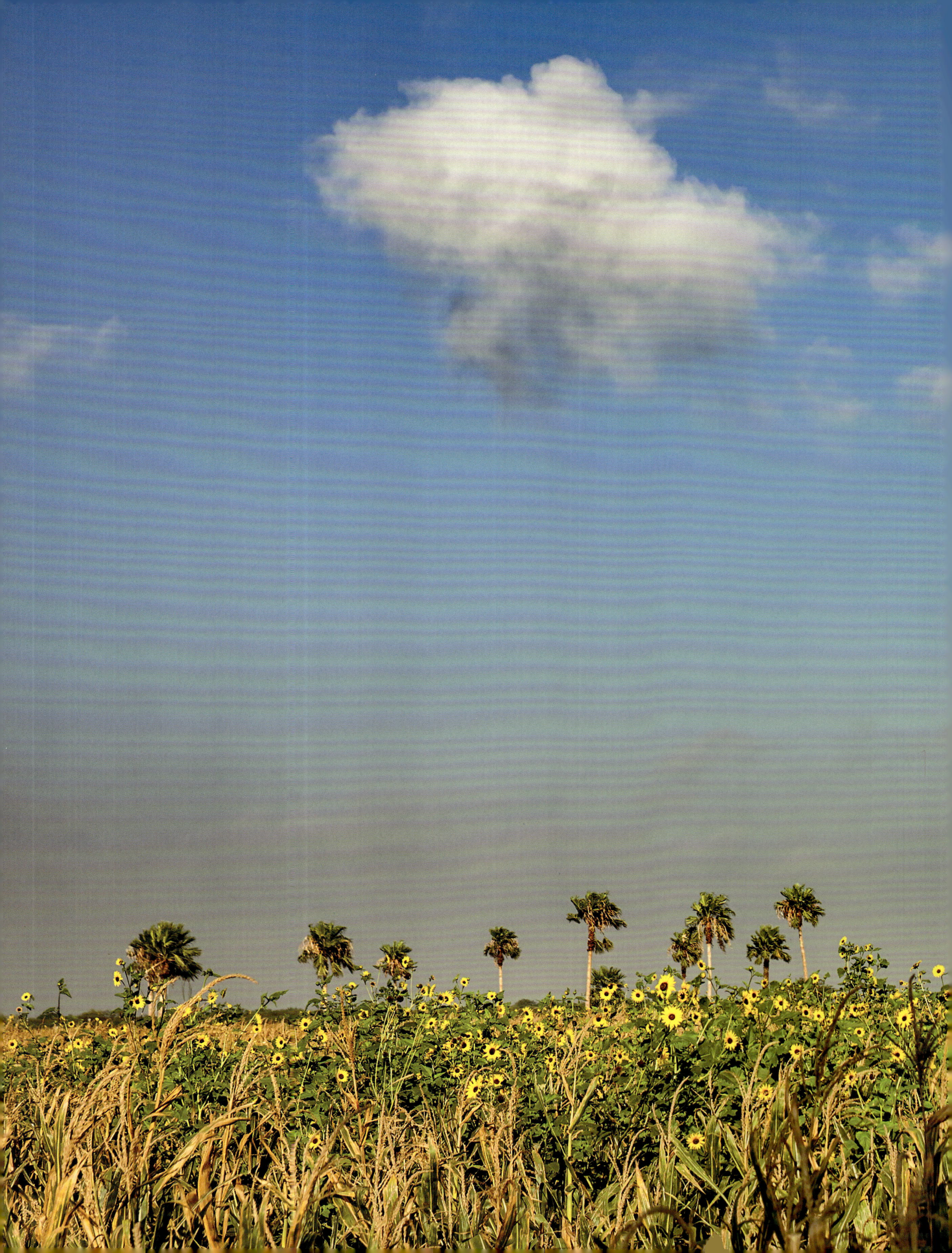

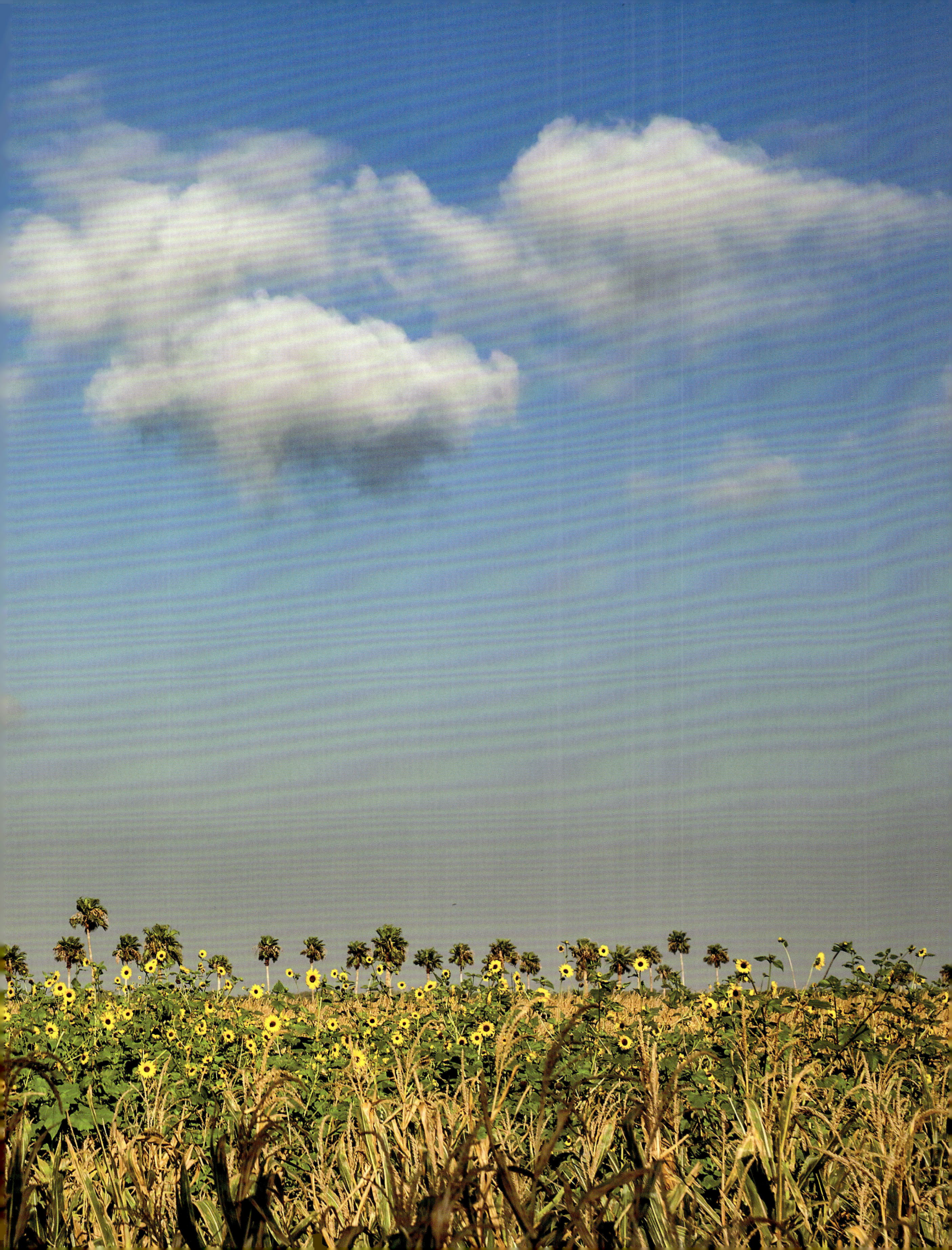

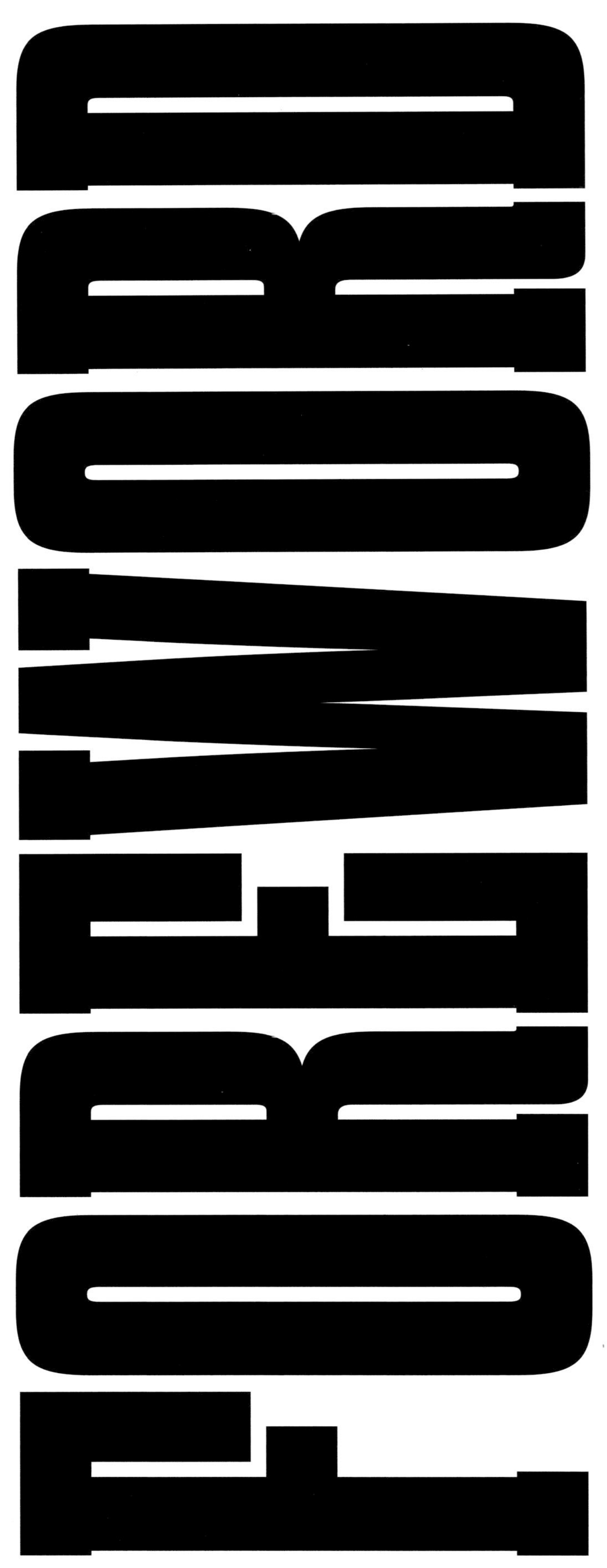

FOREWORD

By **S. C. GWYNNE**

I have spent most of my working life as a magazine writer. Most of that time has been spent at *Texas Monthly* and *Time* magazine, where I have had the privilege of working with some of the country's best photographers. Shooters do not always go out on assignment with writers. In fact, it's pretty rare. Usually the reporter labors in the field for a few weeks or months, then the photog shows up separately, *ex post facto*, to make sense of it. But when the two work together simultaneously, the results are often remarkable. It's a sort of forced collaboration between two different professions with different objectives: one inhabits a tangled universe of words and ideas; the other must deliver—on pain of death—brilliant, clear, singular, evocative images.

In the decade of the aughts I was lucky enough to be sent out on three different assignments with Kenny Braun, all for *Texas Monthly*. He is one of the very best photographers I have ever worked with, and the most gifted at being able to look at the world in front of him, strip it down to some elemental version of itself, and see the single, true photograph embedded in it.

To show you what I mean by that, I offer the following exhibit.

In October 2004, Kenny and I got one of those assignments that writers and photographers dream about: to run the Devils, one of the wildest and most remote rivers in Texas, and chronicle it. Kenny was known as one of the best nature photographers in the state; I was known for nothing that had anything to do with nature.

And so off we went, into the great beyond of West Texas. To give you an idea of what the Devils River was like, I described it in my *Texas Monthly* story as

> an irascible, unforgiving, and quite primitive river that runs through a stretch of raw West Texas outback where few human beings choose to live. It has some of the most violent and sudden flash floods in North America. Its rough limestone will shred your sneakers. Its grooved and rutted rock ledges and boulder gardens will sprain your ankles and break your shins. Its rapids will bend your canoe like a hairpin. You will get lost down its dark, Alice in Wonderland–like chutes of black, rushing water that disappear into canebrake and willow thickets.

You get the idea. There were no maps to tell us where the rapids, waterfalls, low-head dams, dead-end canebrakes, or other hazards were, and the few written accounts were so sketchy as to be mostly useless as guides.

Neither of us had paddled a canoe in white water before. But there we were, in pretty big Class 3 rapids—and one Class 4—in a beaten-up, patched-over, grotesquely overloaded fifteen-foot relic that looked like it had been salvaged from a junk heap and packed by inland, desert-dwelling people who did not understand the concept of a boat. That was not our only problem: the river was swollen and roaring, far above its normal levels. It was a sort of aquatic version of Mr. Toad's Wild Ride. Neither of us will ever forget it.

Throughout the trip, Kenny worked the river hard: snapping away, trying to get that angle of light or ripple of water. I would characterize his approach to taking pictures as sheer doggedness. He persists, and persists, and then persists some more, into tangles of brush, looming rock cliffs, rushing water, and oncoming darkness. This appeared to be a two-step process: 1) he saw things that I did not see, and 2) he would return again and again to the things I did not see, in order to see them better. The result—the photos he delivered to *Texas Monthly*—was a stunning catalogue of our river trip. But it was more than that. His imagery went beyond a graphic record of what happened to the actual *idea* of what happened.

Thus, I offer my exhibit: pages 46–47 of this book, on which you will find two photos of the Devils that convey with uncanny precision the sense of beauty, mystery, anxiety, danger, and exhilaration we felt. The first shot, taken on the first morning of our trip as we pushed off into the unmapped river, shows moody currents of black water, swirling and disappearing into mist. What it conveys is: pretty river, yes, but mostly threat. As we paddled into that mist, we were listening hard for the sounds of approaching waterfalls and rapids. You can feel that tension. The second shot shows the danger itself: Dolan Falls, Texas's largest falls, which we actually found ourselves sliding into and managed a hasty escape from. The latter has been shot many times, but never in a way that showed such lethal, swirling power. Kenny's magnificent take is a treasure all by itself, a way of looking at the falls' massive hydraulics and sculptural formations that I have never seen before.

Though I have spent a lot of time on assignment with Kenny, I can't say I have any idea of how he does it. Or how he can take a smashed-up, massively duct-taped $18 camera and point it at something absurdly ordinary and make a brilliant piece of art. I am referring to his Holga—essentially a toy camera, just a box with a couple of light holes in it, that Kenny uses sometimes. The Holga was my first clue that Kenny was all about simply seeing something, rather than elaborate technology or post-production. He showed me photos he had made from coastal Texas with this primitive equipment that were simply astounding. They gave an entirely new meaning to the idea of "point and shoot."

The second clue was a basket of peaches he had shot for *Texas Monthly*. Nothing more, nothing less. Just peaches. Yet the shot was transcendent. It glowed with a sort of internal light; these were Platonic peaches, ultimate peaches, divine peaches. I had assumed that you could not possibly get that shot without lights and light diffusers or special lenses or fairy dust or something extrinsic to the film itself. Nope. Kenny just saw it that way. He understood it, and once he understood it, he was able to record the image.

I can see that same mind and talent operating throughout this book, this ambitious attempt to decode Texas. I say "decode," because what he has done here is take places that are familiar to most Texans—I have been to many of these places, and love many of them—and show them in a new way, with new components that we did not notice before. Call it the unfamiliarity of familiar places. Kenny is a master at this. There are too many examples to list here, but I offer a few: *Jacob's Well* (pages 106–107), where I have been half a dozen times but never saw as I see it now in Kenny's aqueous, hyper-blue reduction. Or the timeless, archetypal feel of *Deer Crossing* (pages 94–95), shot on the Blanco River, which I have run in a kayak many times but never beheld in such an elemental light. Or the coastal stuff, which is just dazzling. Kenny's coastal stuff is always dazzling. You'll never look at Port A or Matagorda Bay the same way again.

In his novel of Texas, *The Gay Place*, Billy Lee Brammer famously wrote that "the country is most barbarously large and final." And indeed it is. Few artists and writers and photographers are big enough to embrace it. This book is proof that Kenny Braun is one who does, which is great news for the rest of us.

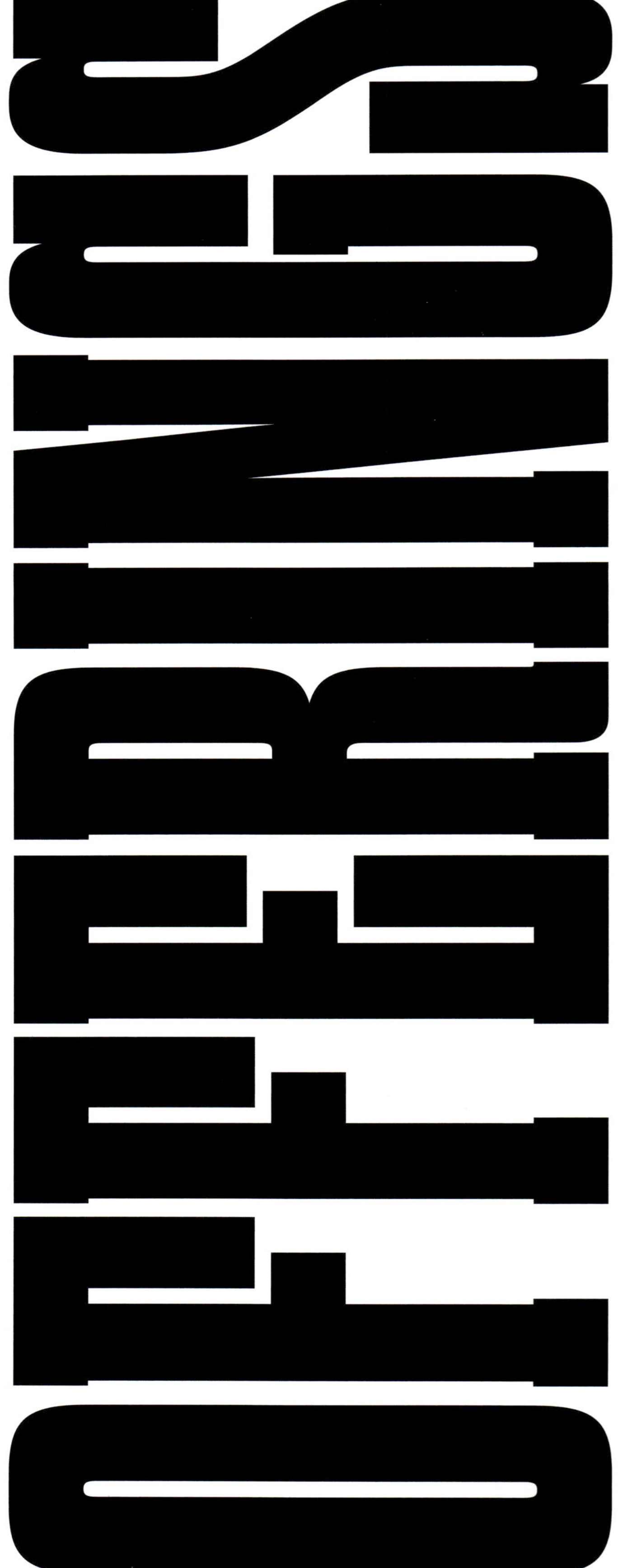

By **KENNY BRAUN**

I grew up in Houston, Texas, during the sixties and seventies. My parents grew up on small farms near small towns in south central Texas. Both farms were about an hour-and-a-half's drive from Houston, and we would visit them often. I remember playing in the dirt with my Tonka trucks; I loved to be outdoors as much as possible. When I got older, I hunted and fished with my family and friends. We would wake up early in the morning, pack sandwiches and drinks, and stay out all day, following creeks and roaming the woods. It was a wonderful feeling of freedom and adventure: we were out on our own with no real agenda, and we never knew what we would stumble upon.

I lost interest in hunting with guns around the same time I got my first 35mm camera, in high school. Looking back, I now realize that photography and hunting are very similar. You carry a highly specialized piece of precision equipment that takes skill to operate. You become hyperaware of your surroundings as you hunt for worthy subjects. The adrenaline kicks in as you zero in to make the shot. If you are successful and your quarry is worthy, you bring it home, mount it, and proudly hang it on the wall.

After spending so much of my youth outdoors, I was innately drawn to nature as subject matter when I started to take photography more seriously. When I was in high school, my best friend and I would go out and see who could make the best picture of a log, for example. We started bringing our cameras on campouts and surf safaris. We would shoot slides and later host slide shows for our friends, who would sit around and critique. "Oh, that one's great! Who shot that one? That one sucks!" And so on. It was friendly competition, and showing my work to others helped to build confidence, along with thicker skin.

I still feel that same rush of freedom and adventure that I felt as a kid, or as a teenager, when I set out to make a picture today. I'm never sure exactly what I'll find, but I know that if I keep an open mind and stay in the present, I'll discover something that works. Sometimes I'll have an idea of the kind of image I want before I set out, and every so often that's what I'll find. But other times it leads to something even better than I could have imagined. The thing that I have come to realize is that it's mostly out of my control. I know that I can make a good picture when I try. But my goal is to make a great picture. And as hard as I might try, it will only happen when the stars are aligned. That's why I've come to consider my best photos to be gifts. All I can really do is put myself out there and hope for an offering.

To me, it's not surprising that nature is among the most generous photographic subjects, and this book collects some of her greatest gifts to me. I am continually awed, and surprised, by the natural beauty of Texas. That's why I keep going out, hoping for a great photo. This book is about beautiful images, but it is also personal. It reflects my twenty-plus years in photography and a lifelong relationship with the natural wonders of Texas. It is my honor and privilege to share some of the gifts I have received along the way.

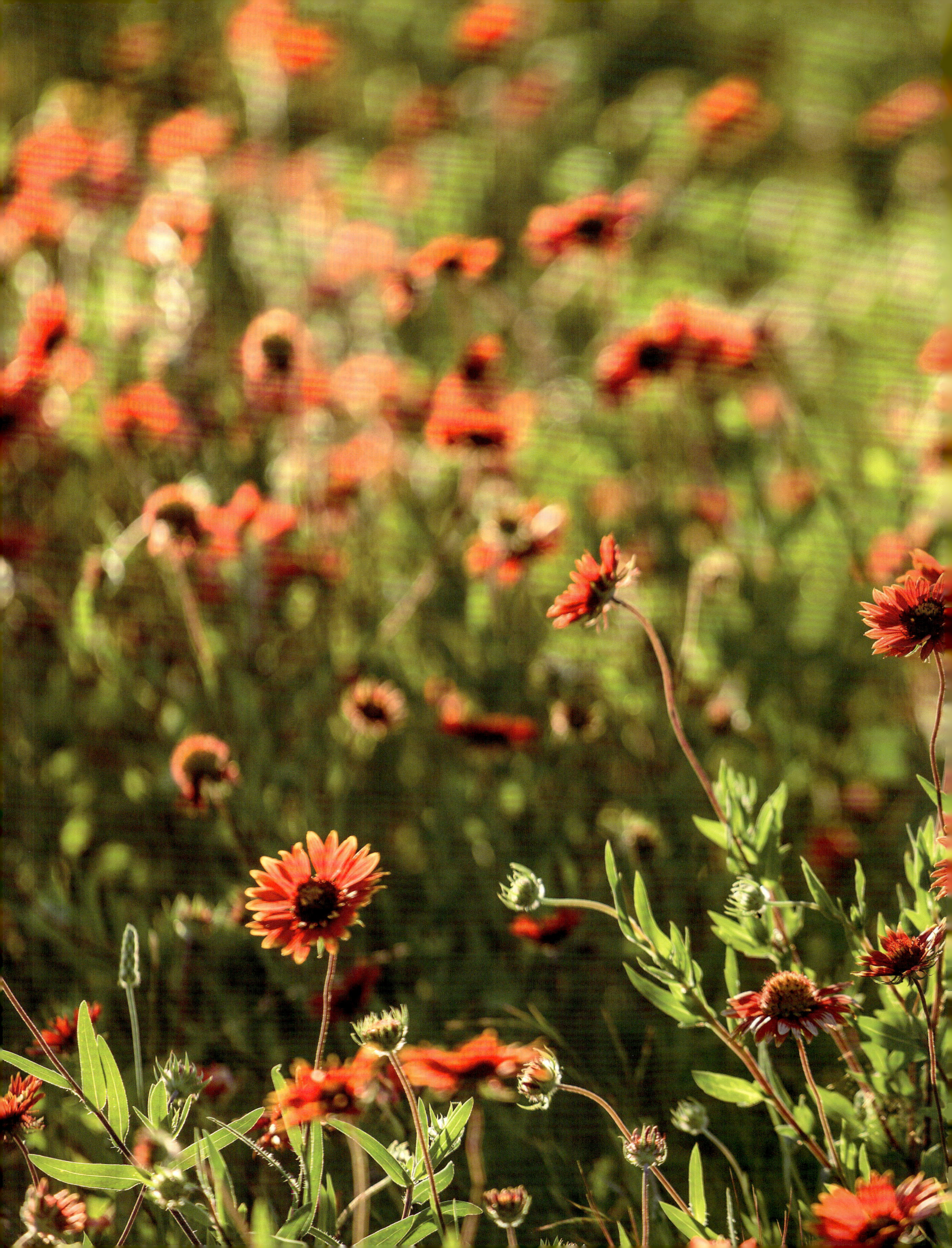

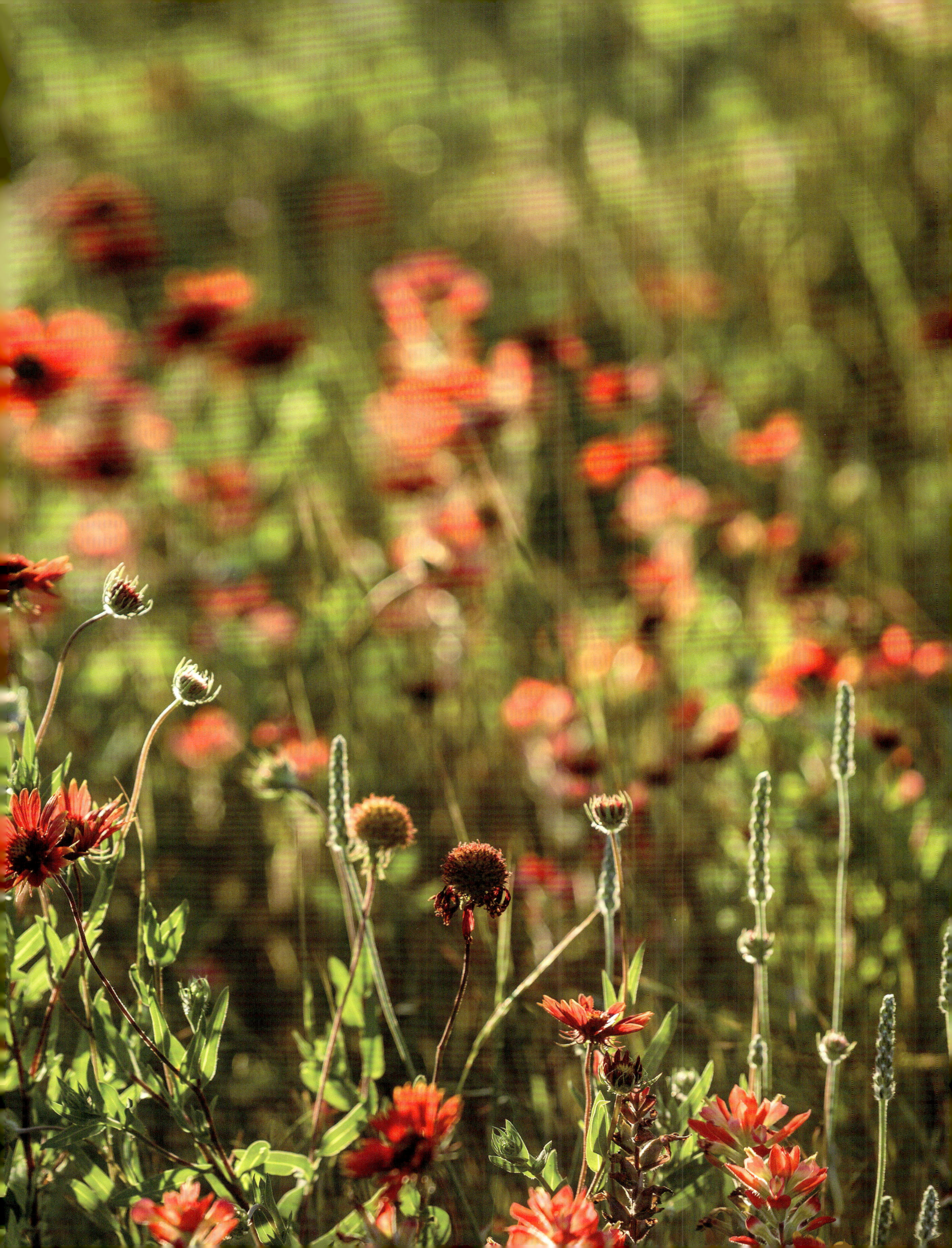

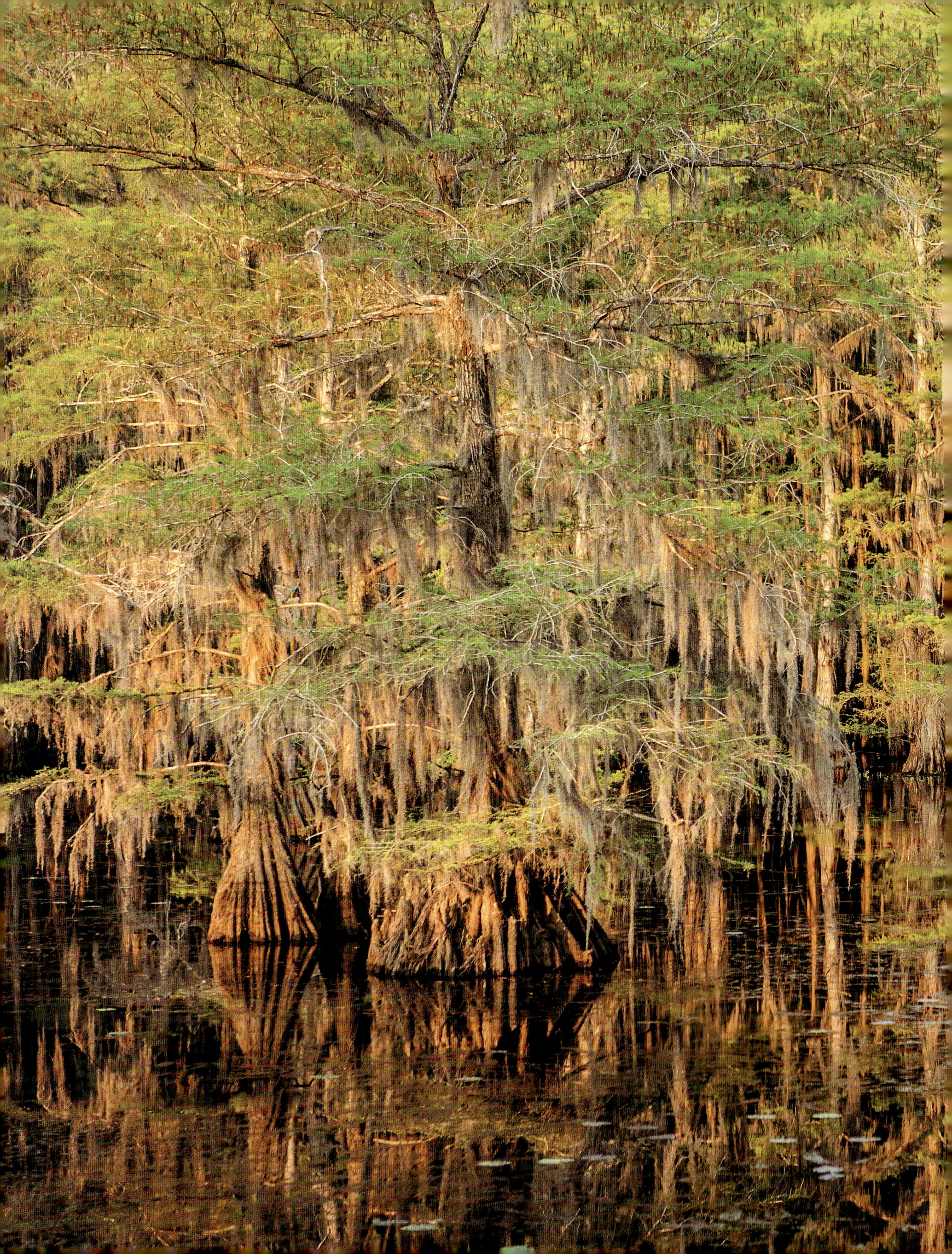

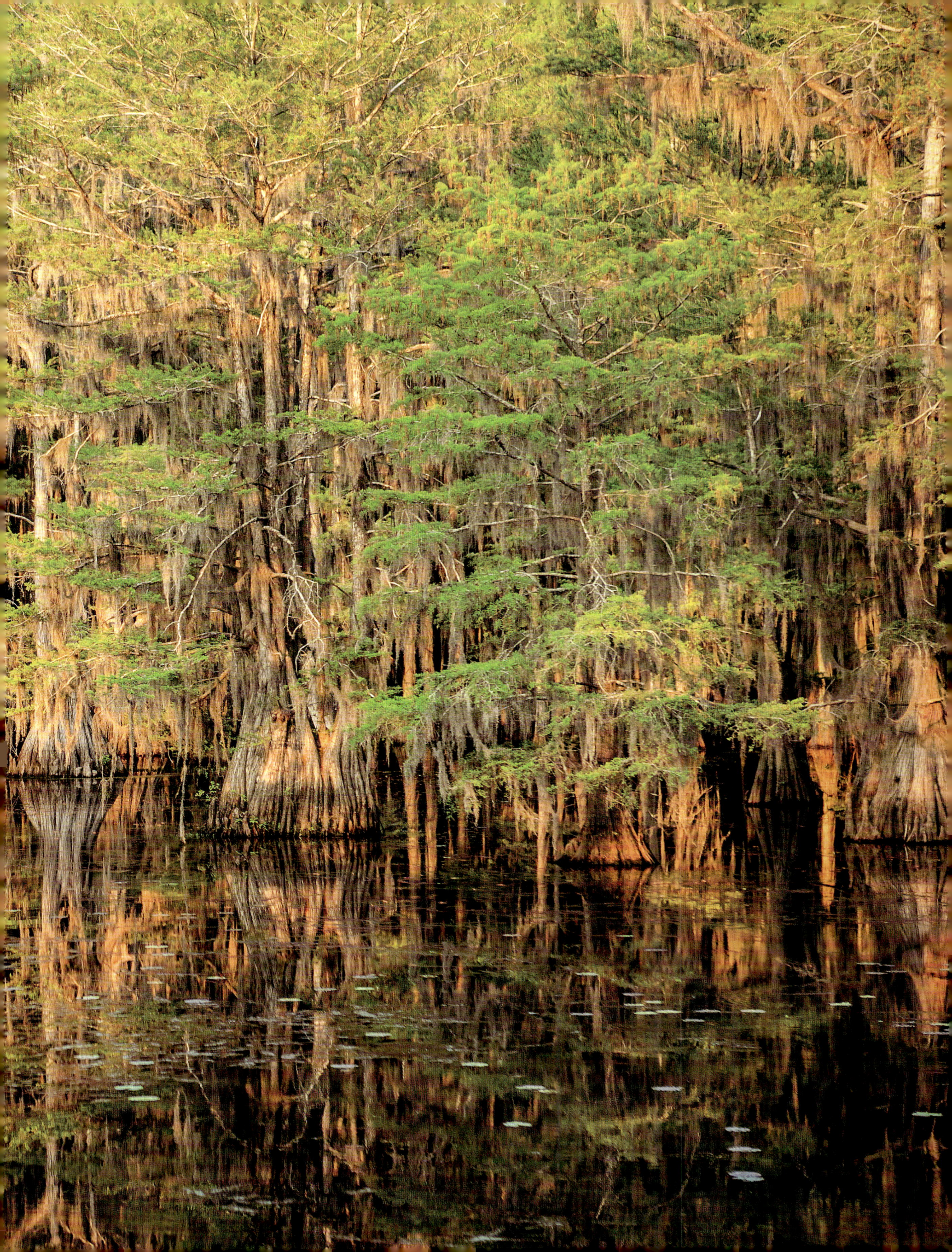

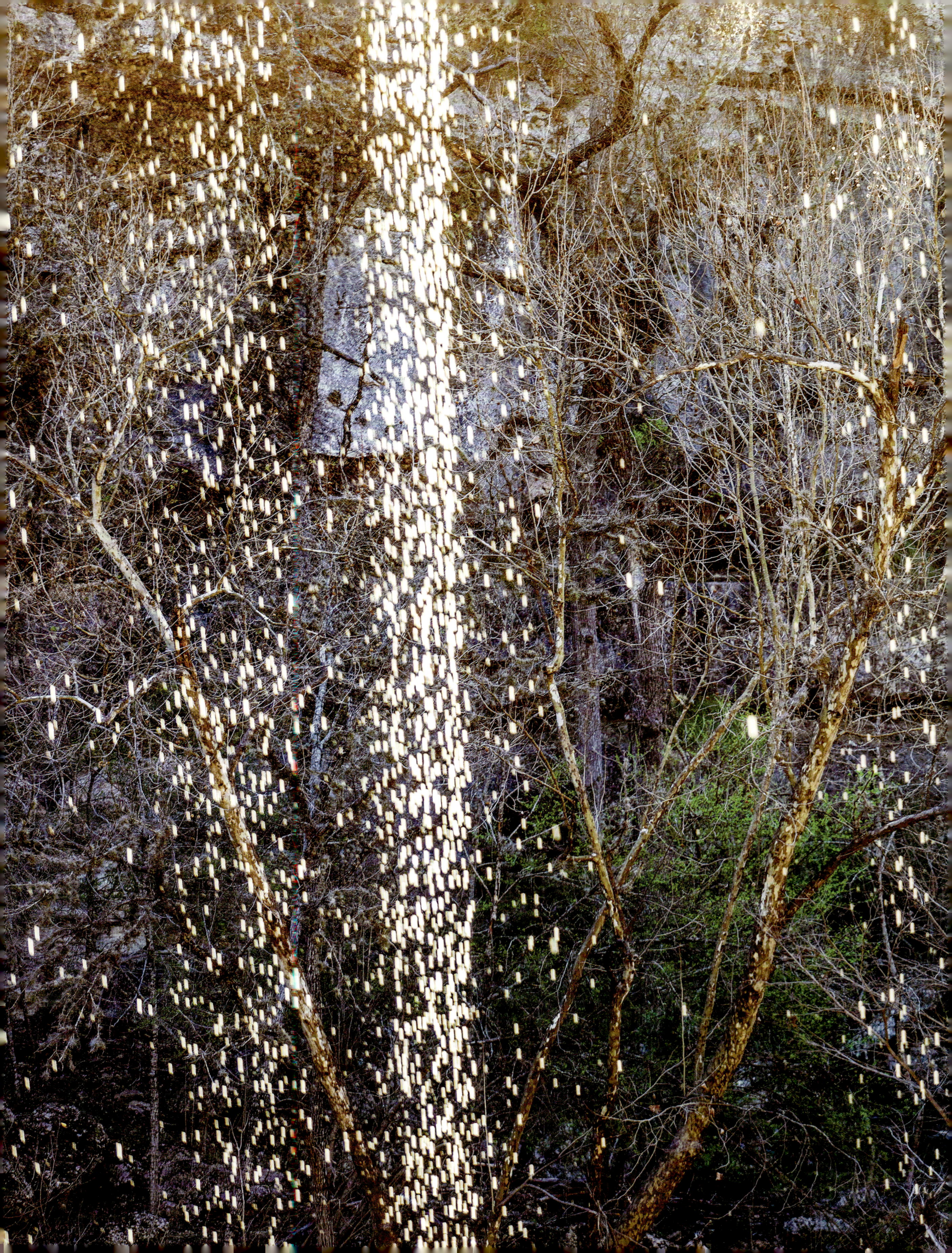

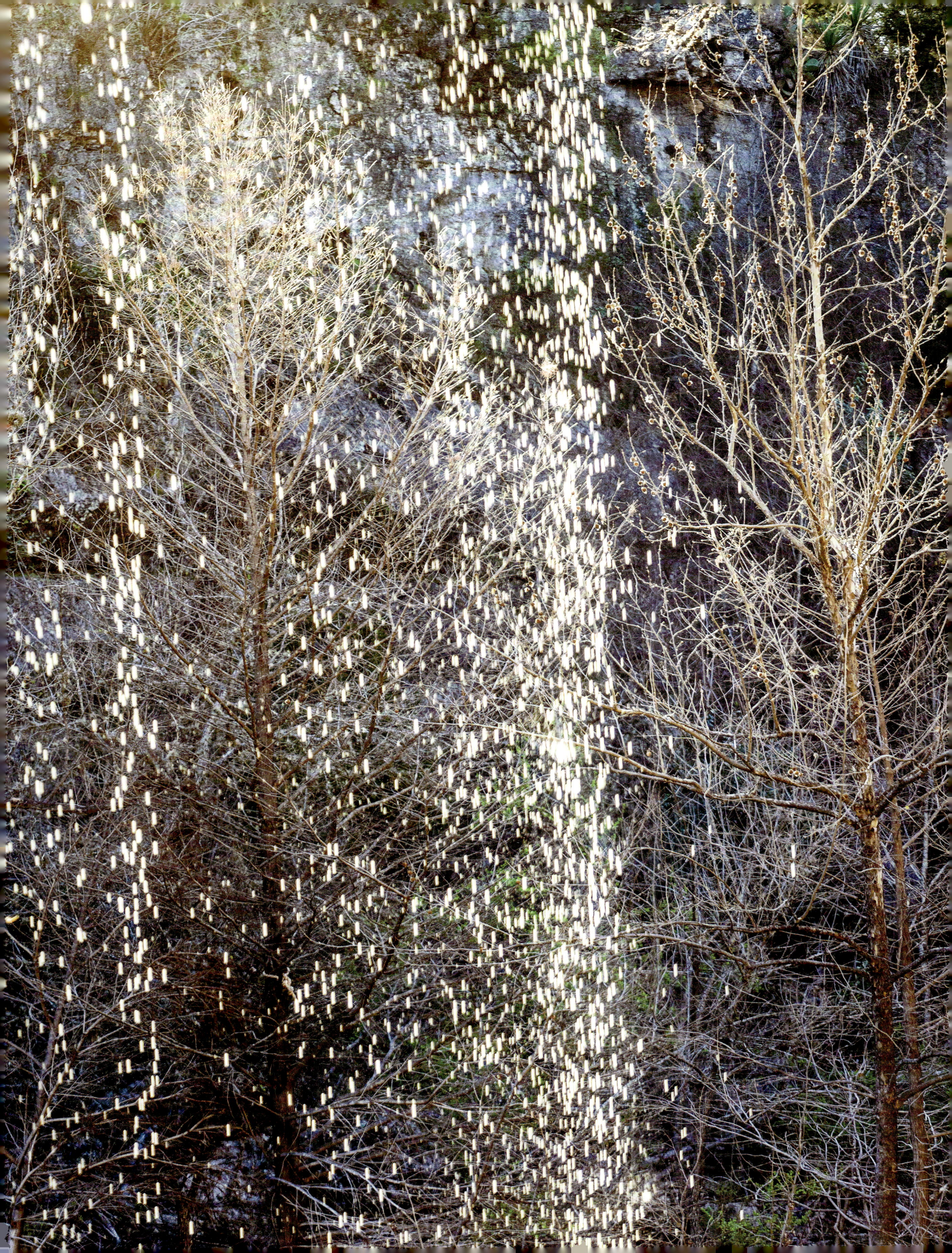

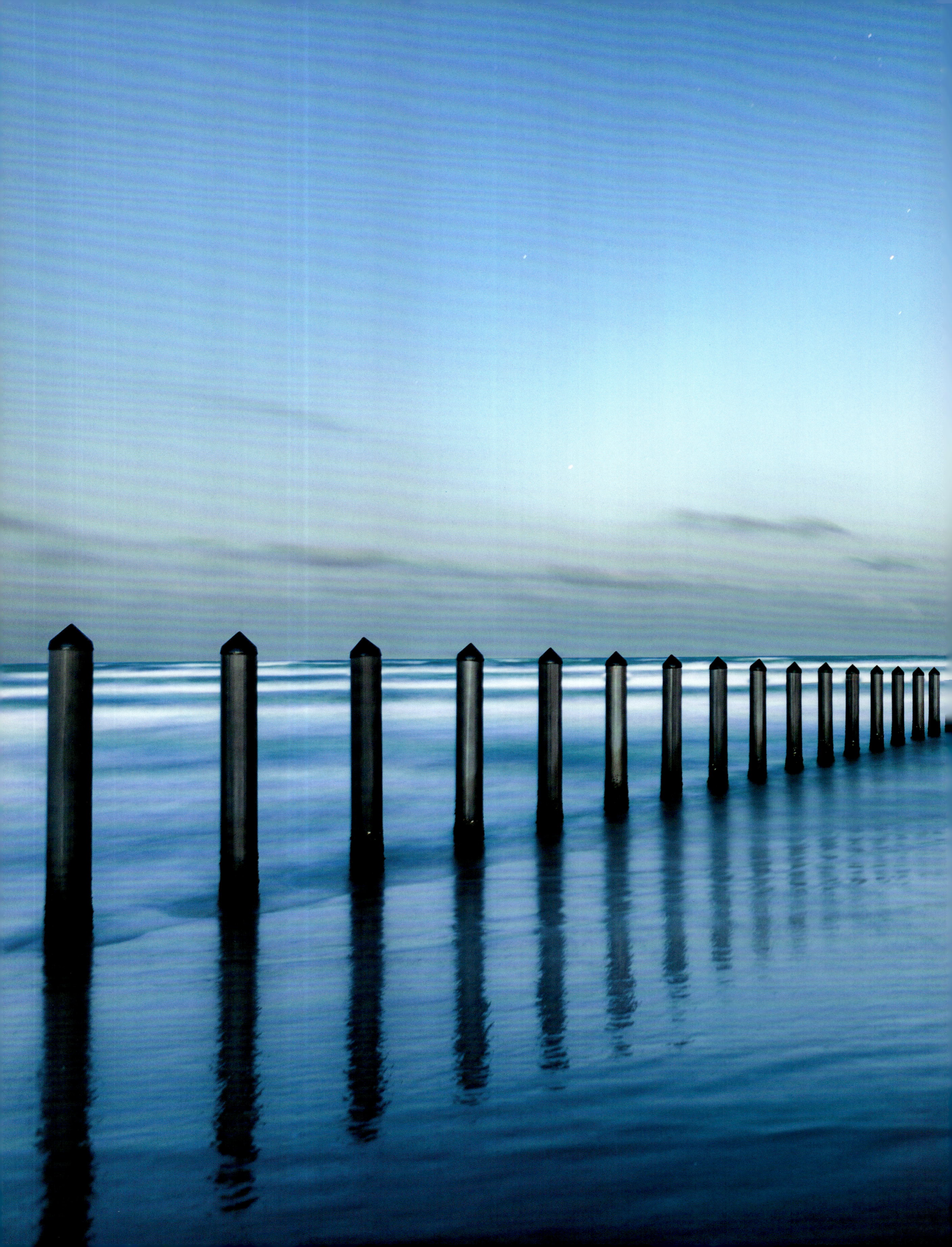

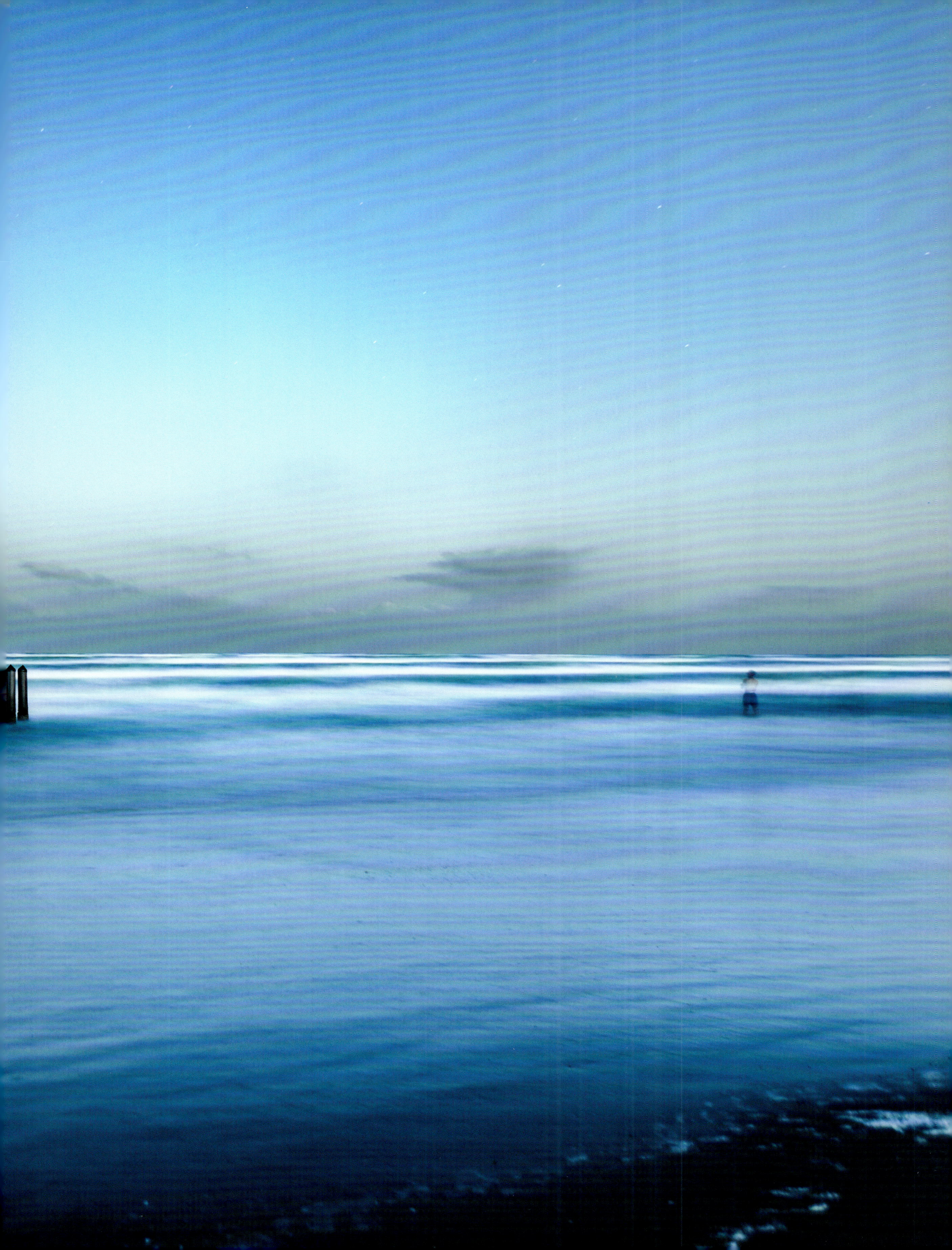

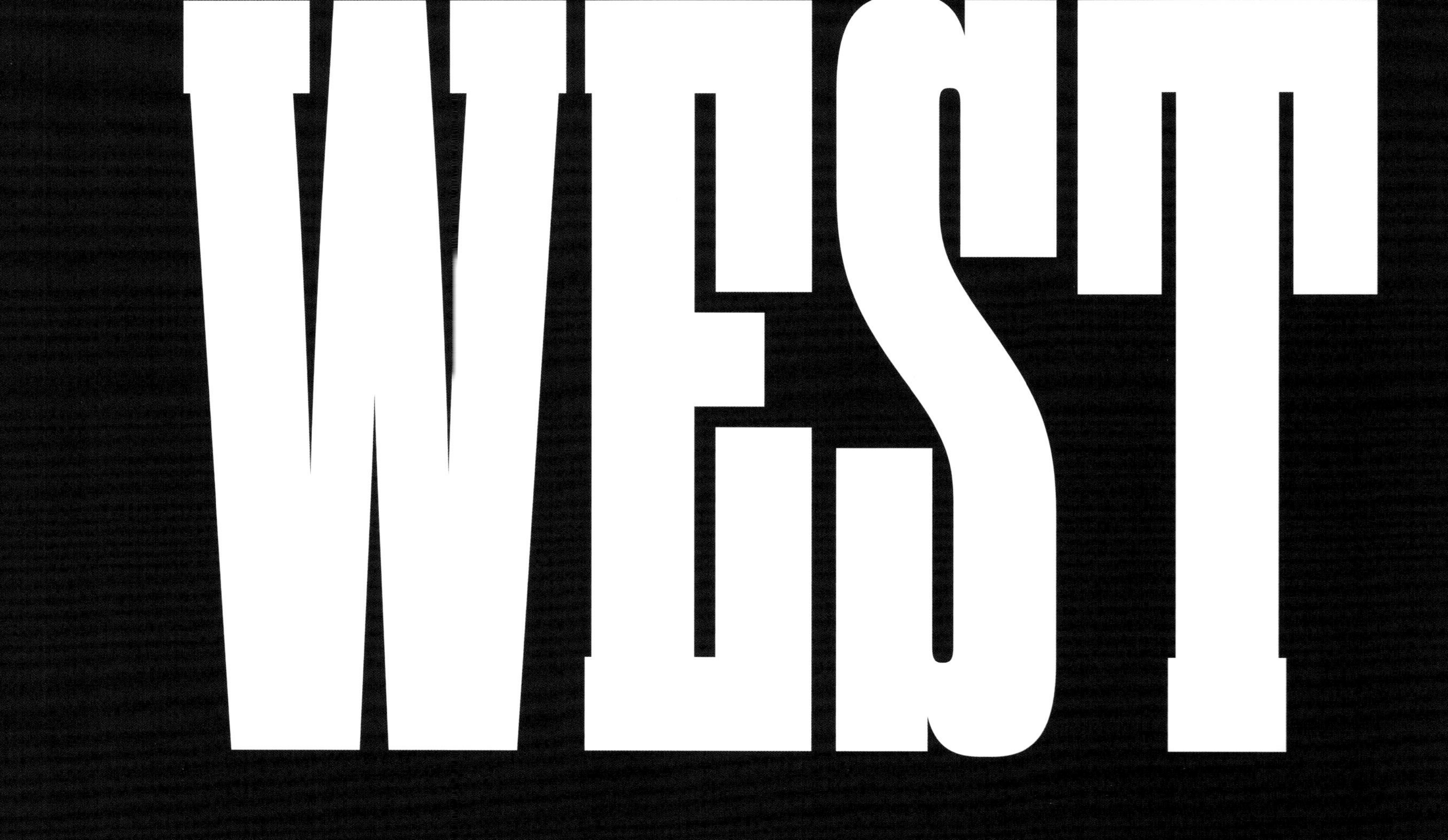
WEST

TEXAS

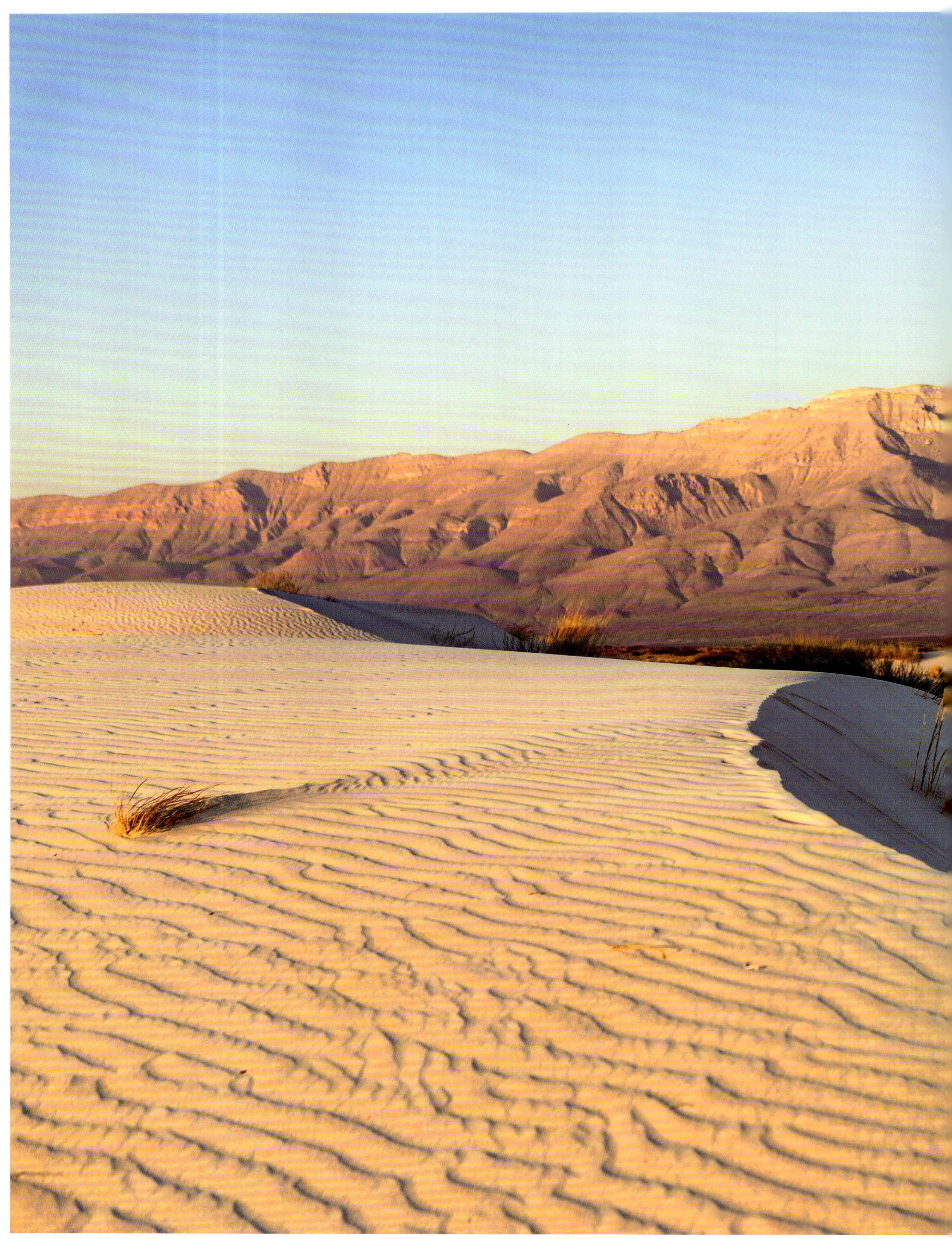

GYPSUM DUNES AND MOUNTAINS Salt Basin Dunes, Guadalupe Mountains National Park, 2017

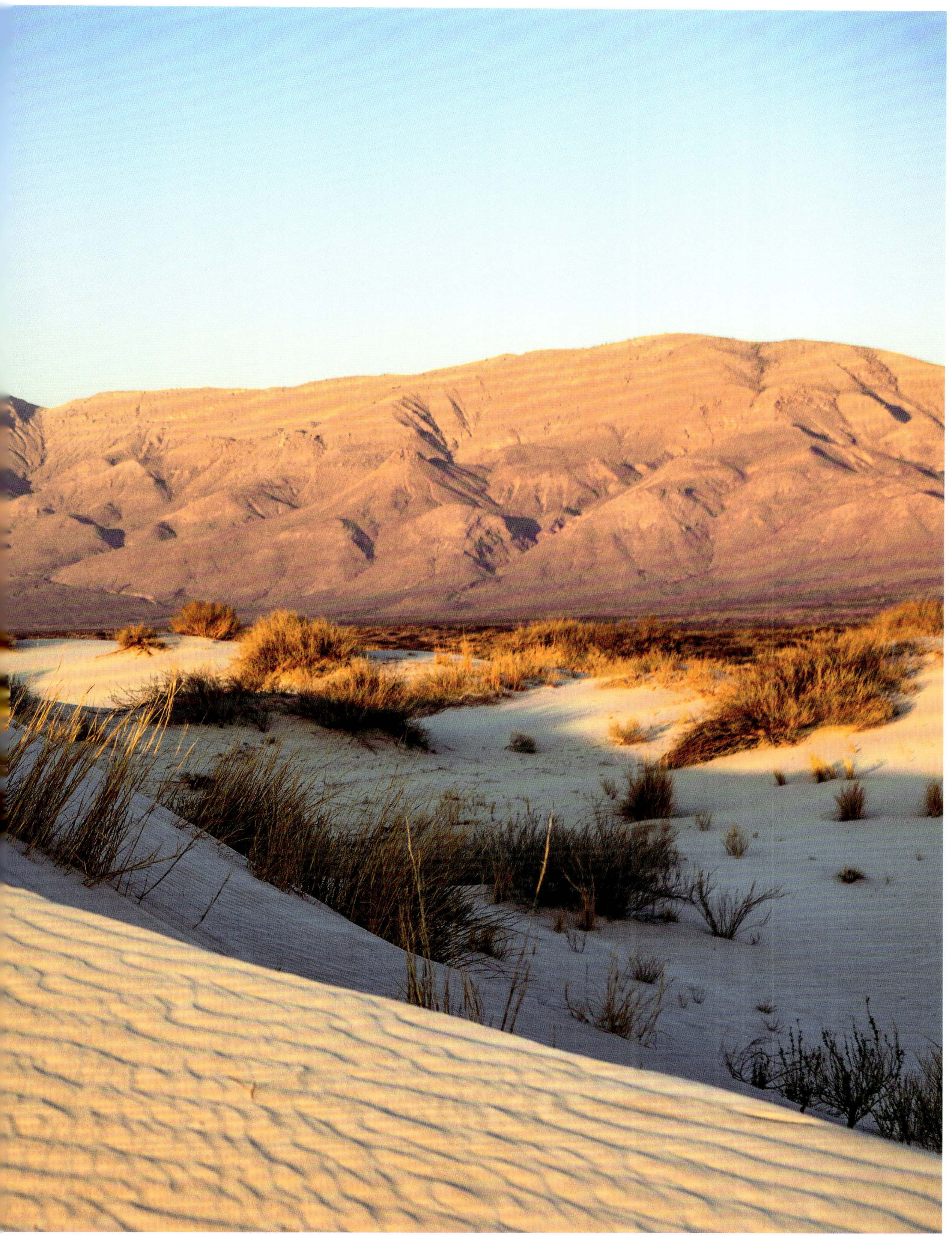

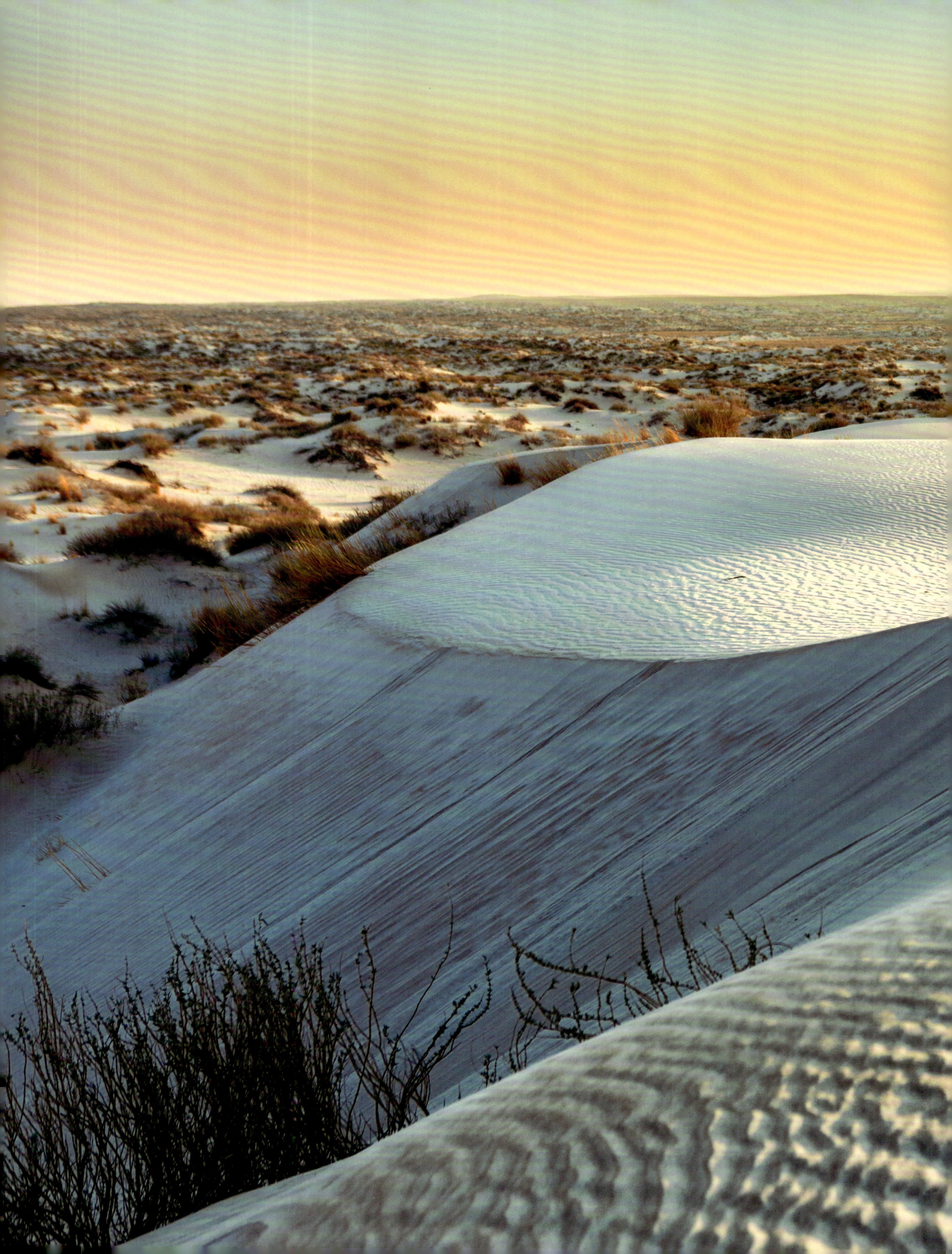

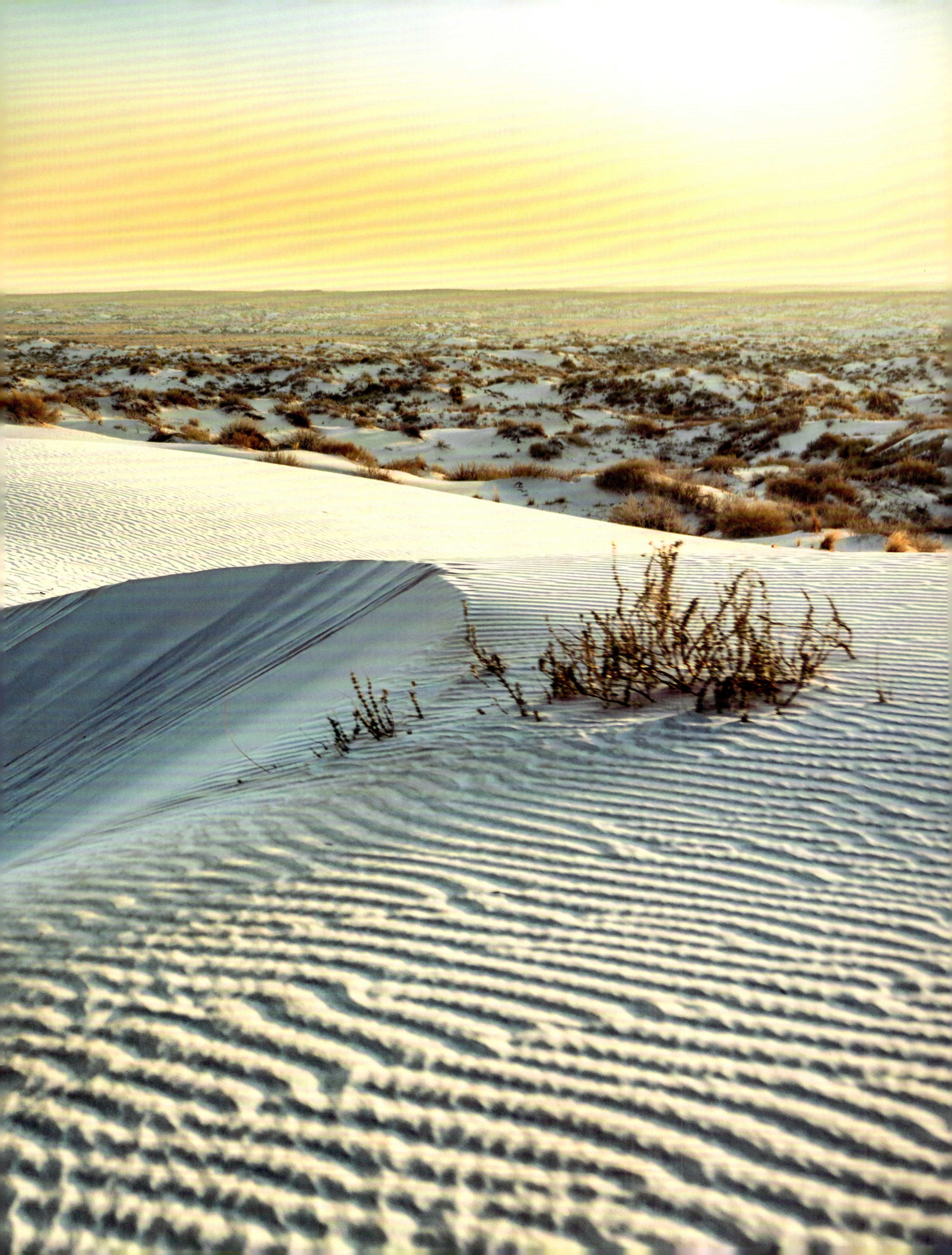

< **SALT BASIN DUNES** Guadalupe Mountains National Park, 2017

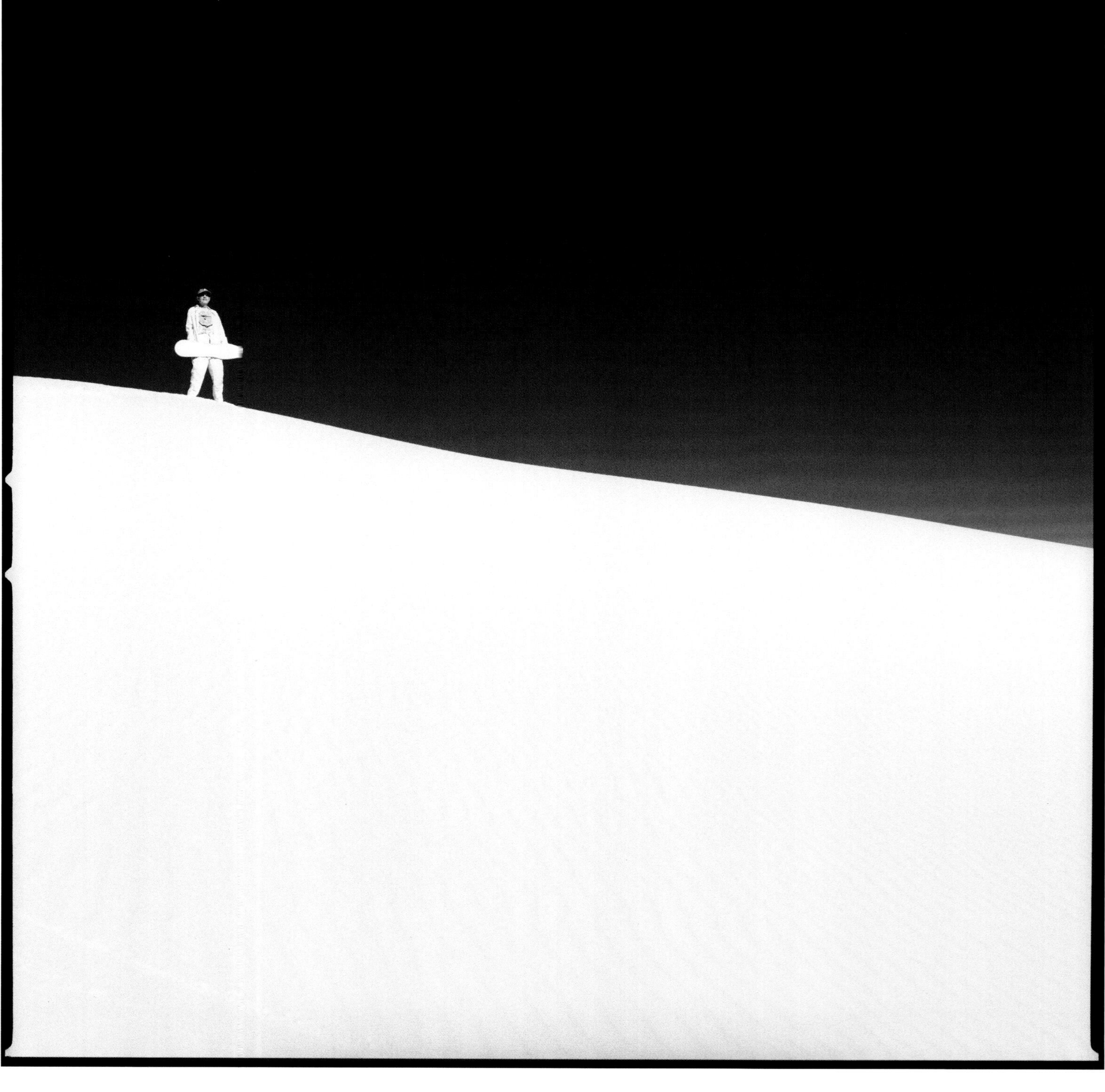

SAND SURFER Monahans Sandhills State Park, 2004

SUNSET OVER CORNUDAS MOUNTAINS Salt Basin Dunes, Guadalupe Mountains National Park, 2017 >

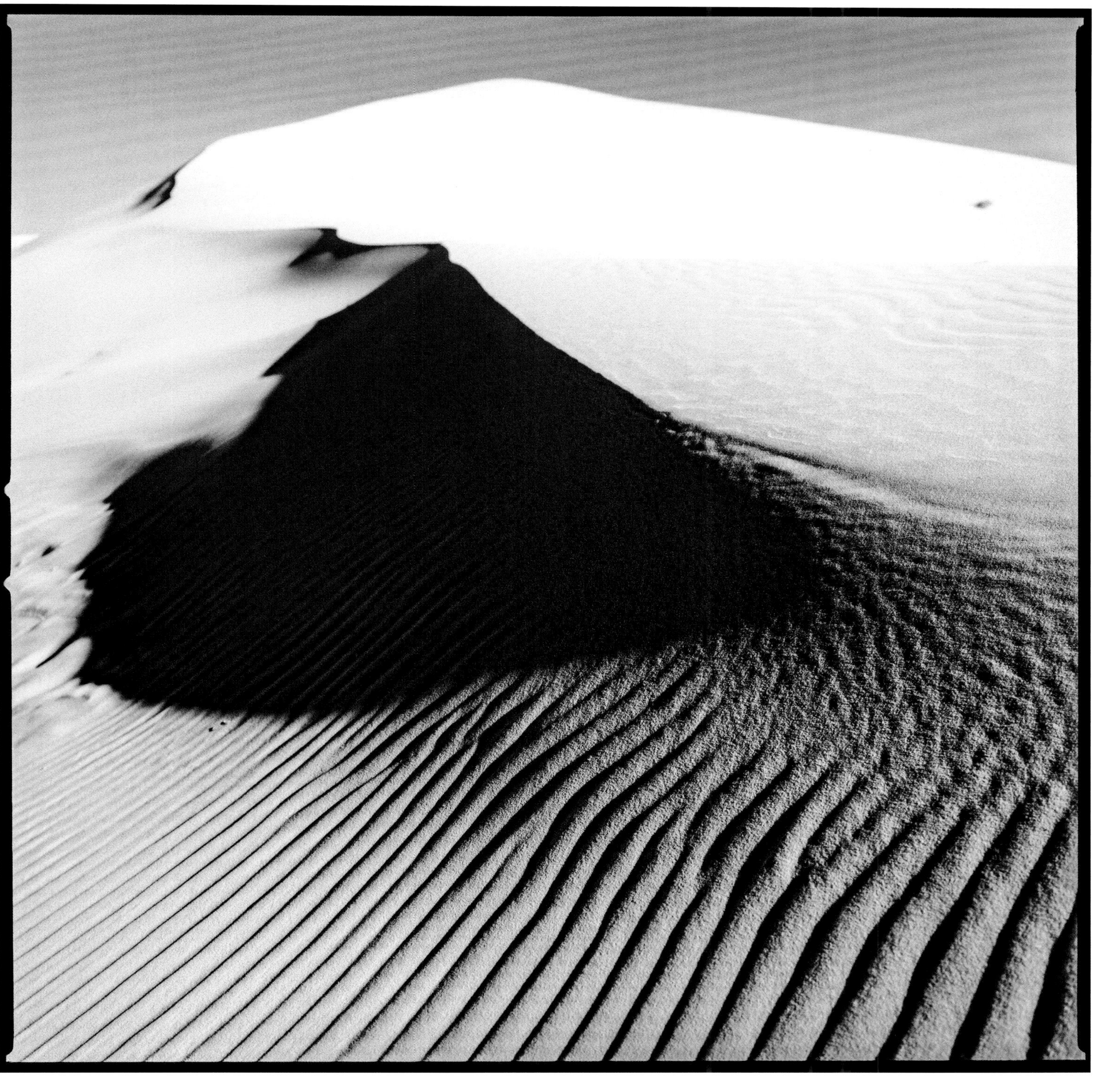

DUNE Monahans Sandhills State Park, 2004

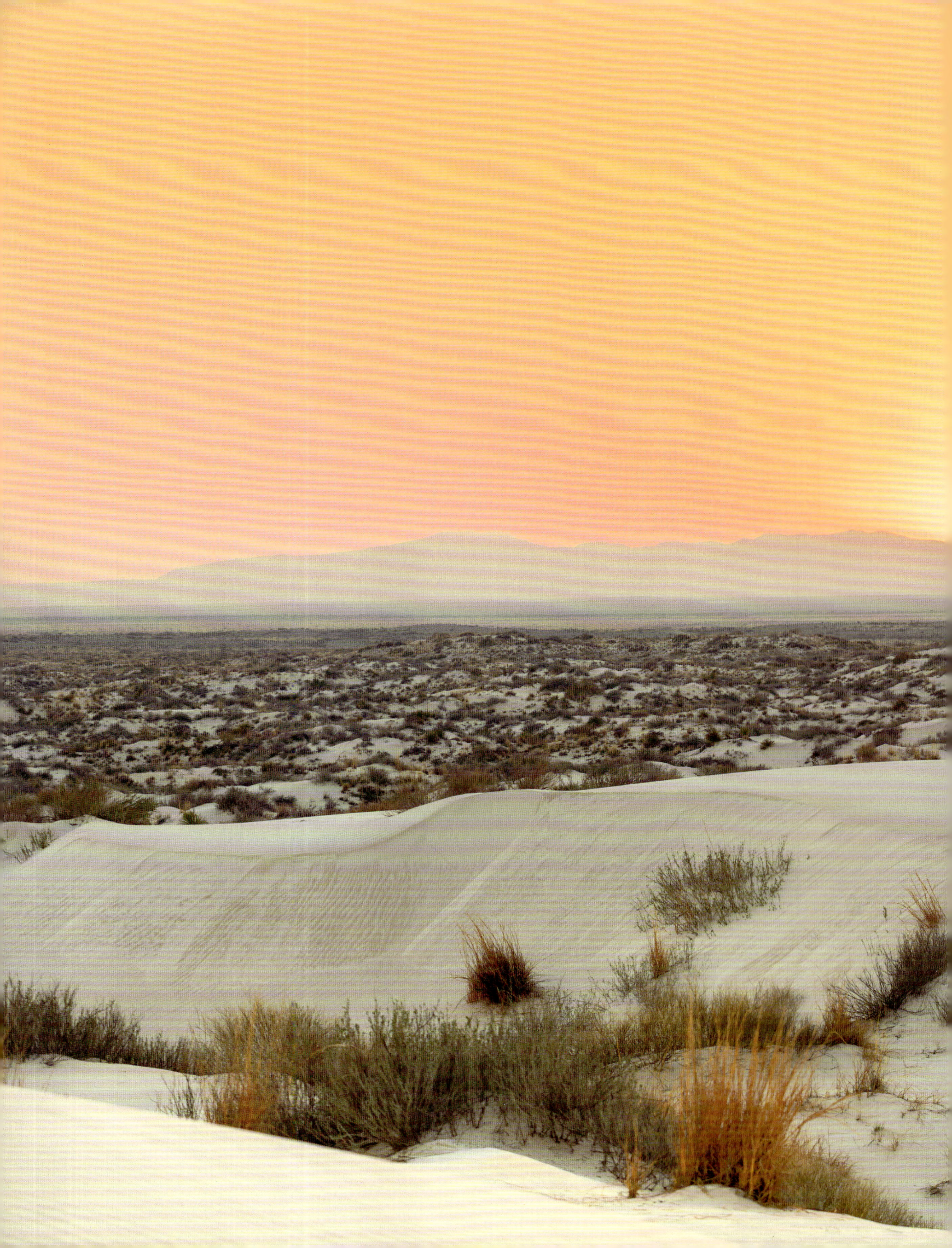

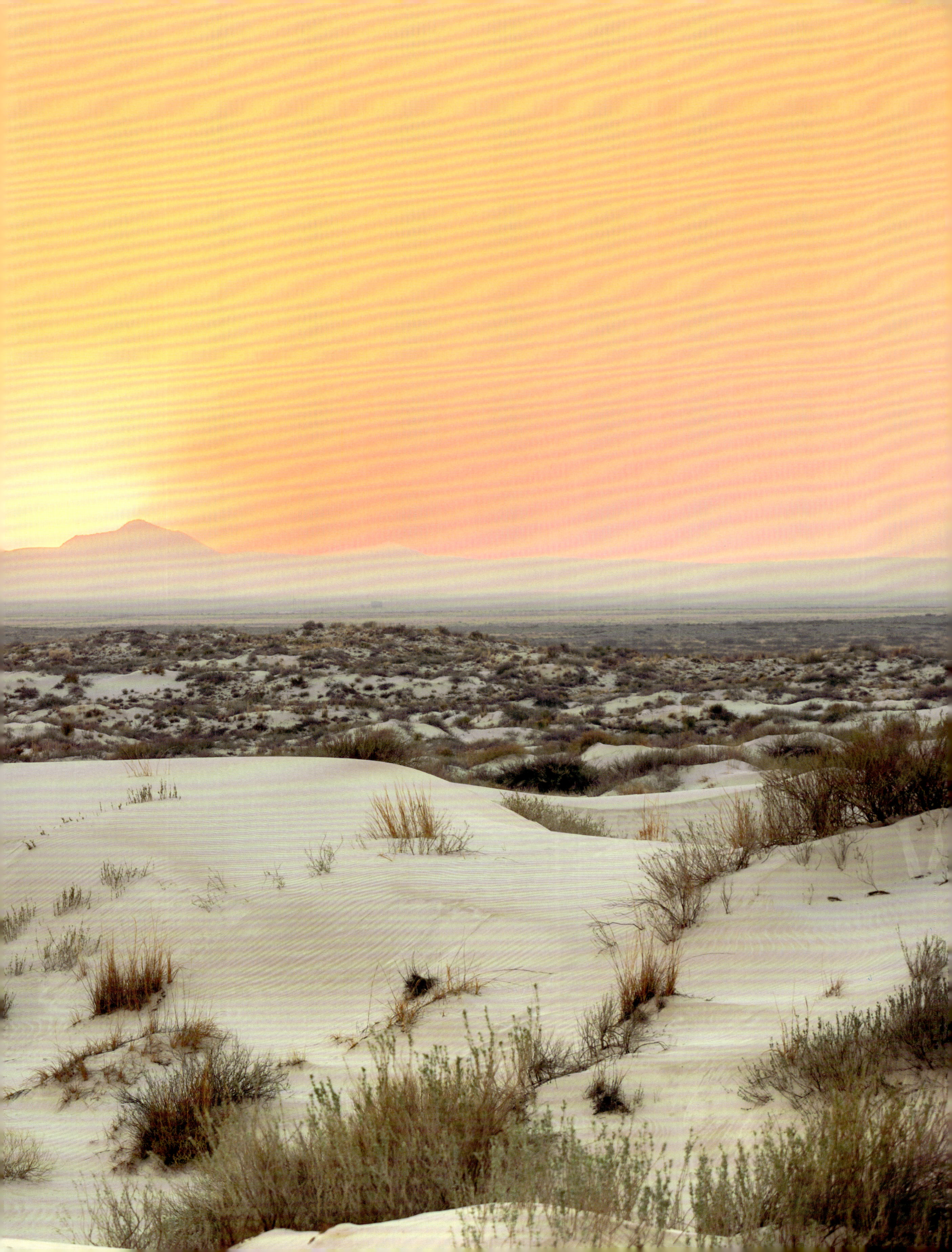

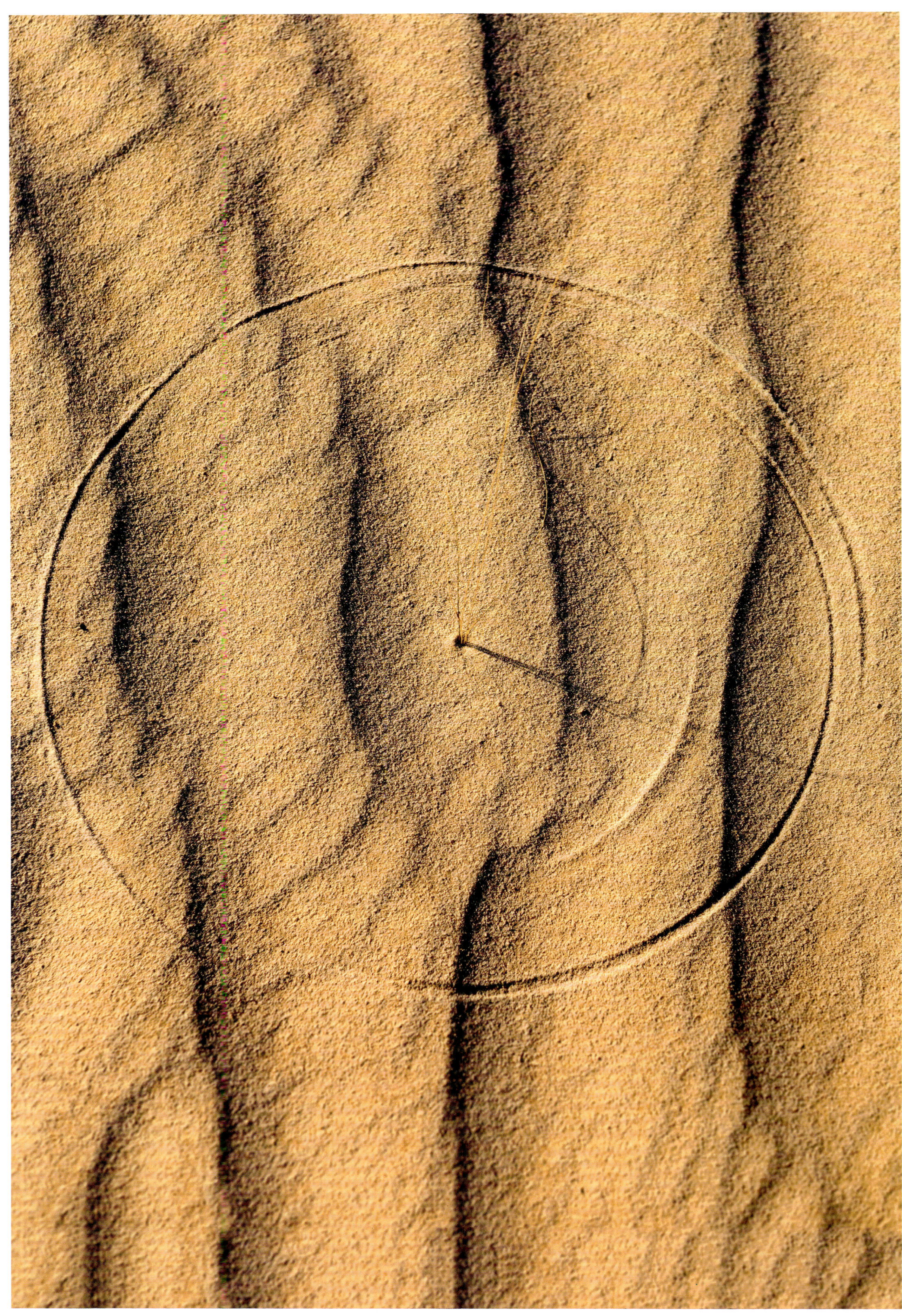

SCRATCH CIRCLE Salt Basin Dunes, Guadalupe Mountains National Park, 2017

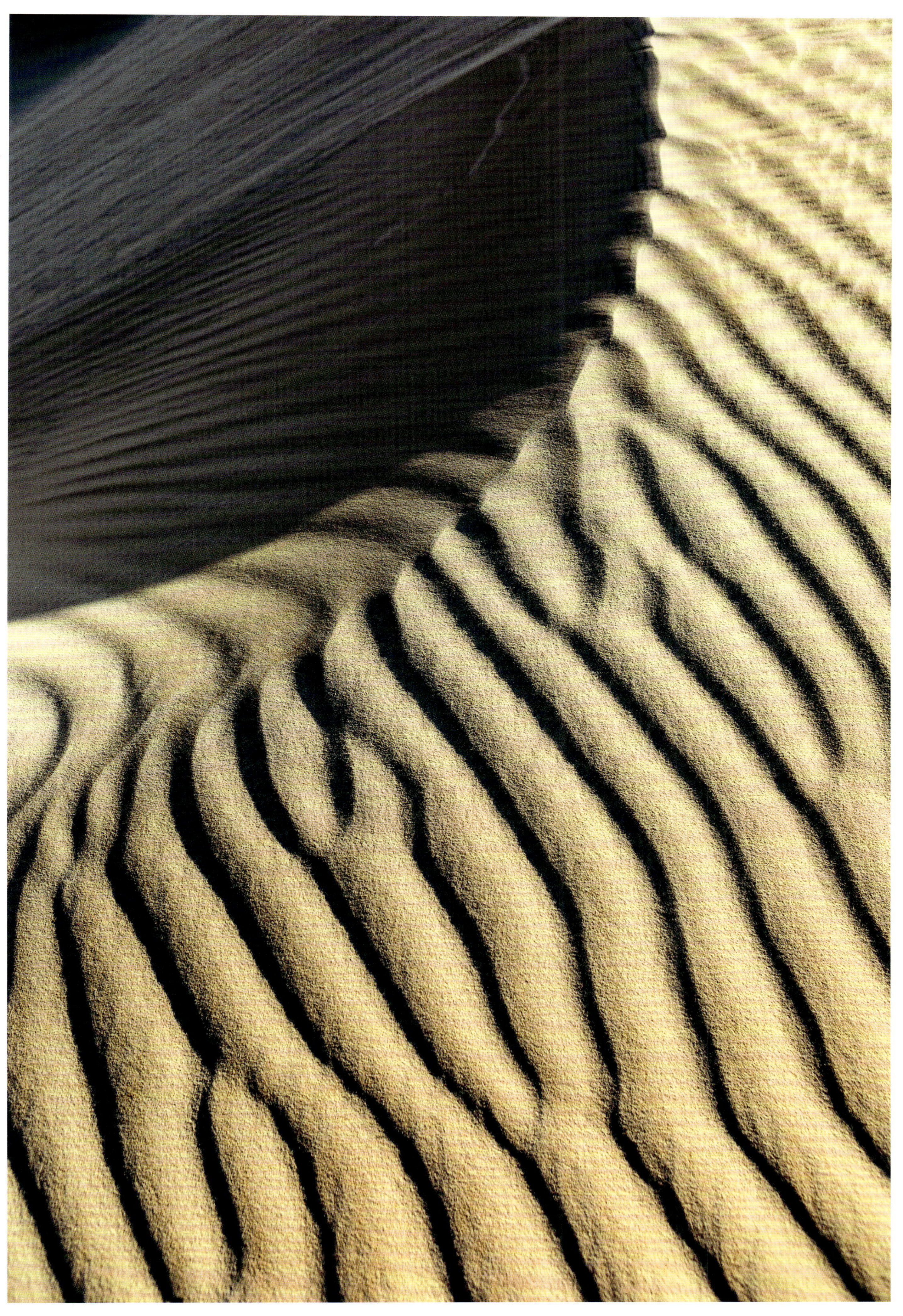

SAND DUNE Salt Basin Dunes, Guadalupe Mountains National Park, 2017

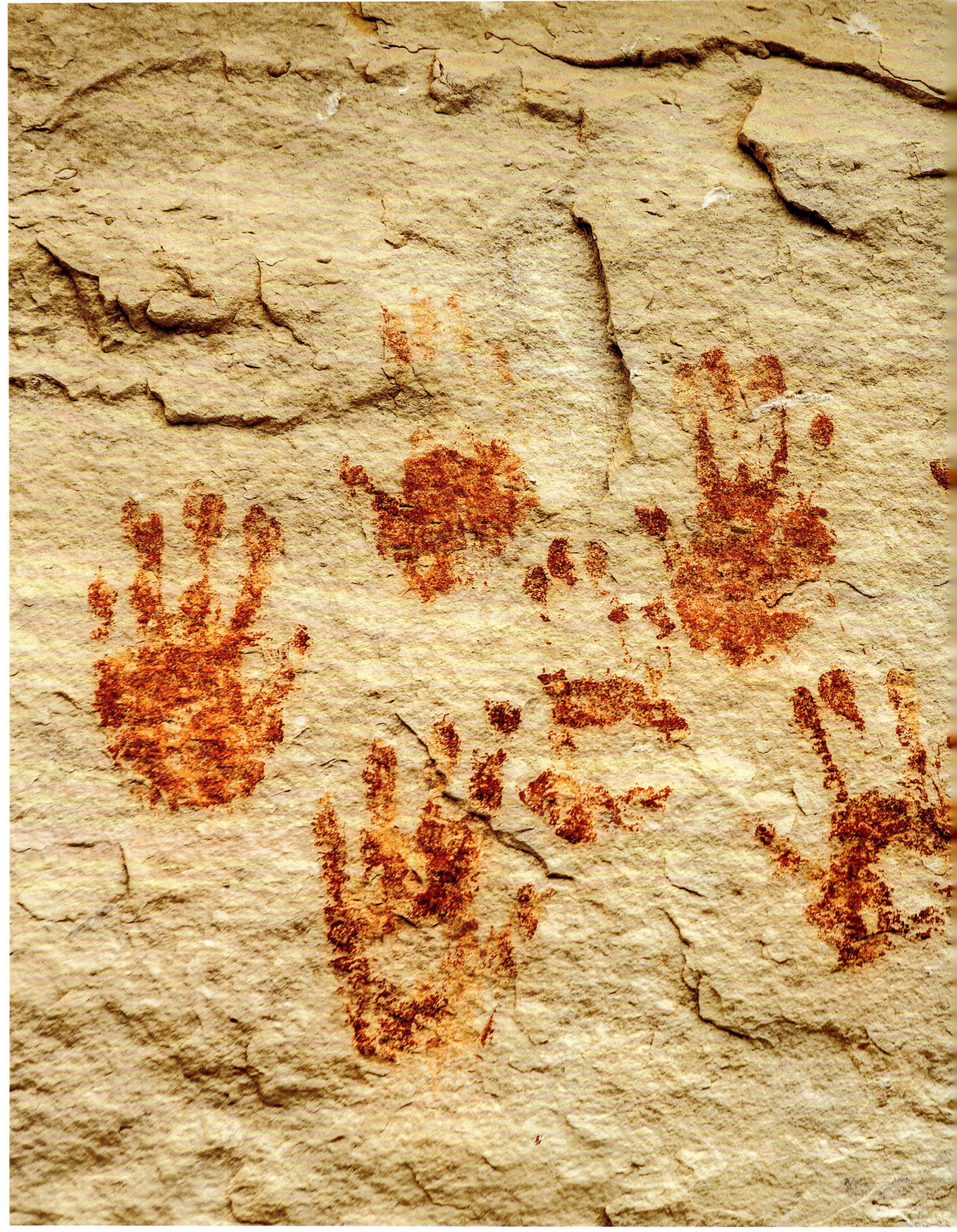

CONTACT ancient hand print site on the Devil's River, near Comstock, 2012

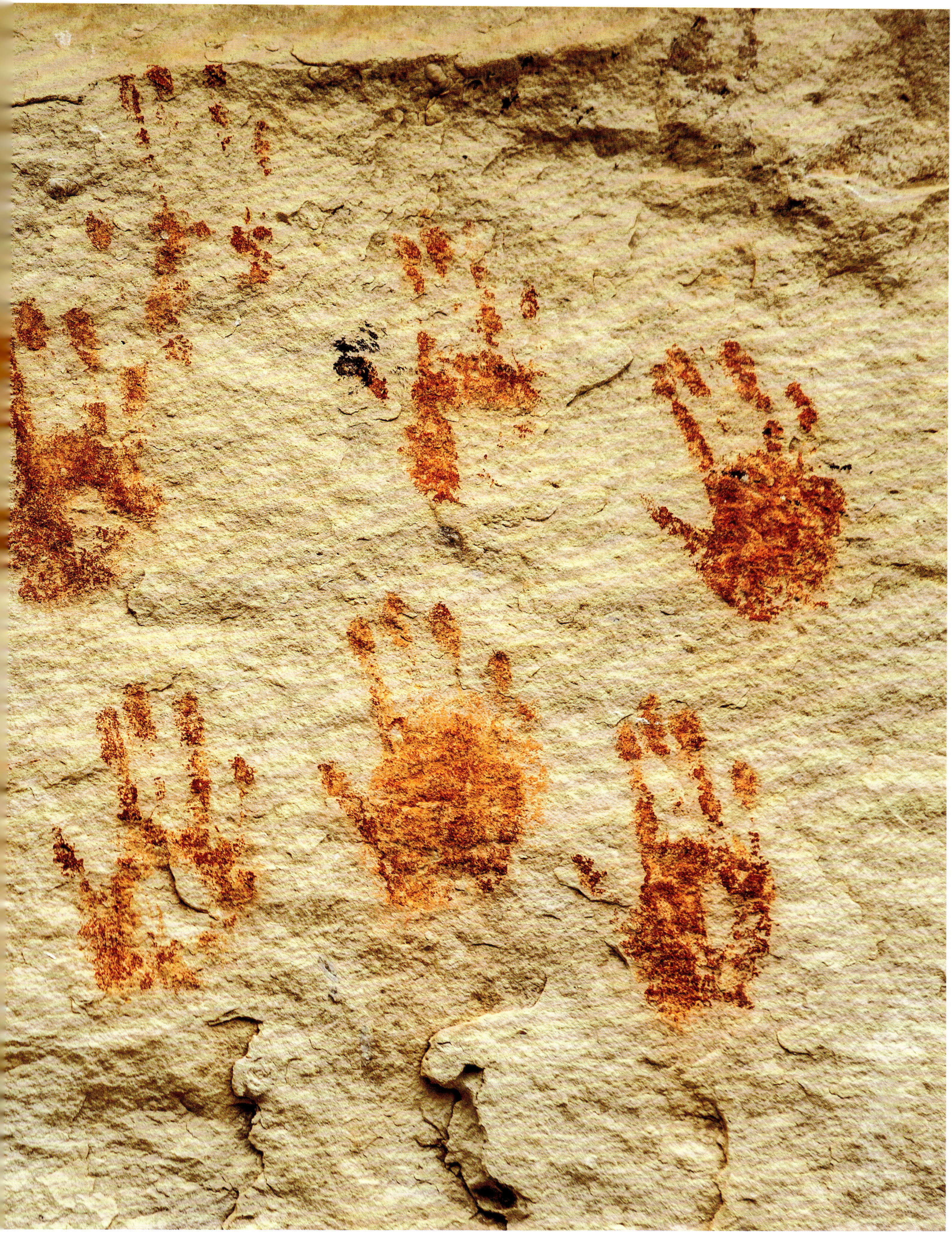

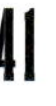

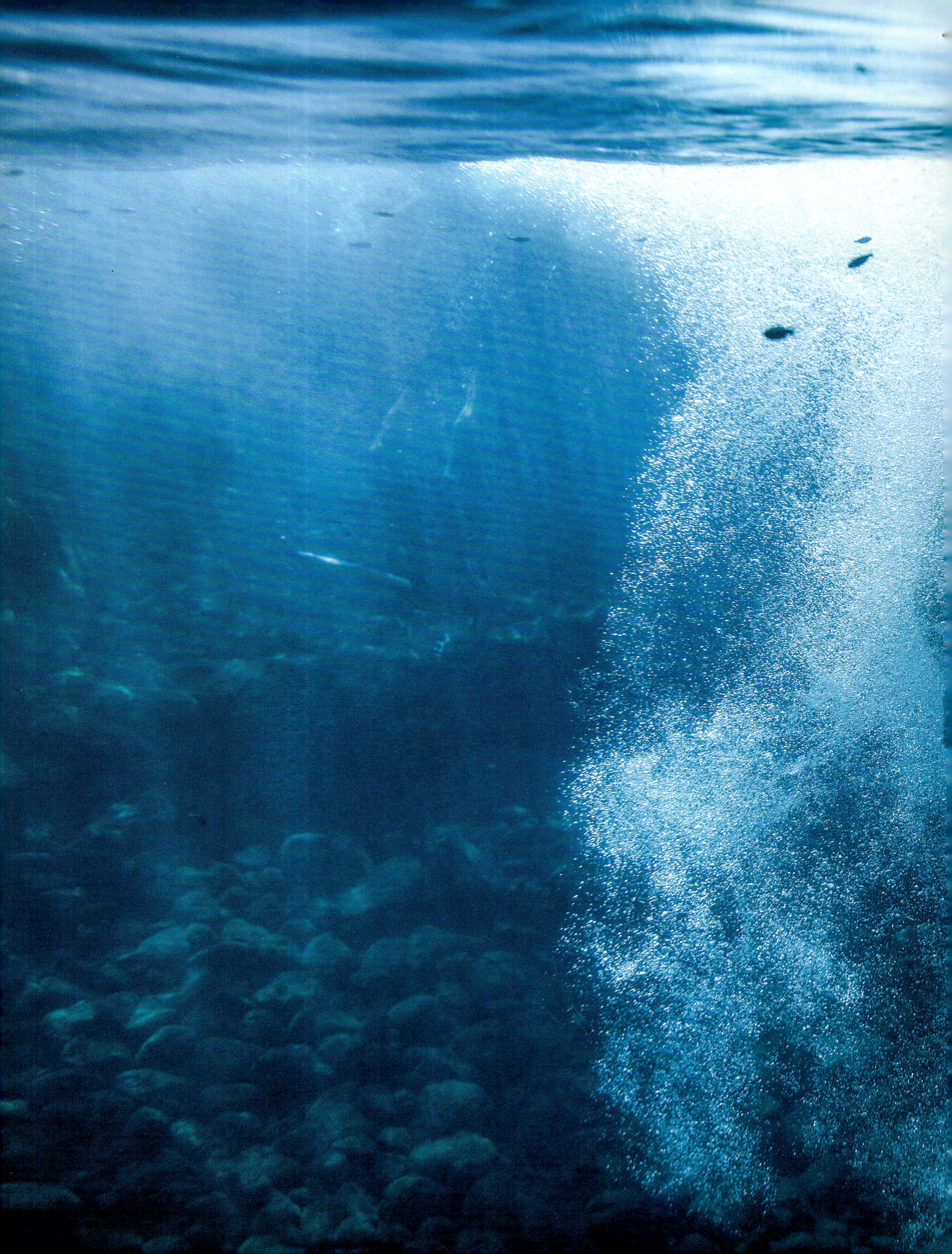

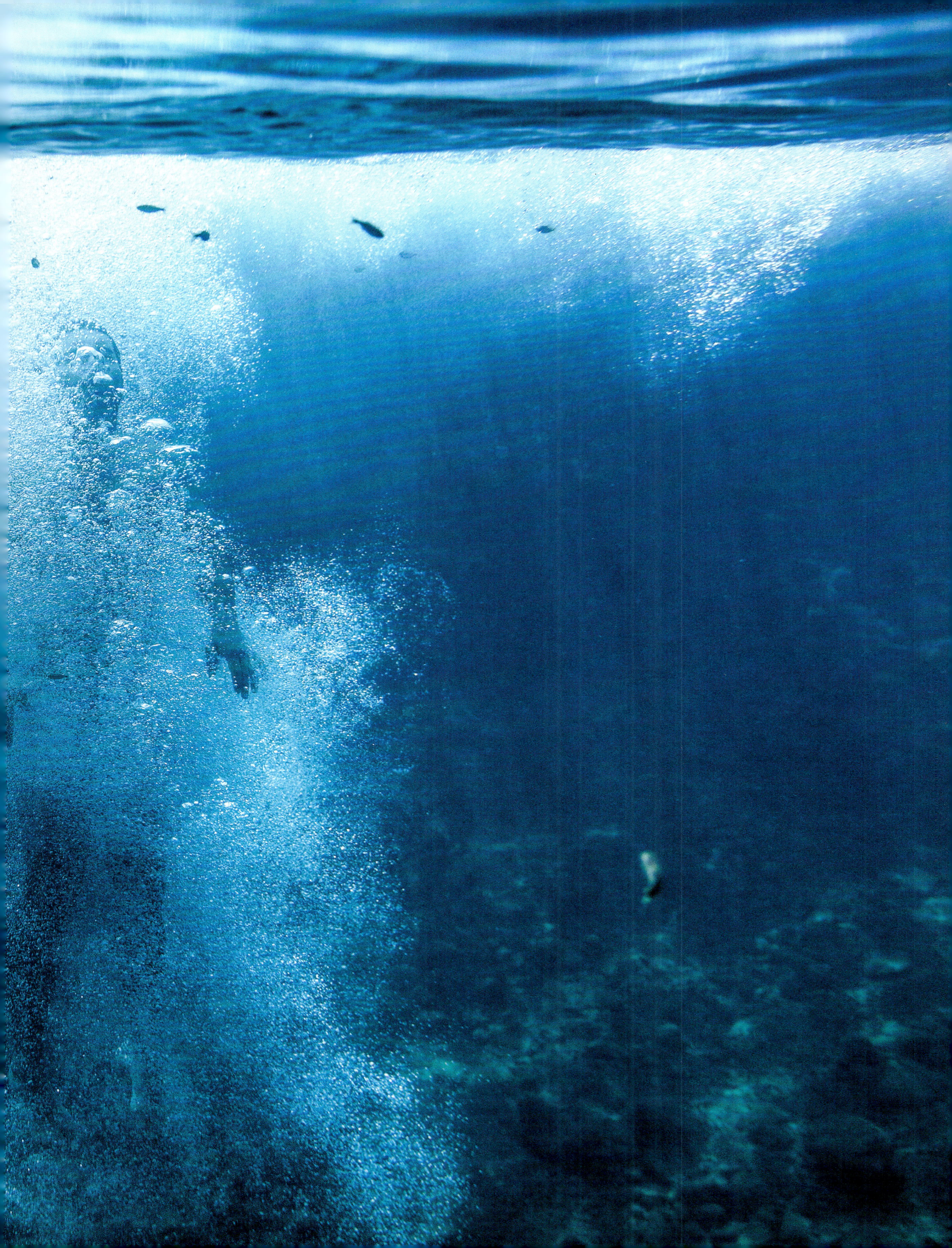

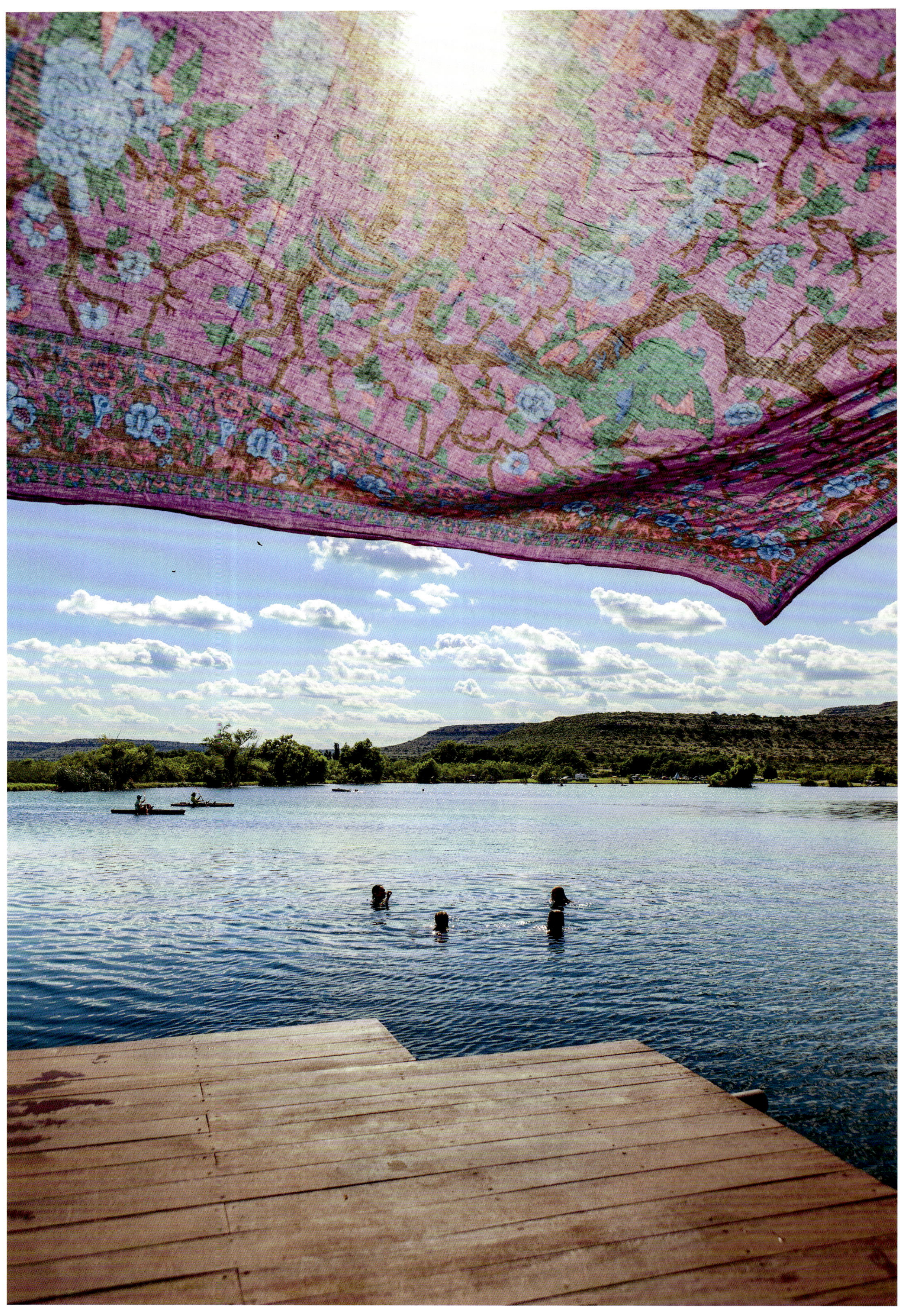

DESERT OASIS Independence Creek Preserve, near Sheffield, 2016

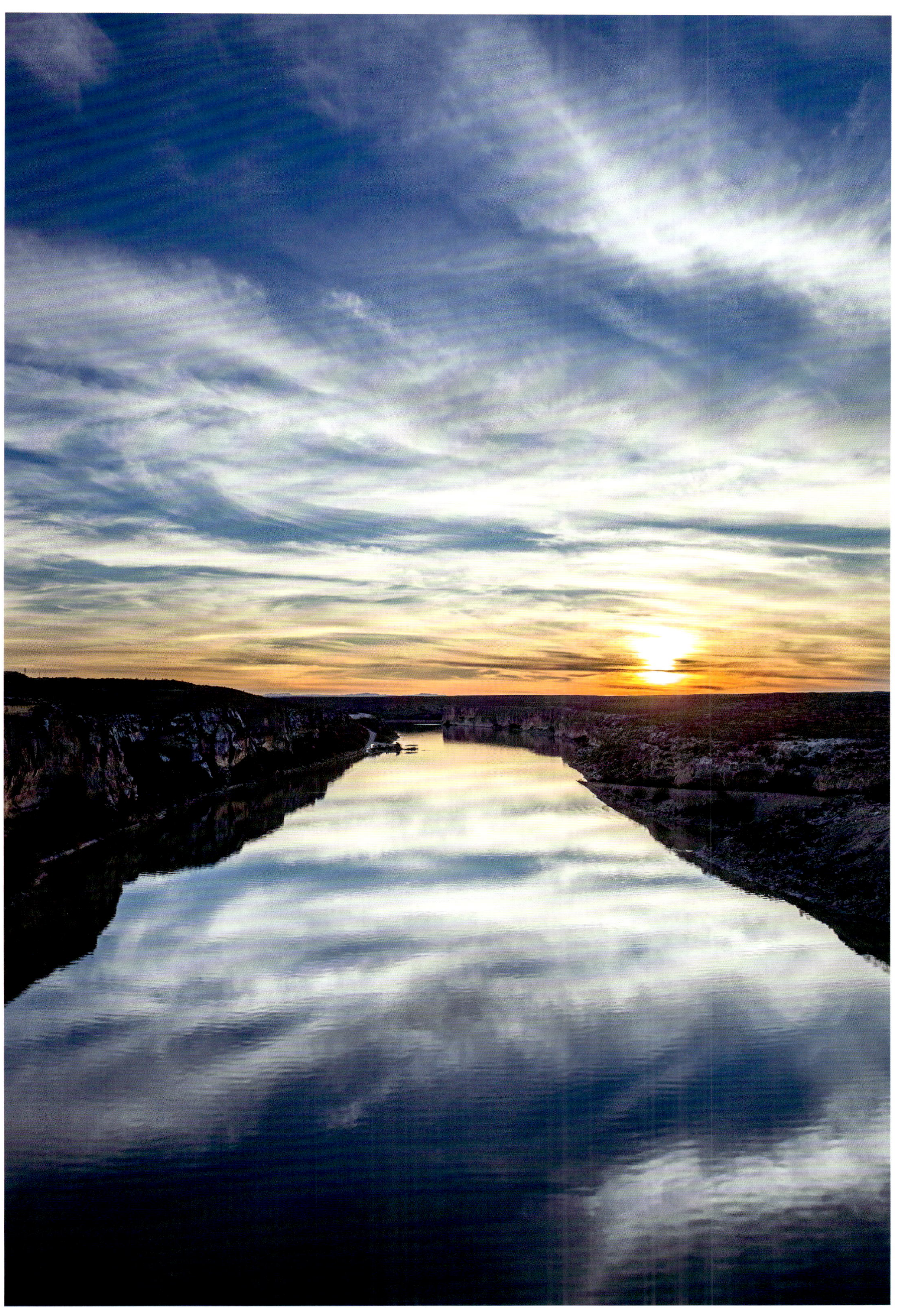

PECOS RIVER from Highway 90 bridge, Comstock, 2010

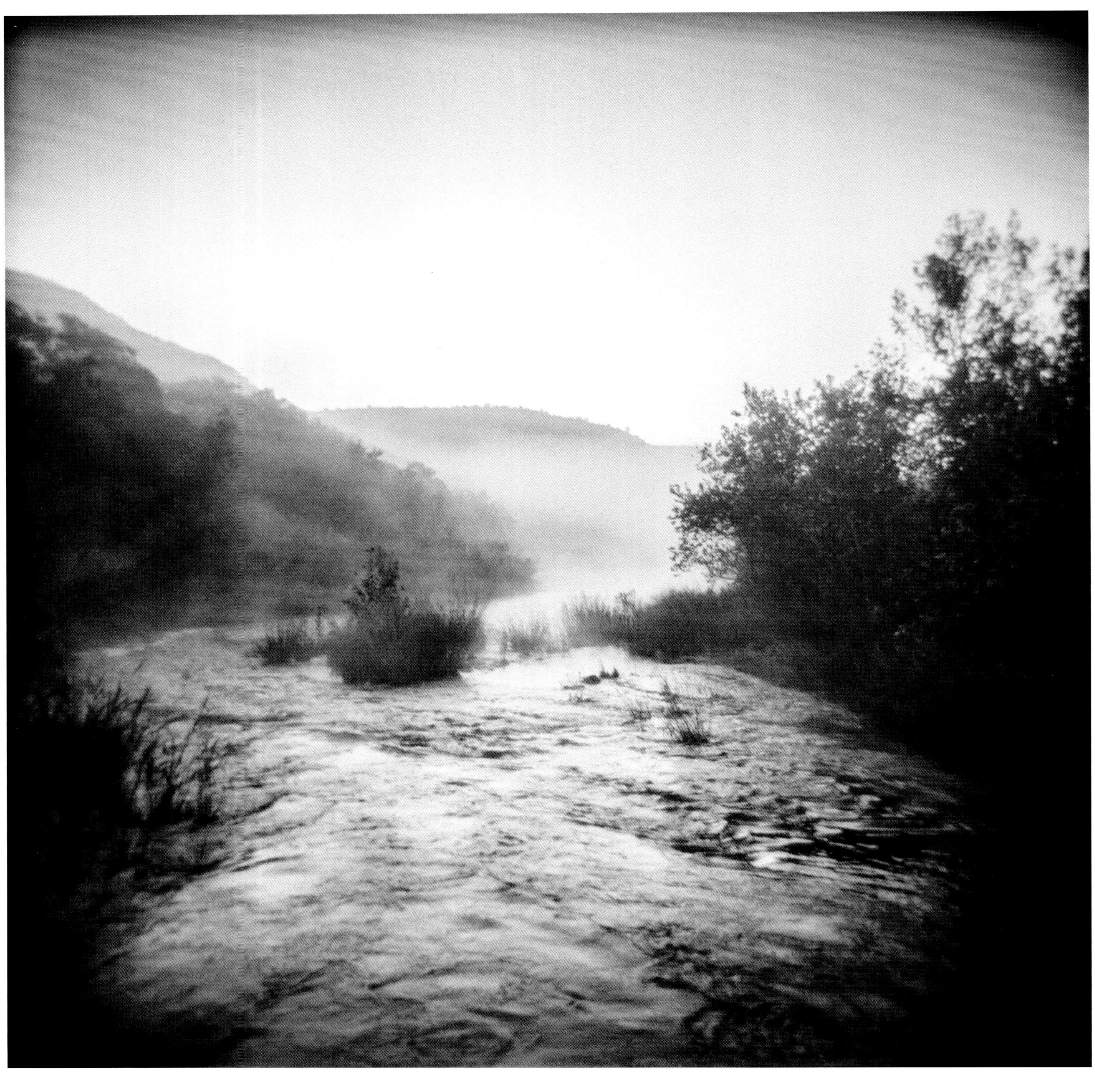

DEVIL'S RIVER AT BAKER'S CROSSING near Del Rio, 2004

MOUNTAIN MIST near Alpine, 2014 >

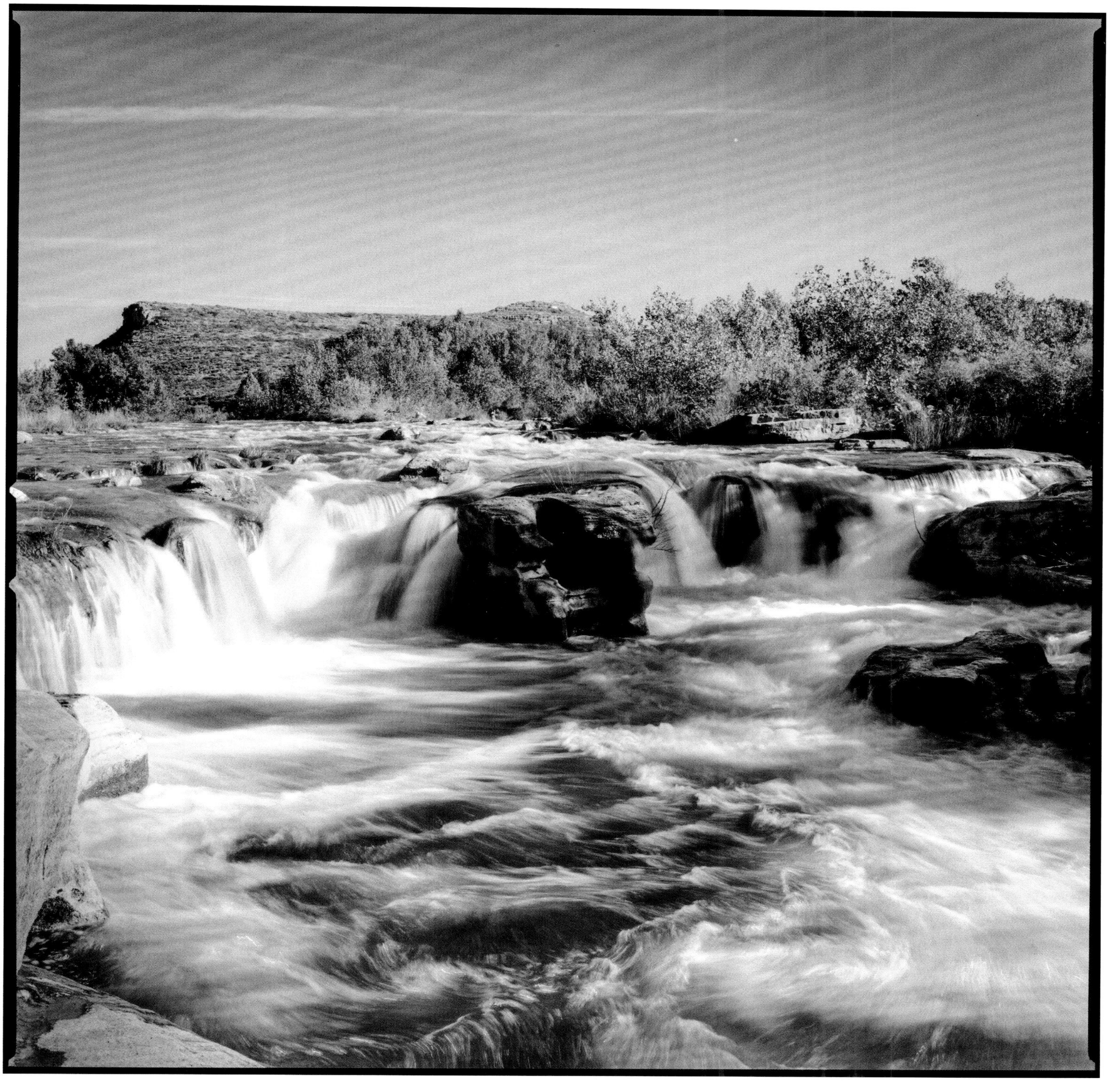

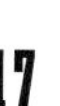

DOLAN FALLS near Del Rio, 2004

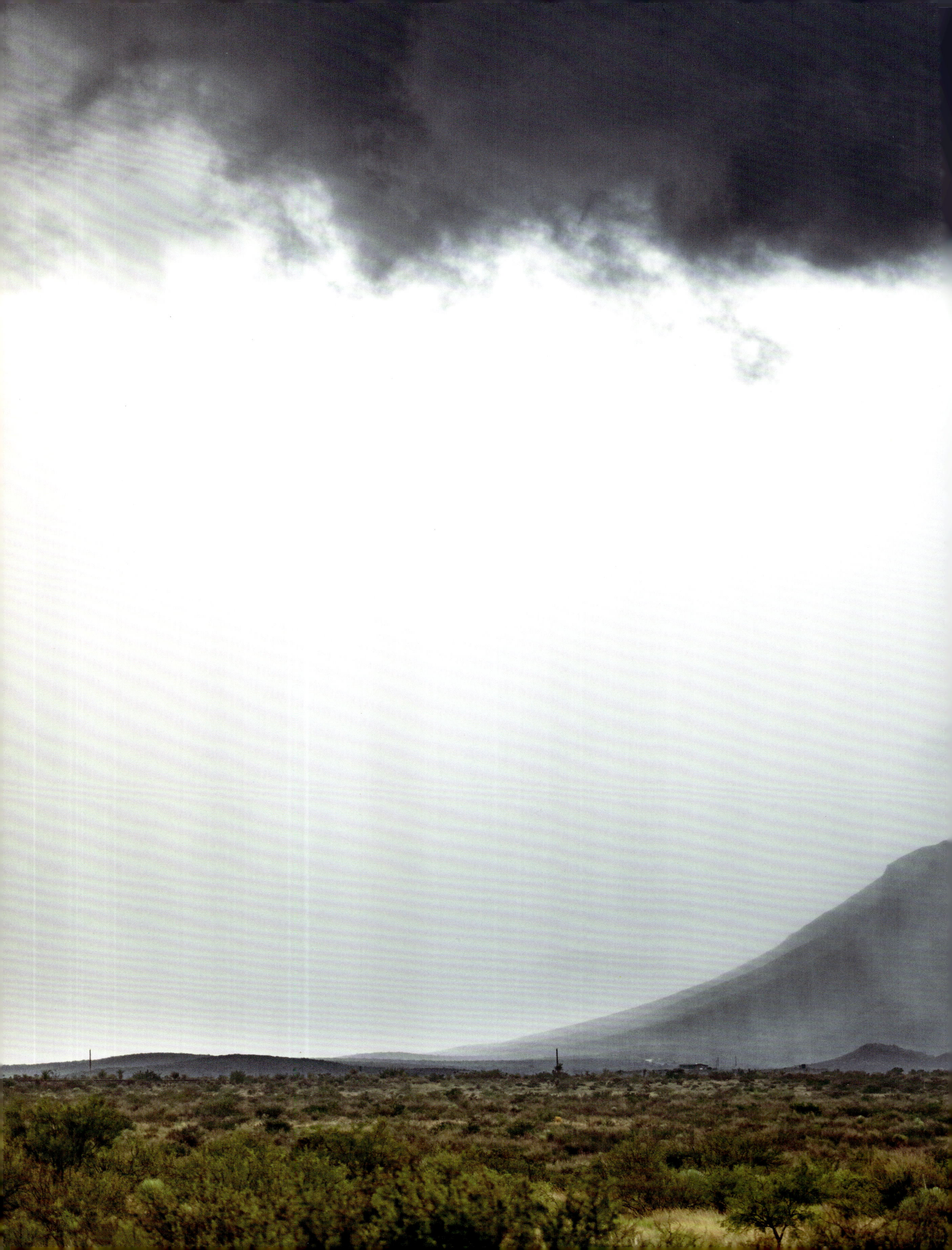

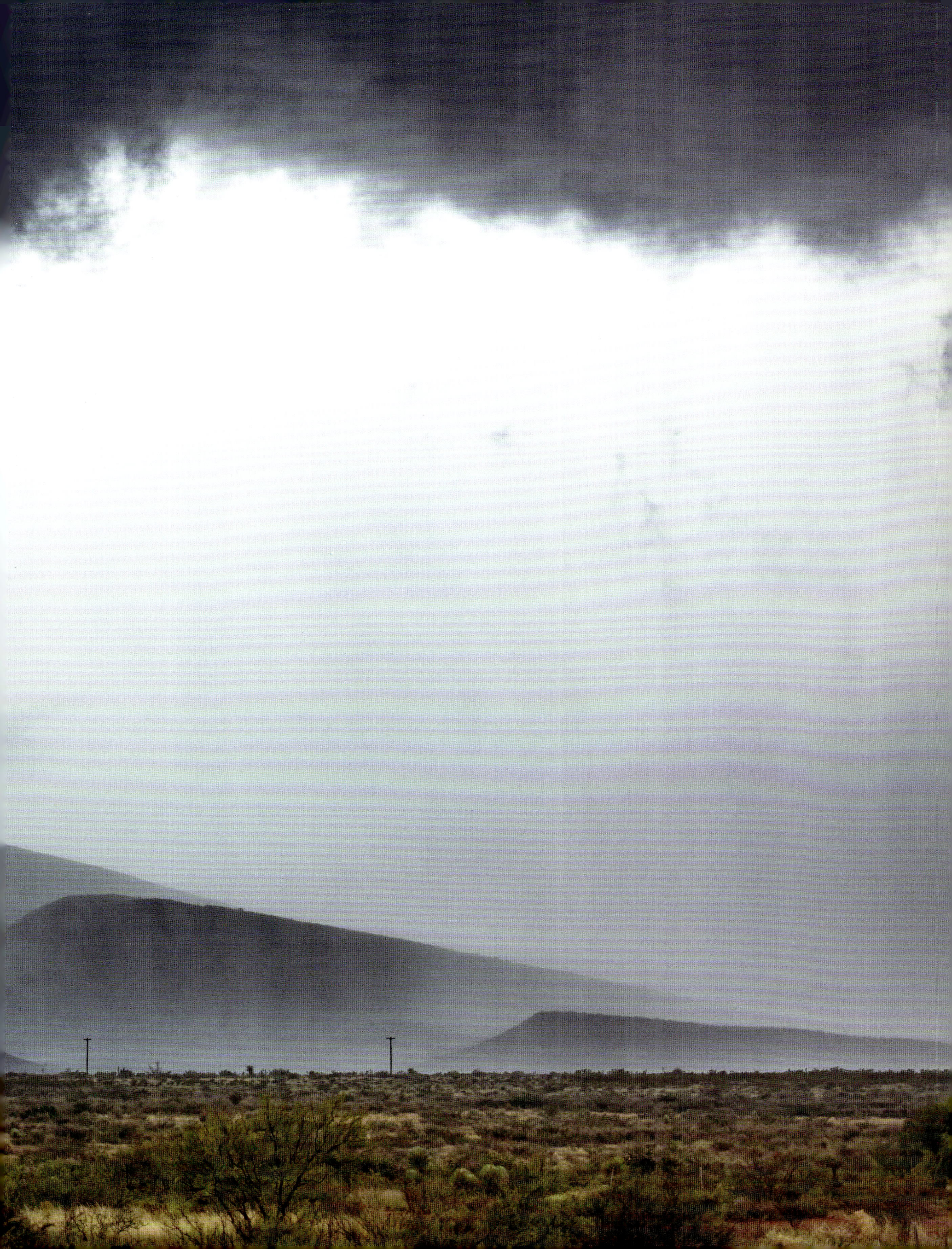

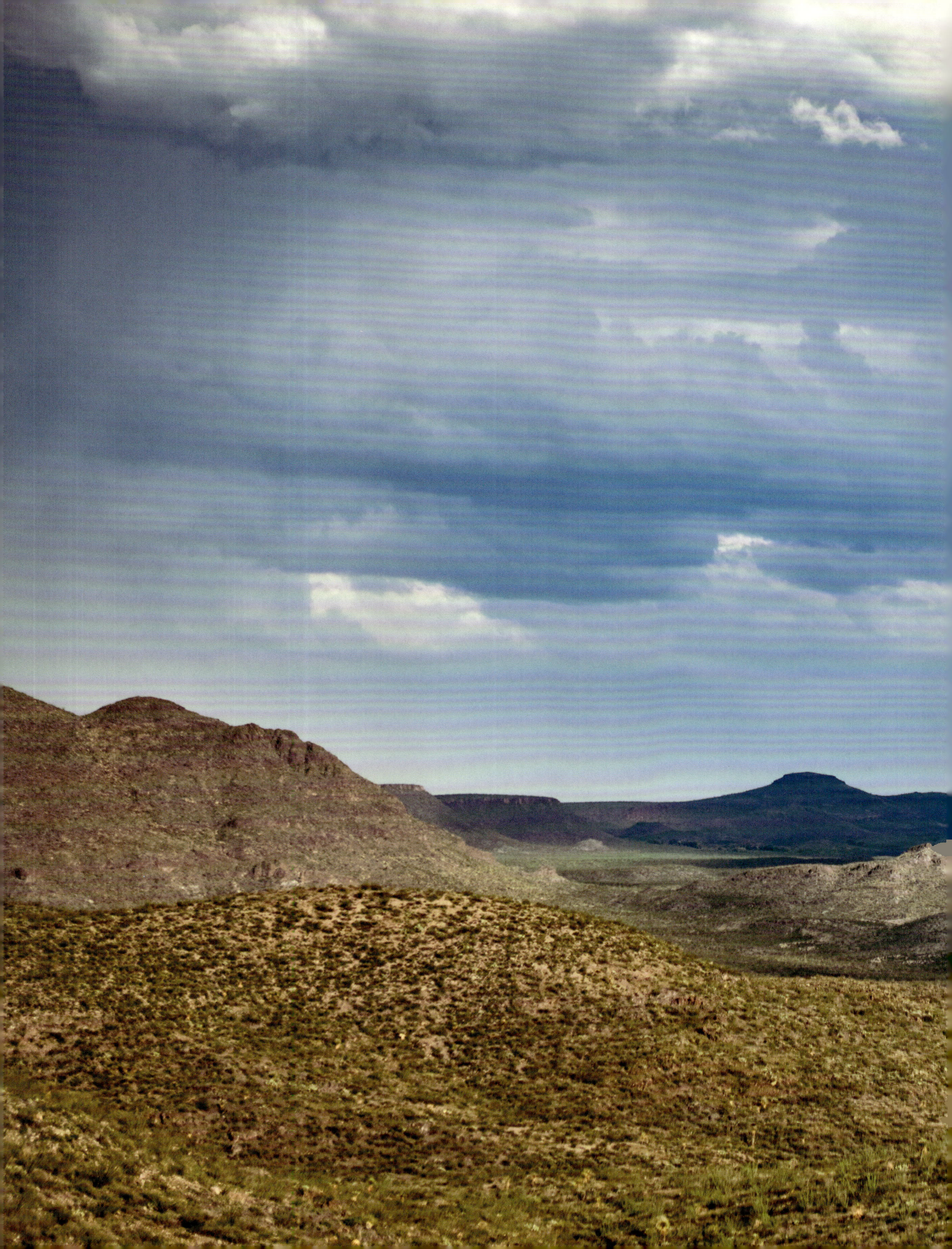

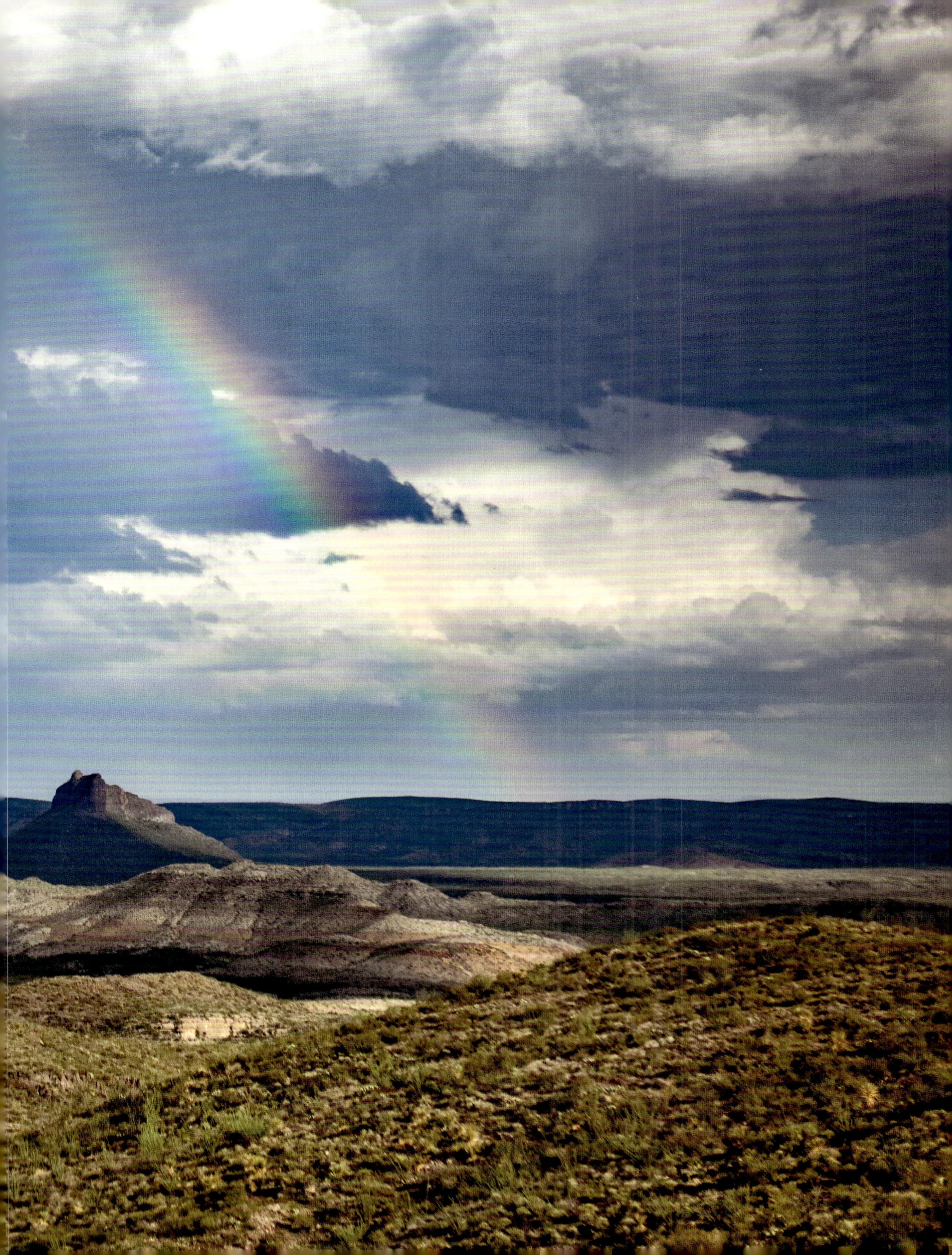

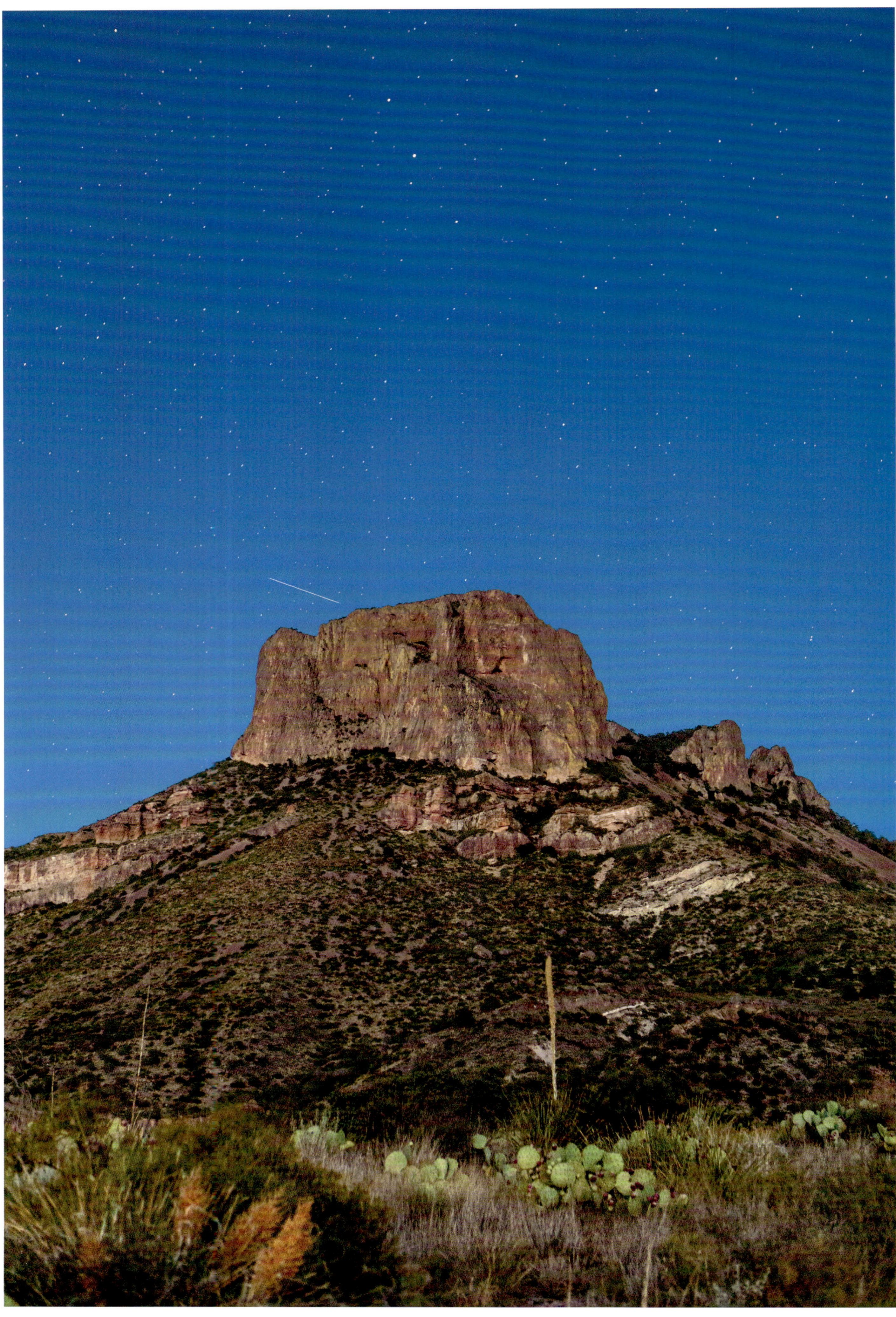

CASA GRANDE Big Bend National Park, 2015

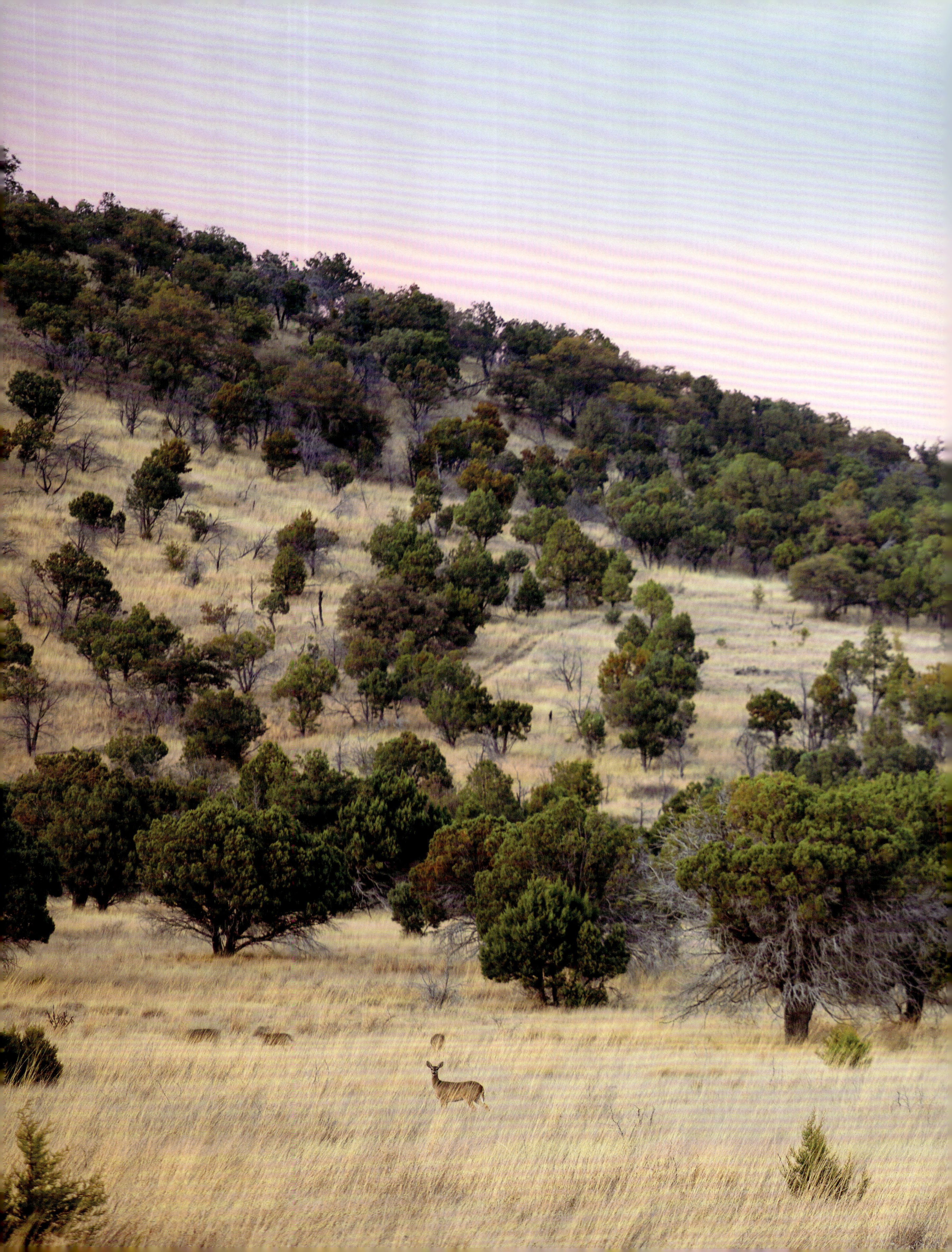

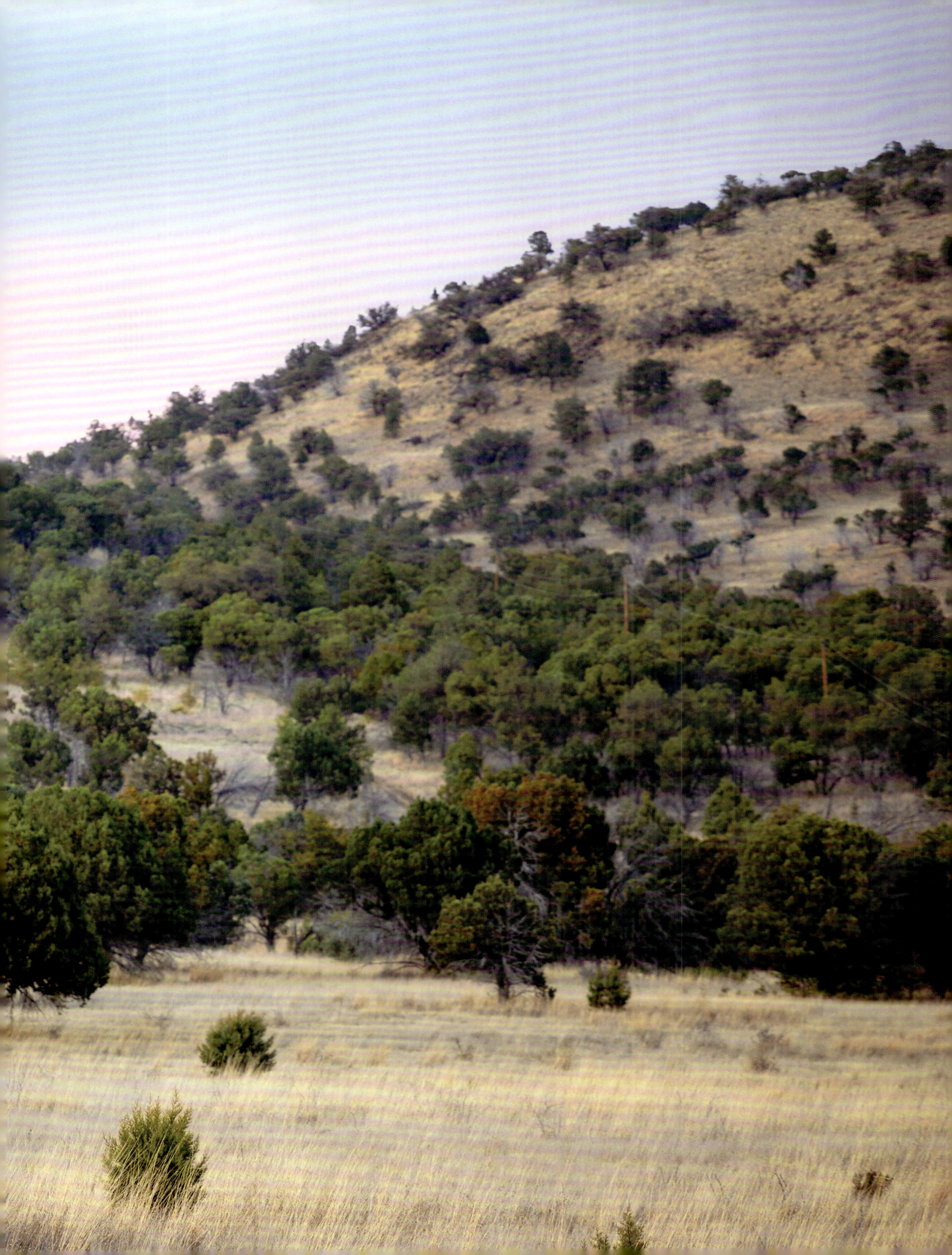

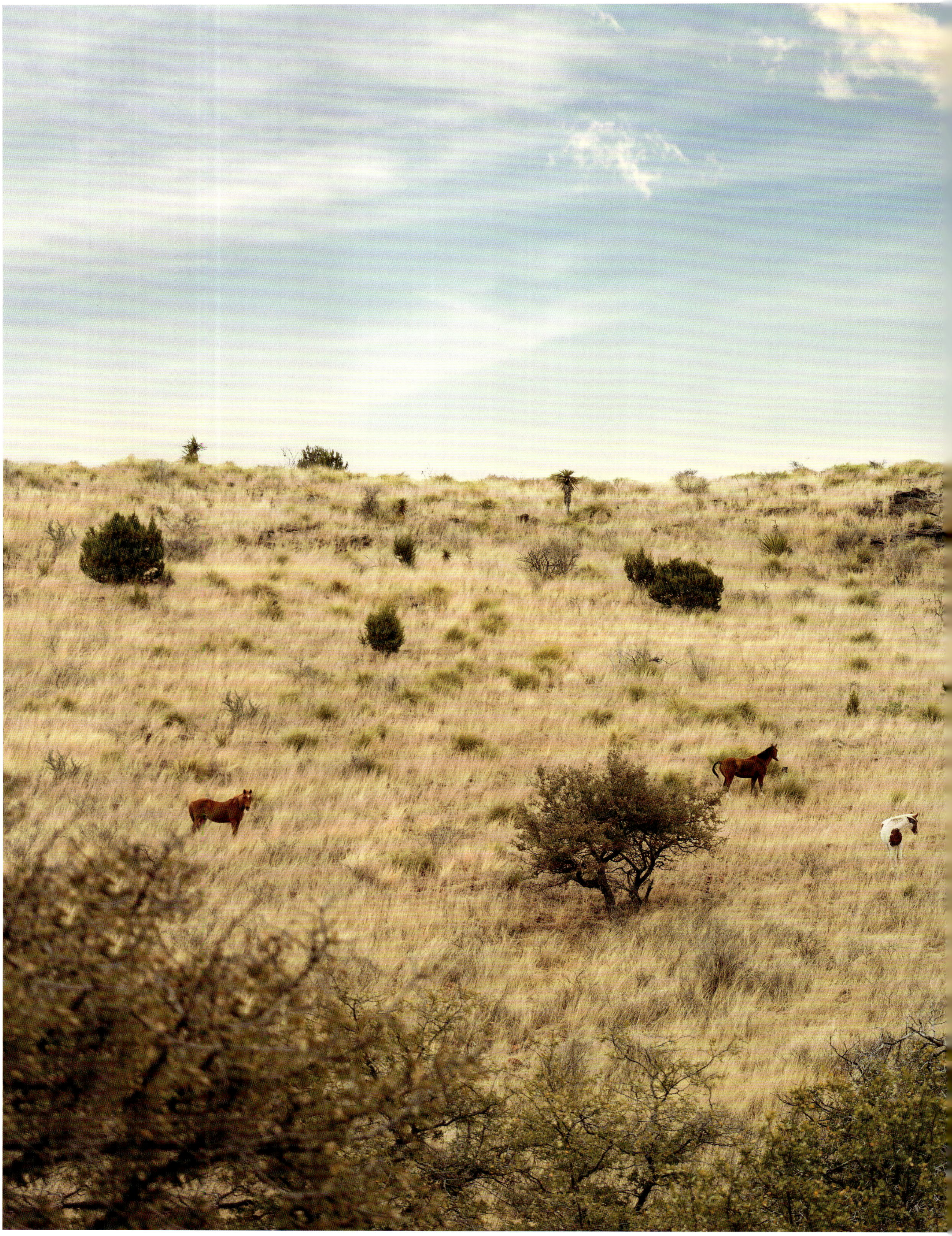

GRAZING Davis Mountains, 2017

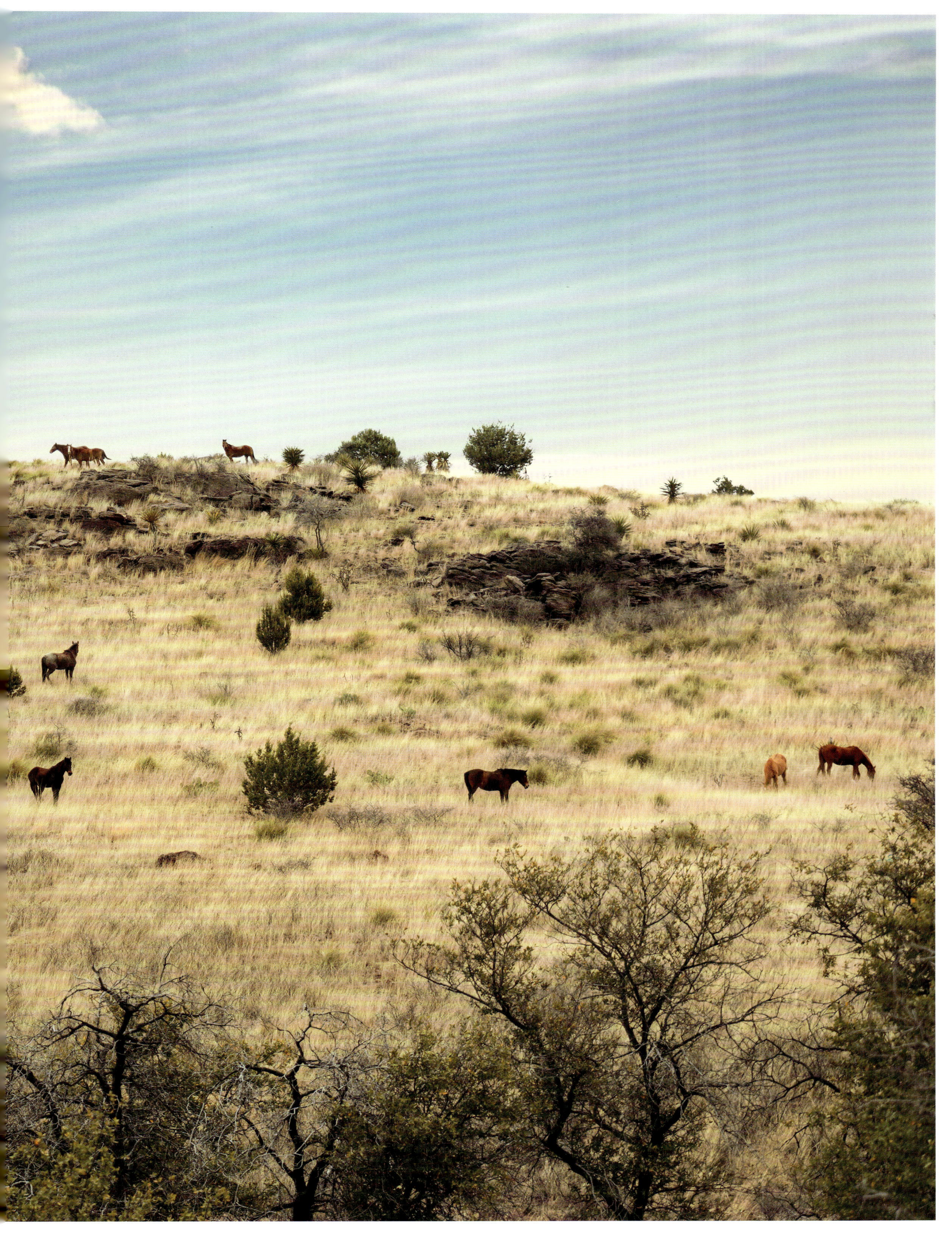

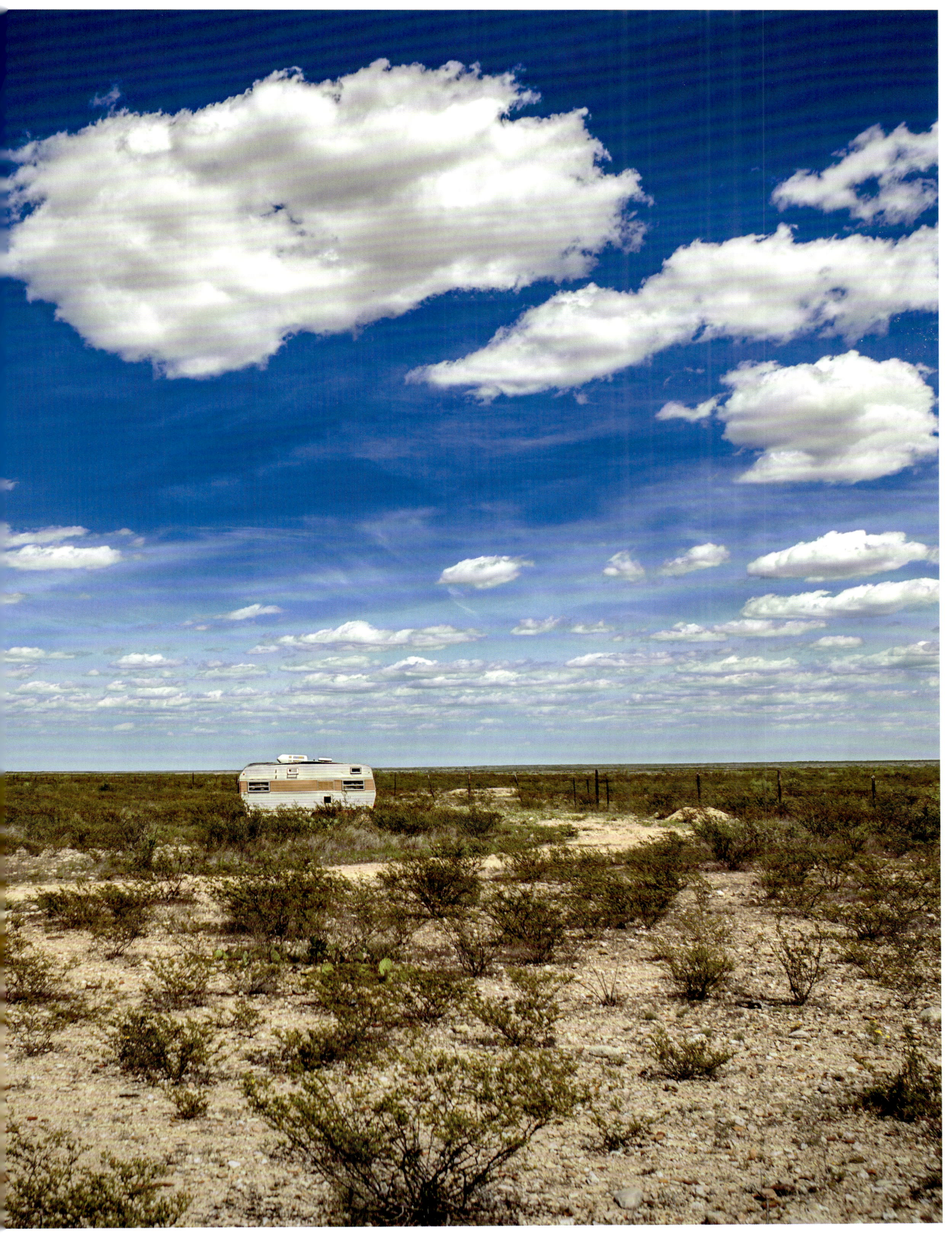

OFF THE GRID near Dryden, 2016

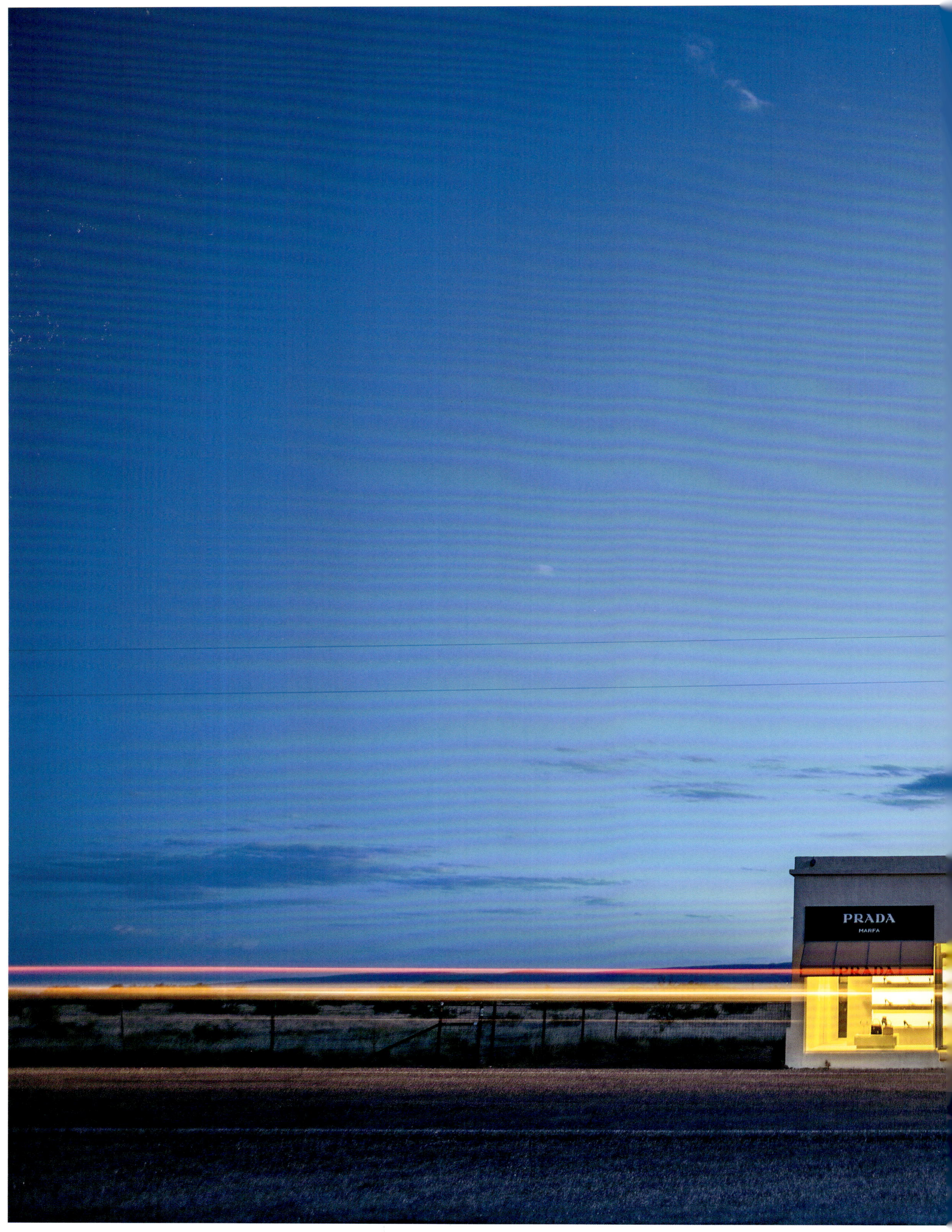

PRADA MARFA near Valentine, 2015

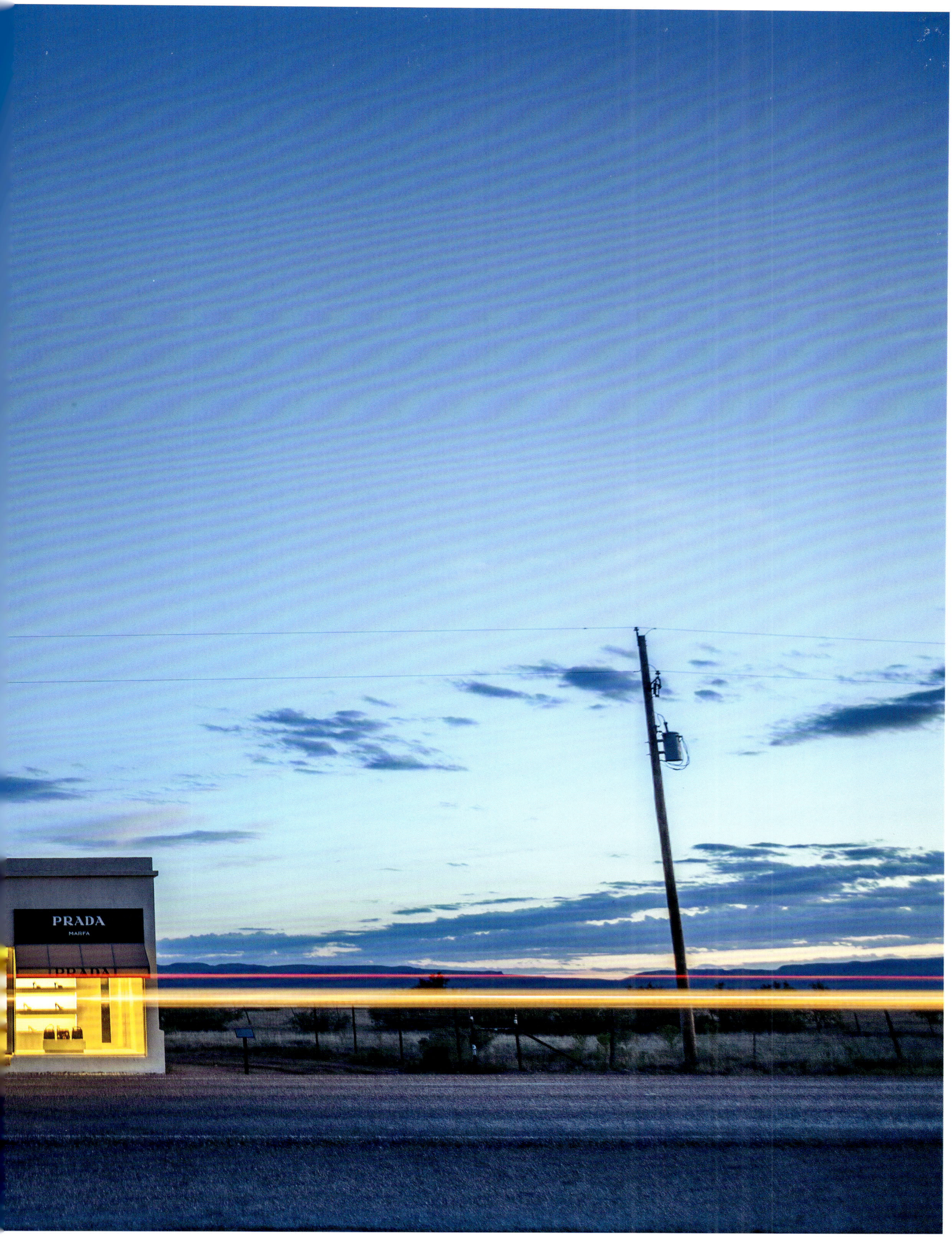

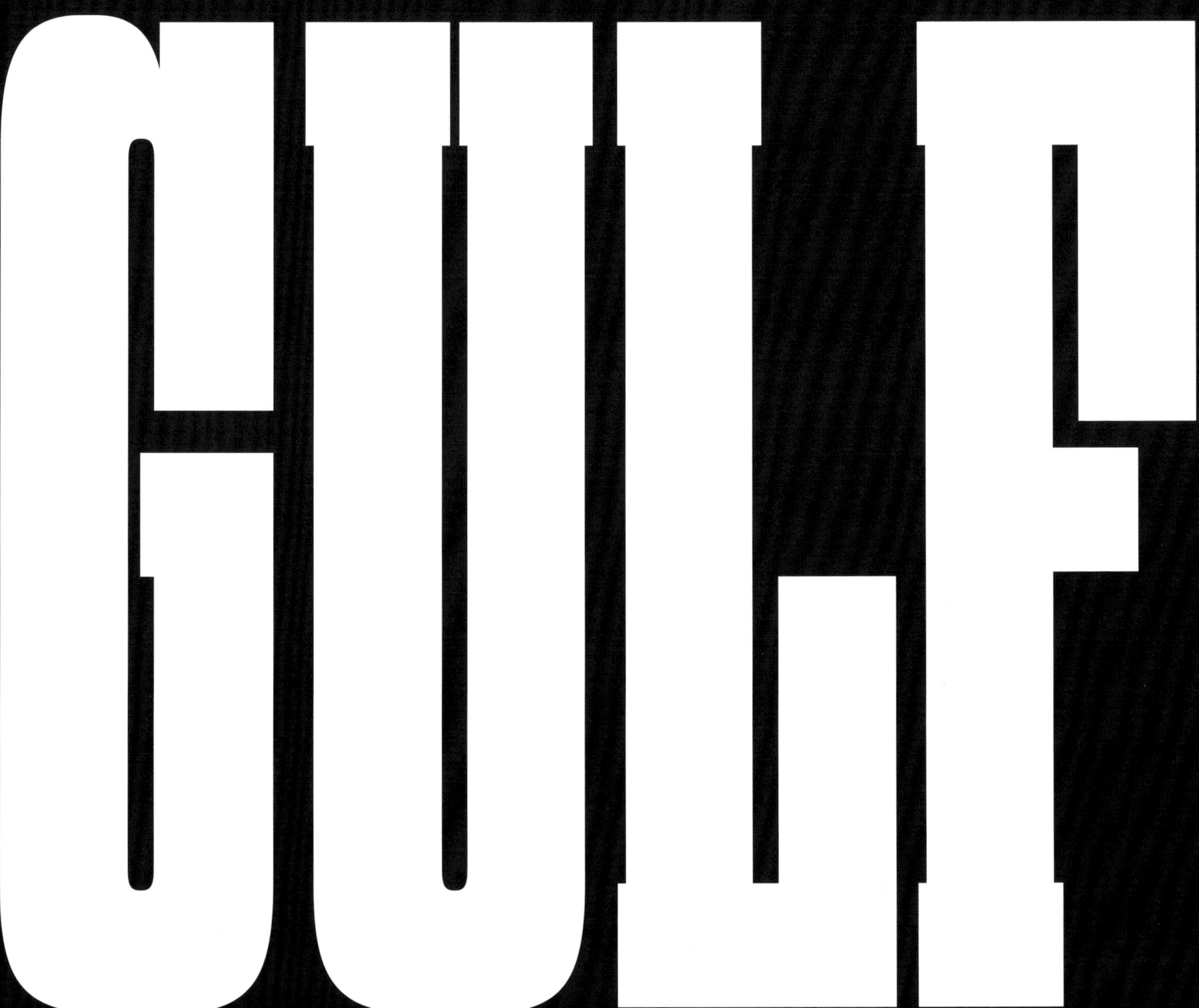
GULF

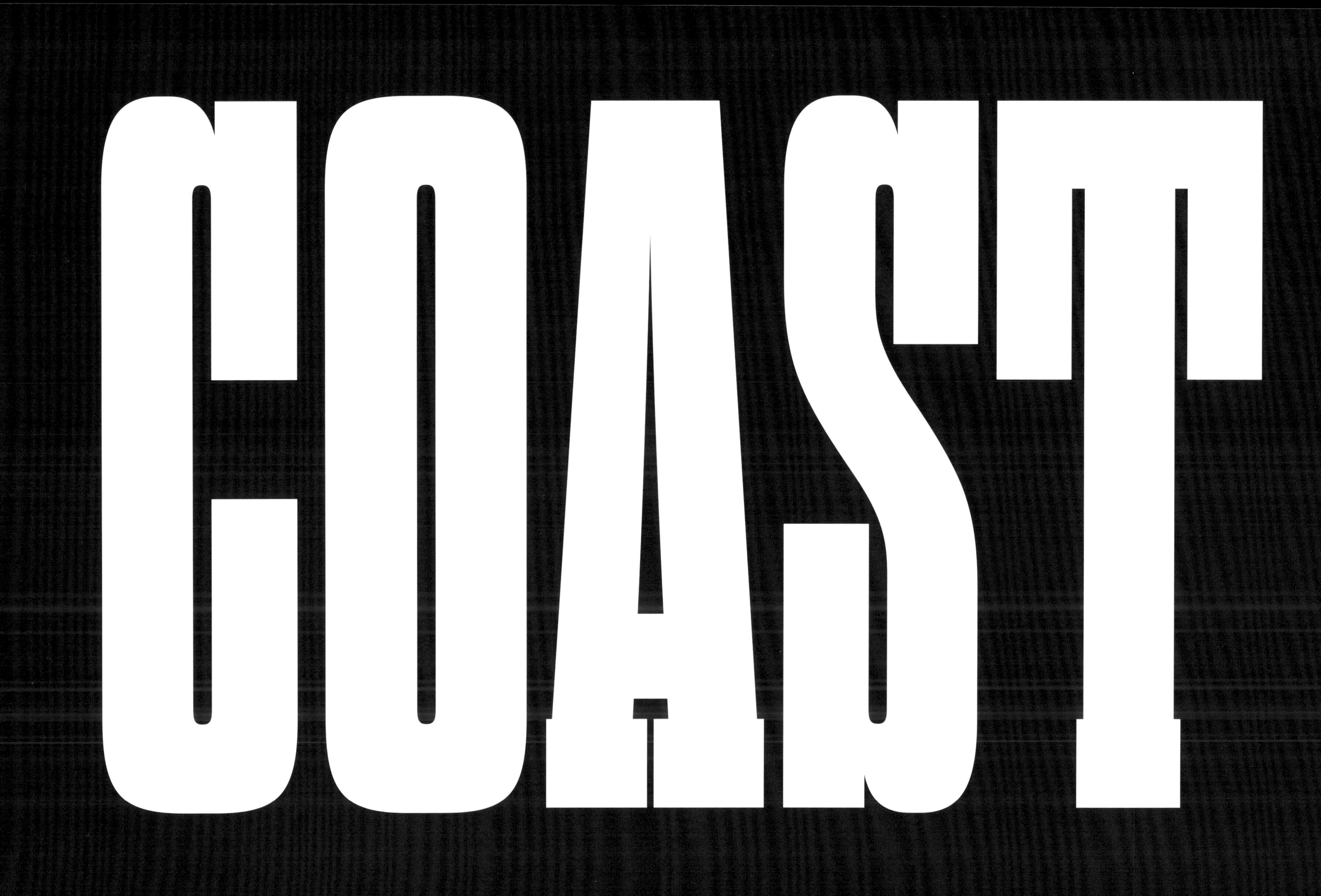
COAST

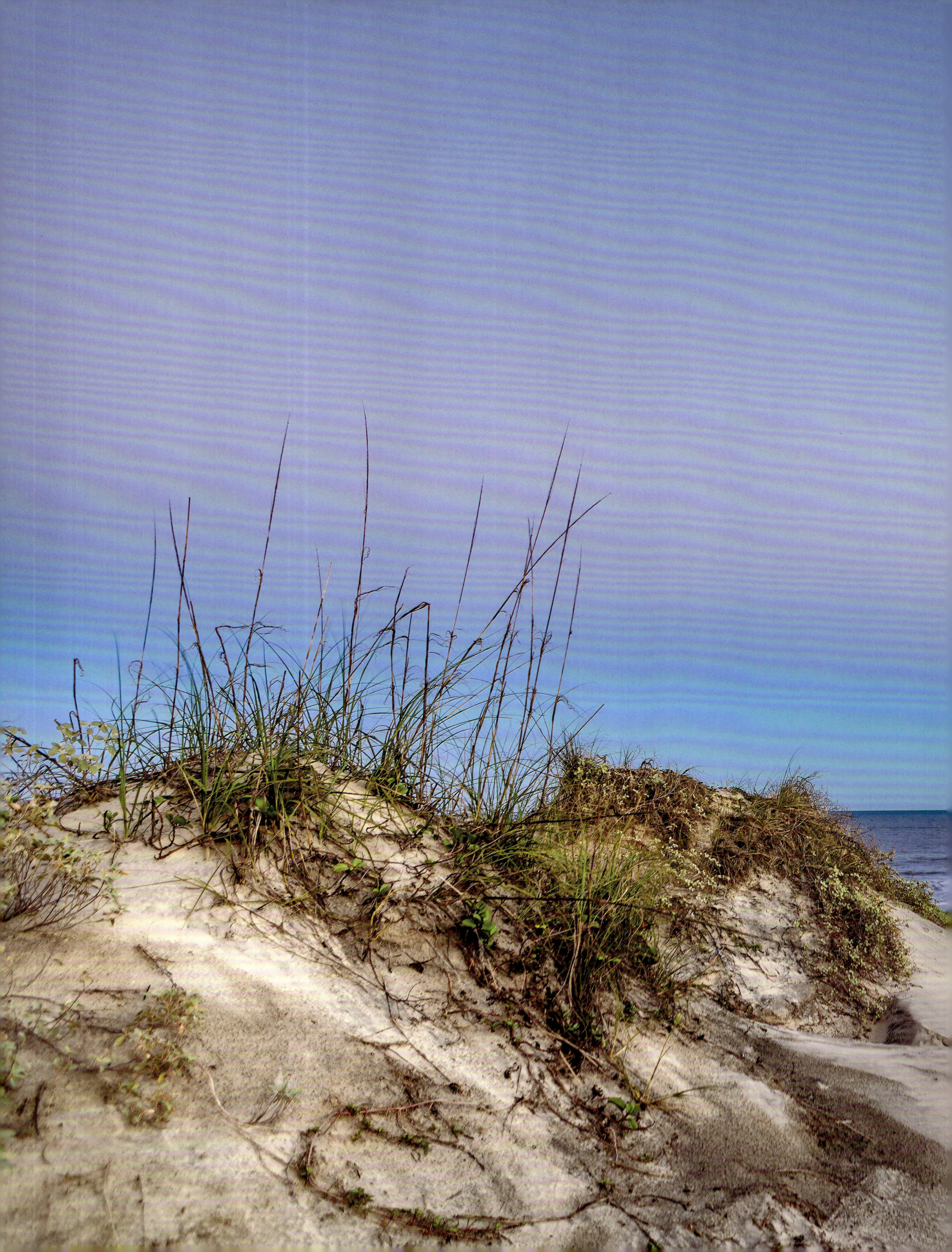

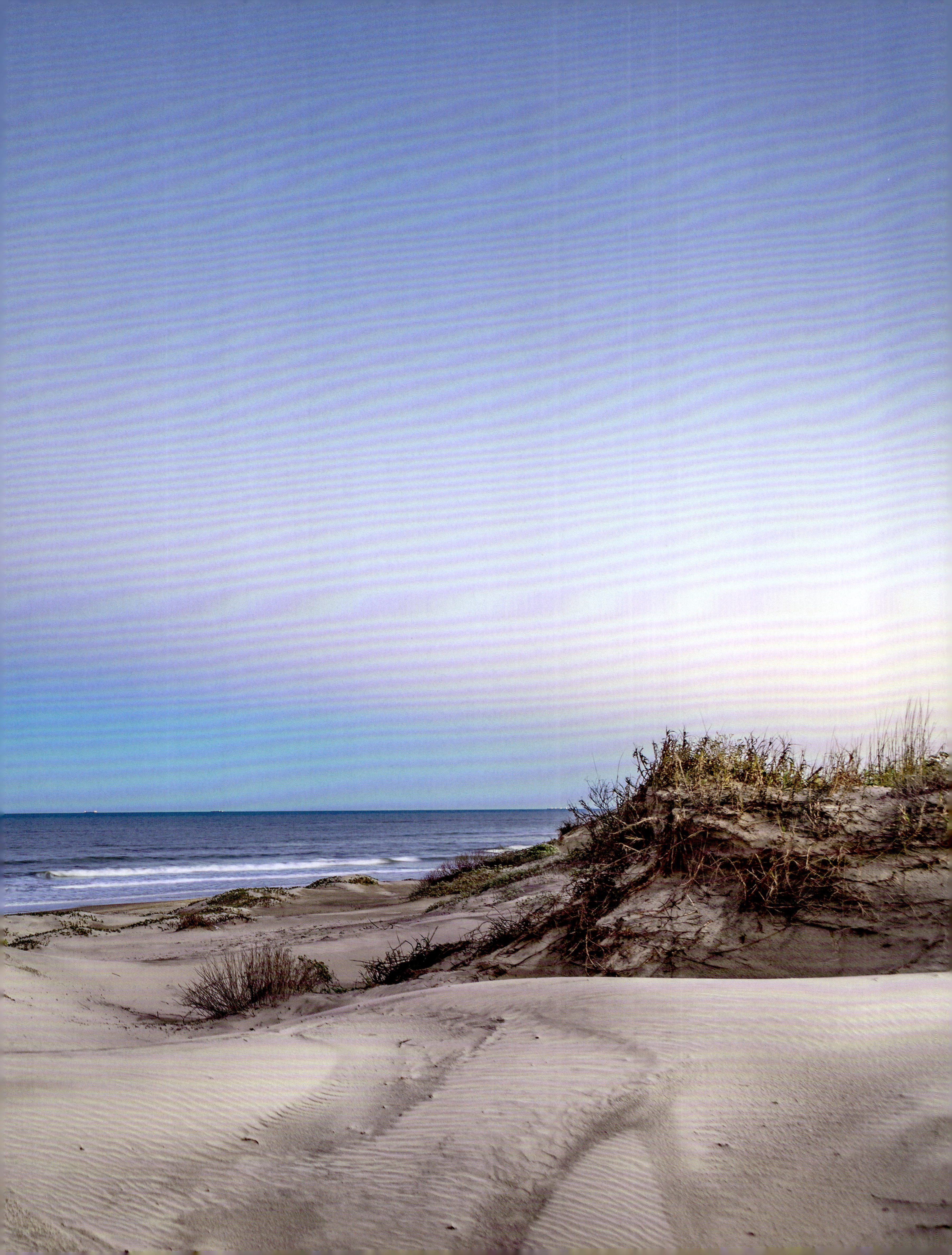

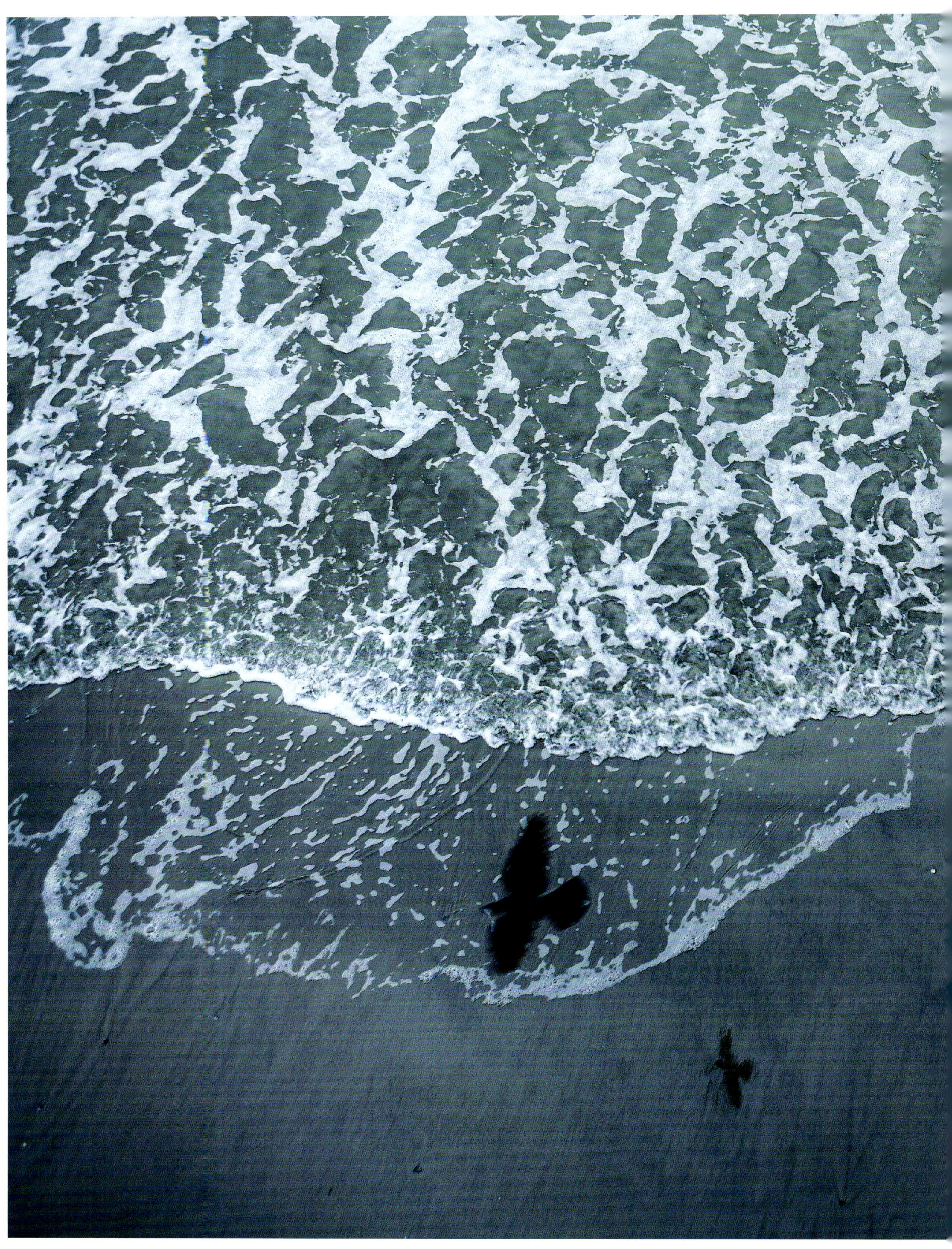

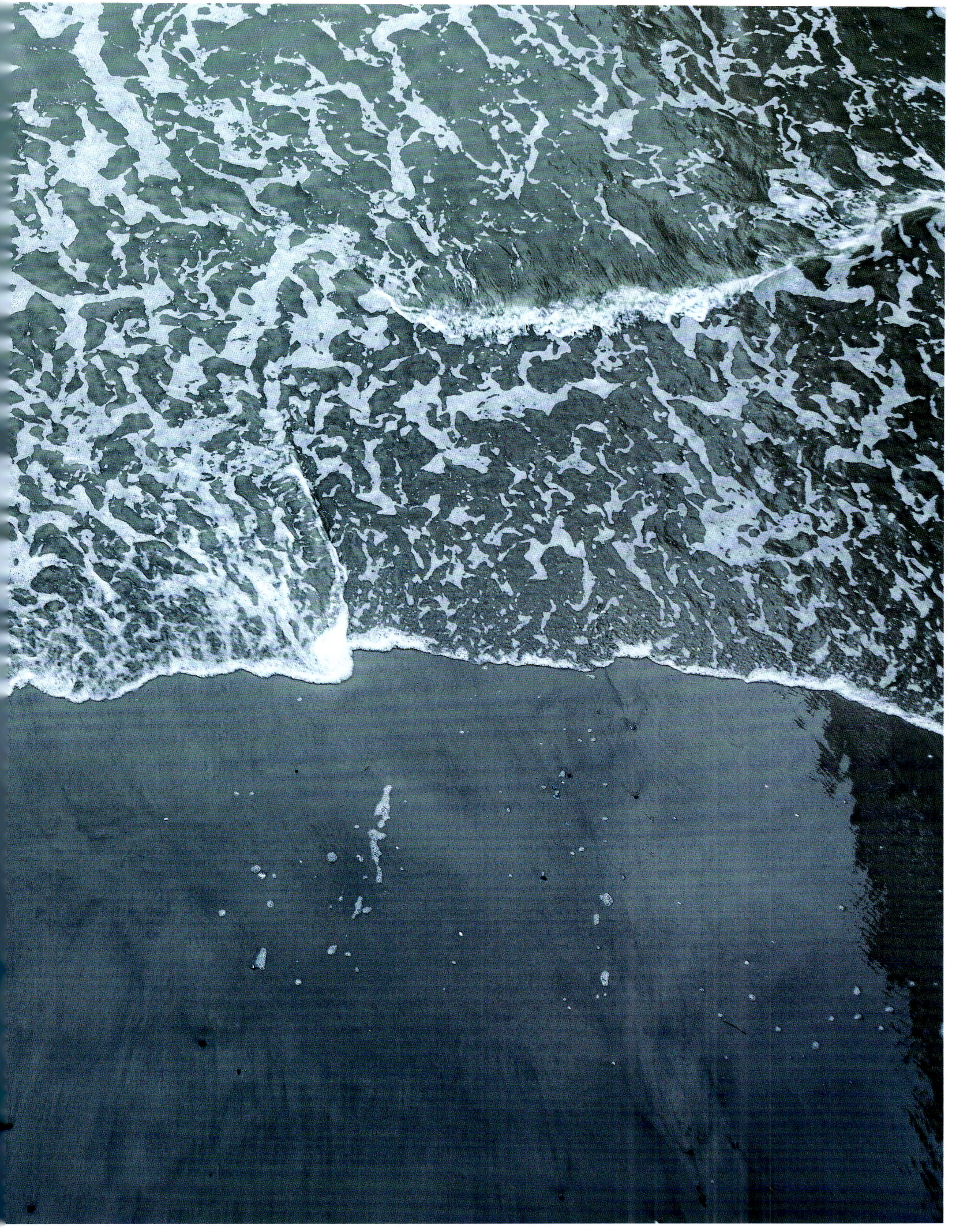

FLY BY Port Aransas, 2016

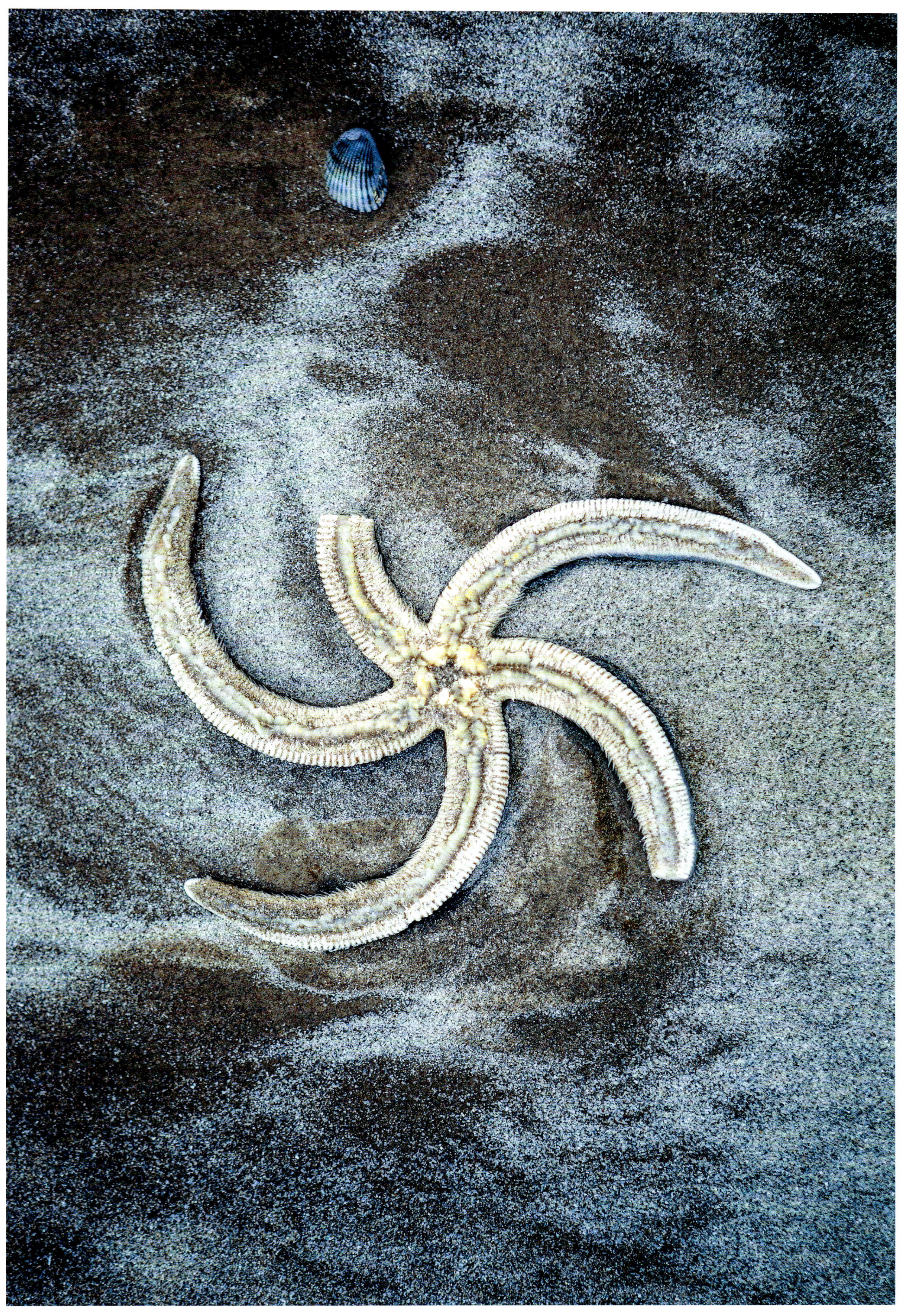

GRAY STAR South Padre Island, 2014

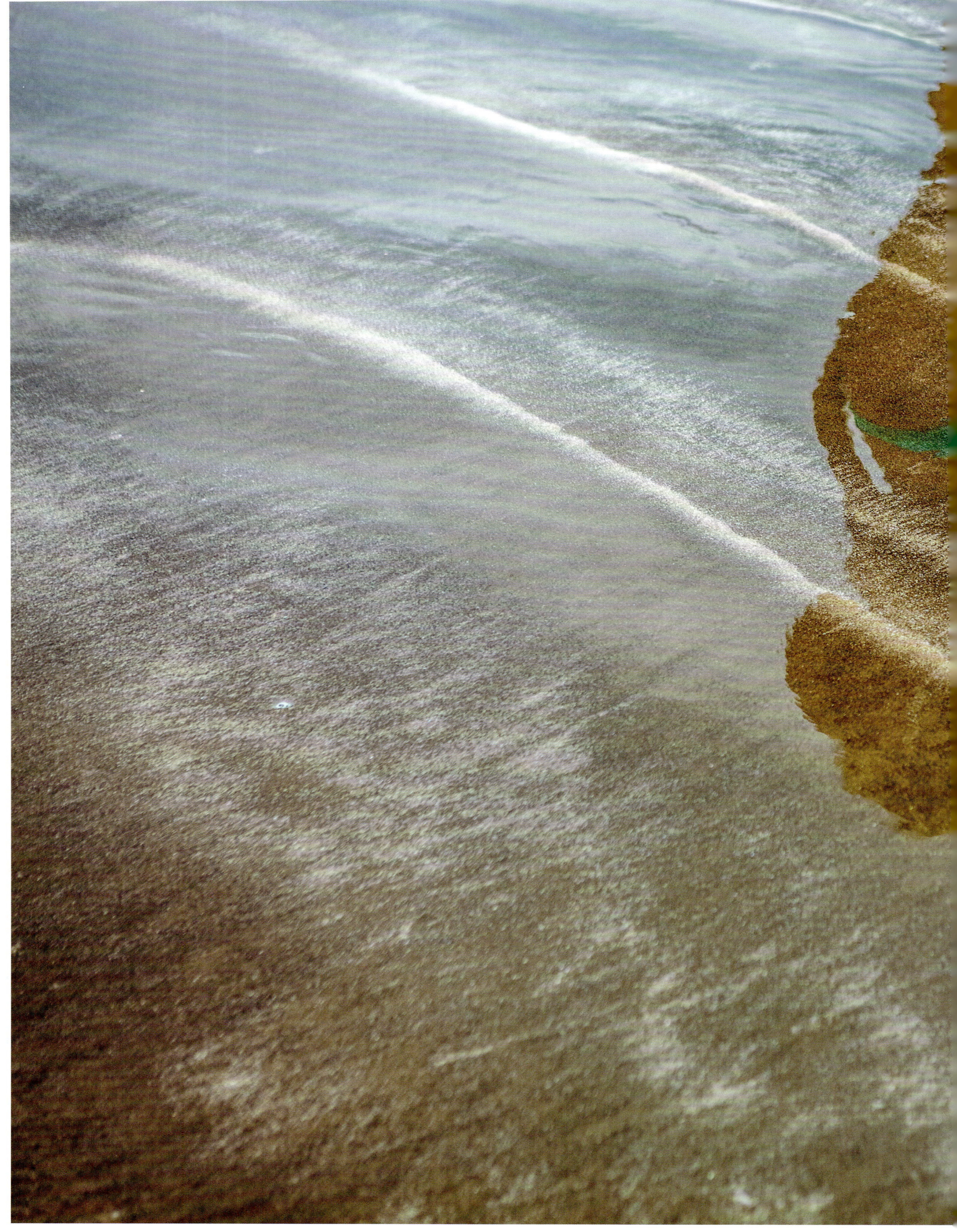

SIRENA Port Aransas, 2016

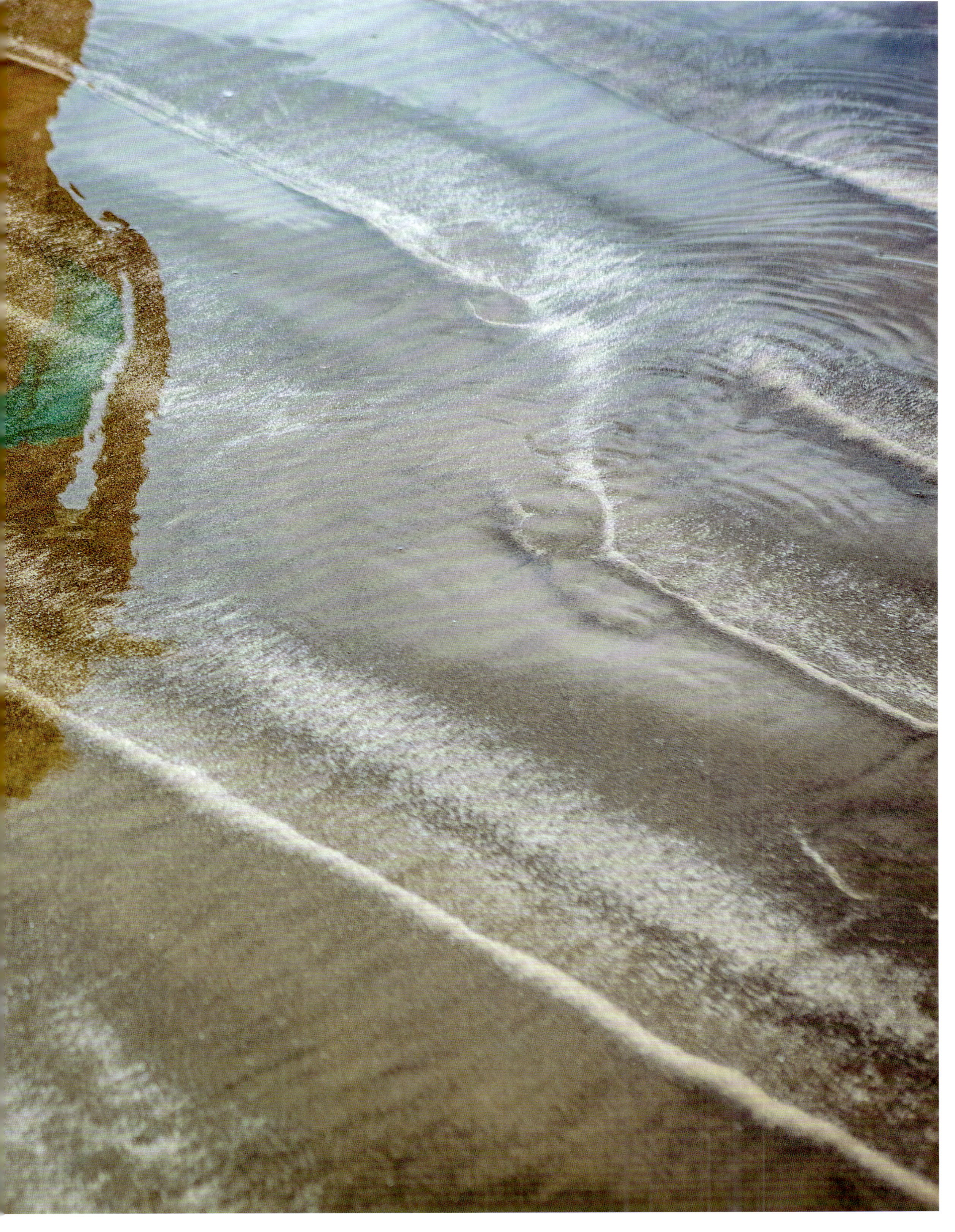

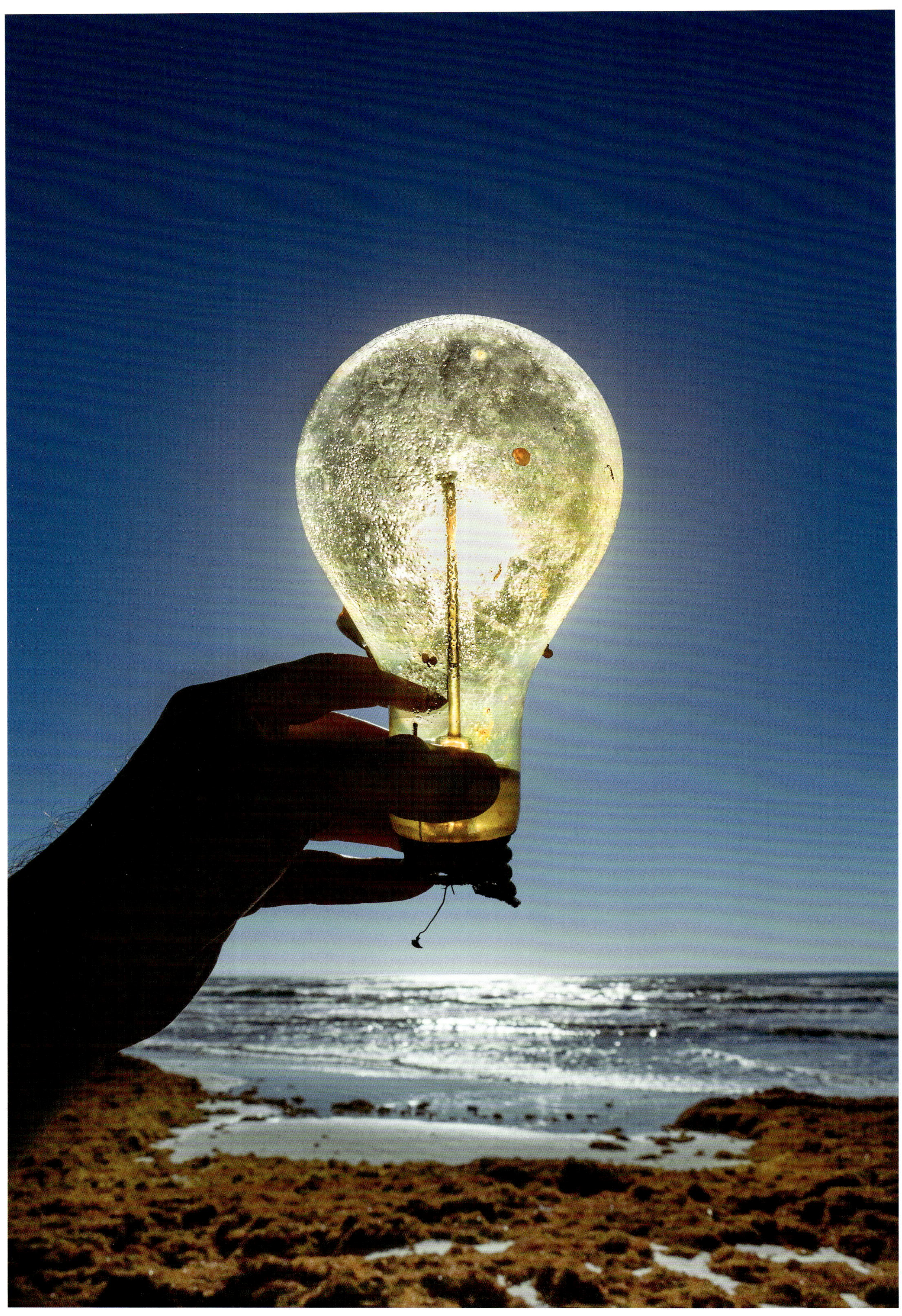

SOLAR Padre Island National Seashore, 2007

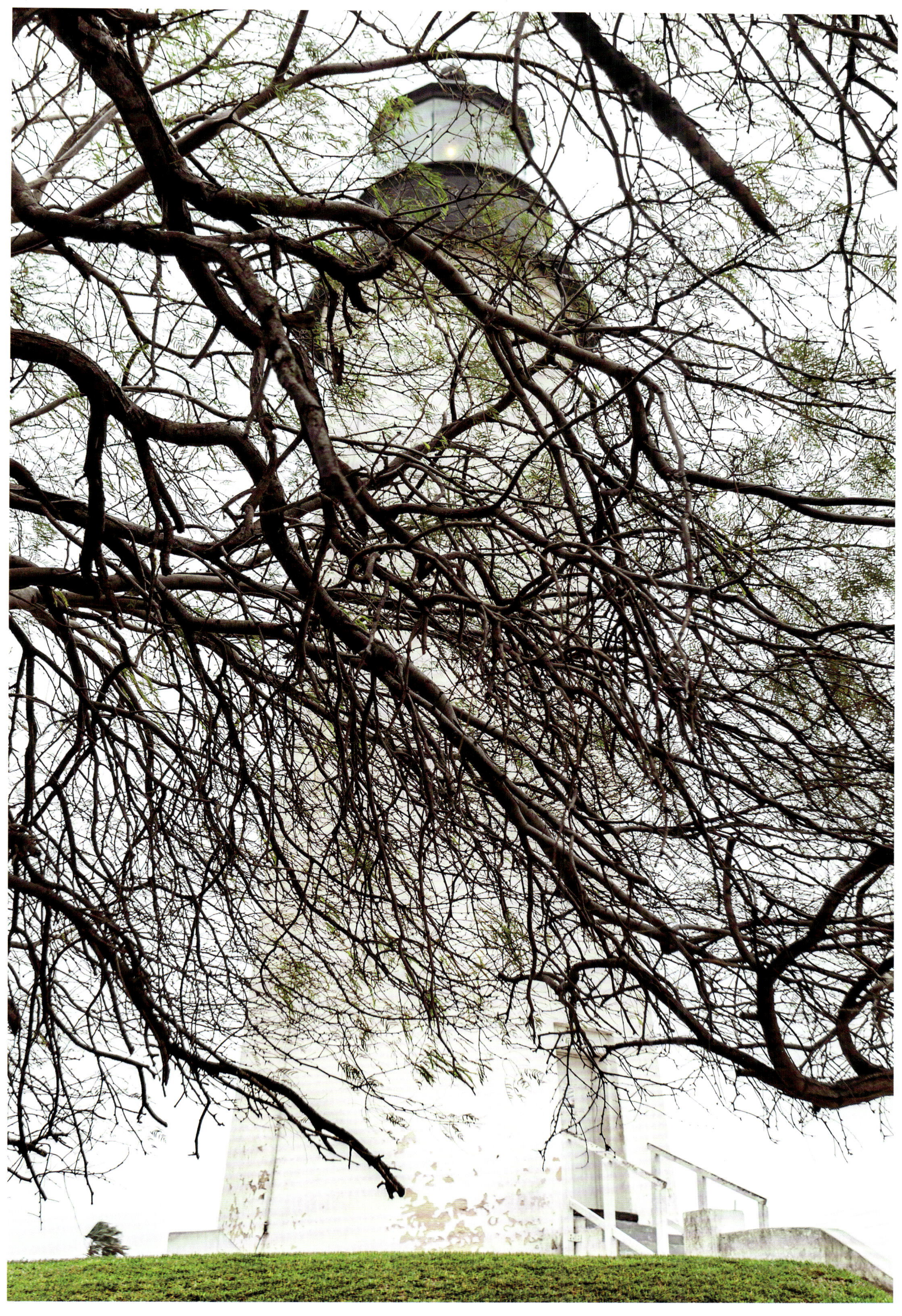

PORT ISABEL LIGHTHOUSE Port Isabel, 2015

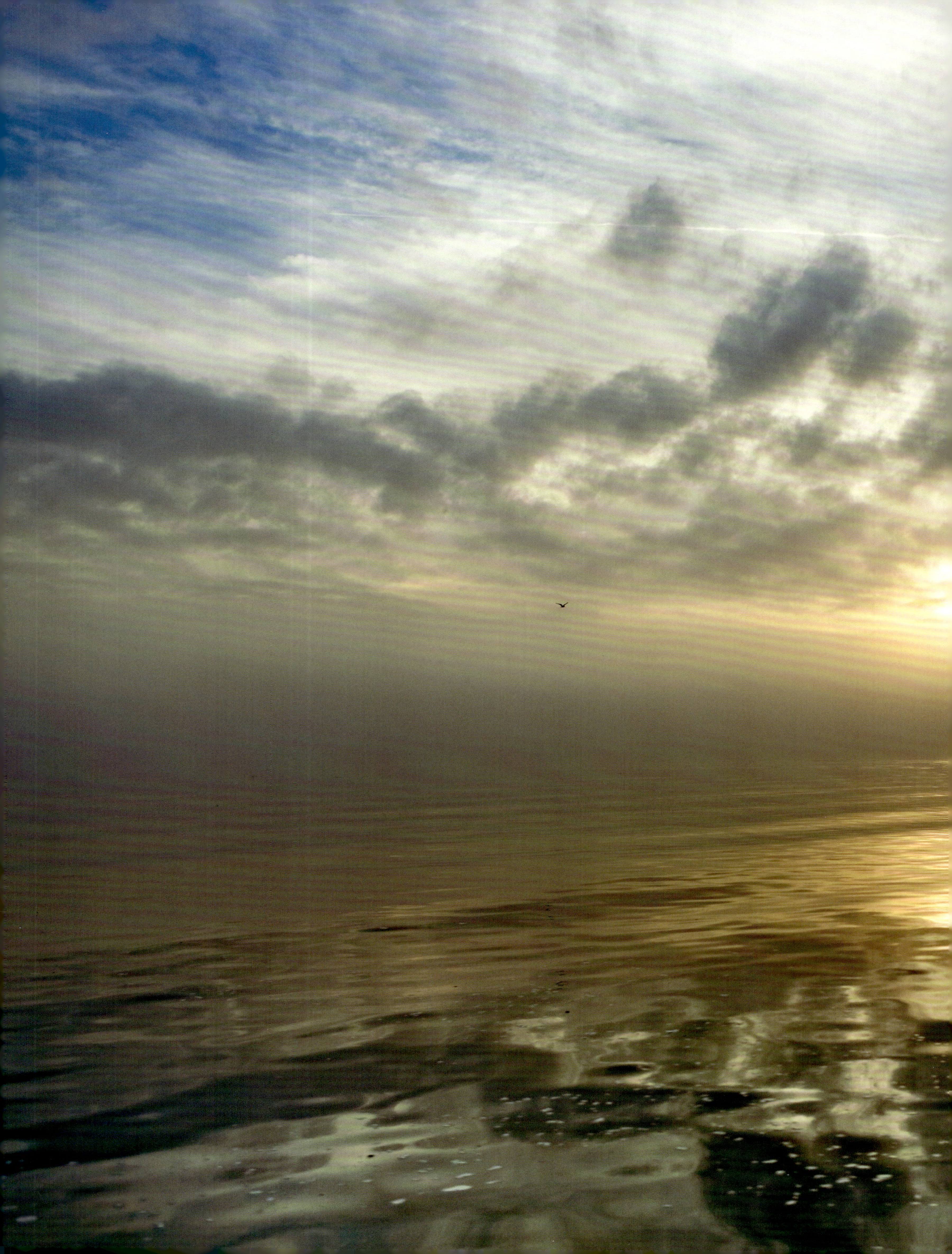

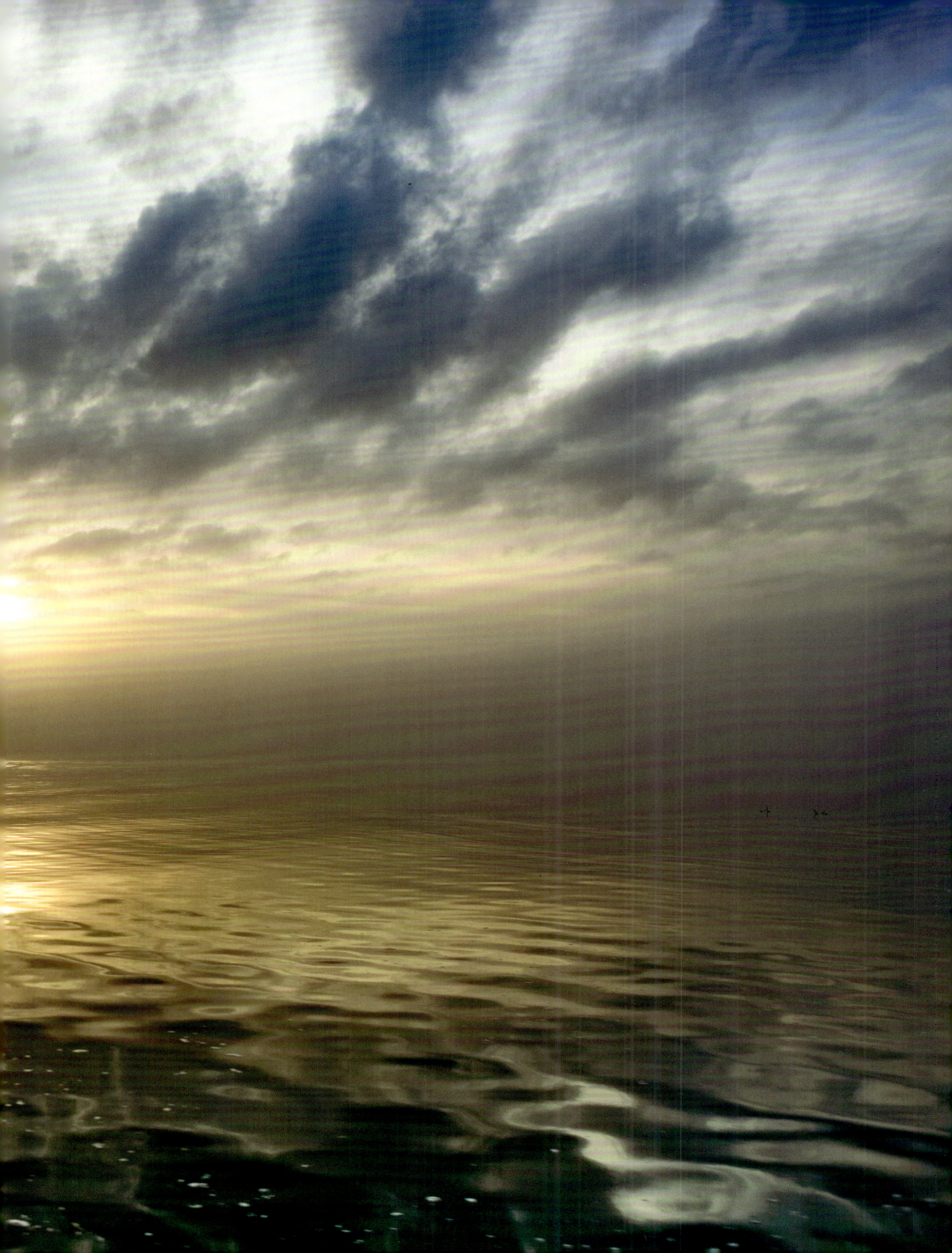

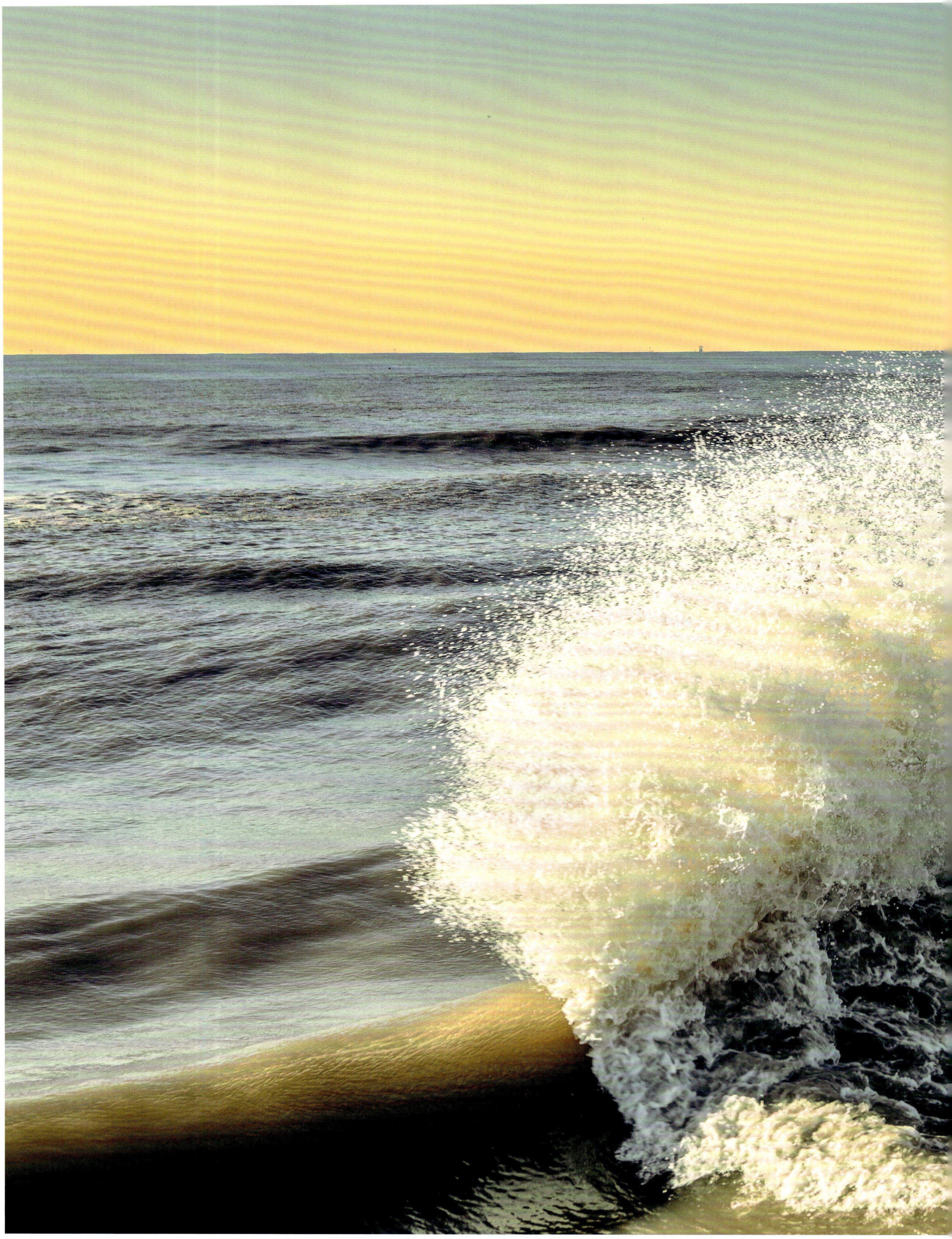

< **LOST HORIZON** Port Aransas, 2012

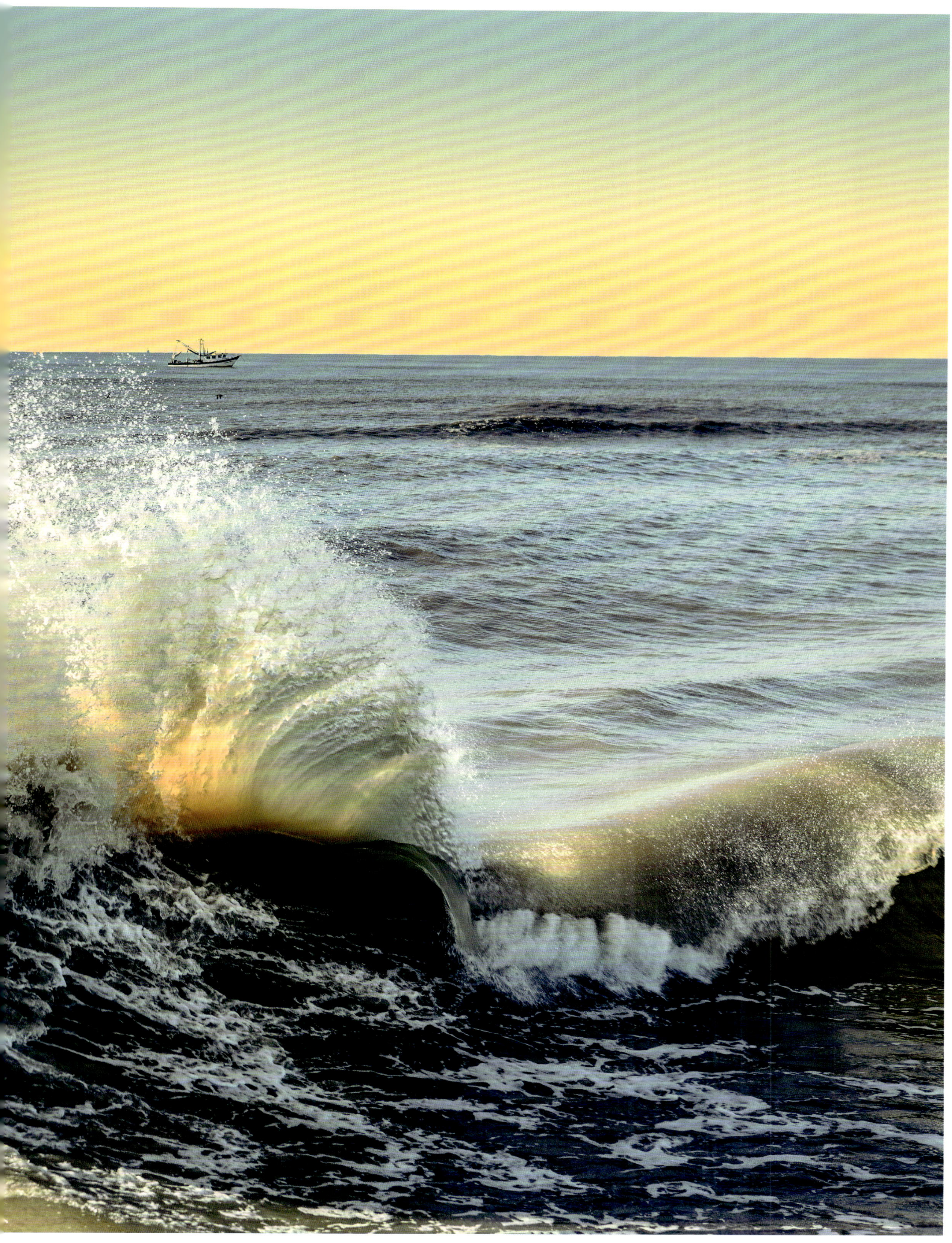

WAVE INTERFERENCE Matagorda, 2017

SOLE SURFER South Padre Island, 2012

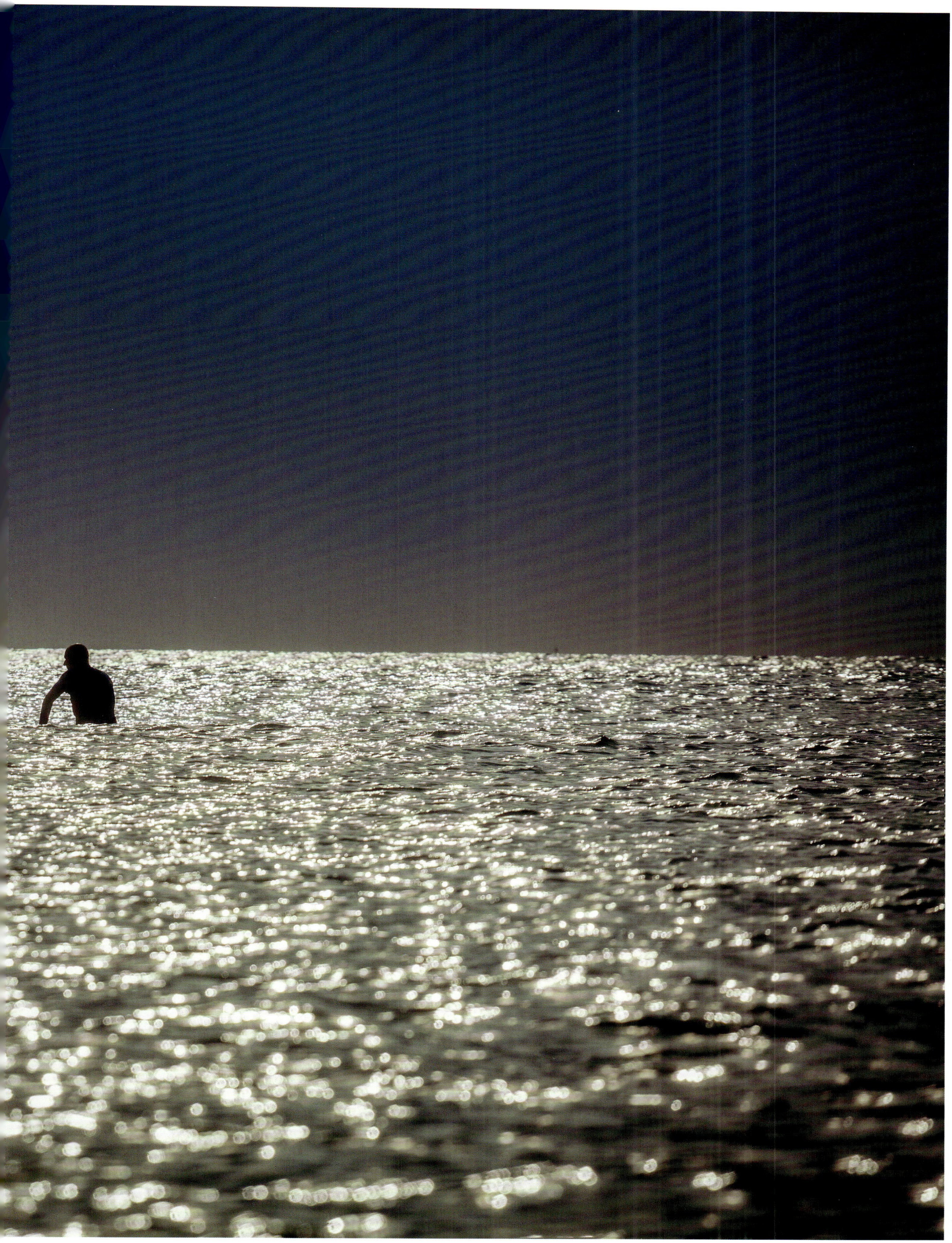

HURRICANE ISAAC #5 South Padre Island, 2012 >

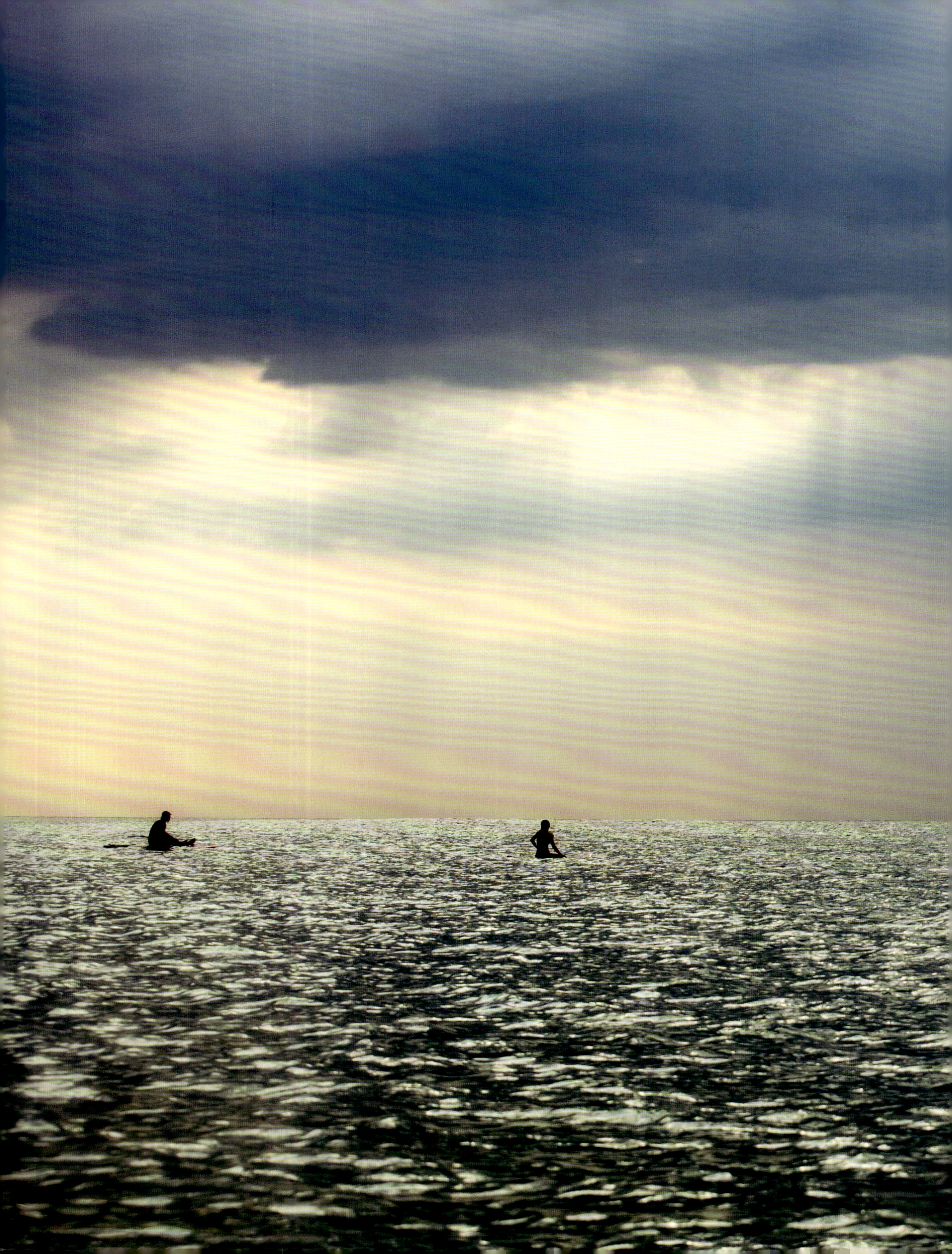

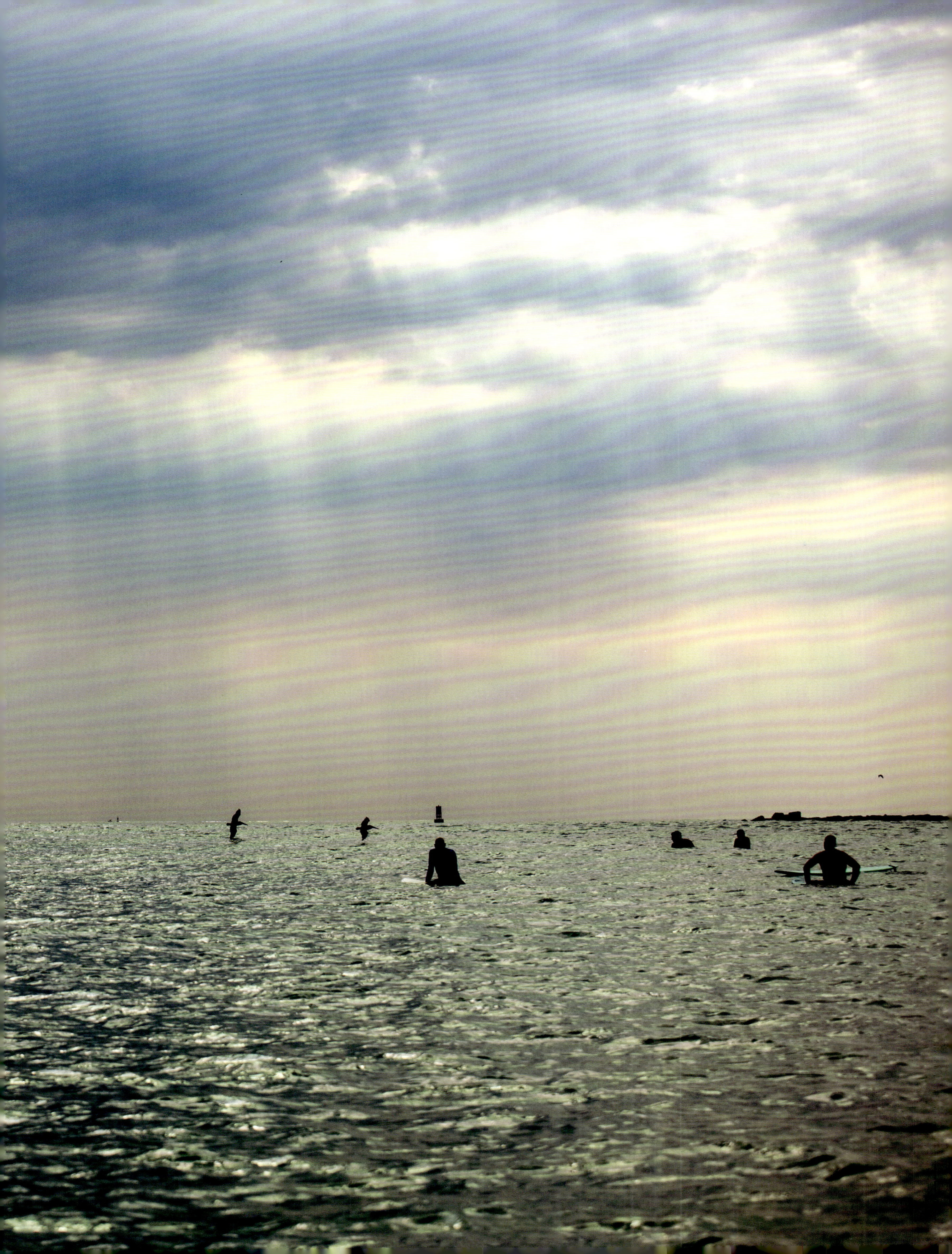

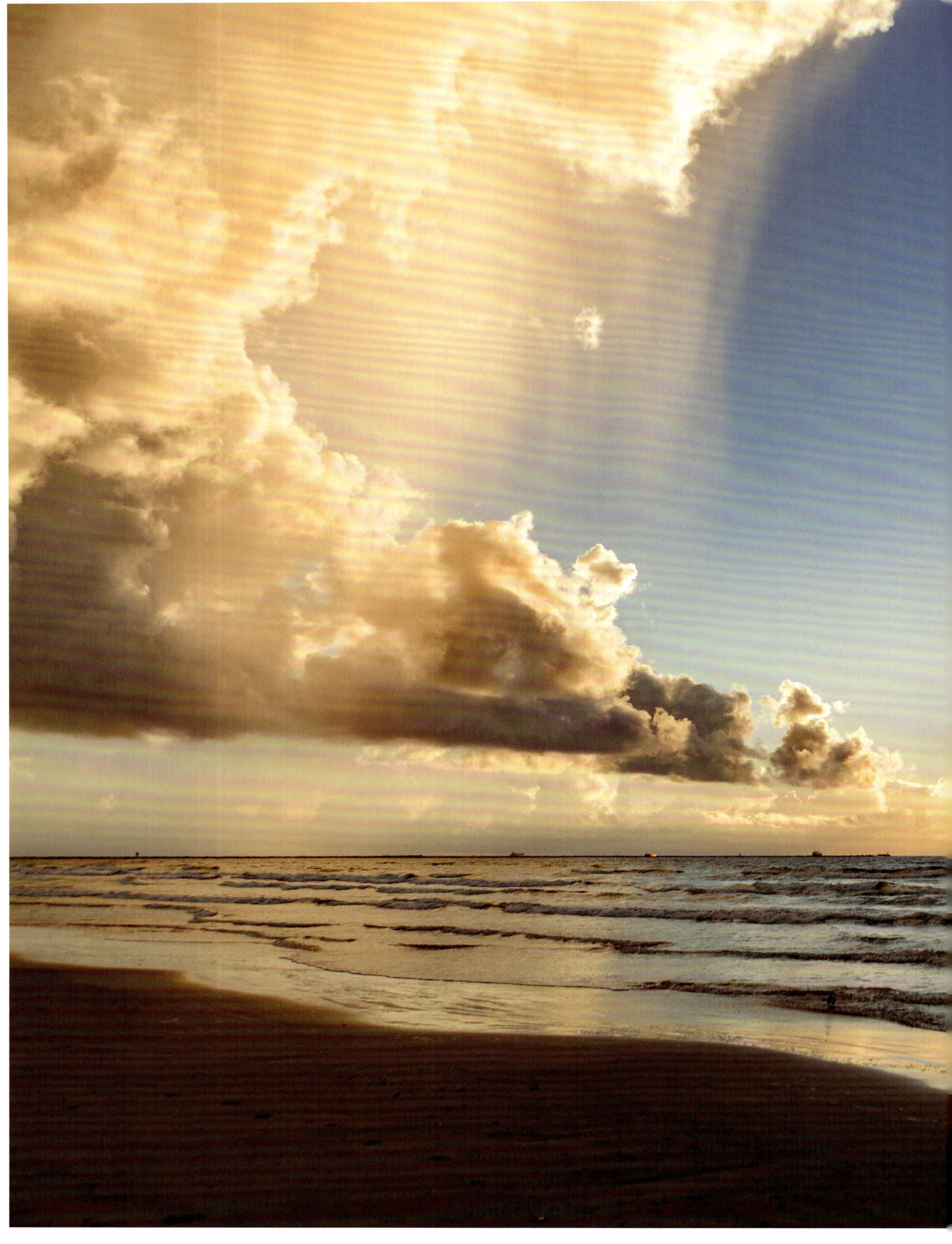

BLUE SKY AND RAIN Port Aransas, 2016

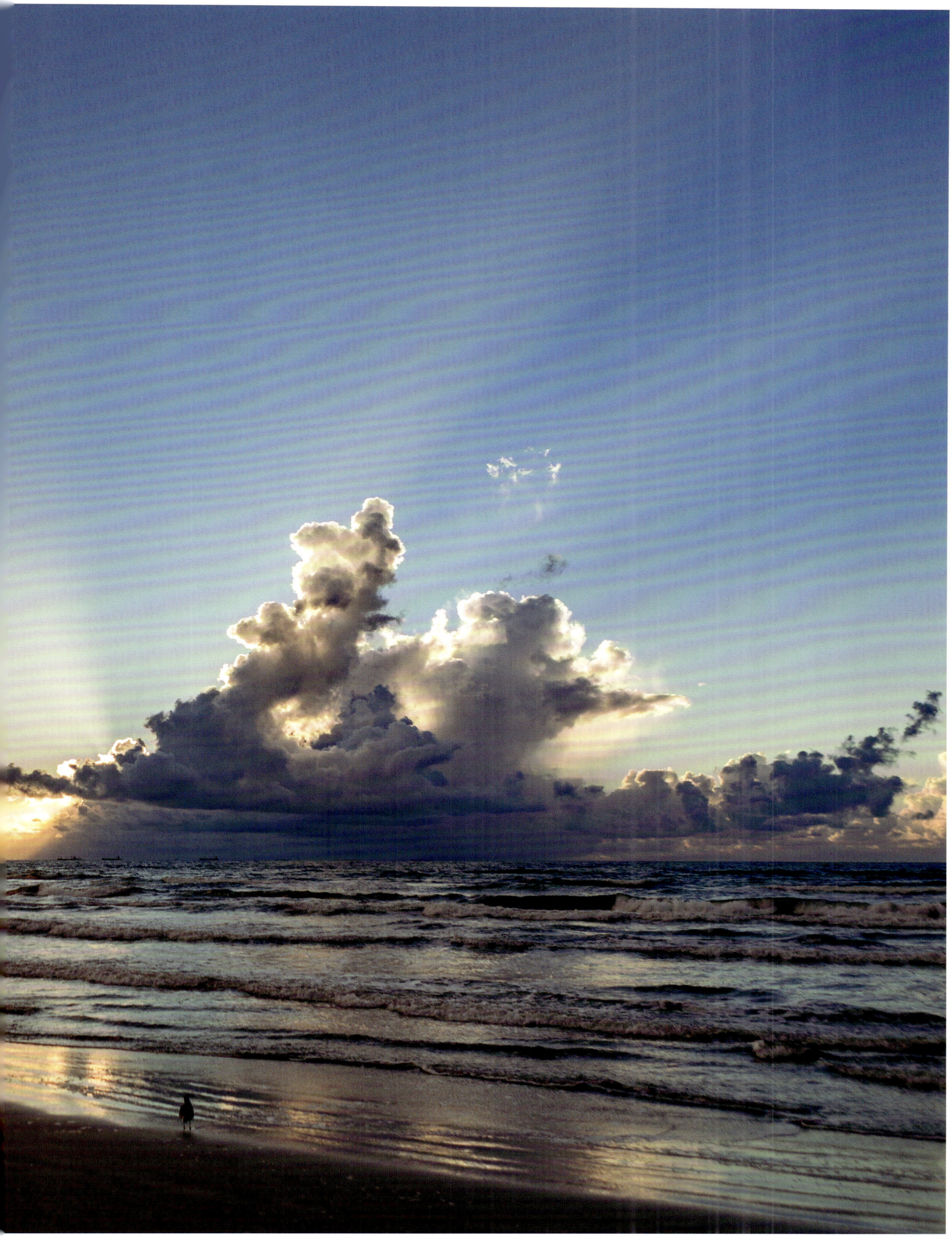

HORACE CALDWELL PIER Port Aransas, 2012 >

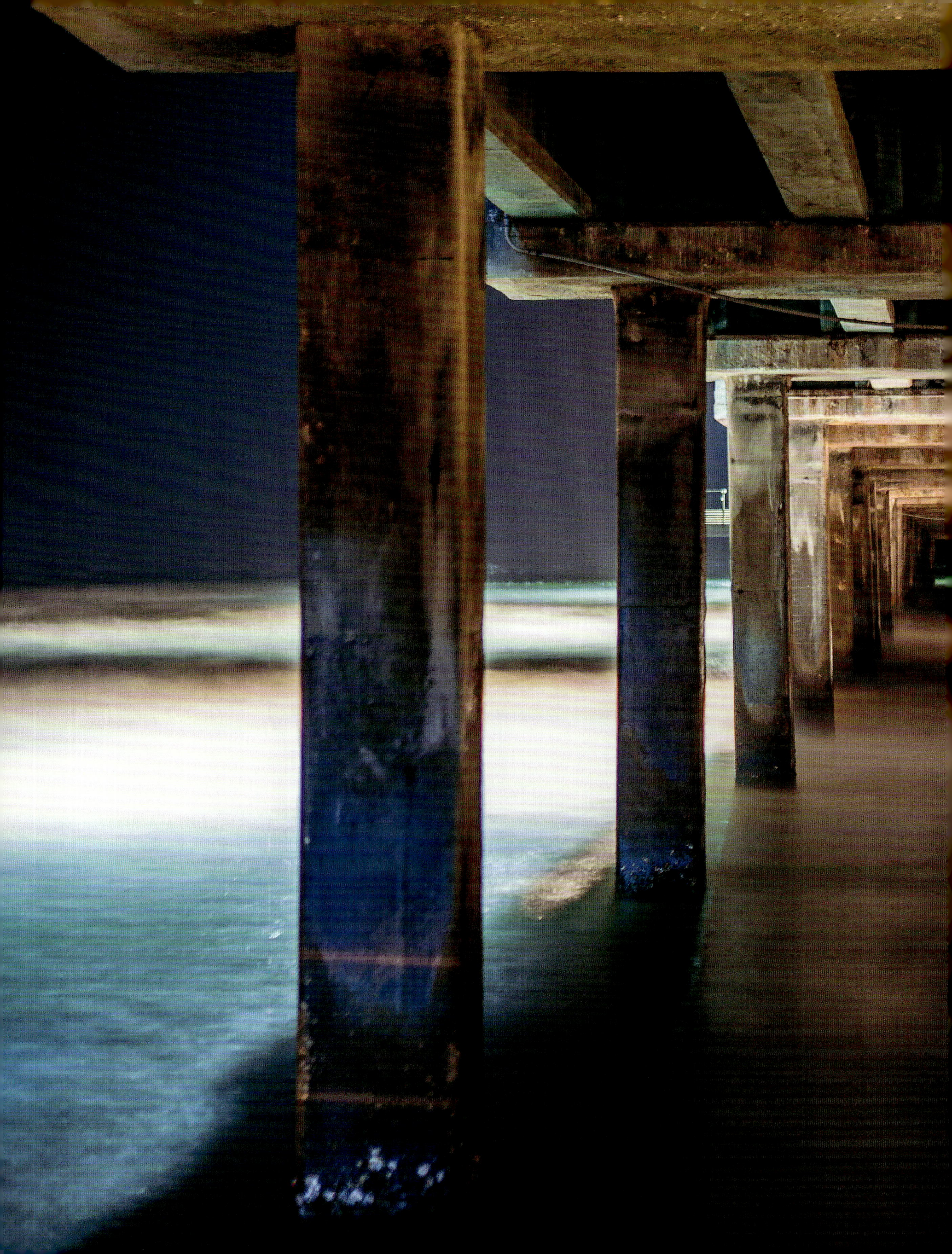

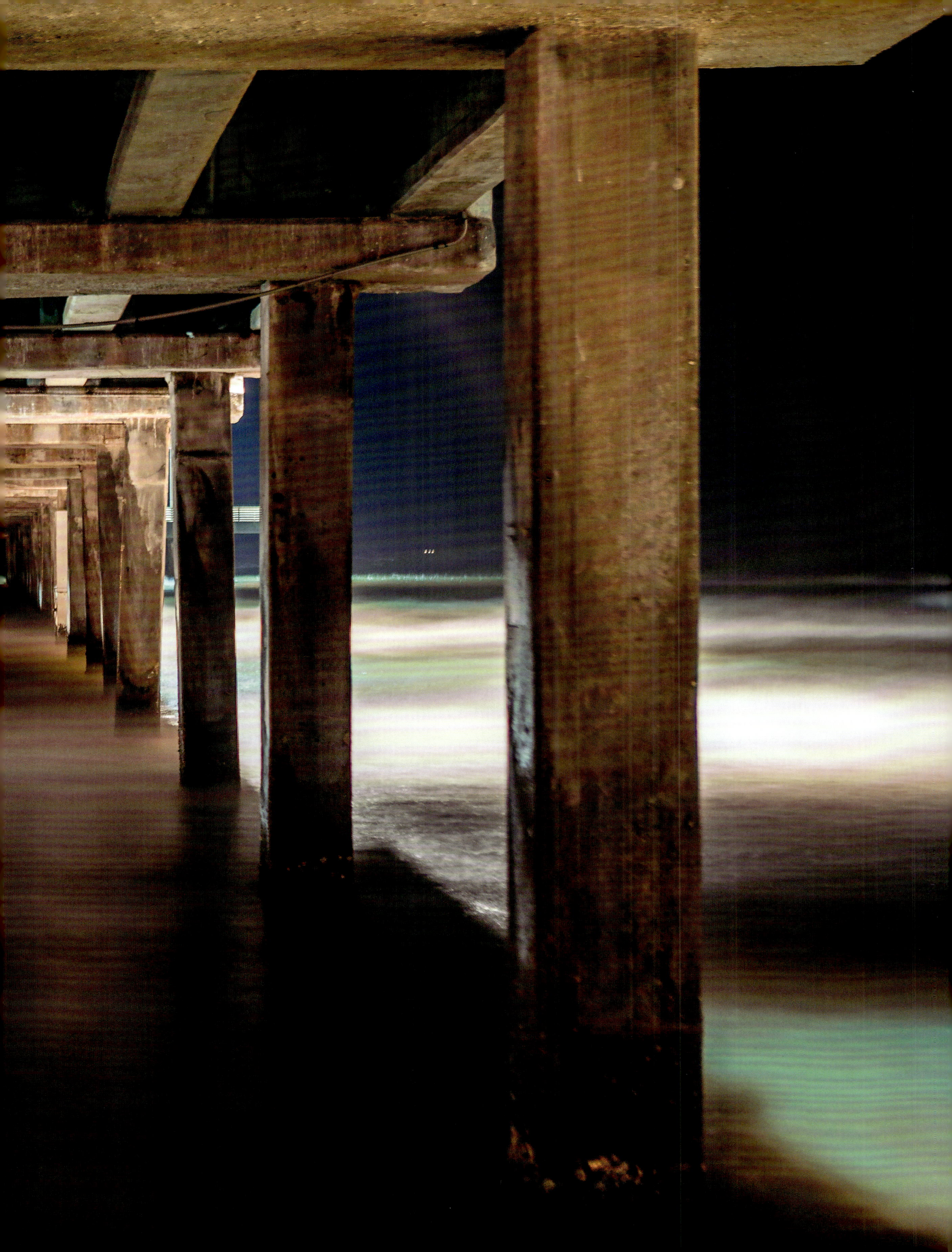

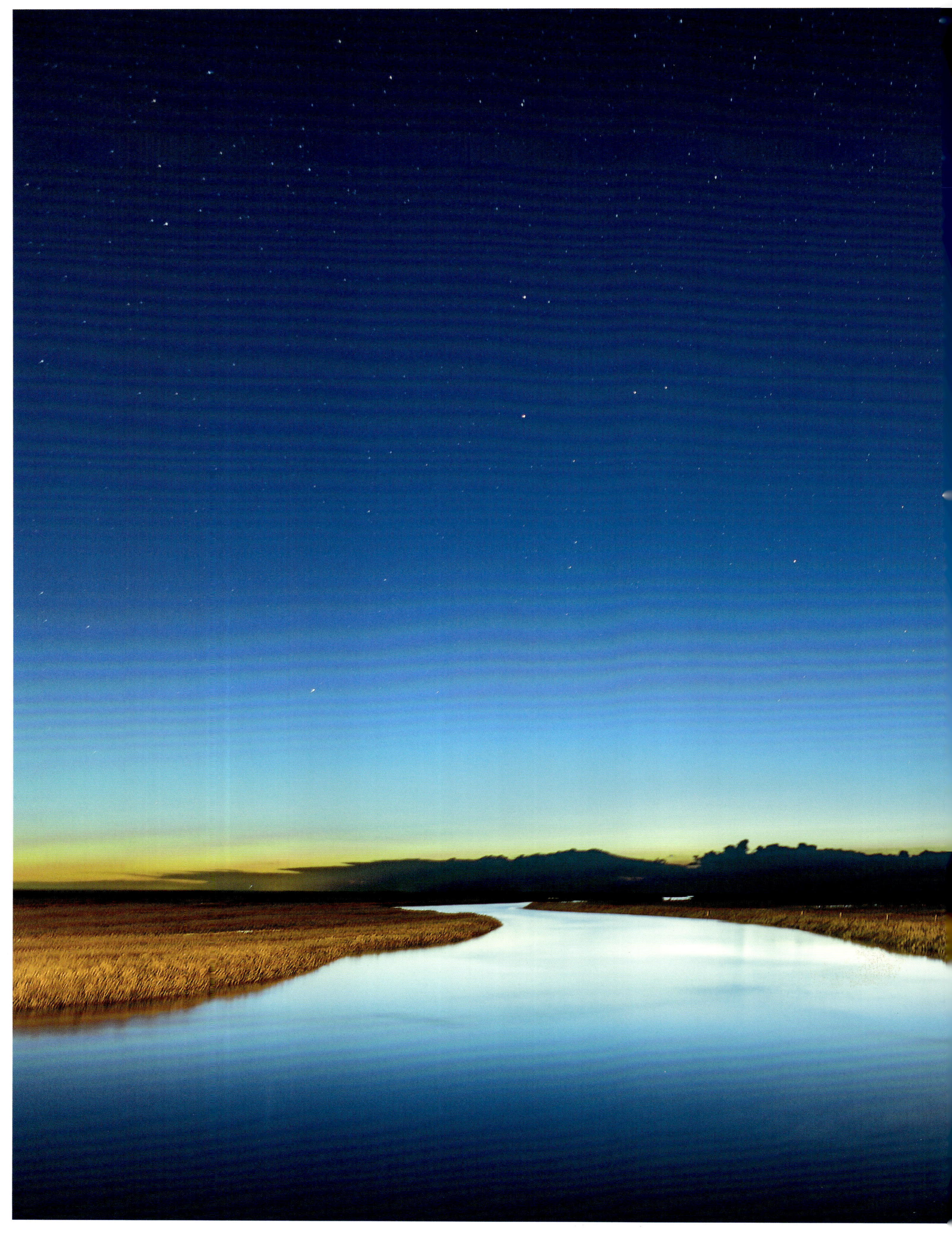

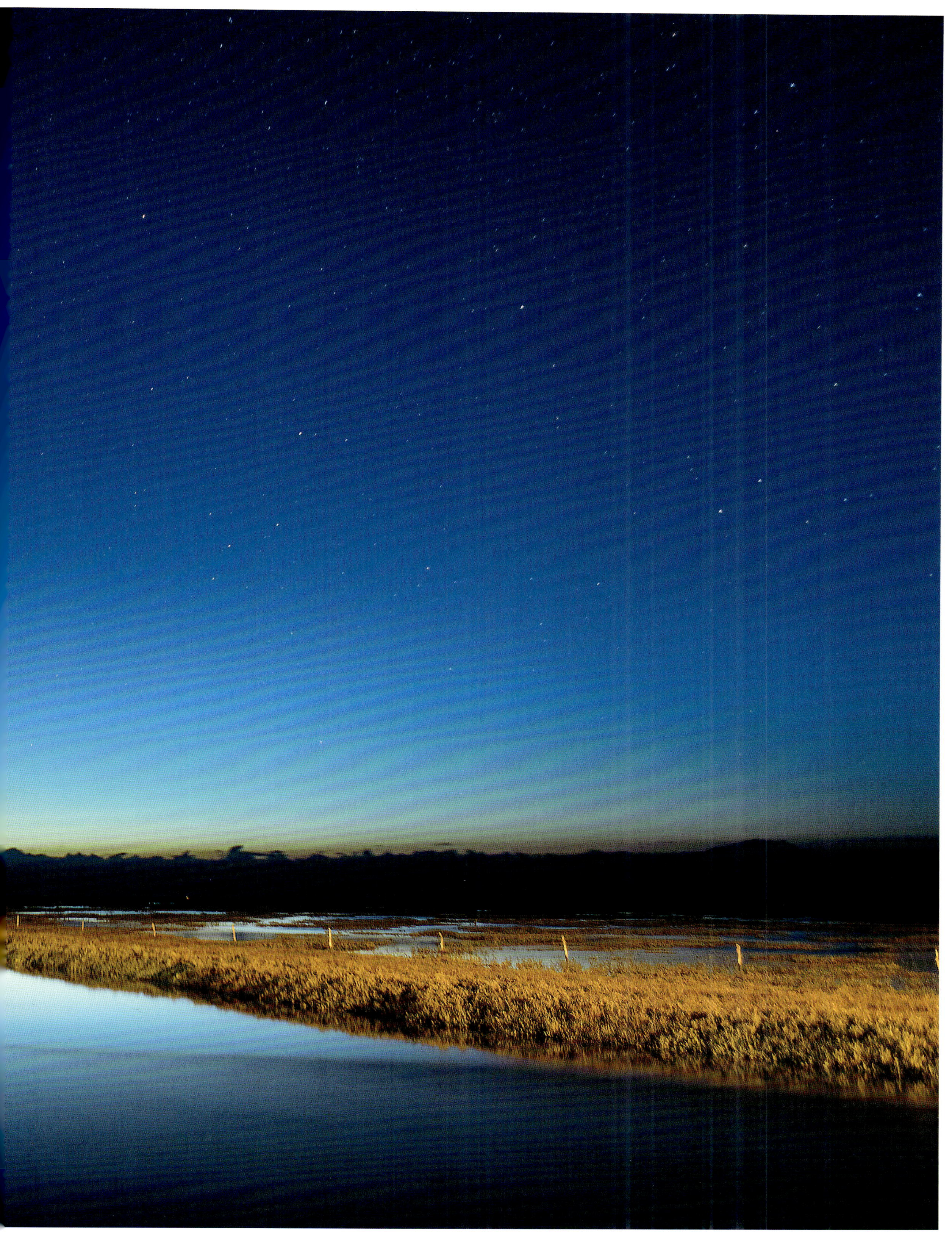

PREDAWN Matagorda, 2017

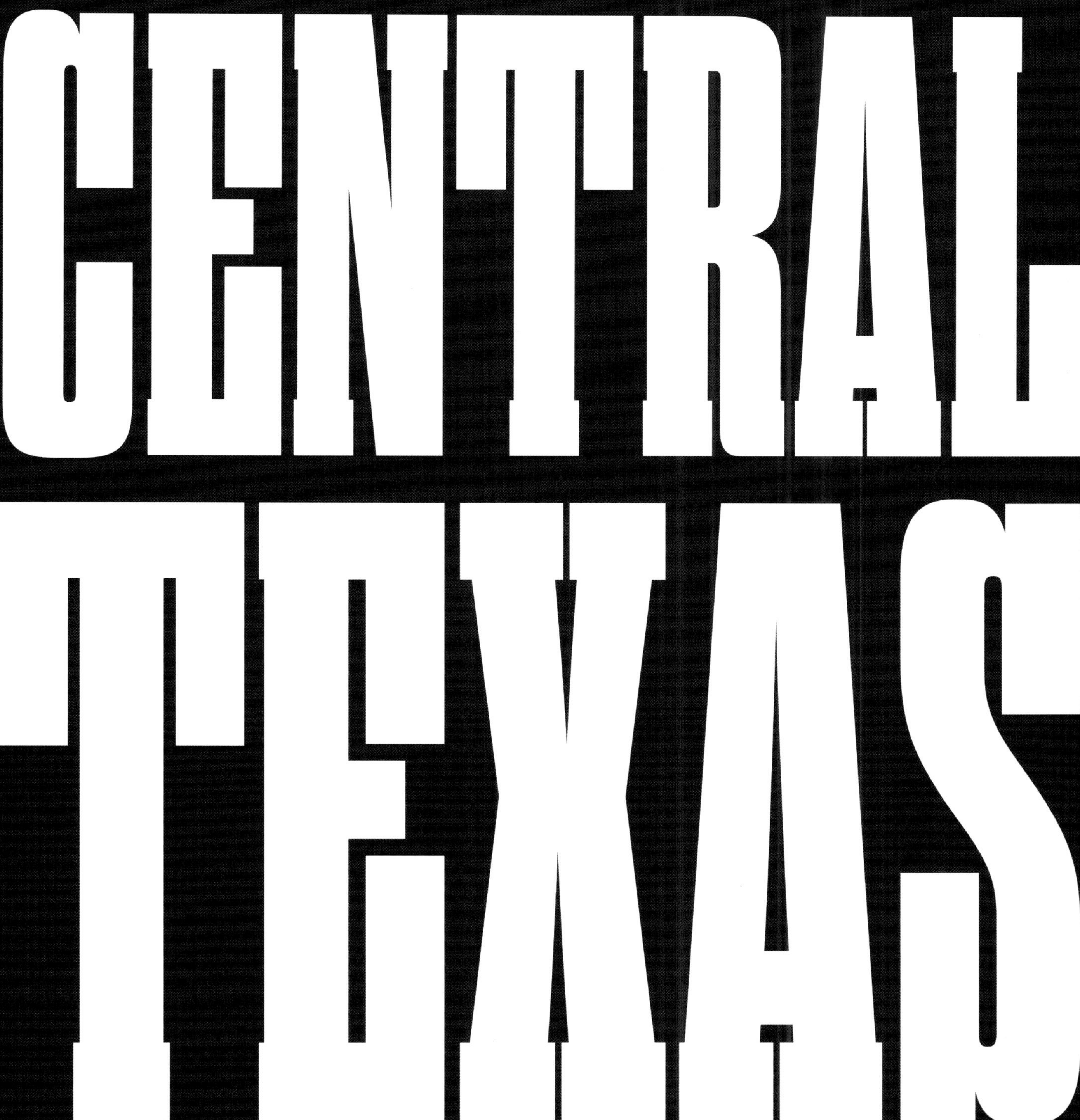
CENTRAL
TEXAS

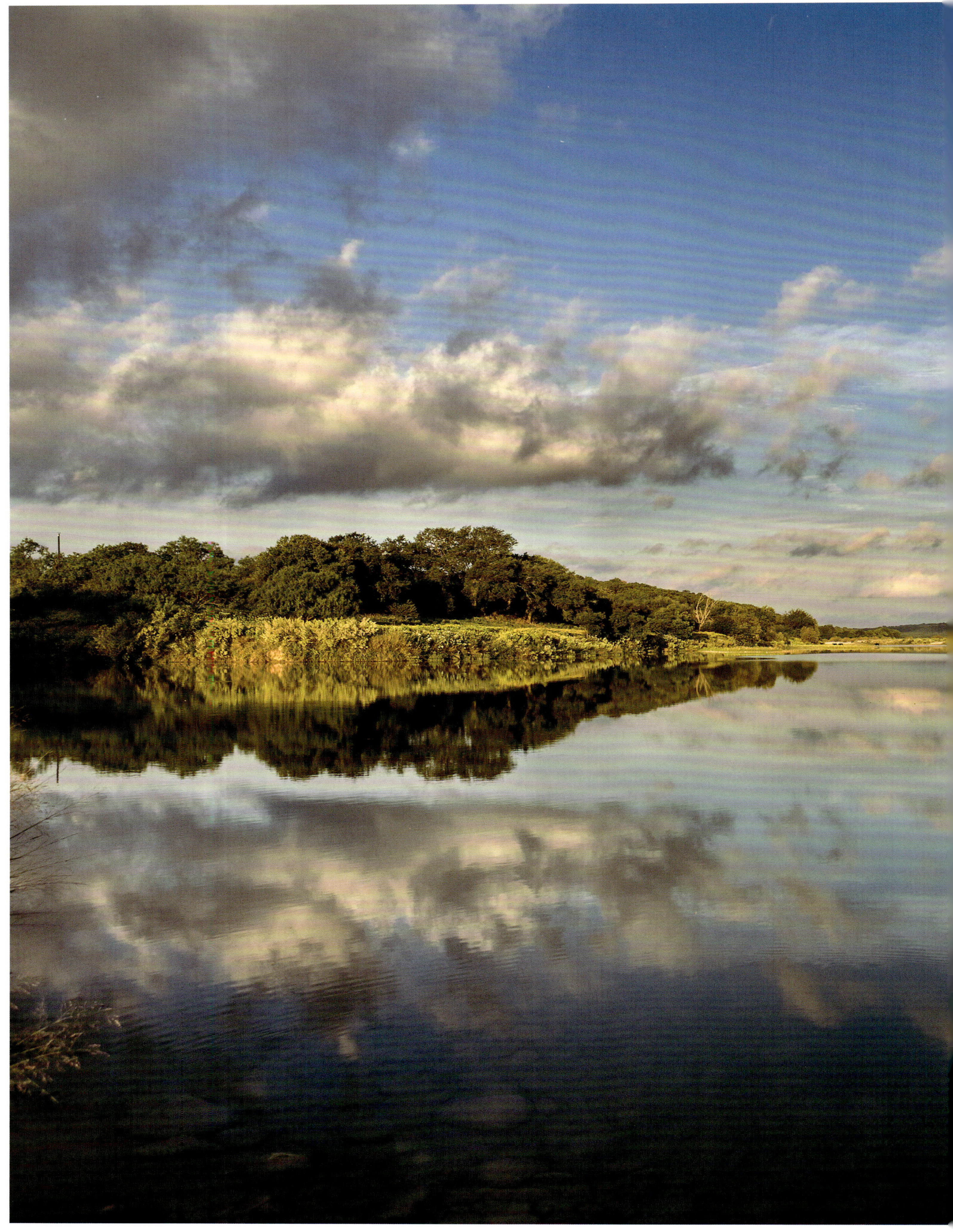

DOS RIOS confluence of Llano and James Rivers, near Mason, 2006

DEER CROSSING Blanco River, near Kyle, 2016 >

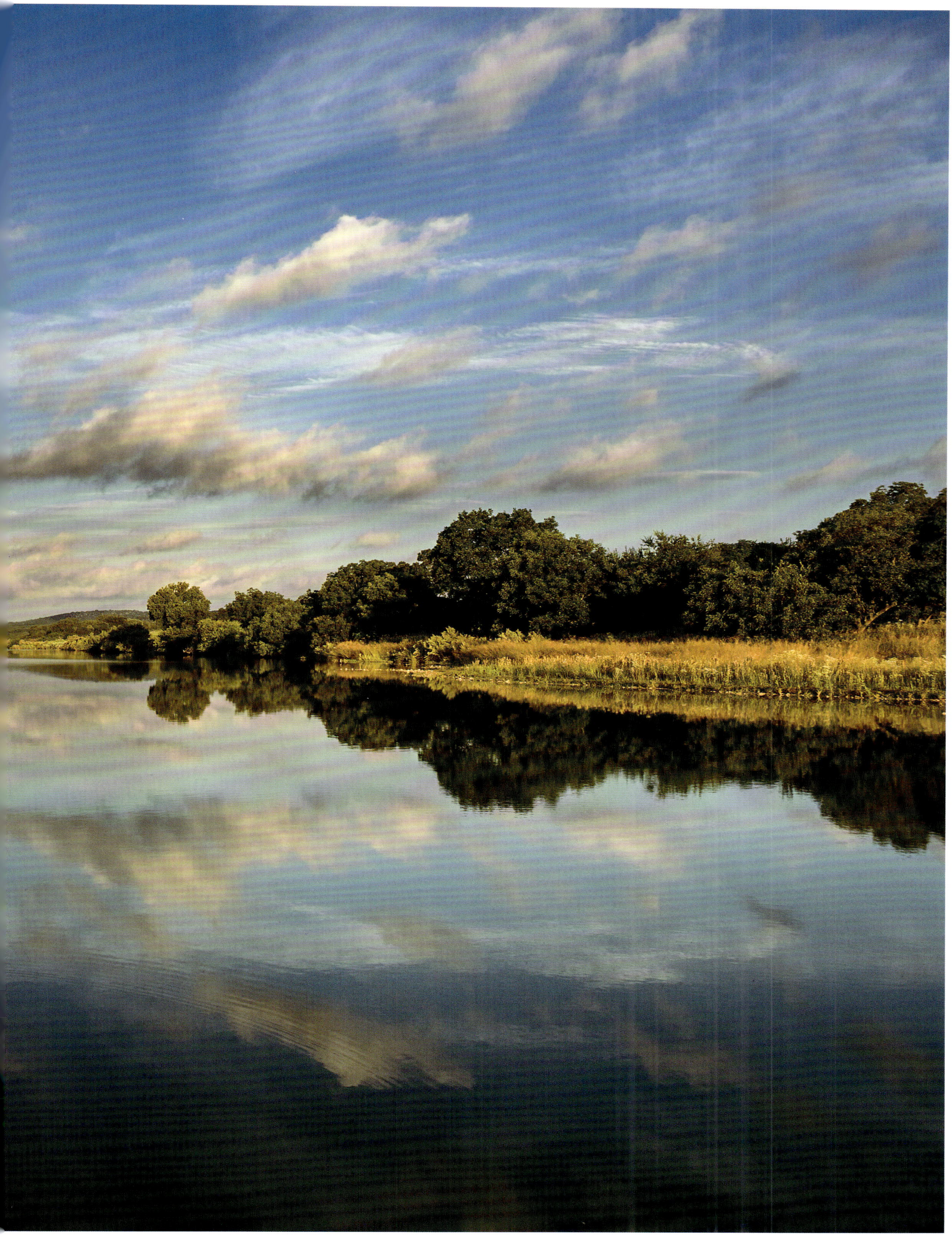

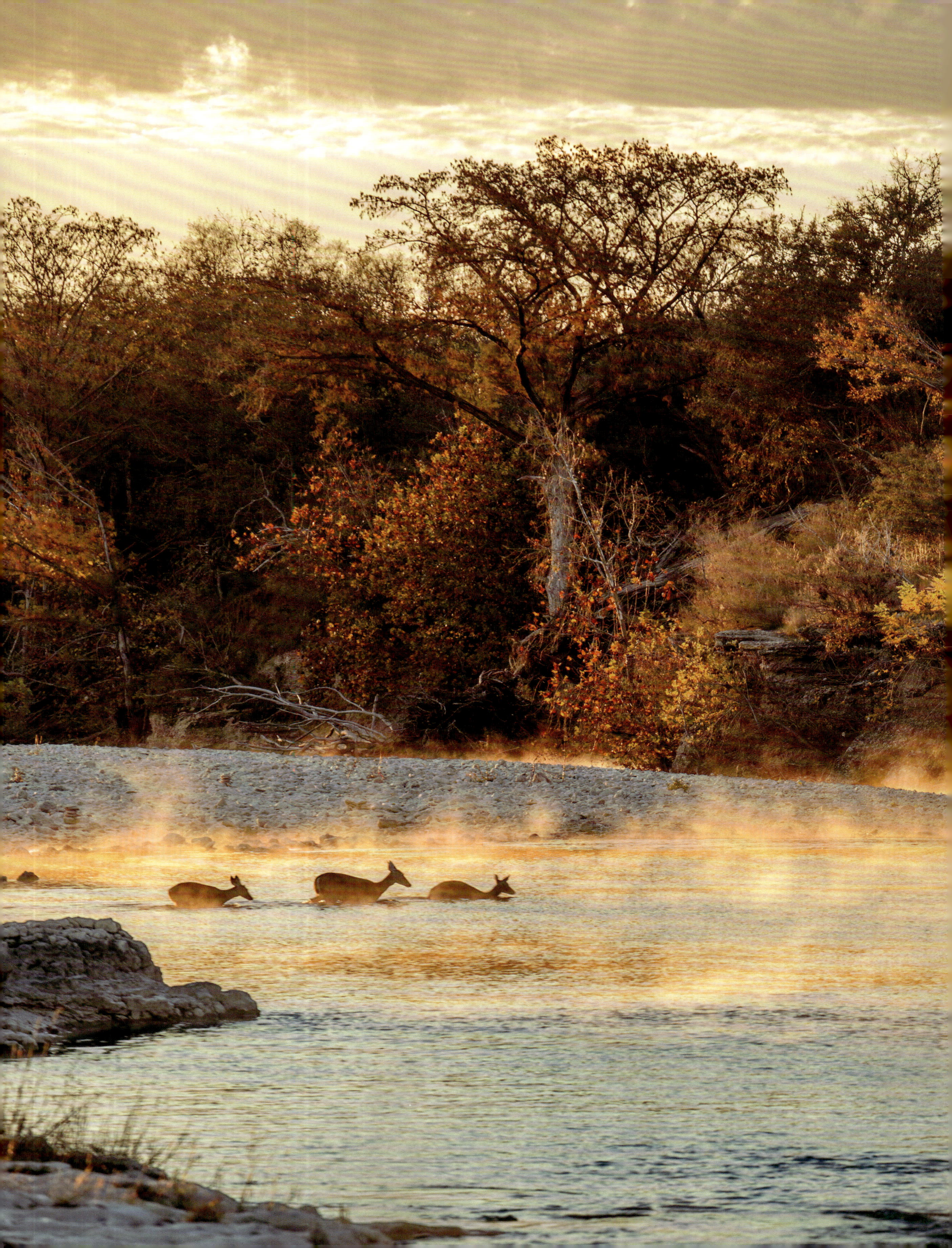

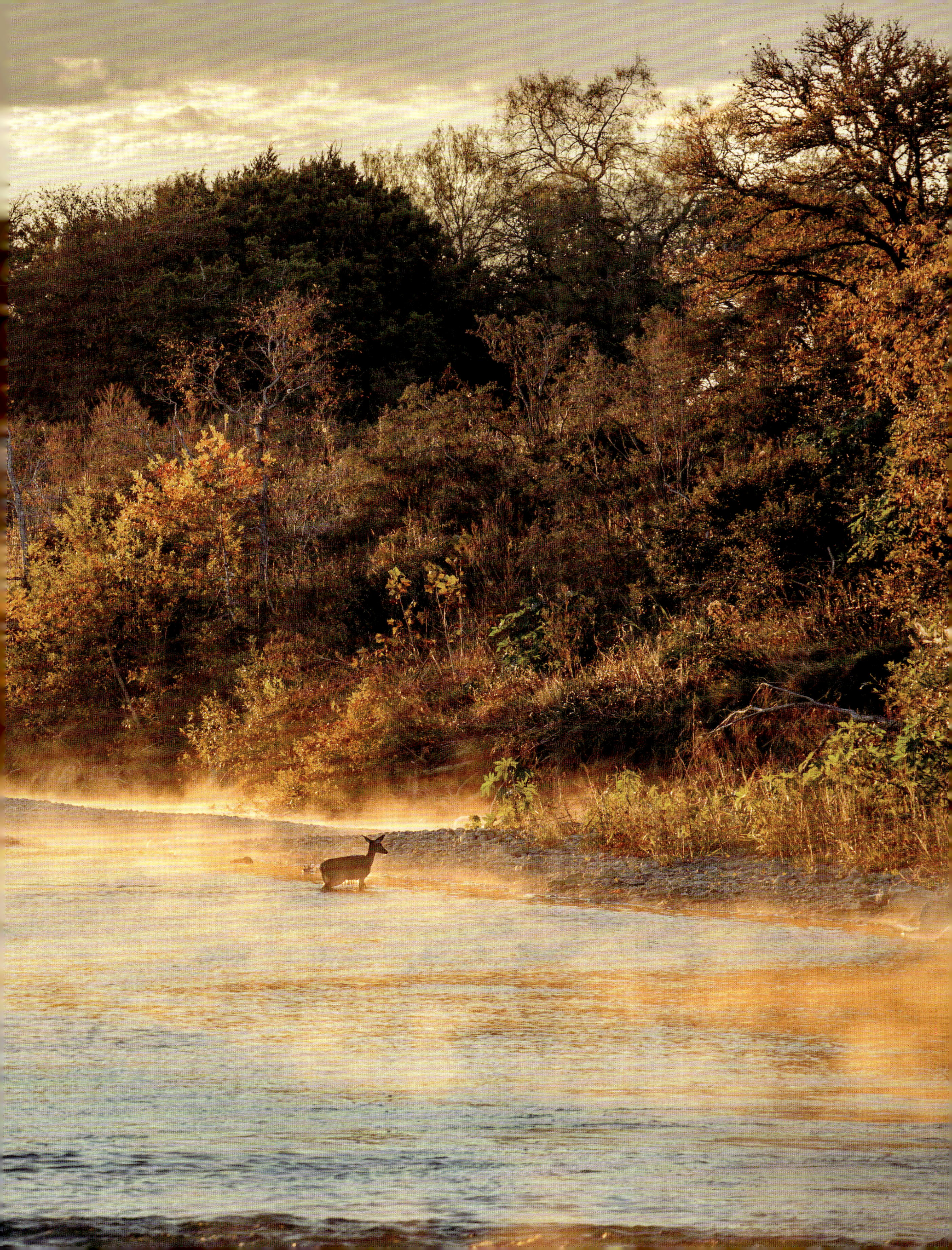

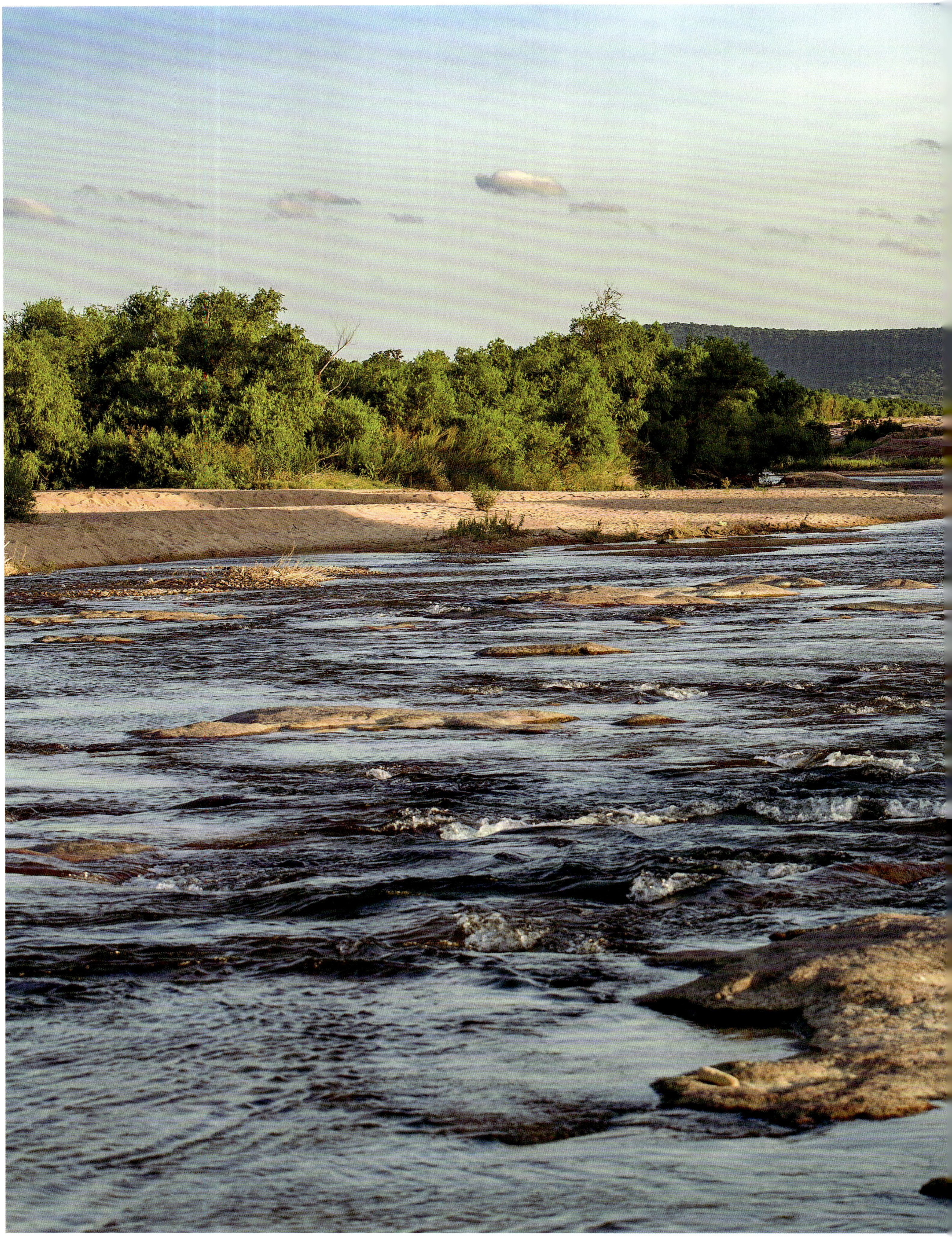

THE SLAB, Llano River, near Kingsland, 2008

MARTIN BLUFF, Llano River, near Mason, 2010 >

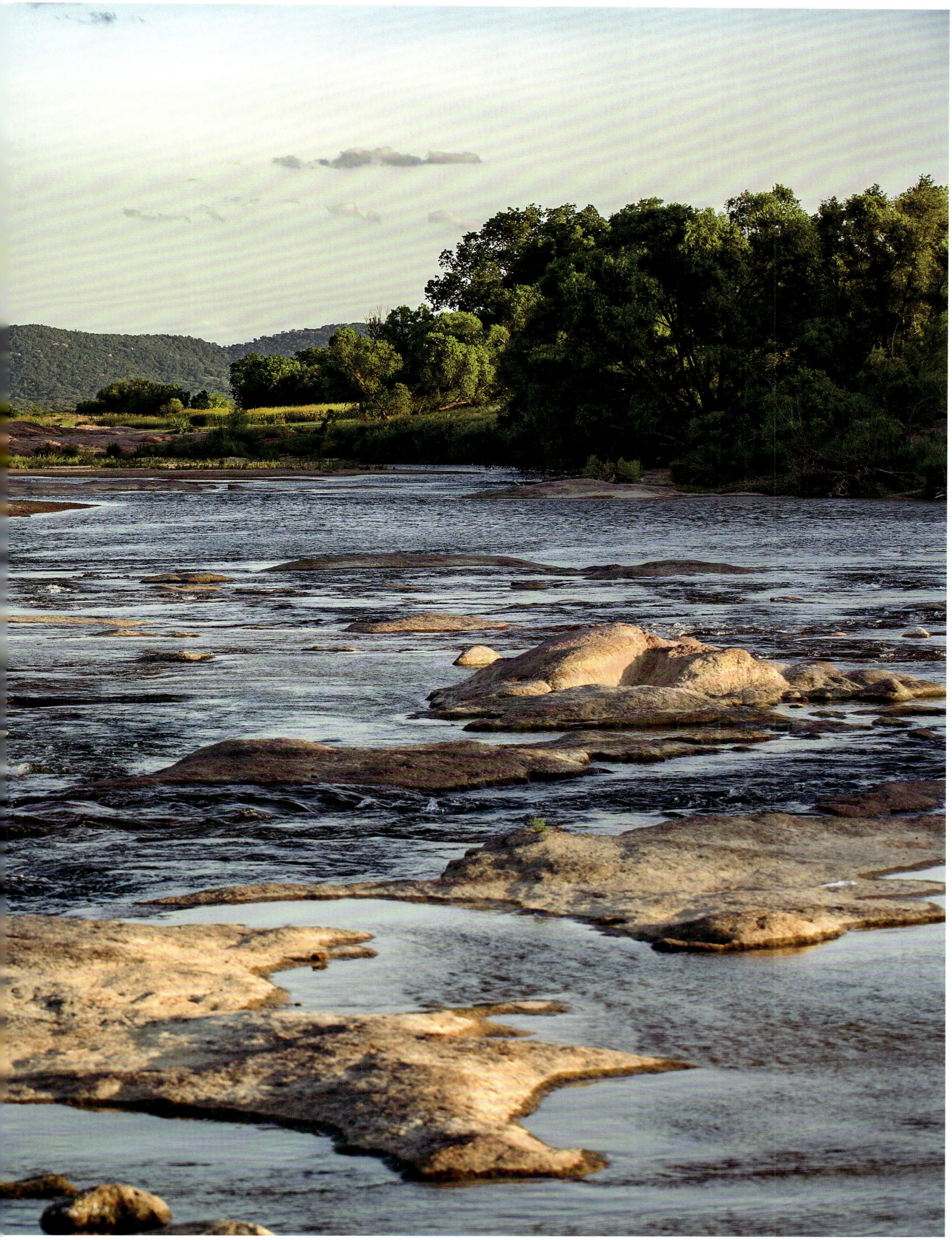

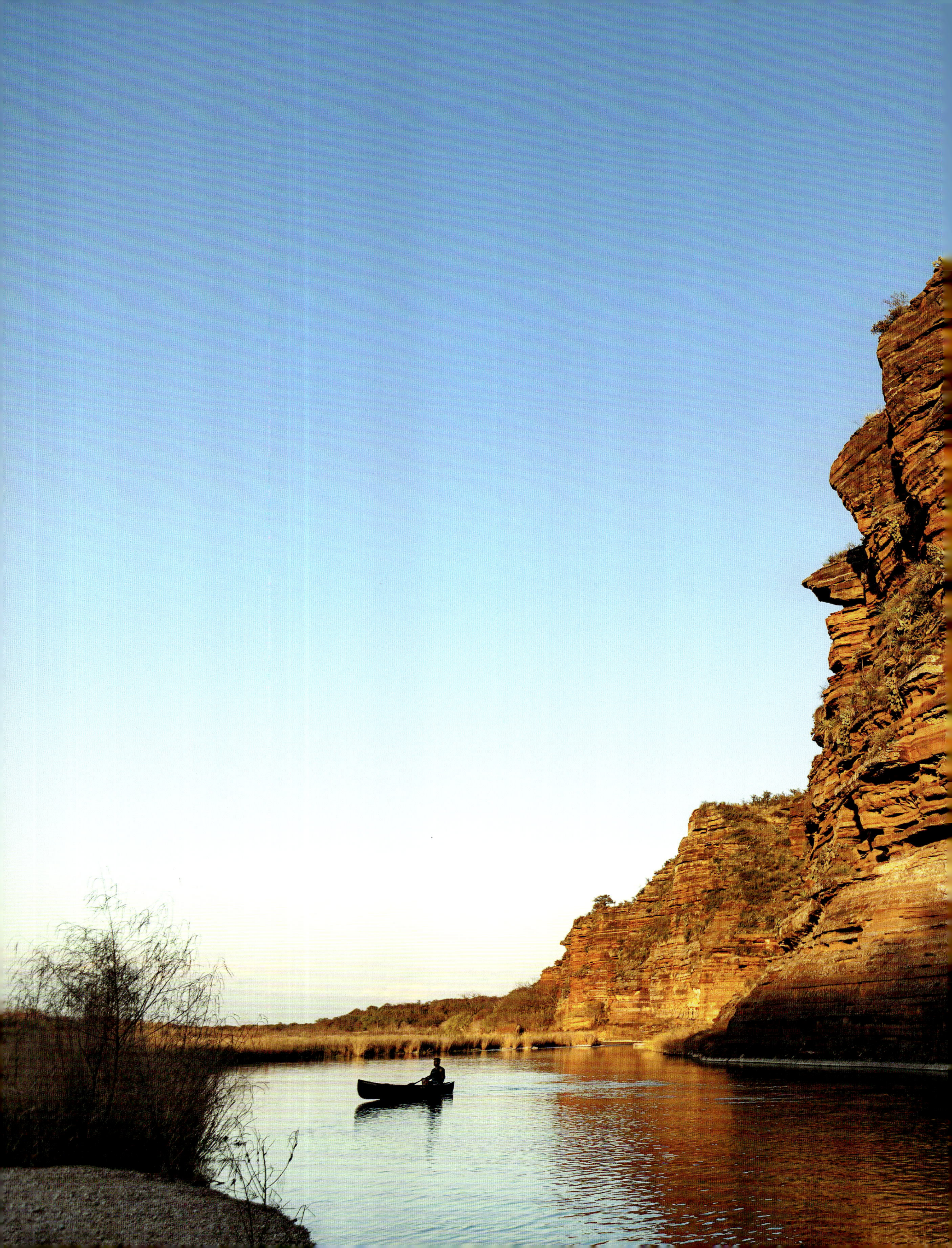

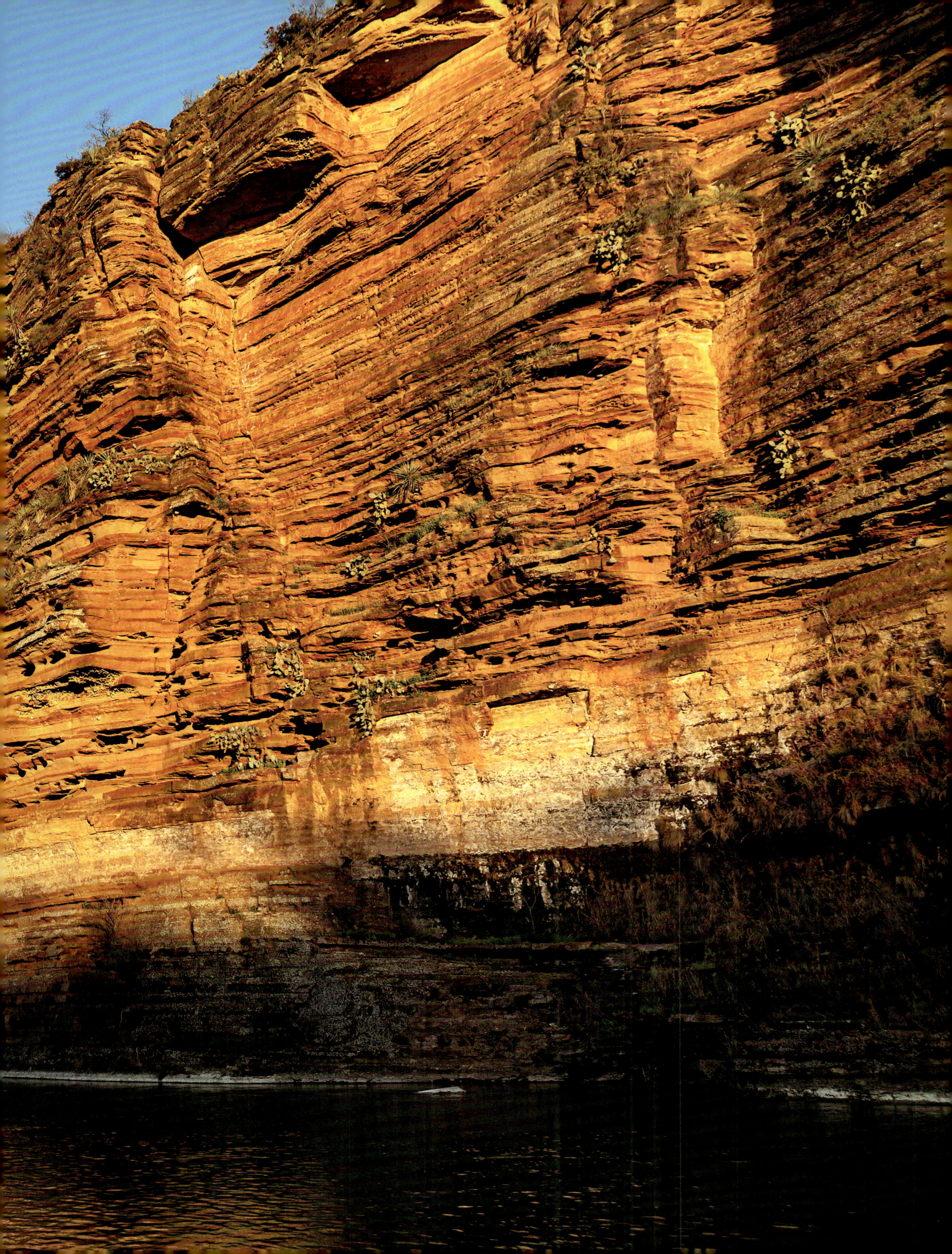

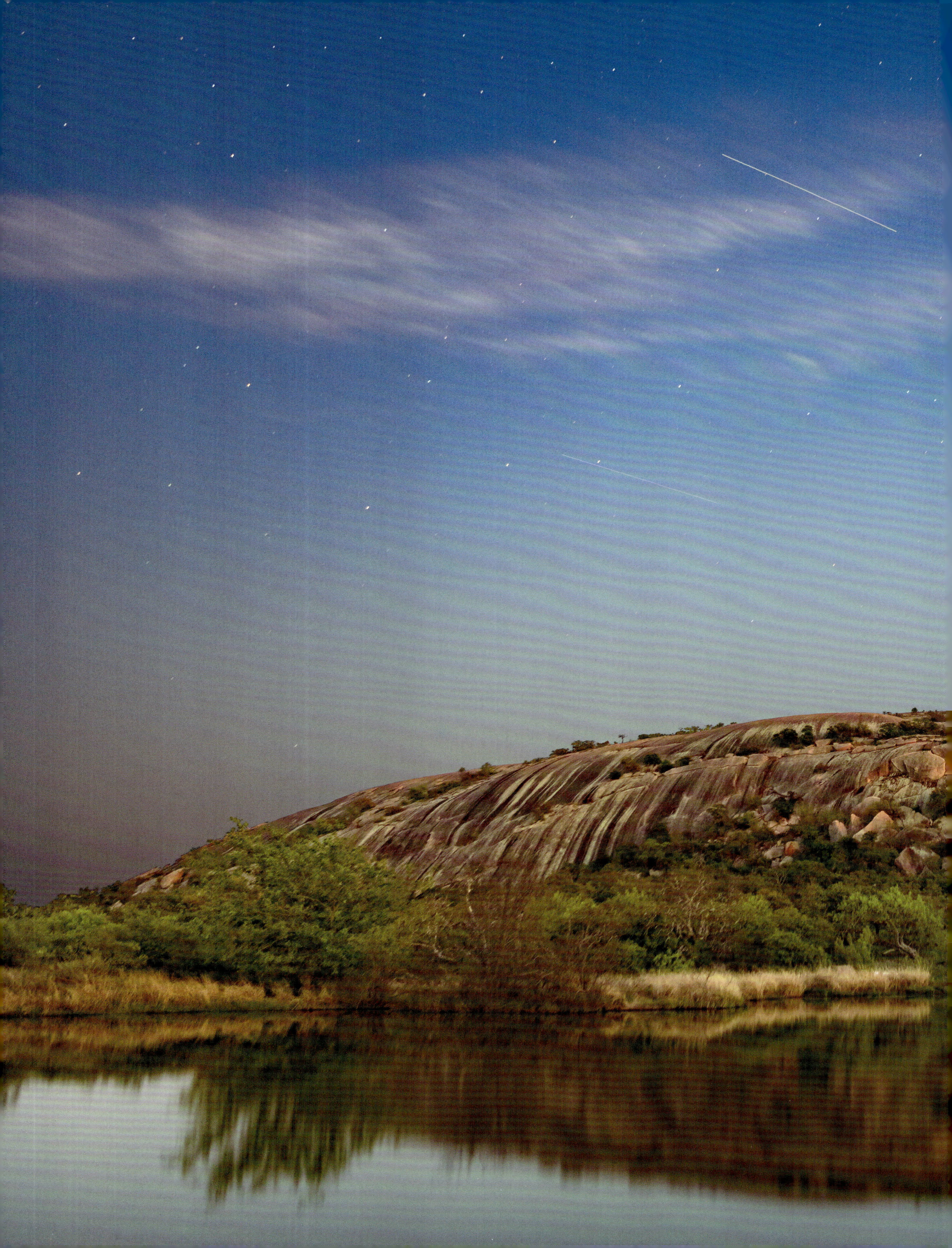

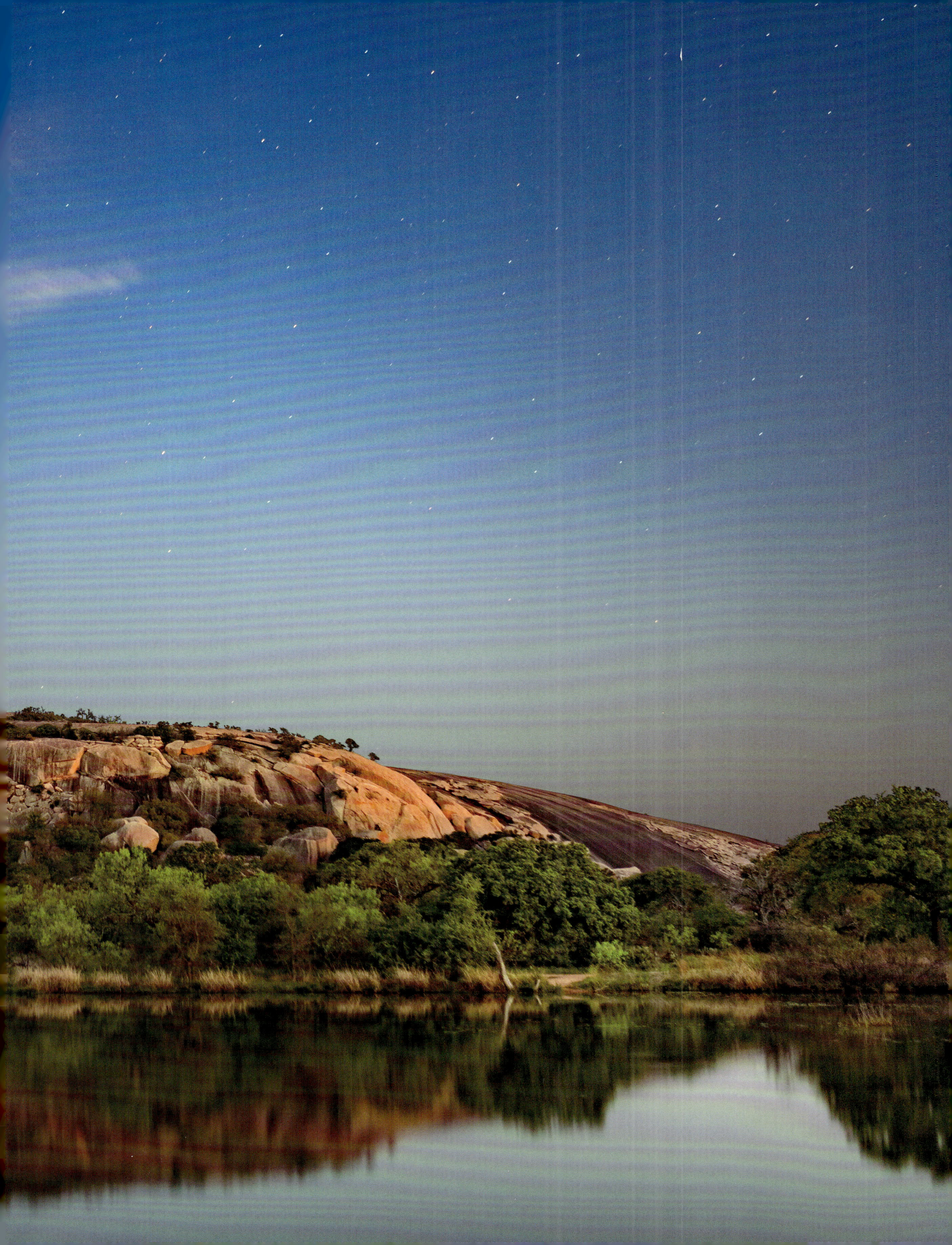

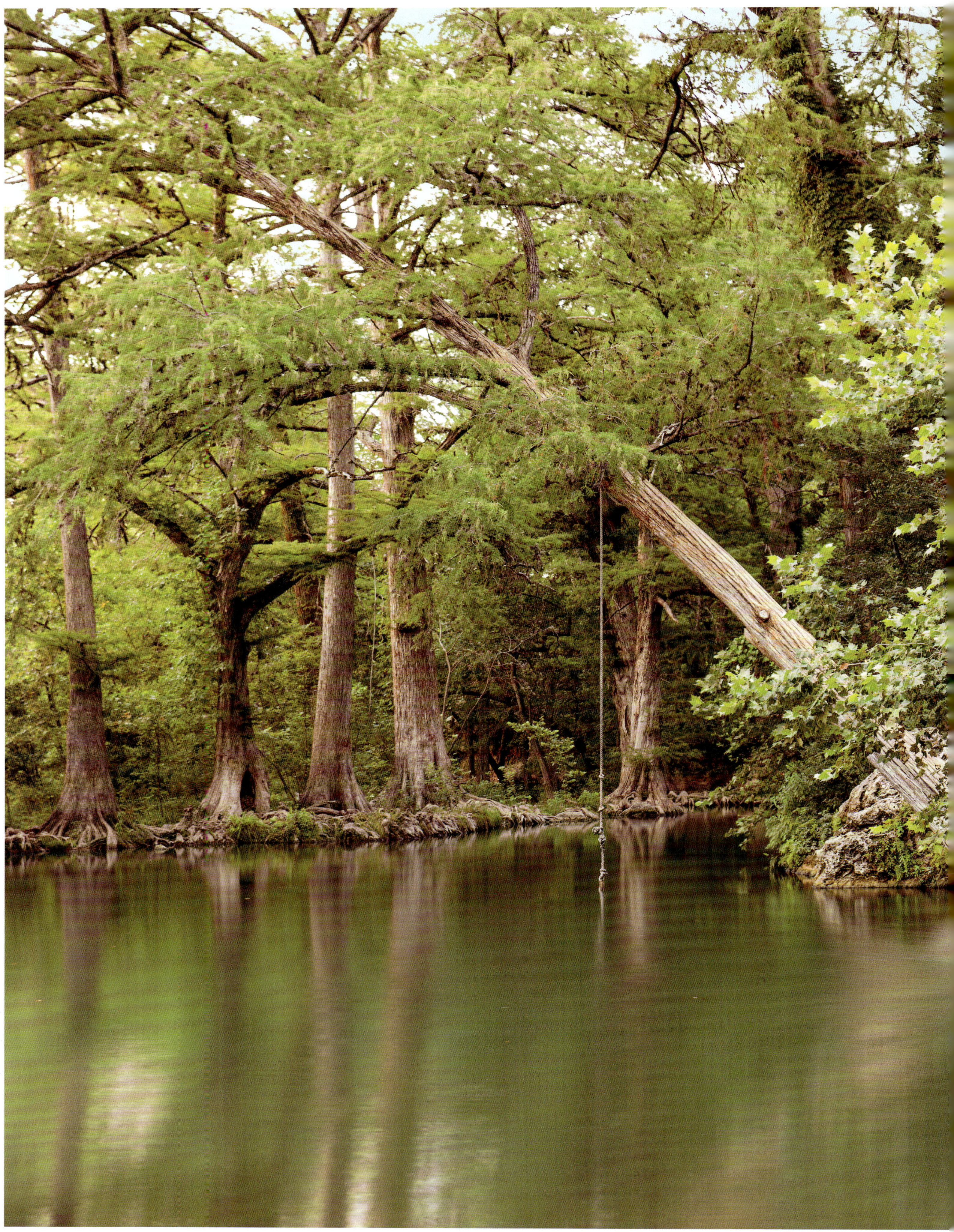

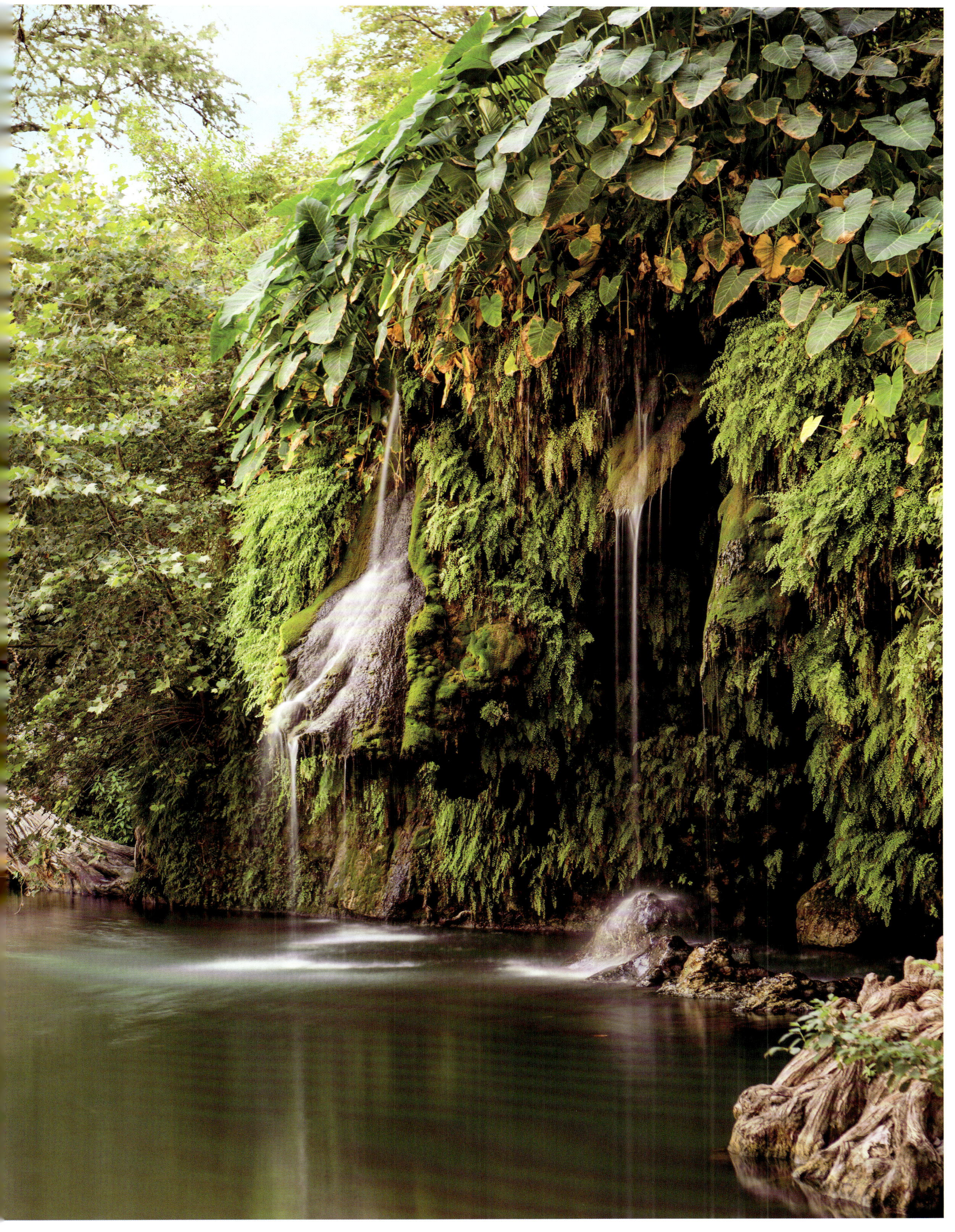

KRAUSE SPRINGS Spicewood, 2017

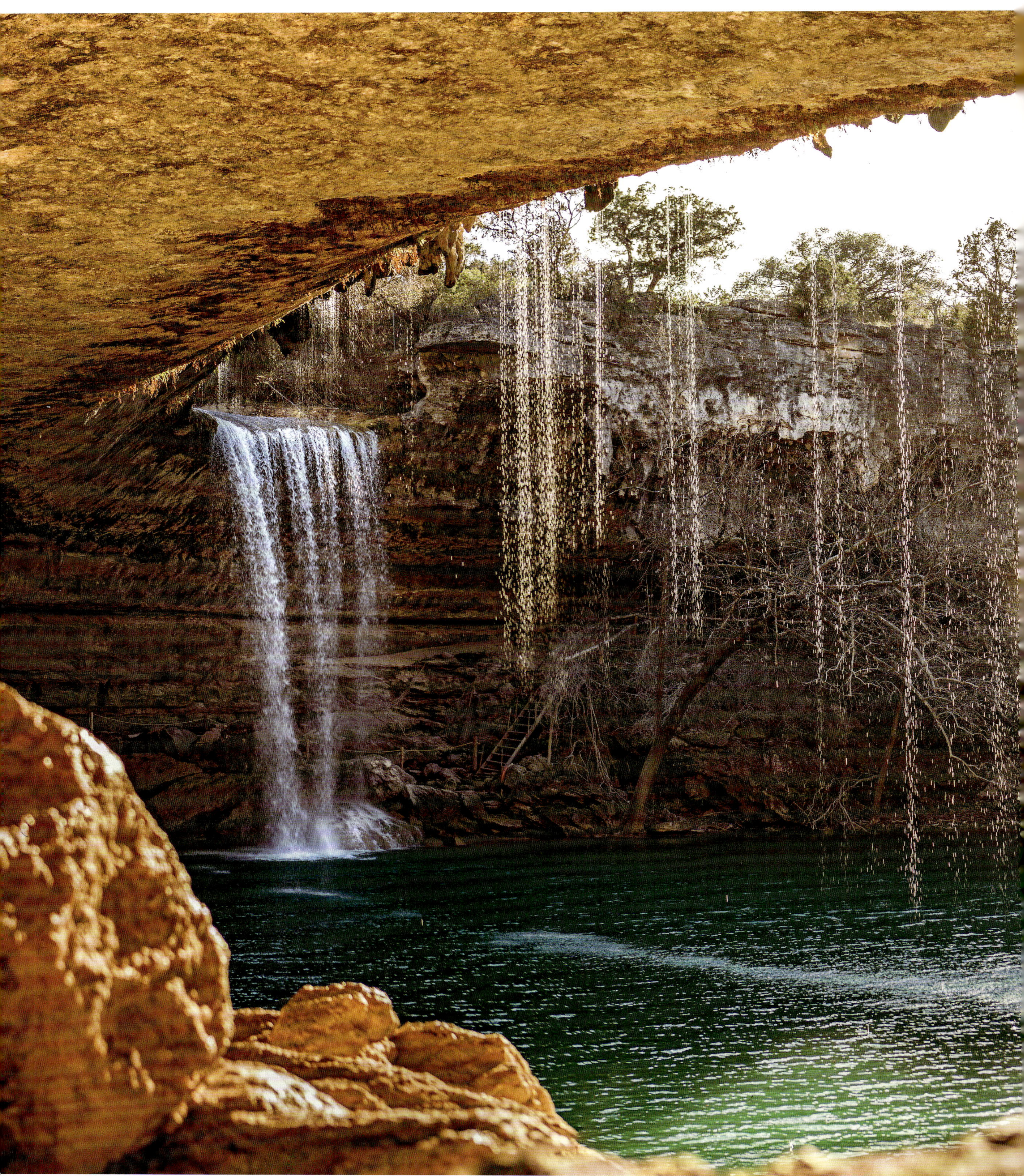

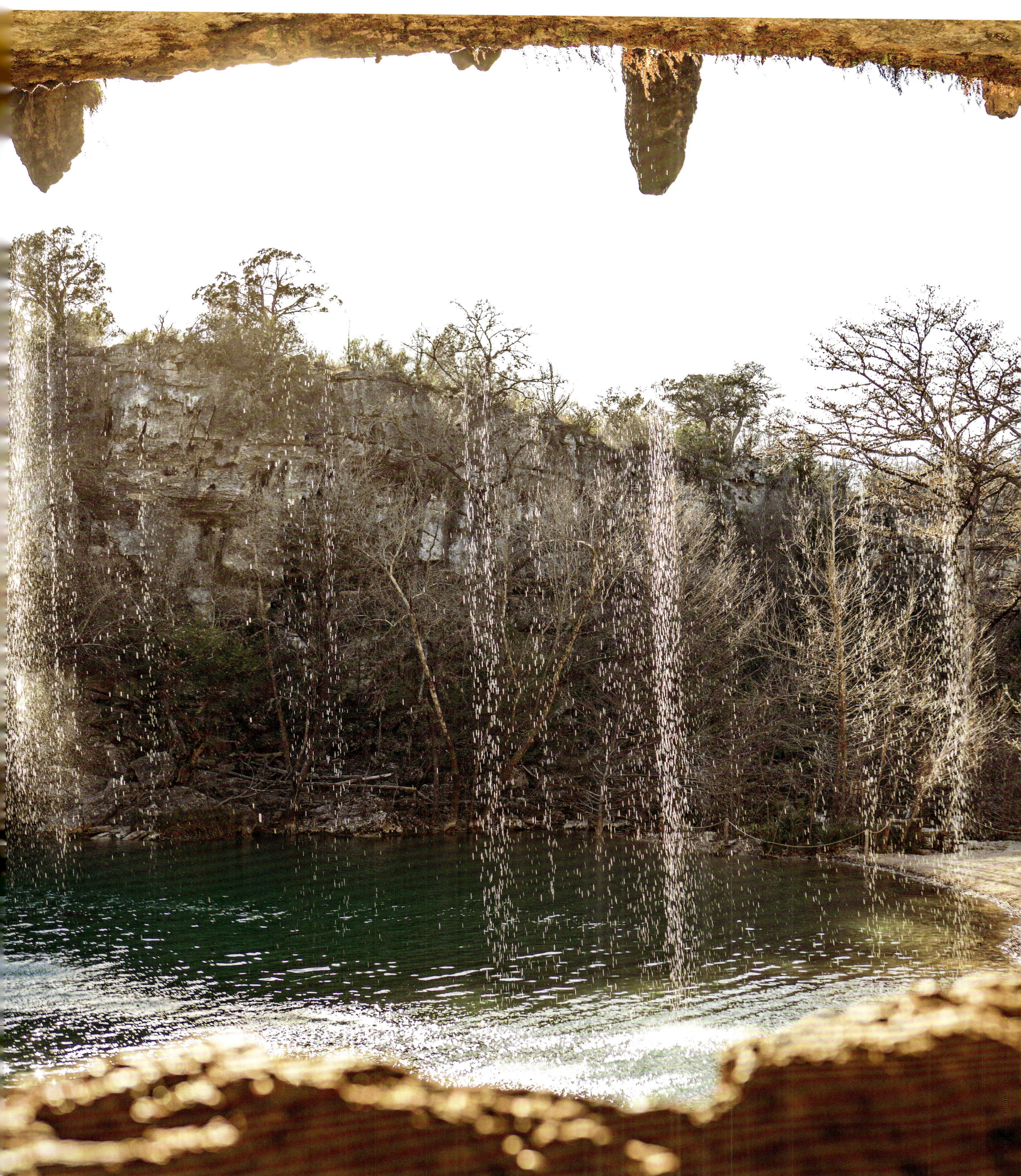

HAMILTON POOL Dripping Springs, 2017

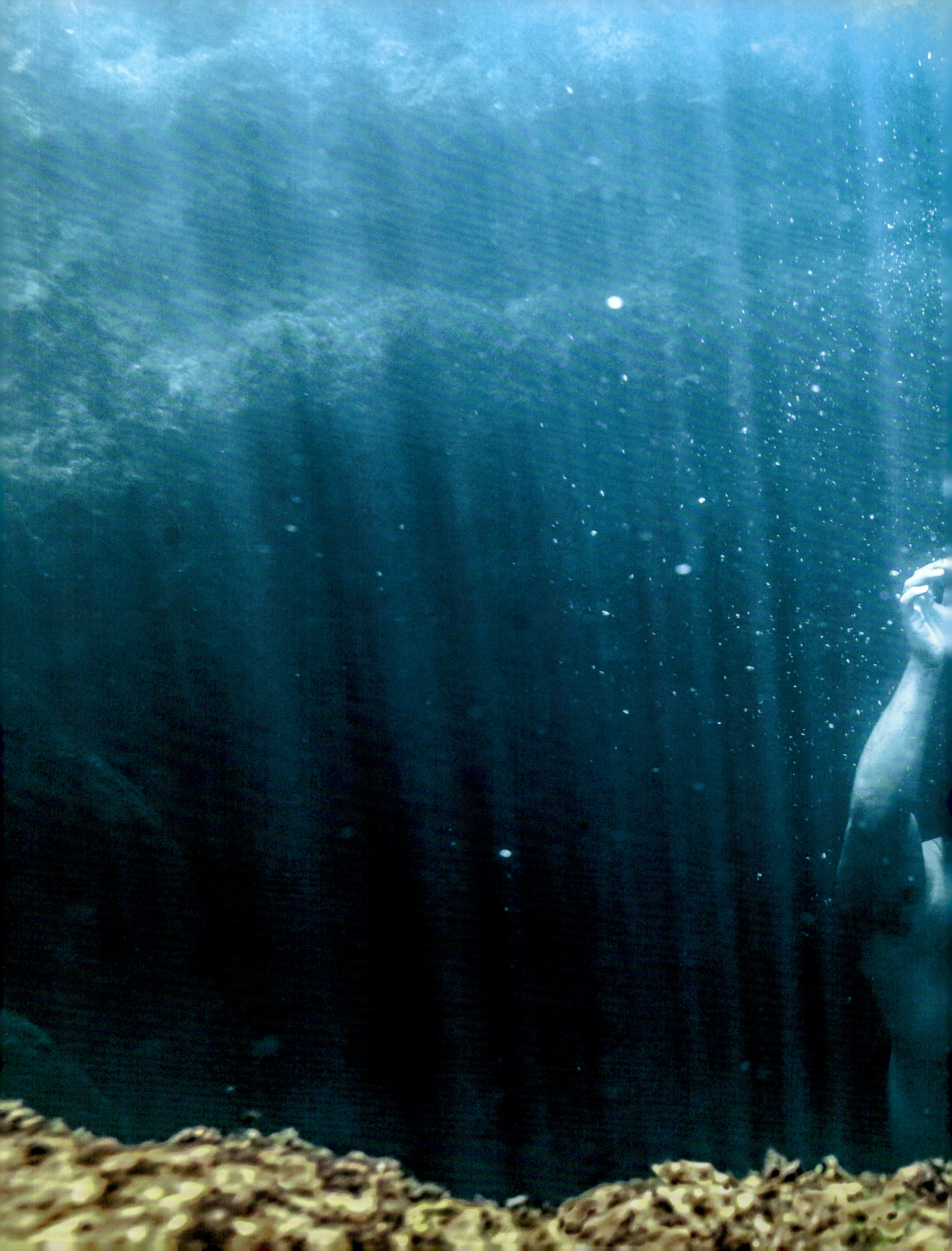

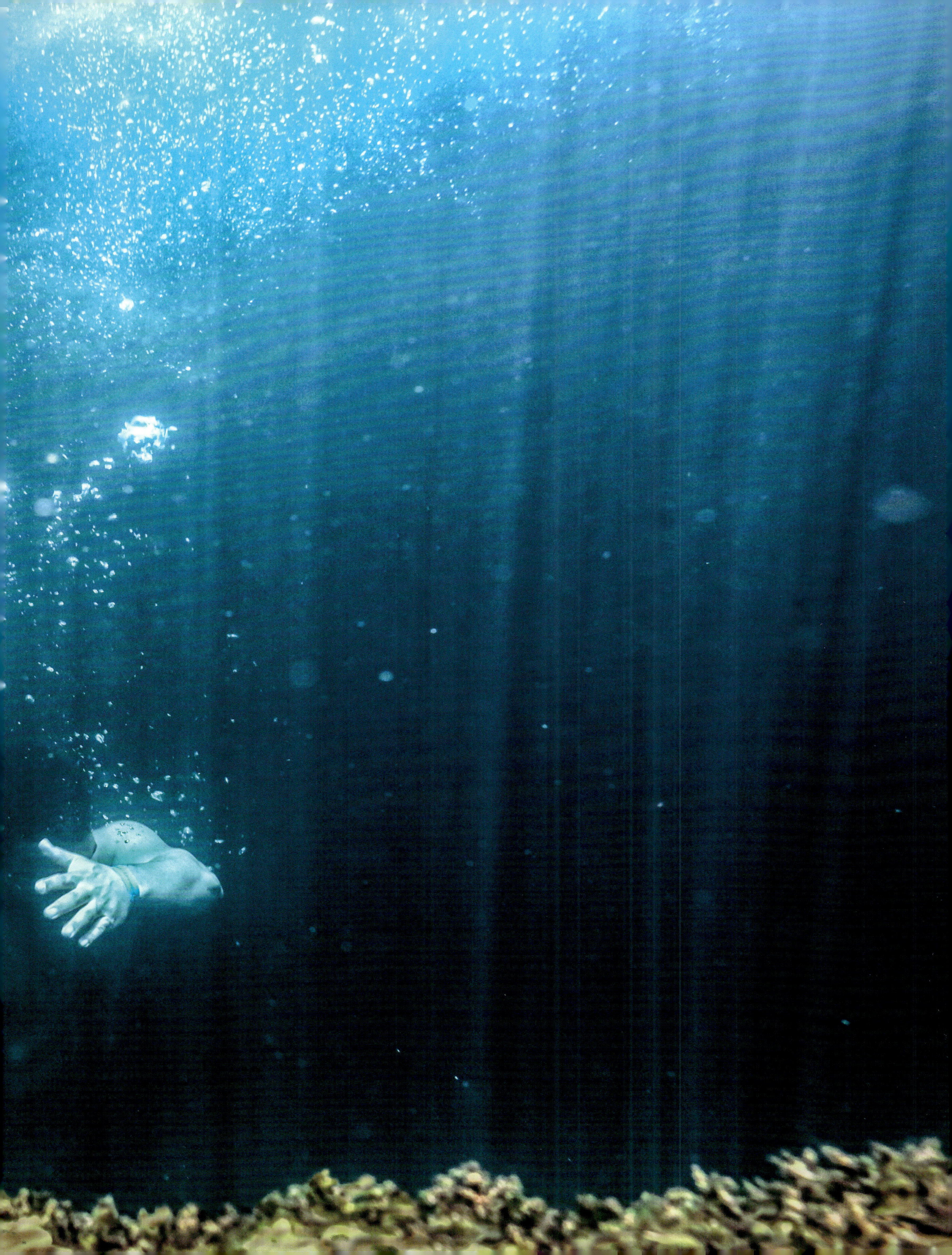

< **JACOB'S WELL** Wimberley, 2016

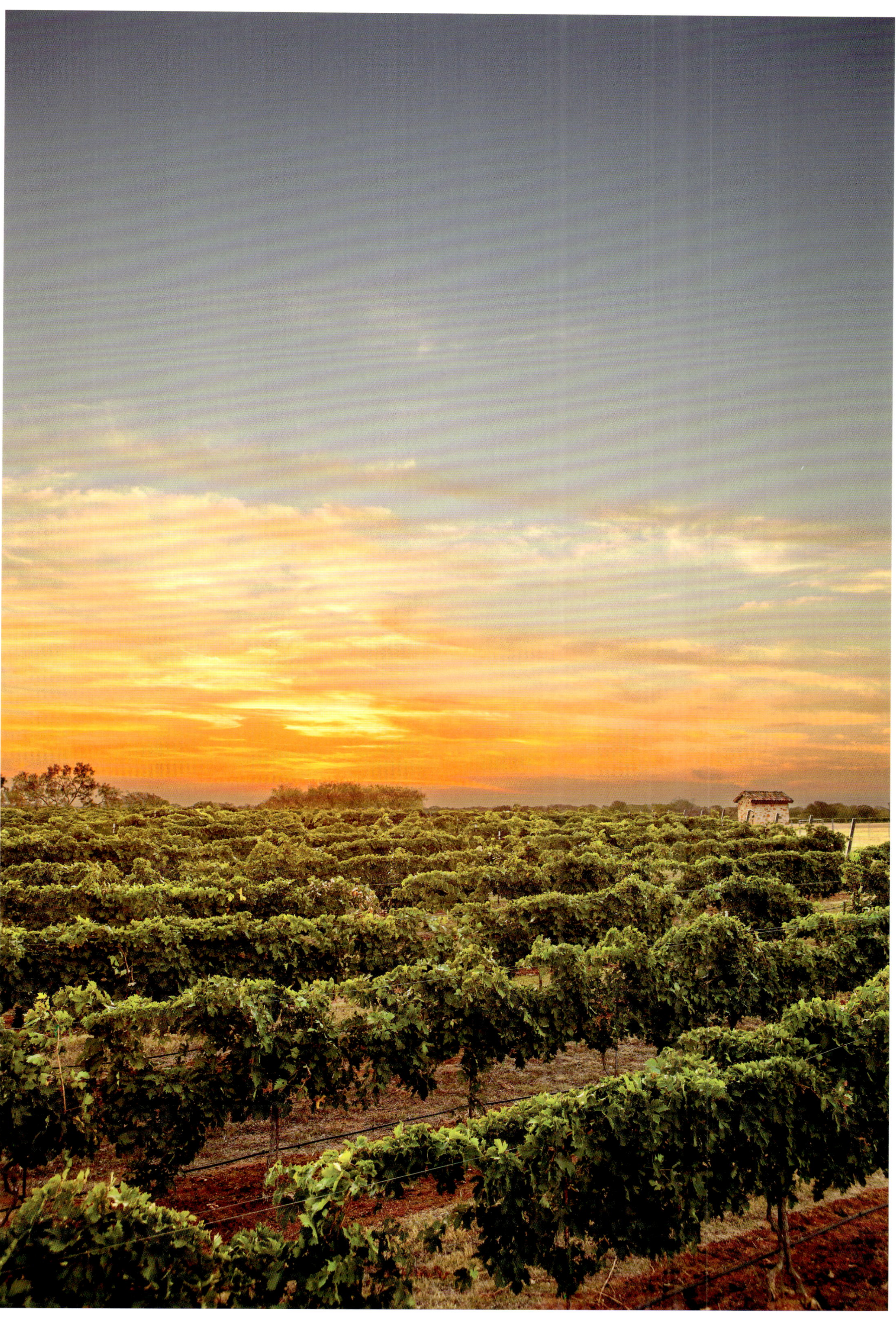

VINEYARD near Fredericksburg, 2014

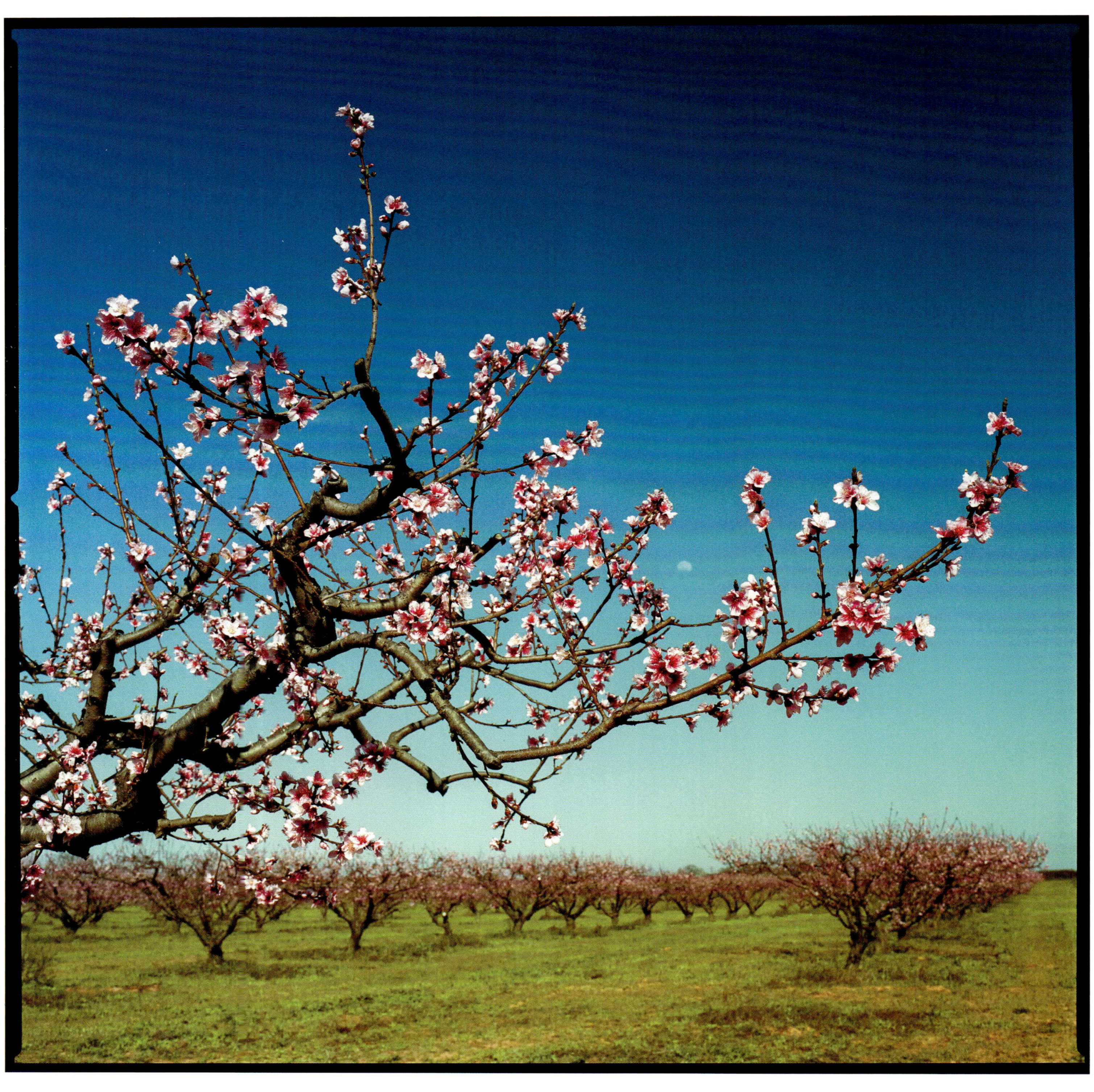

PEACH BLOSSOMS Stonewall, 2003

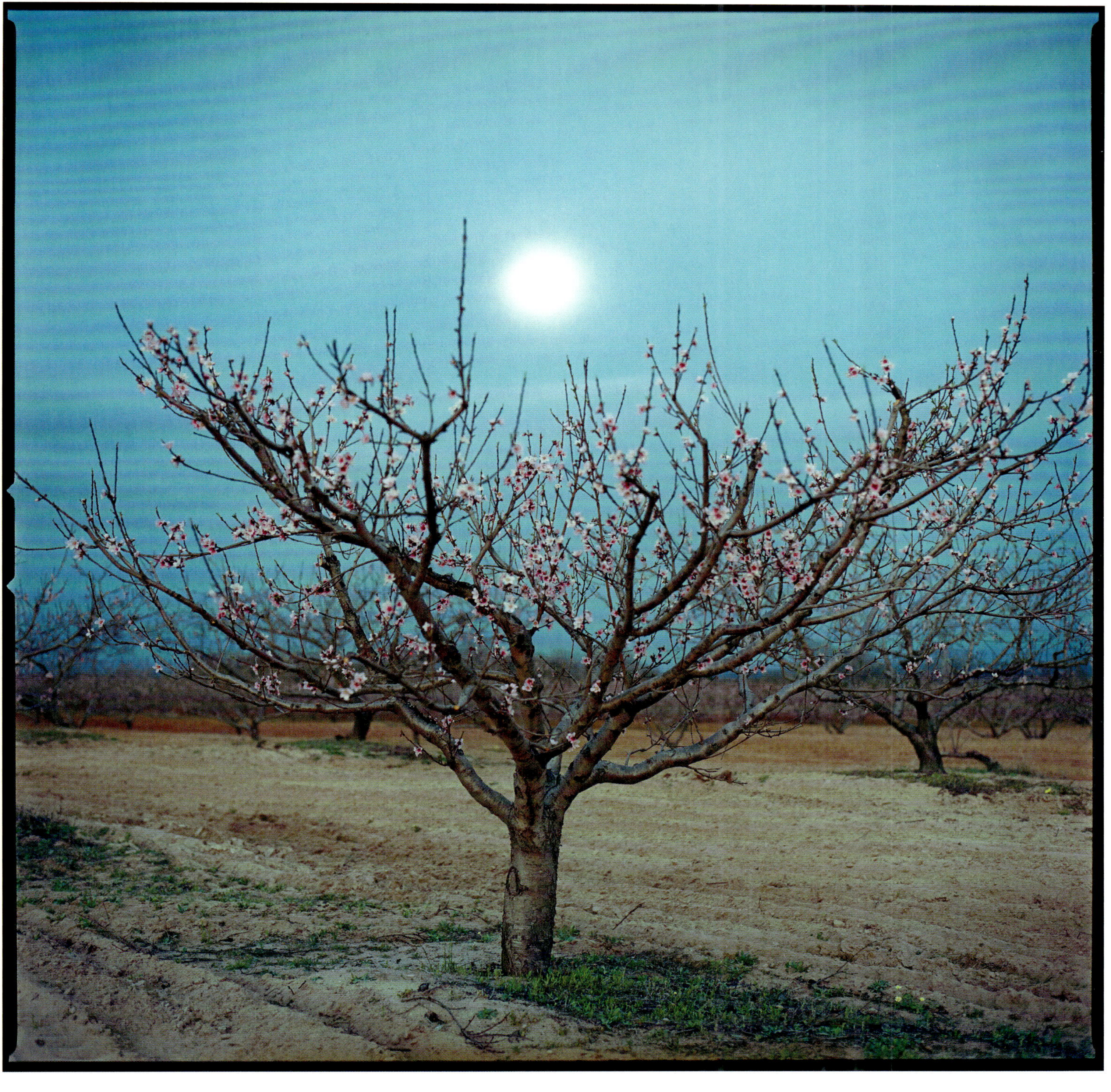

ORCHARD MOONRISE Stonewall, 2003

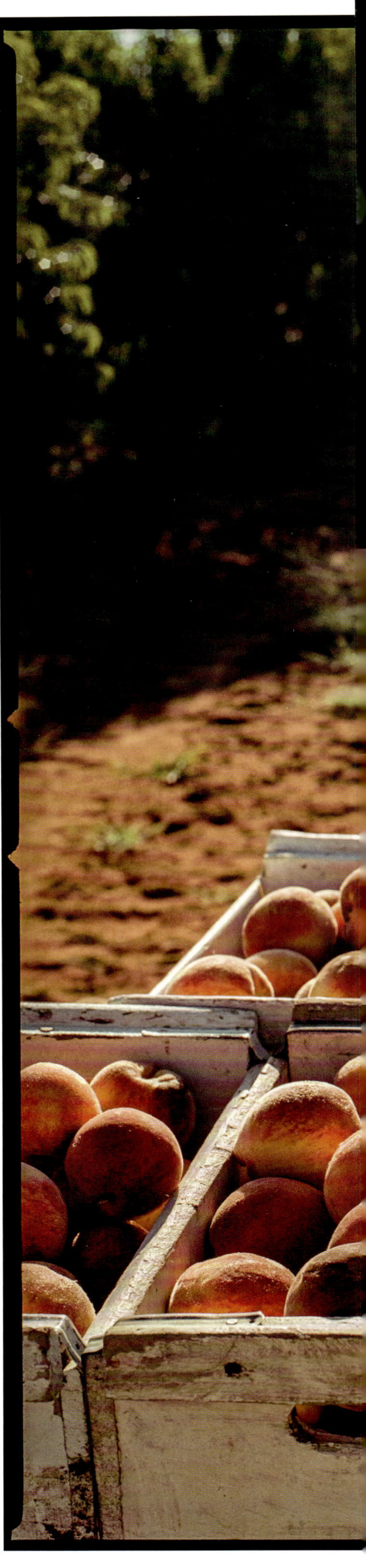

FOGGY BOTTOM, near Hochheim, 2016 >

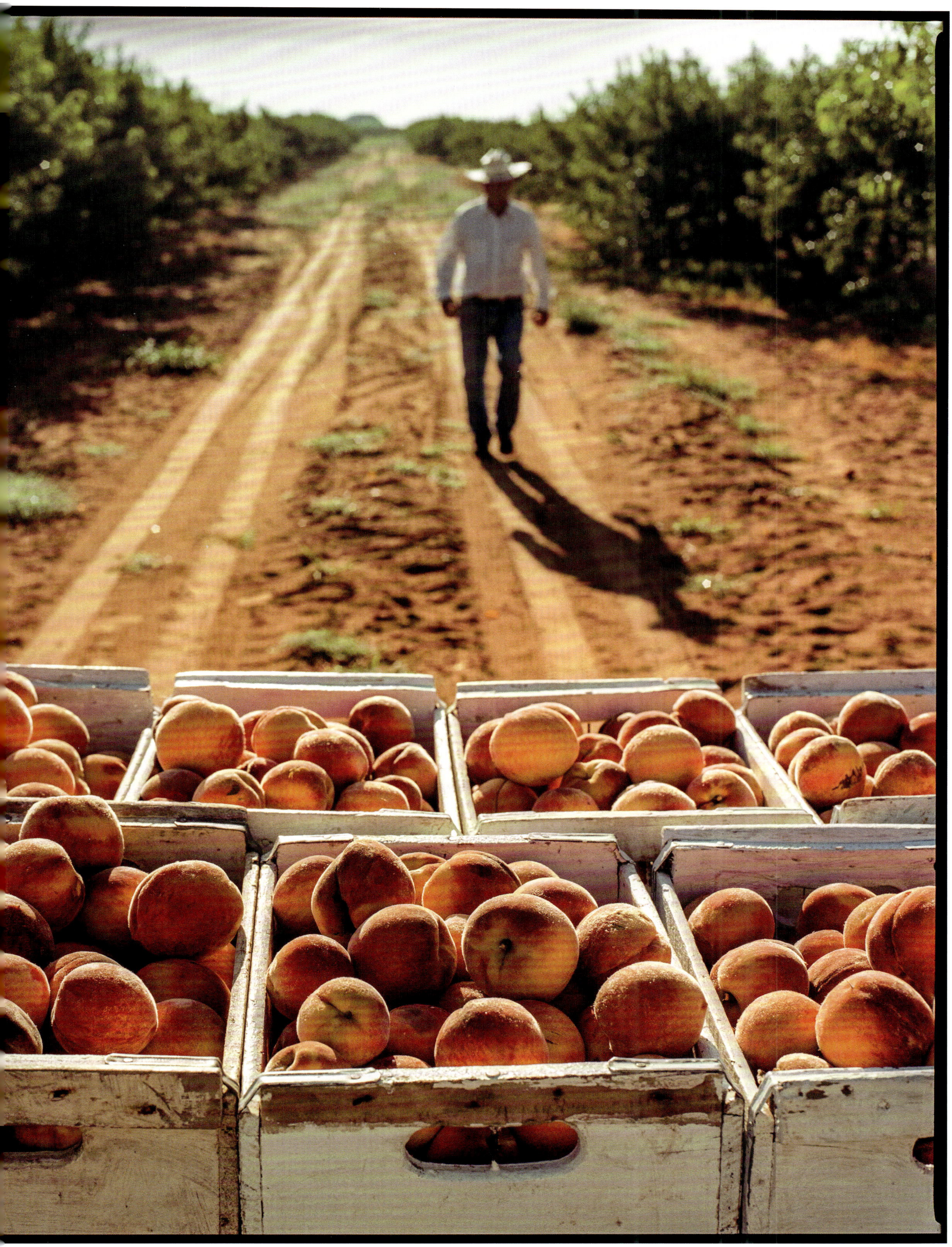

PEACH CRATES Stonewall, 2003

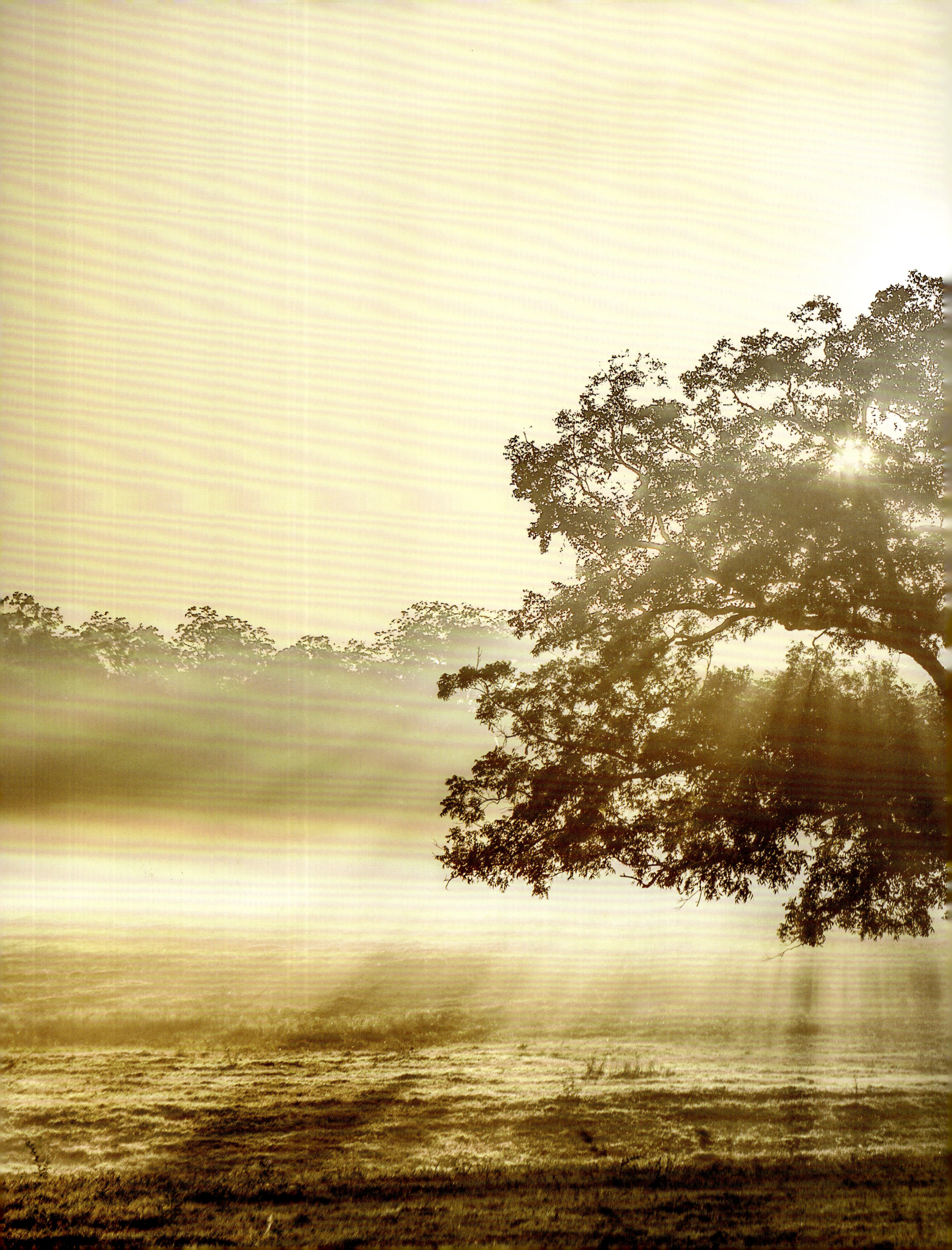

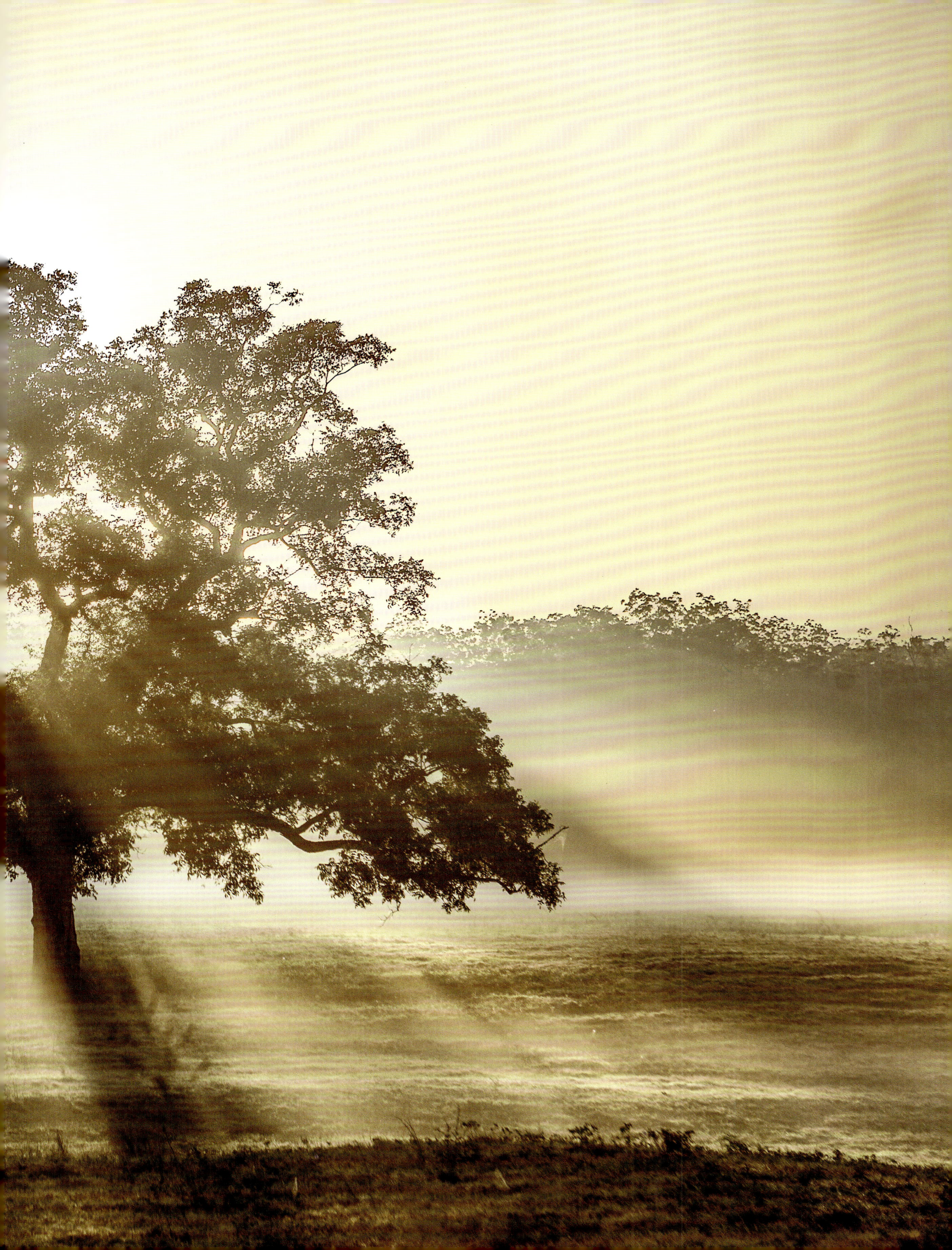

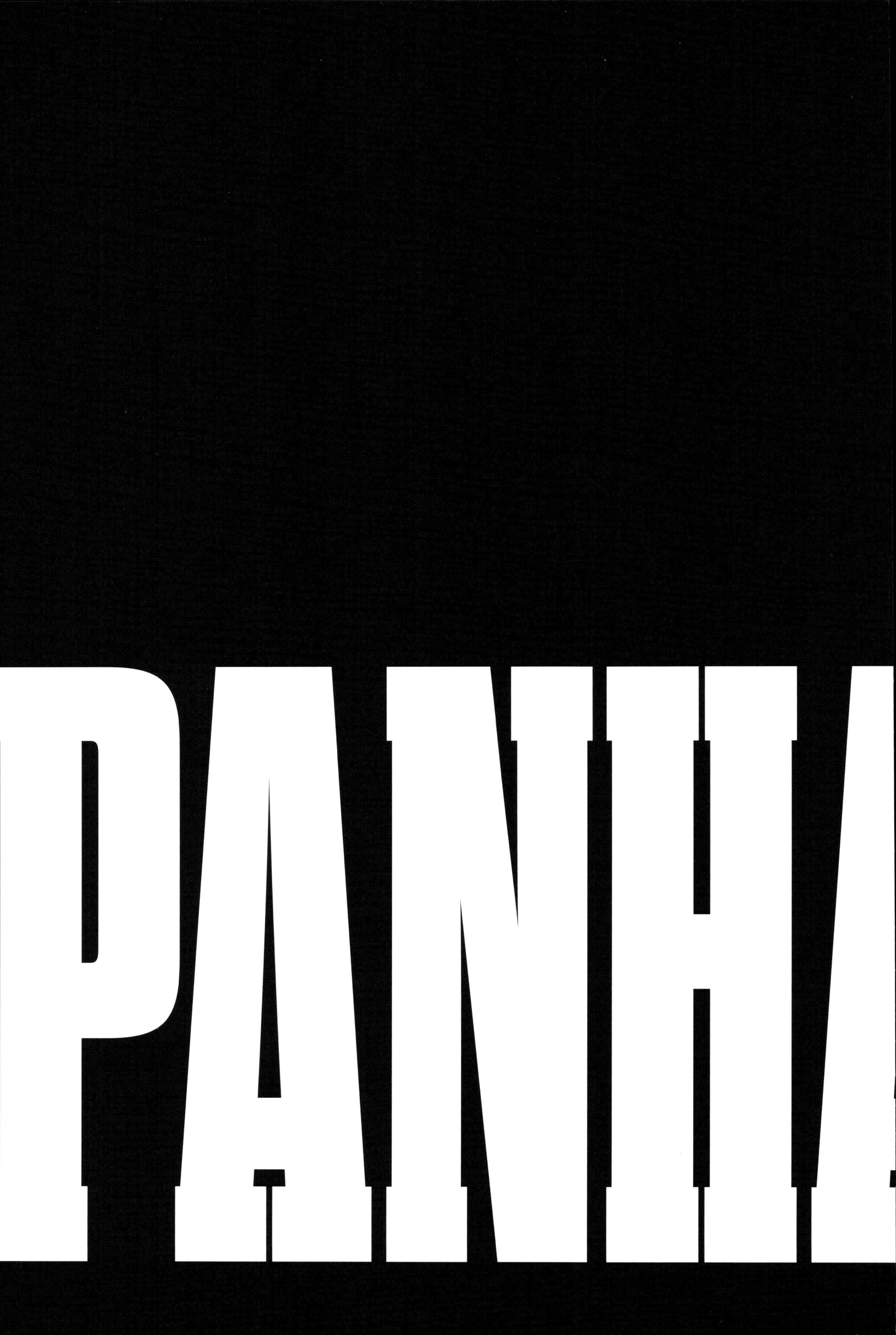
PANHA

ANDLE

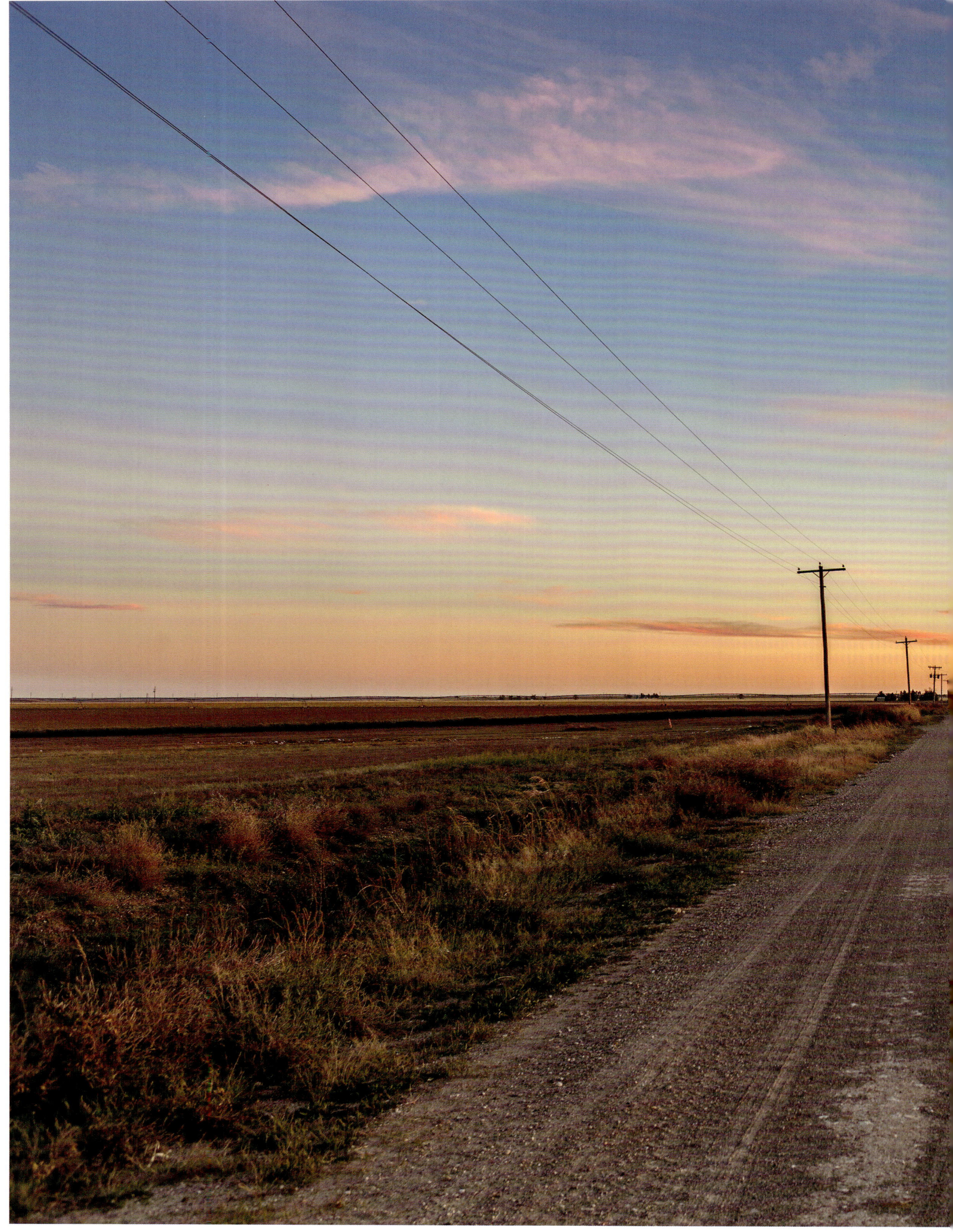

FARM ROAD near Cotton Center, 2017

STARS AND COTTON near Tahoka, 2017 >

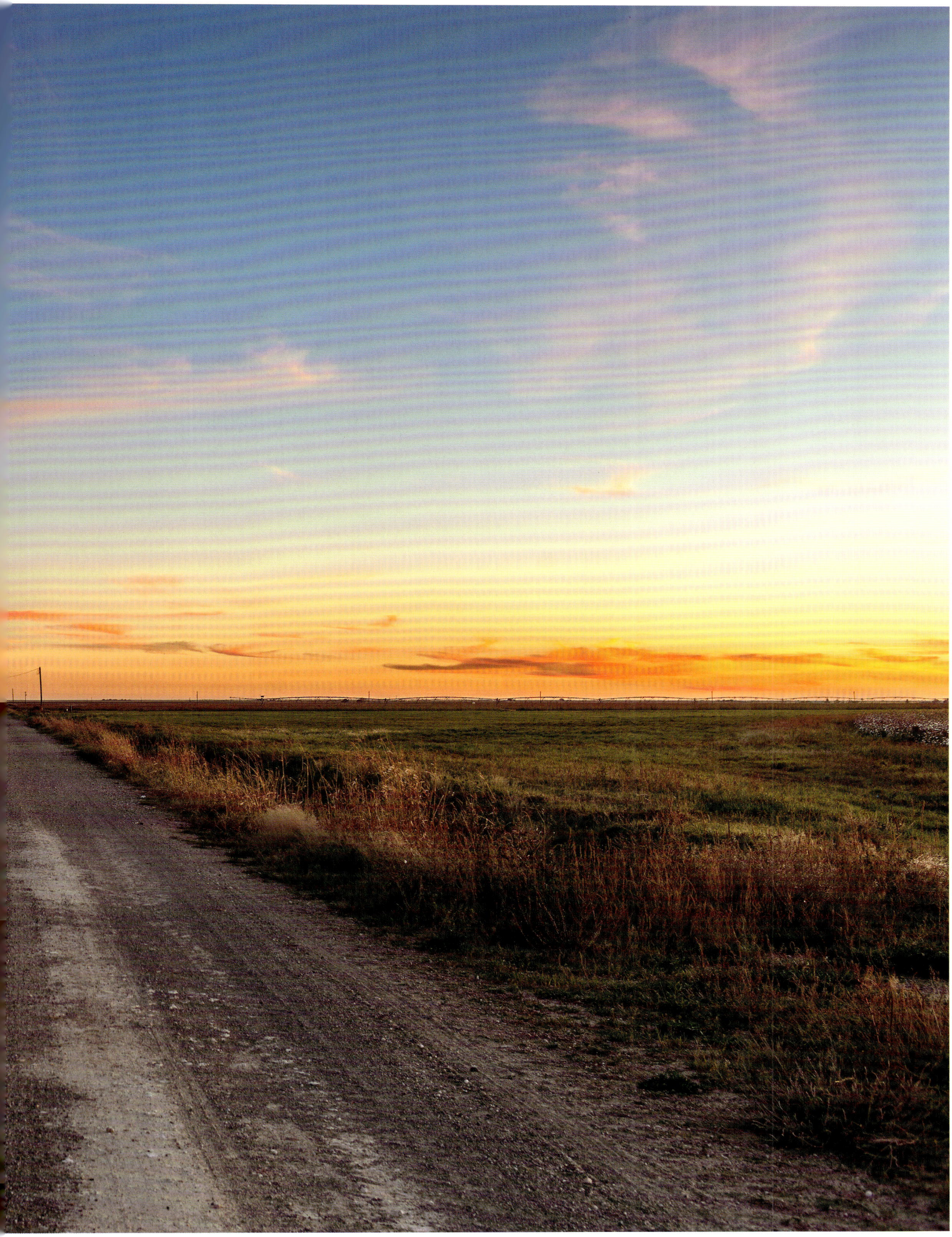

HIGH COTTON near Cotton Center, 2017

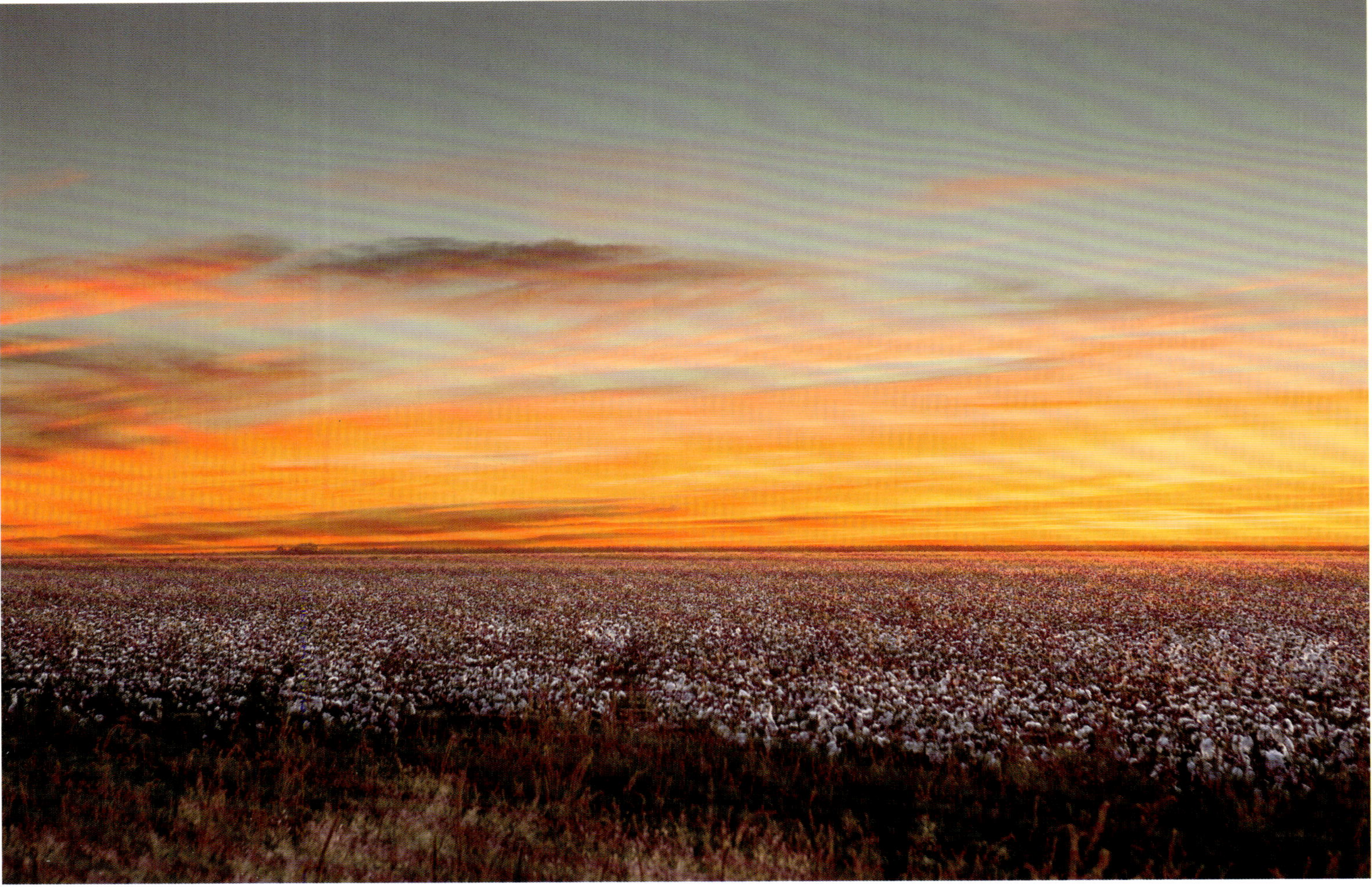

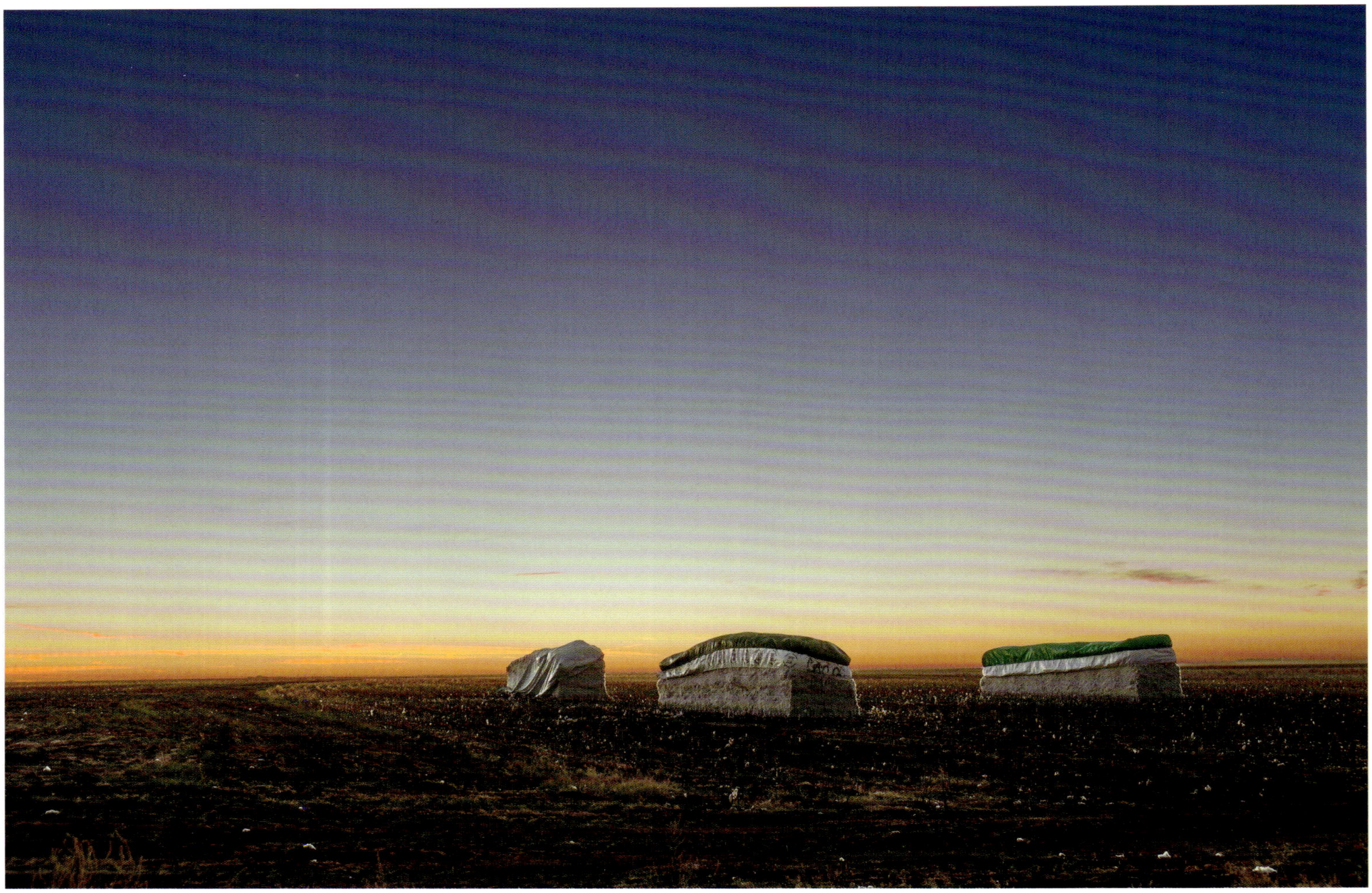

COTTON FIELD near Post, 2016

COTTON BALES Silverton, 2017

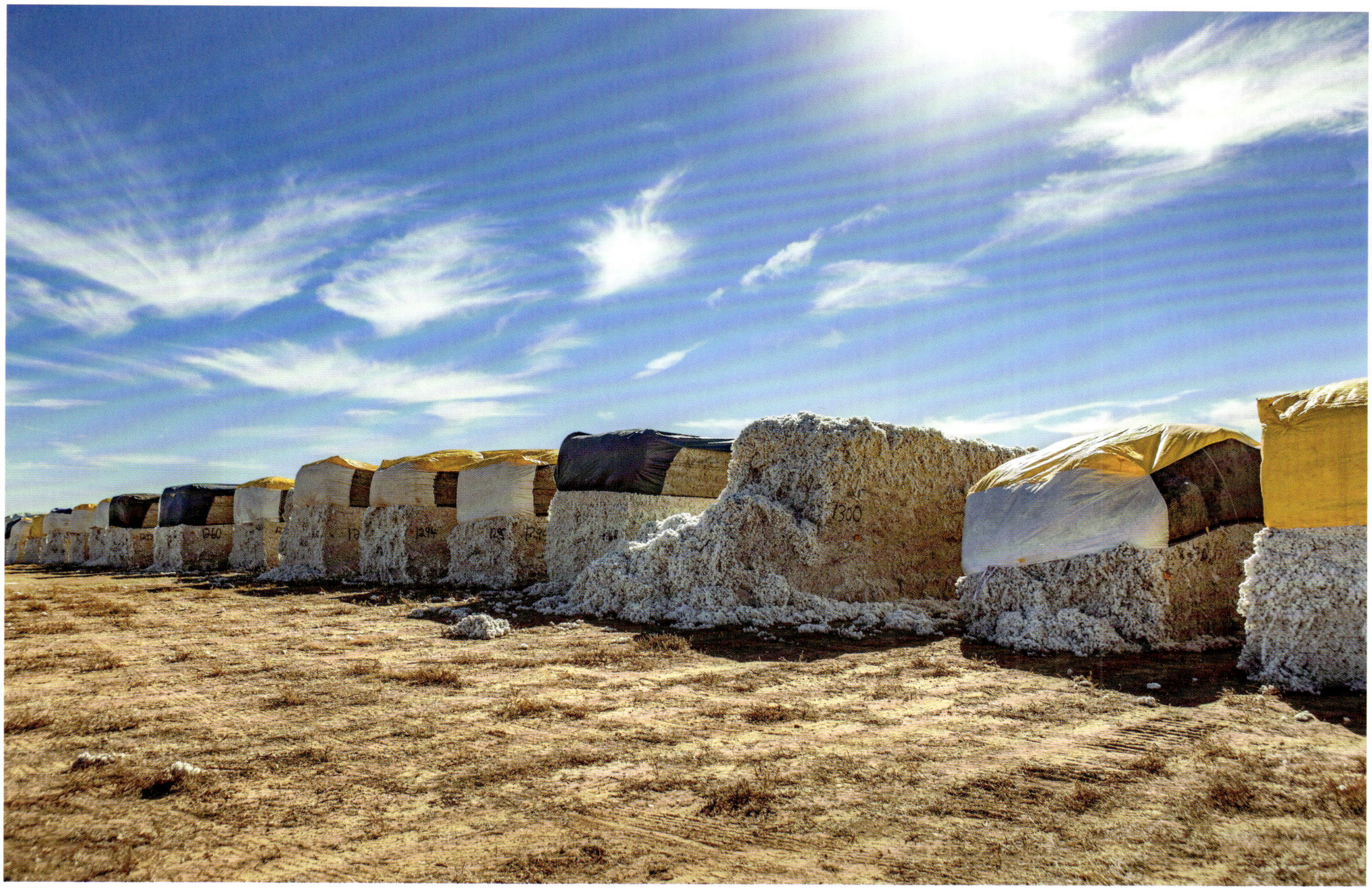

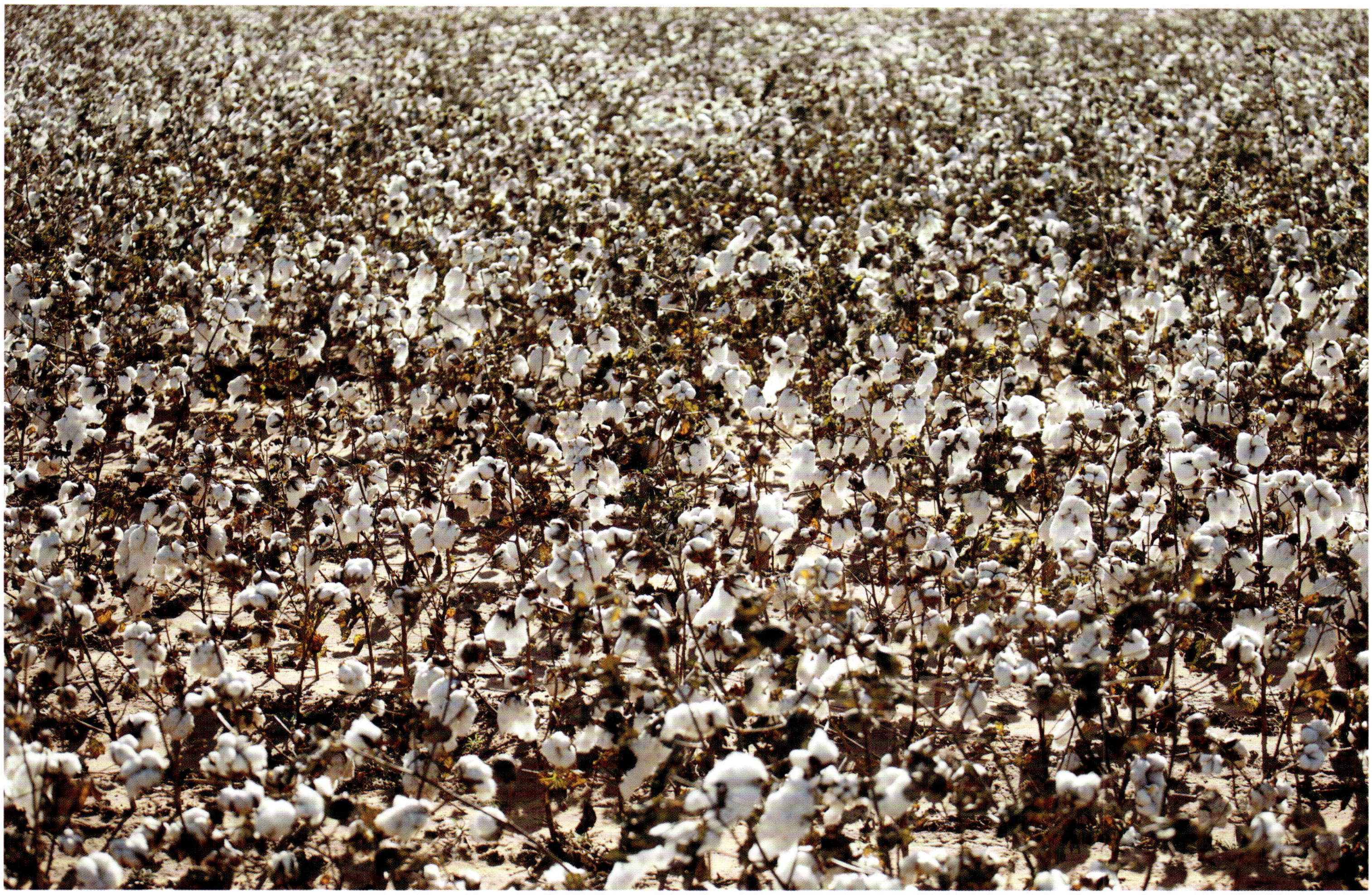

100% COTTON Quitaque, 2016

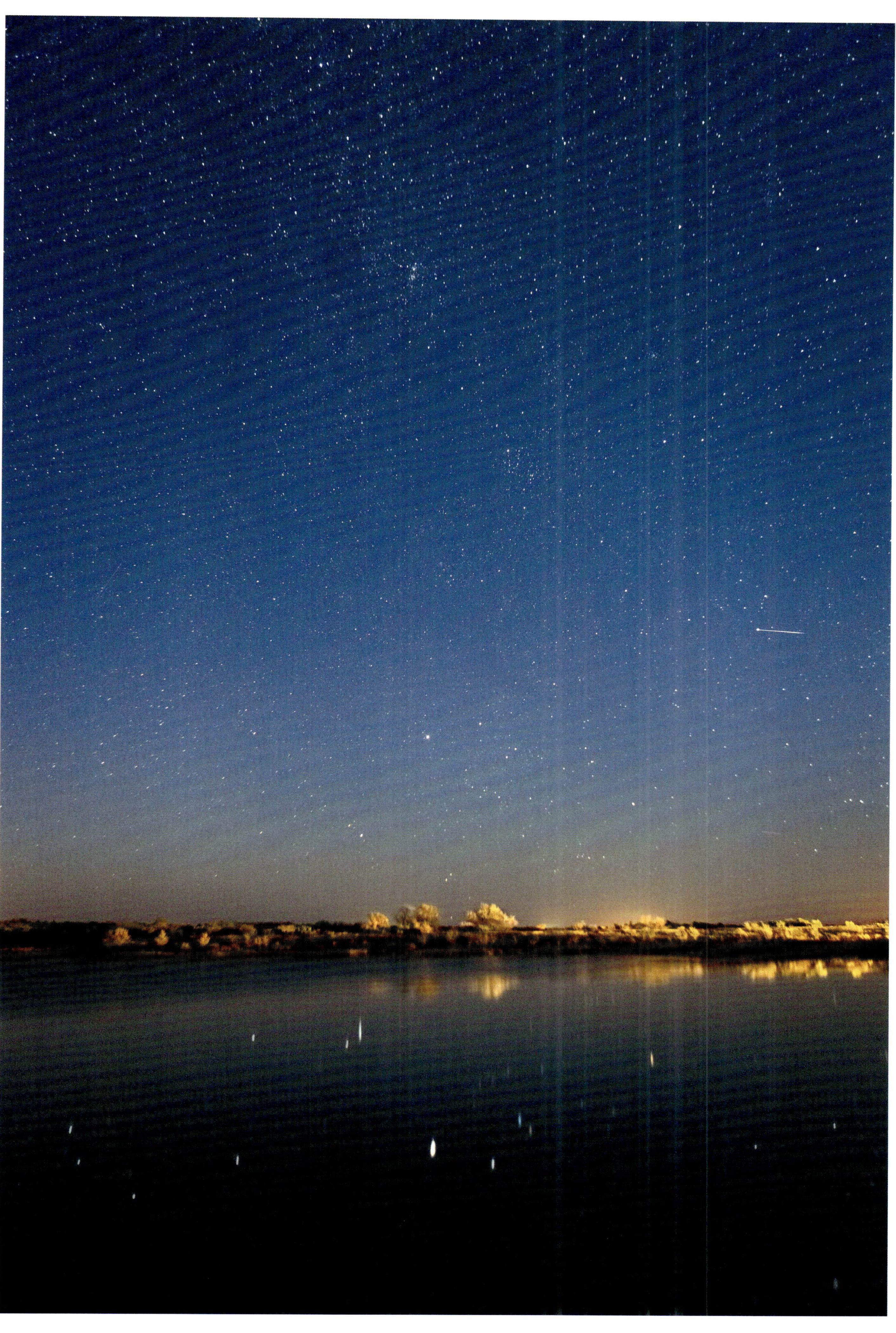

STARS OVER LAKE THEO Caprock Canyons State Park, 2017

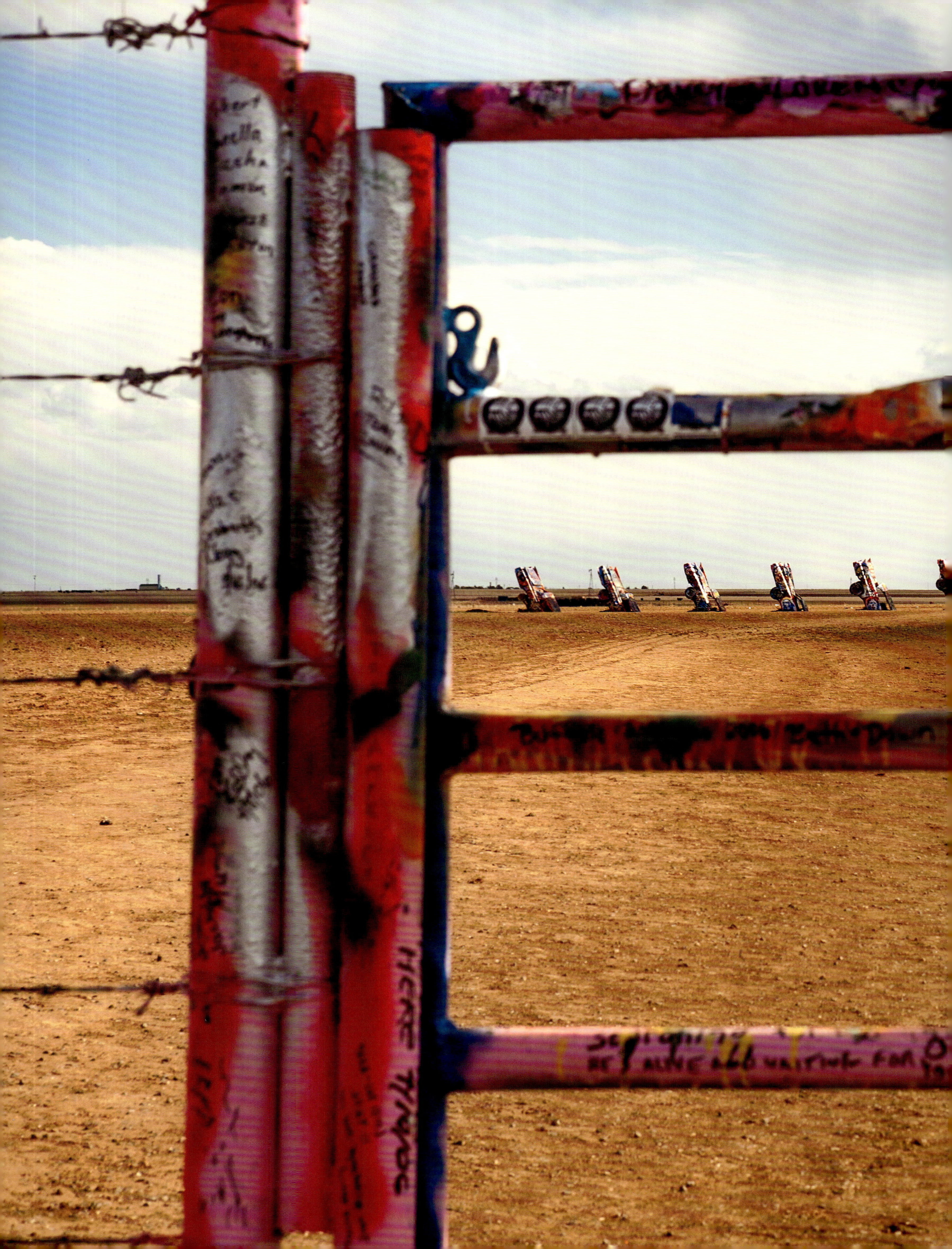

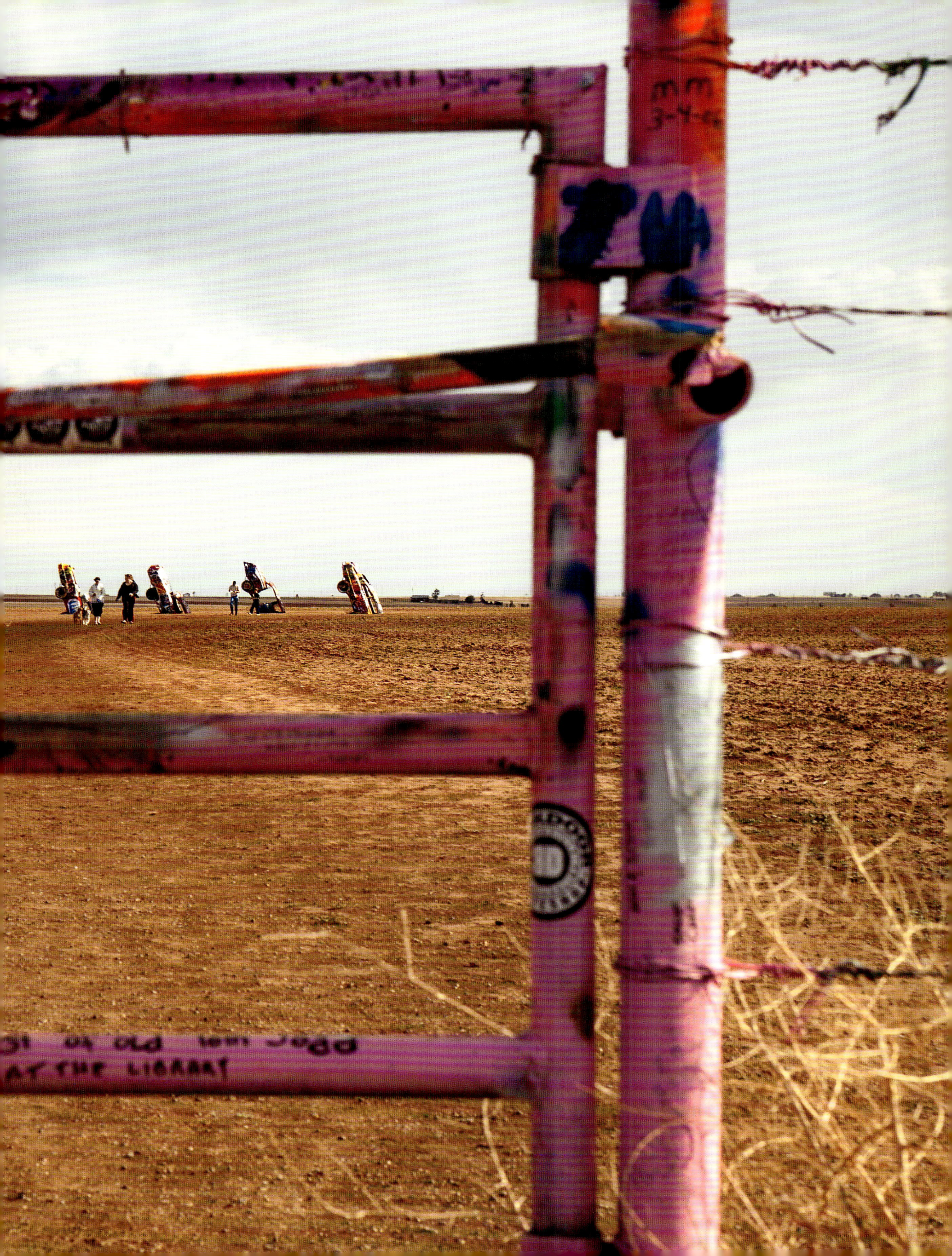
mm
AT THE LIBRARY

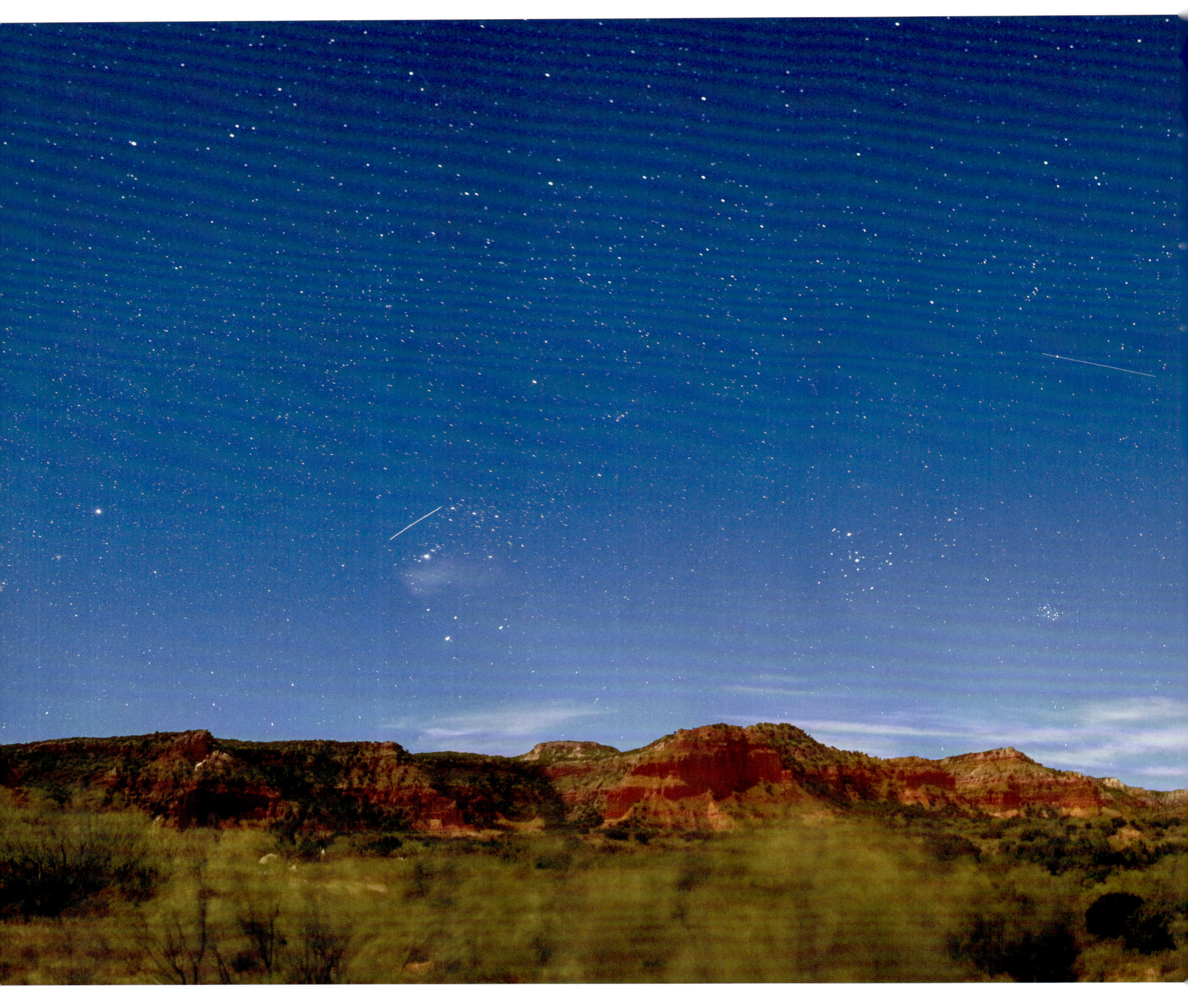

BEFORE SUNRISE Upper Canyon Trail overlook, Caprock Canyons State Park, 2017

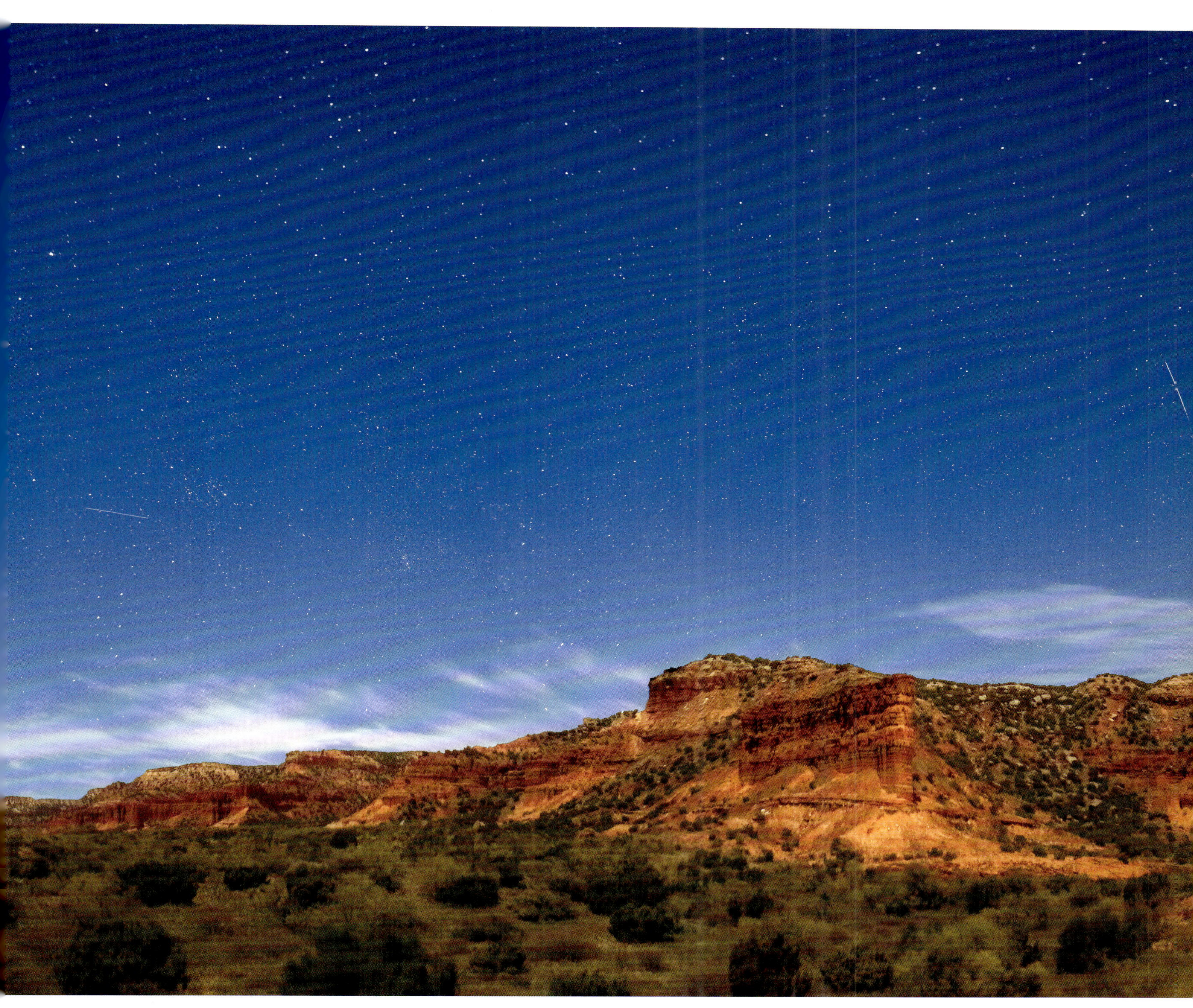

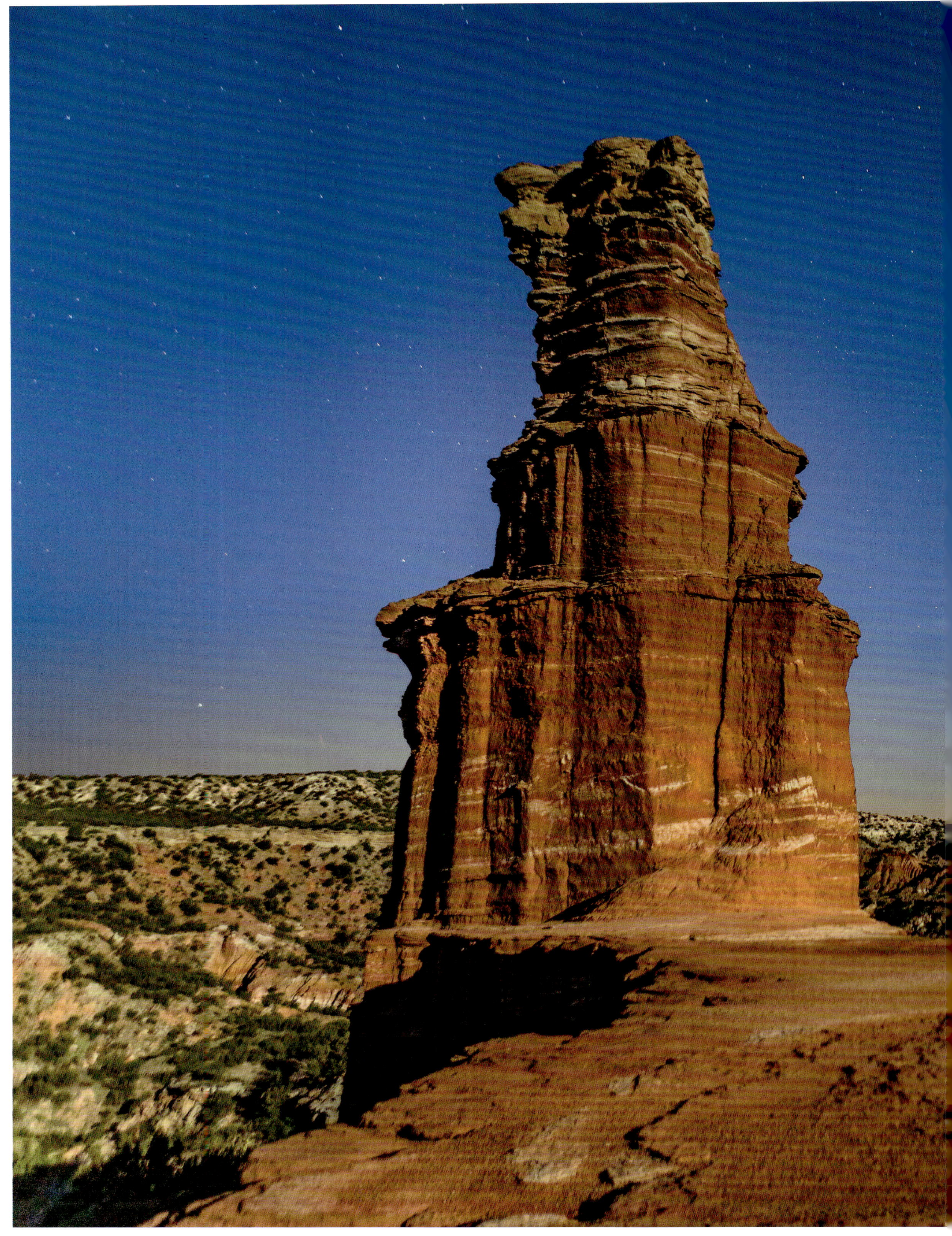

THE LIGHTHOUSE Palo Duro Canyon State Park, 2017

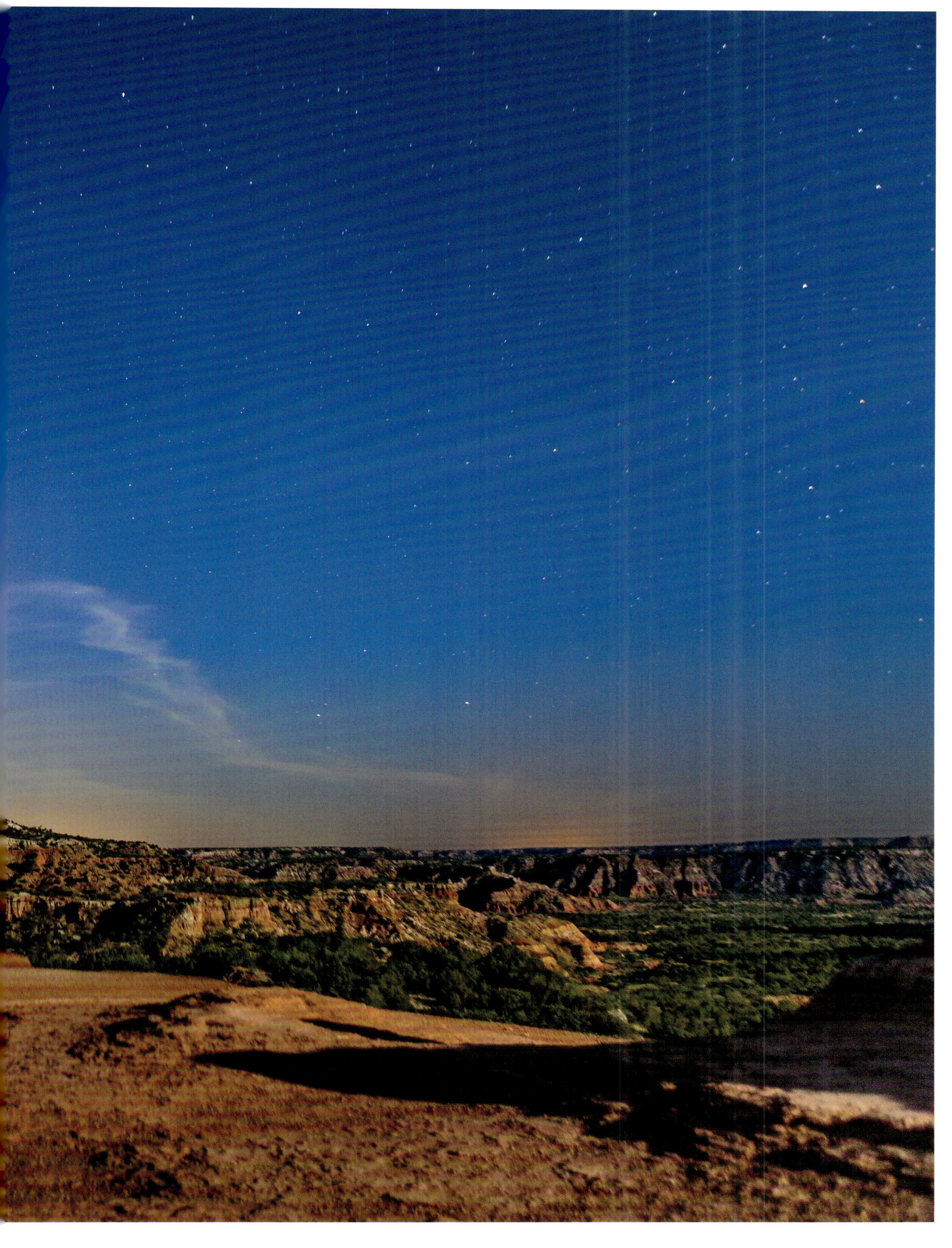

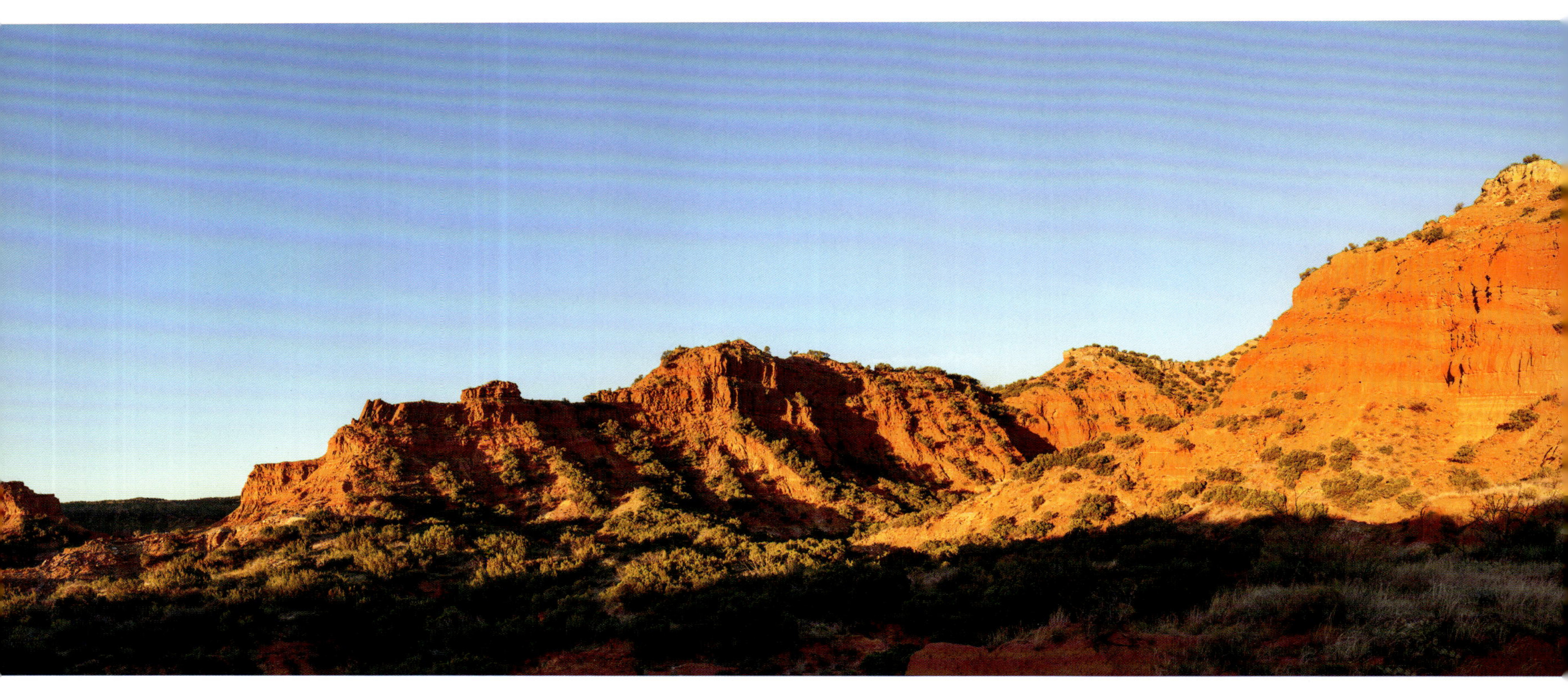

FIRST LIGHT Upper Canyon Trail, Caprock Canyons State Park, 2017

ARROYO Caprock Canyons State Park, 2017 >

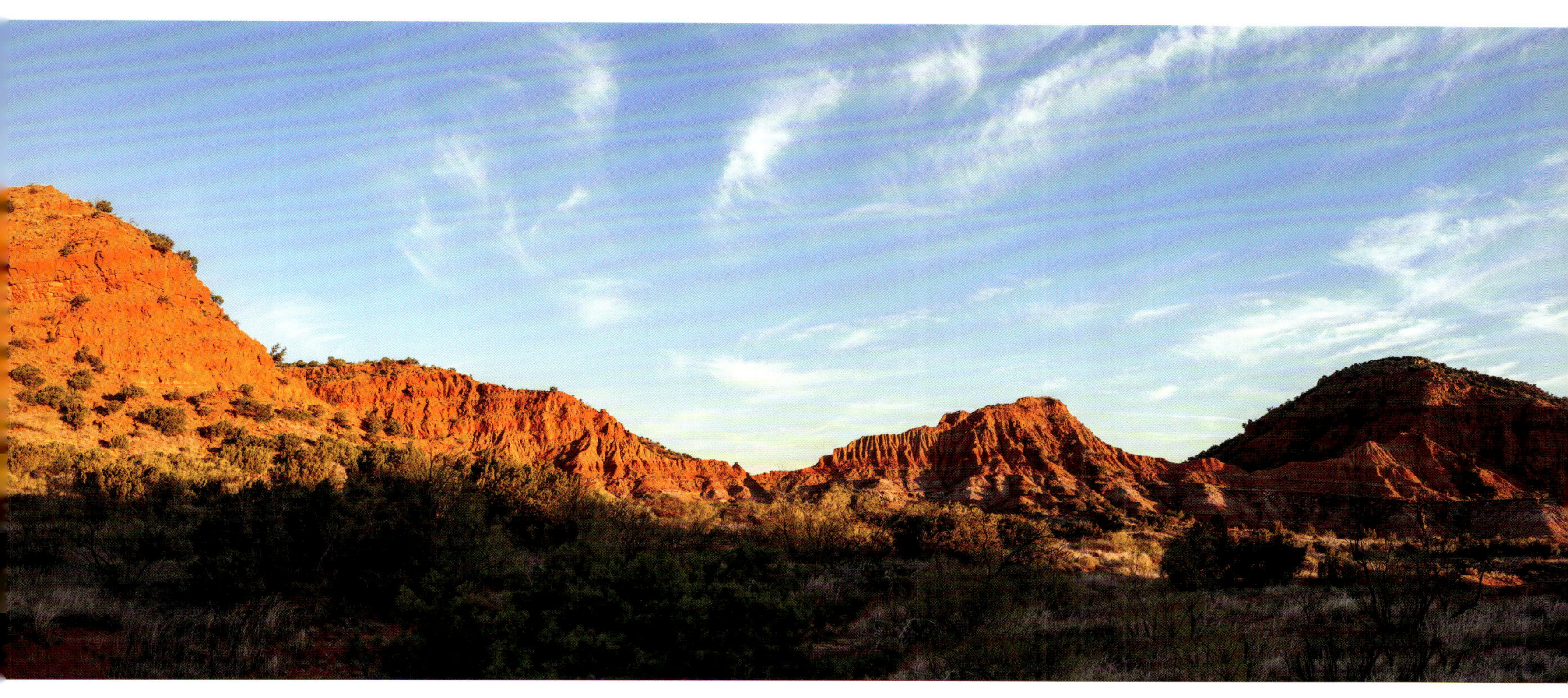

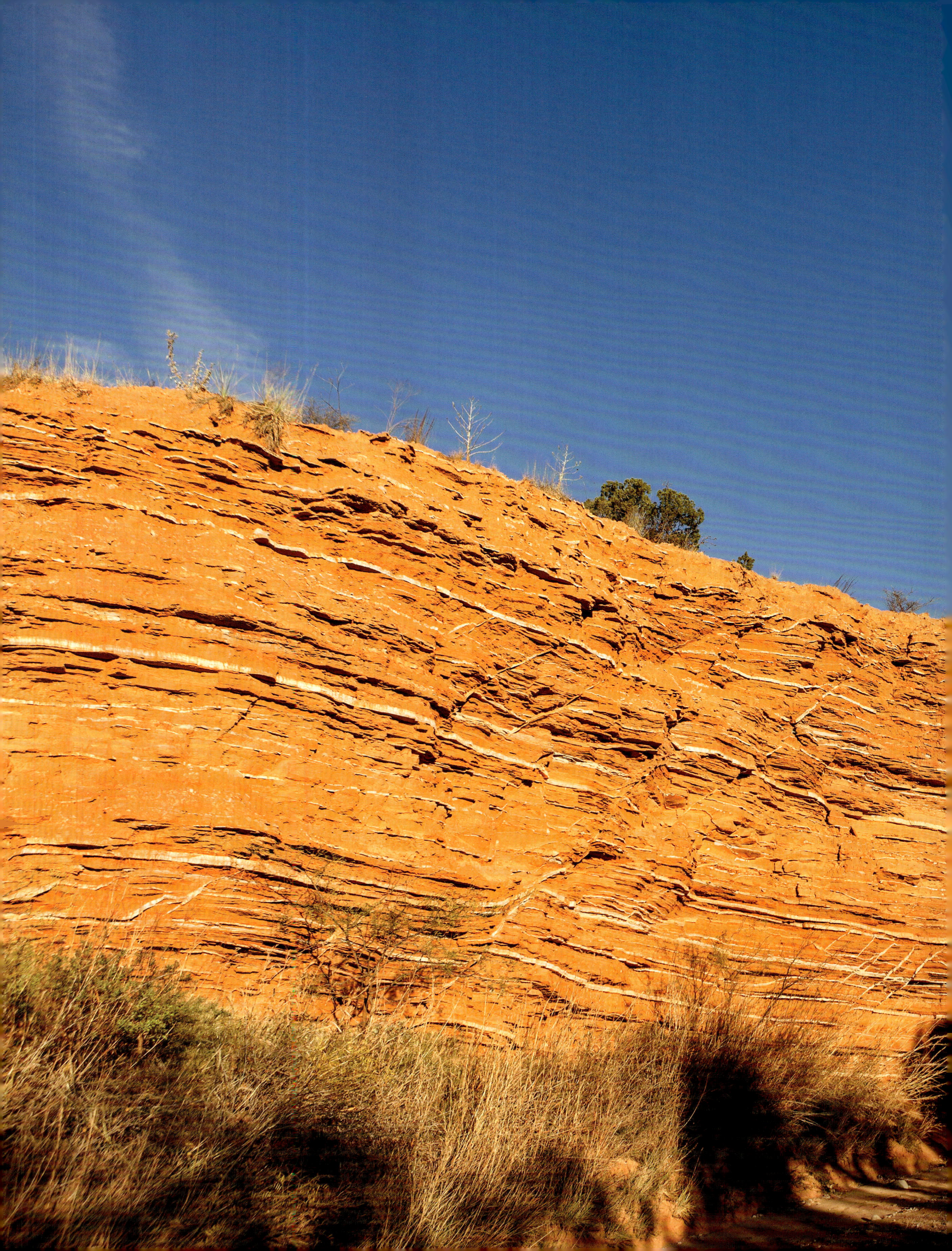

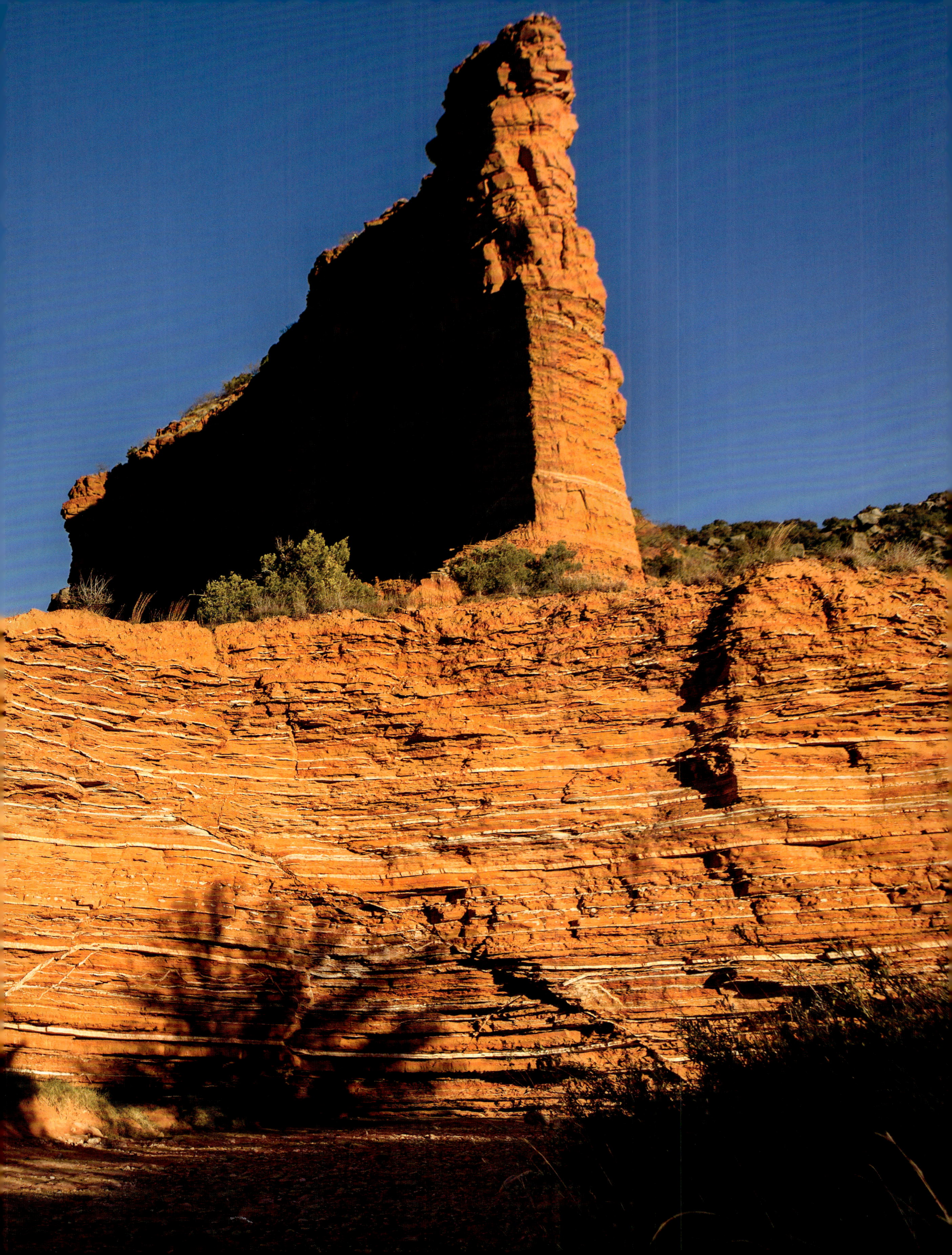

EAST TEXAS

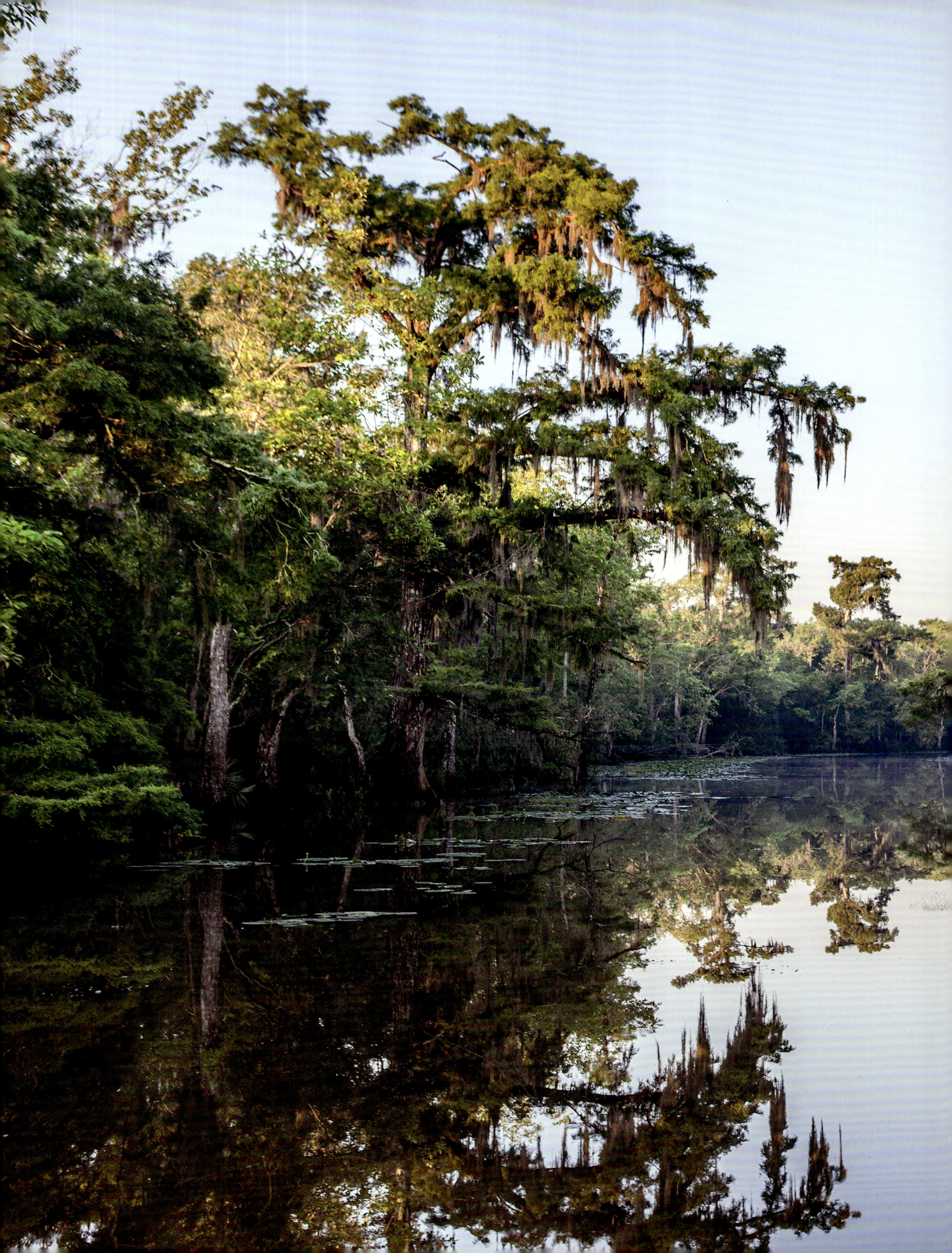

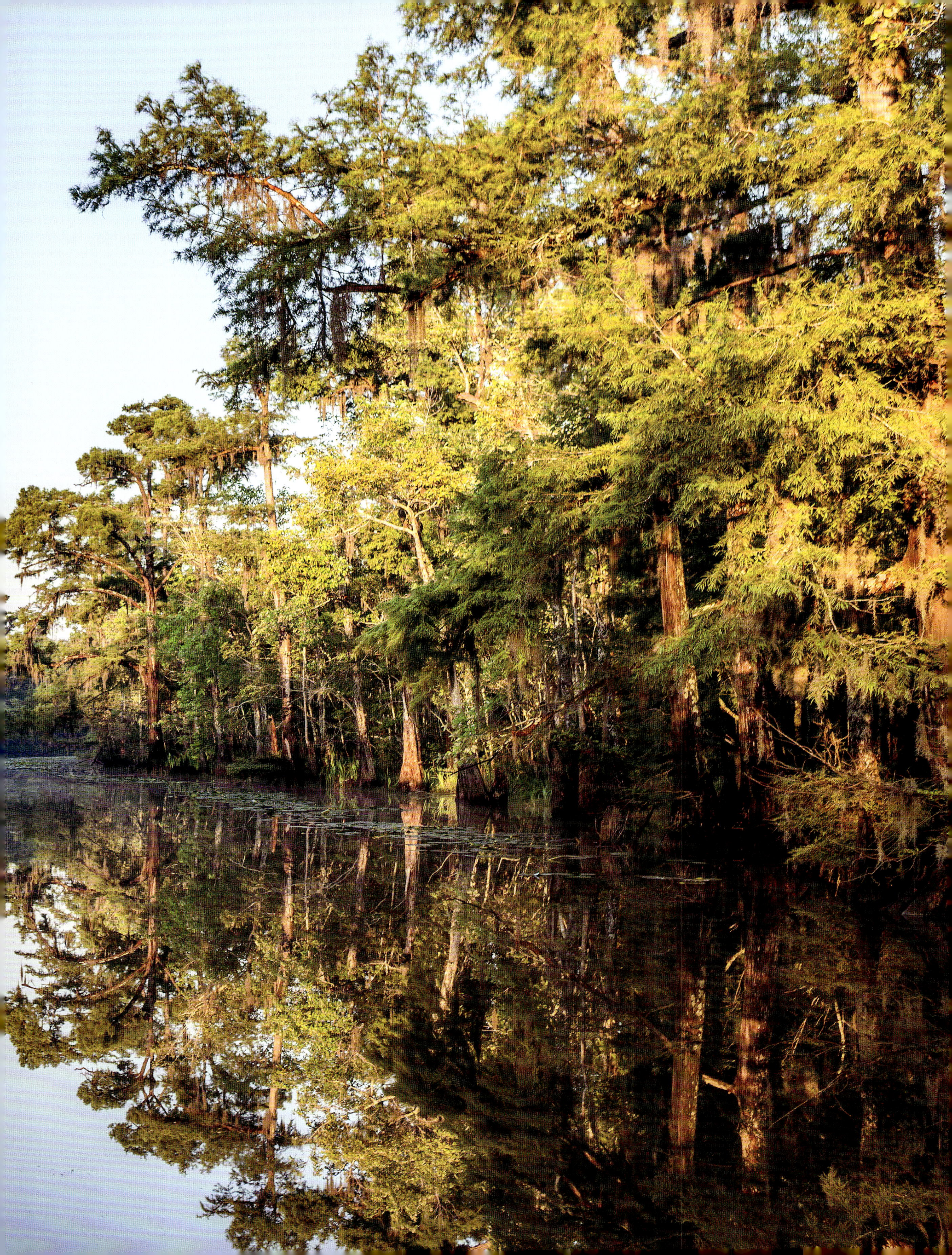

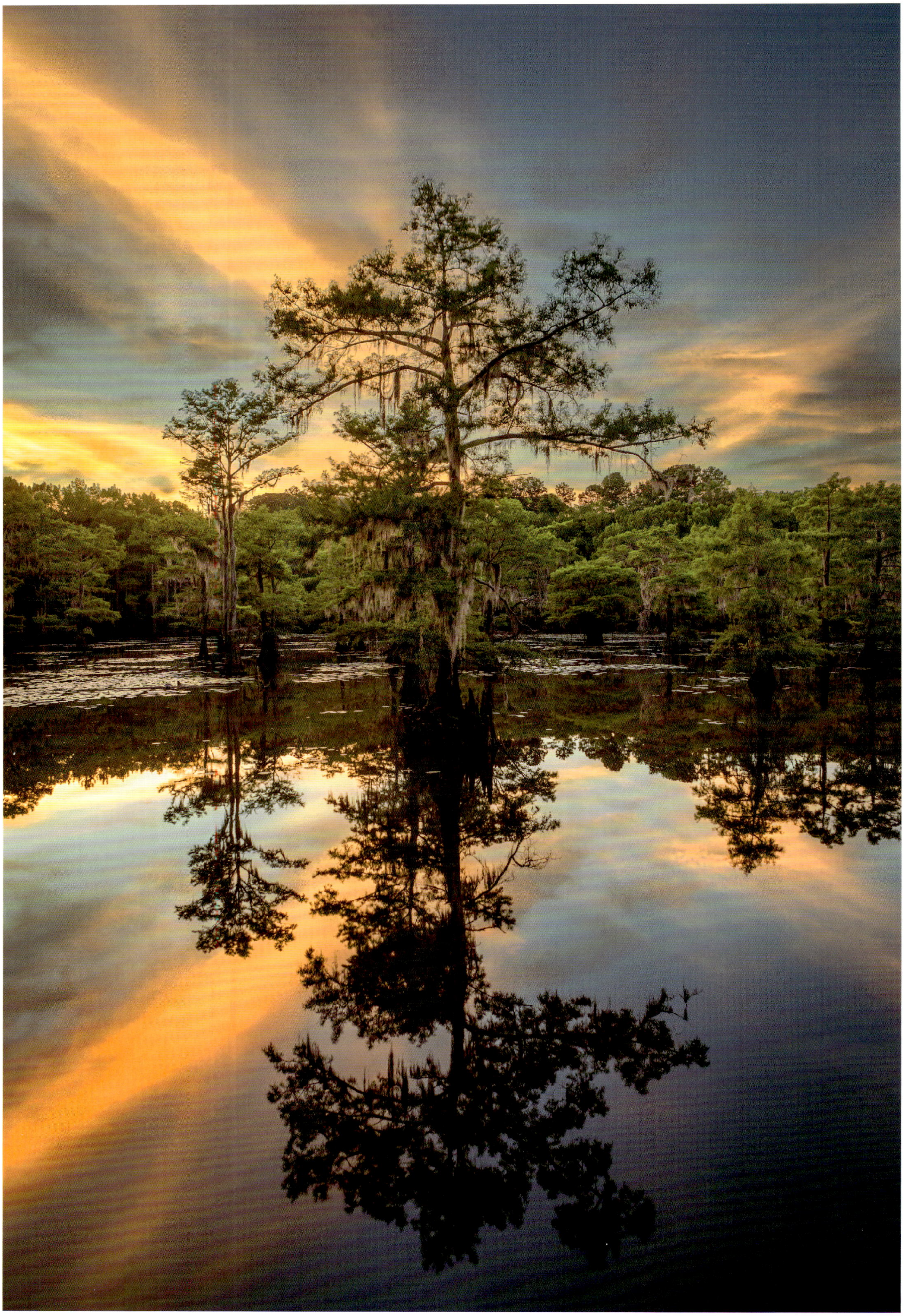

< **SWAMP** Sabine River, near Orange, 2012

SAW MILL POND Caddo Lake State Park, Karnack, 2017

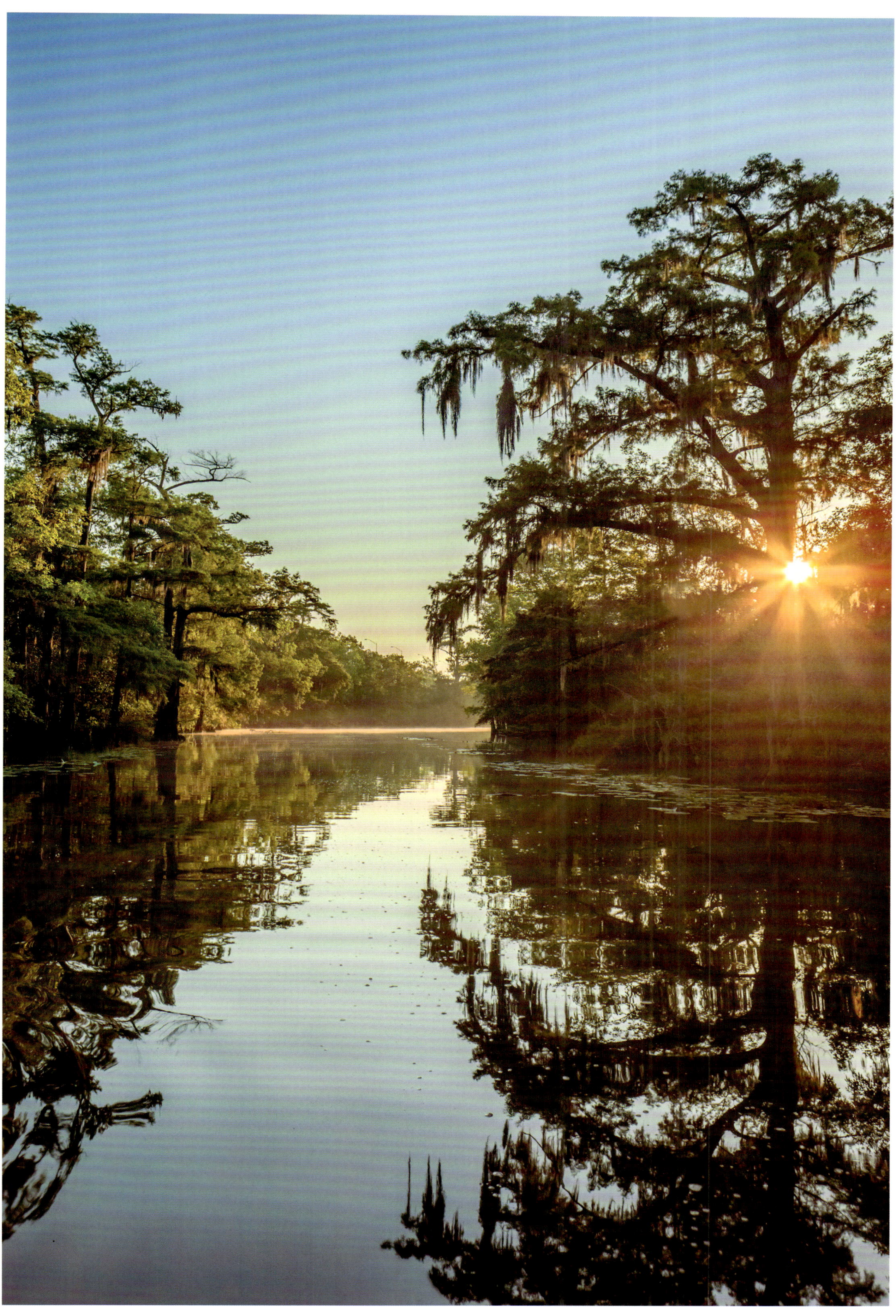

SUNRISE Sabine River, near Orange, 2012

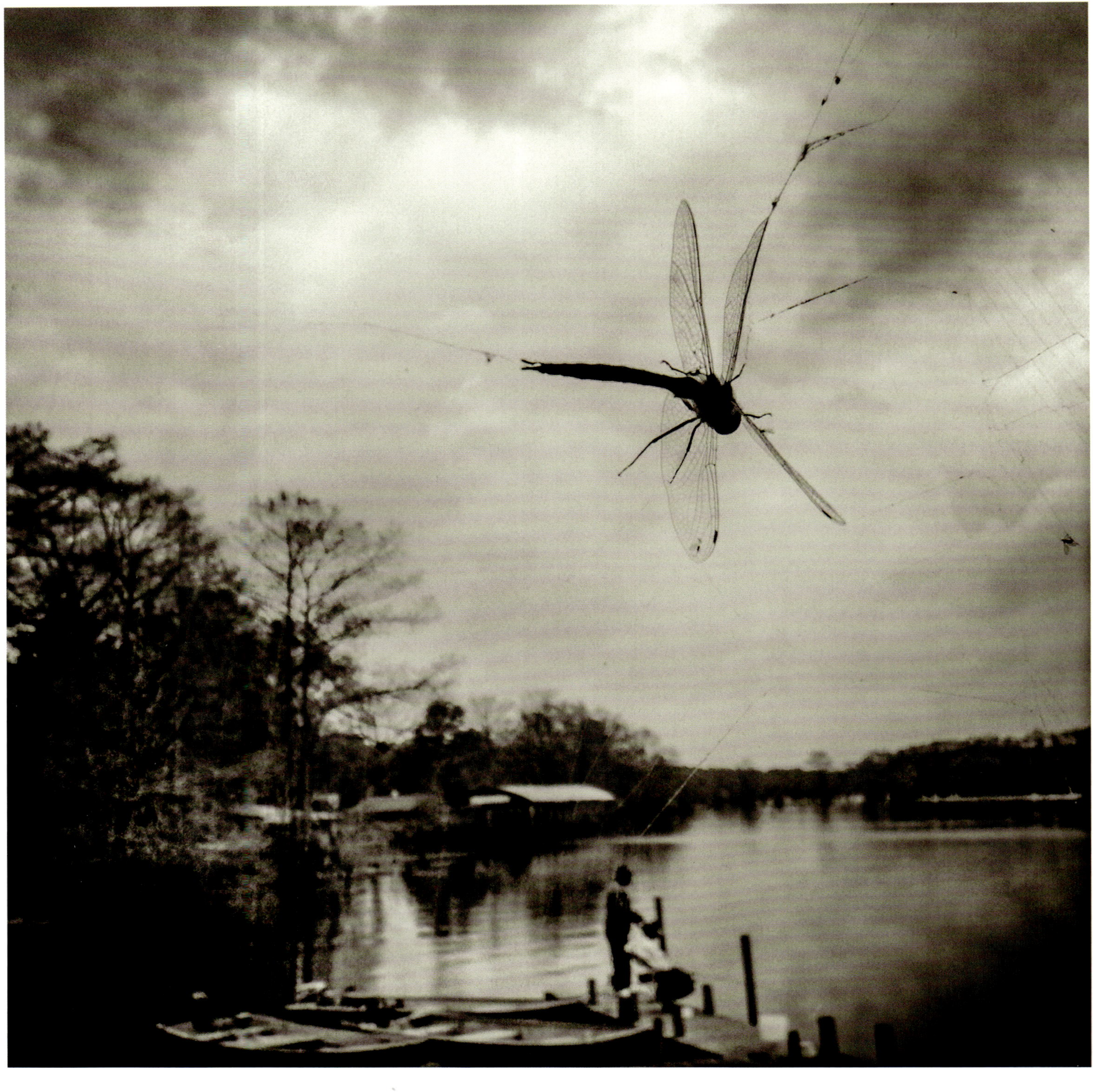

DRAGONFLY Caddo Lake, 2015

LAKE CHARLOTTE near Wallisville, 2010 >

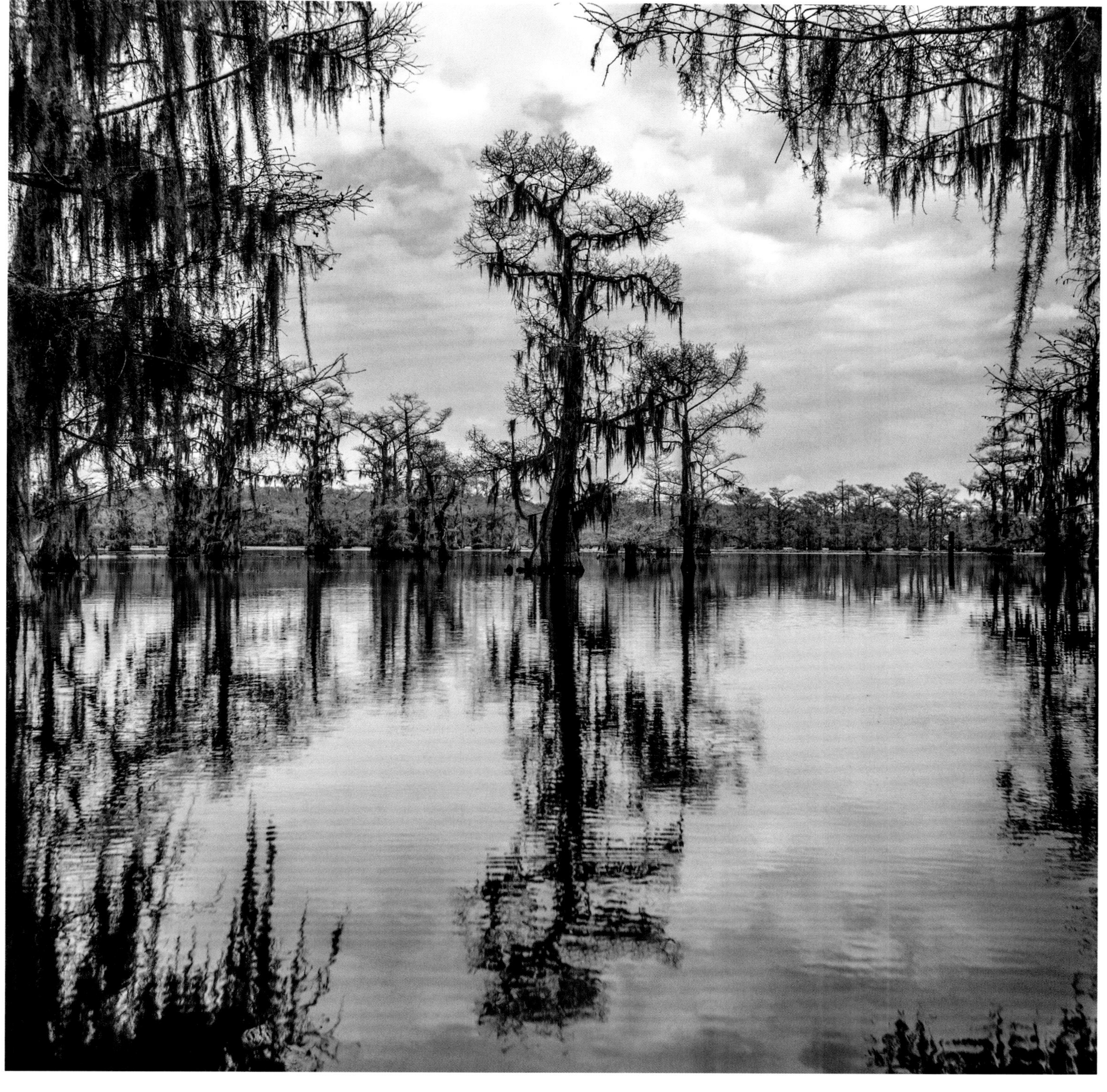

143

WATER TRAIL Caddo Lake, 2015

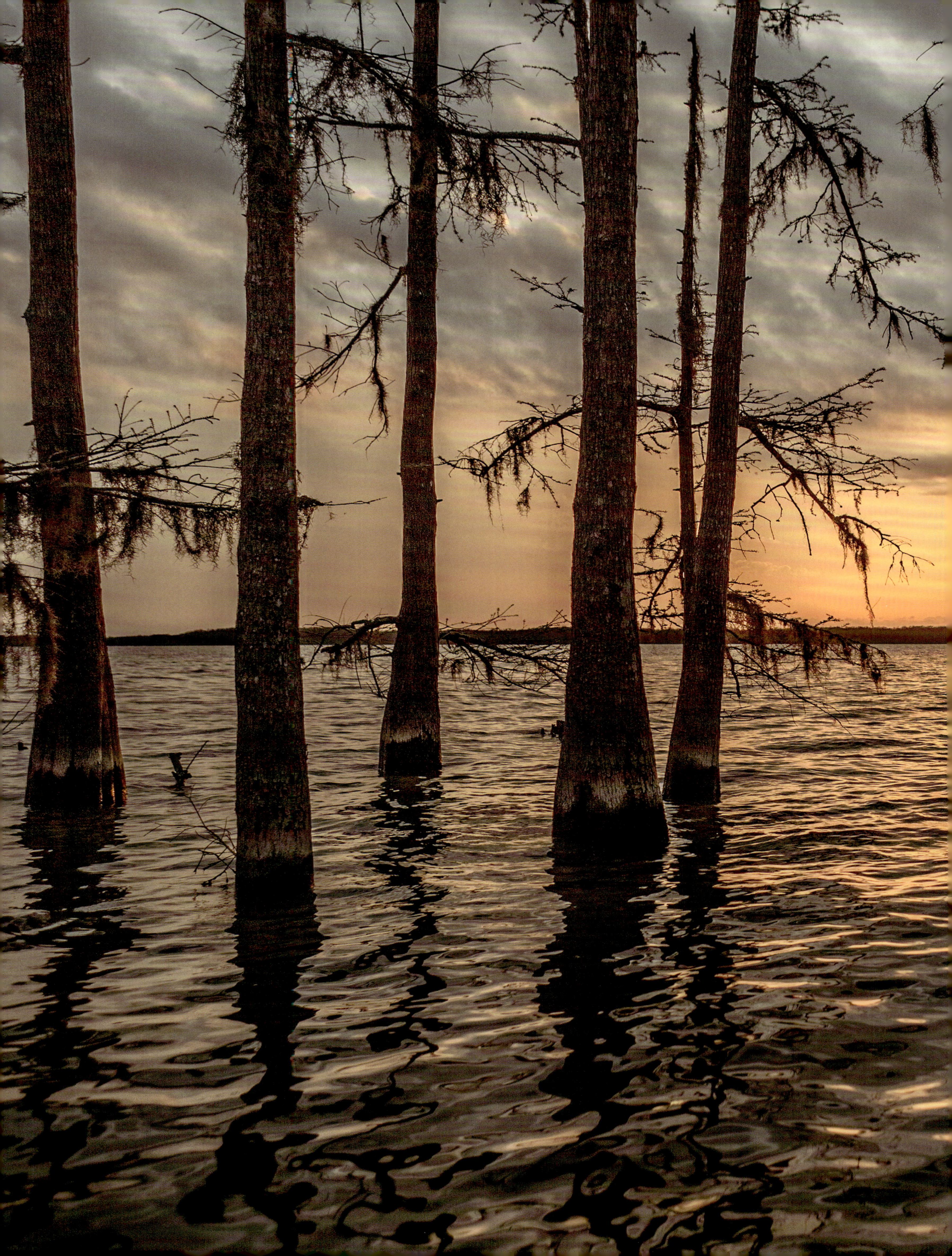

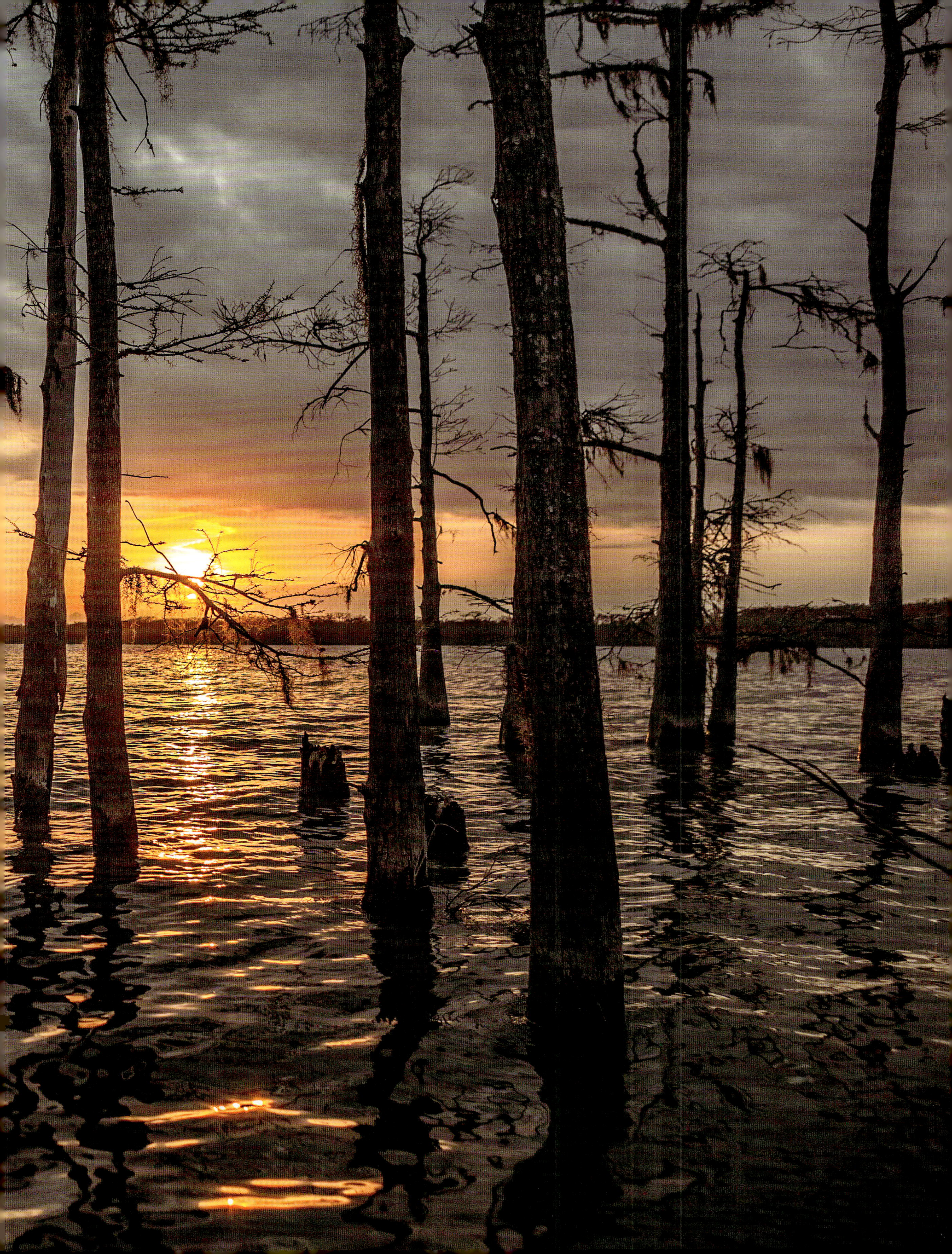

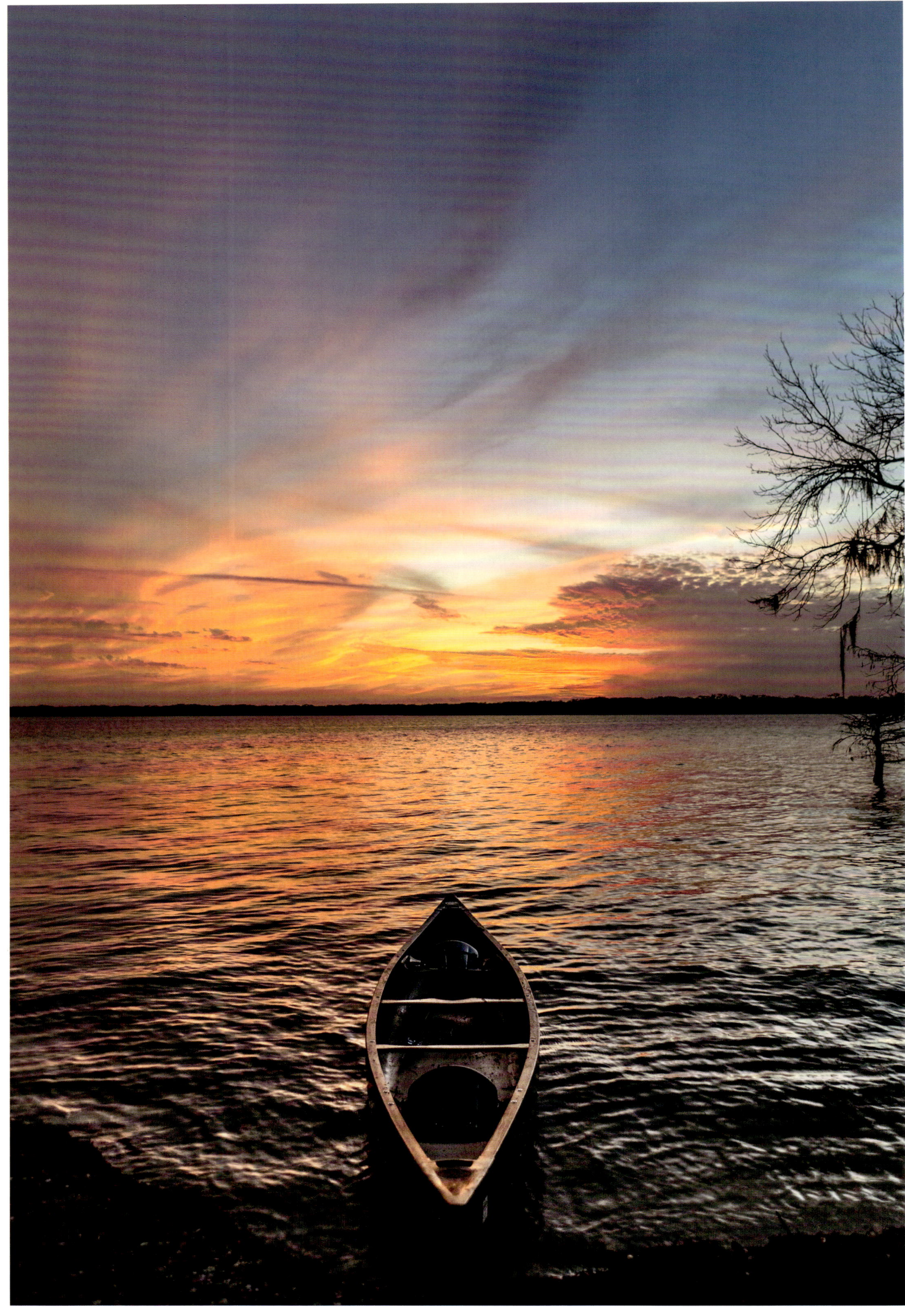

CANOE Lake Charlotte, near Wallisville, 2010

TWELVE FEET DEEP Camp Tonkawa Springs, Garrison, 2012 >

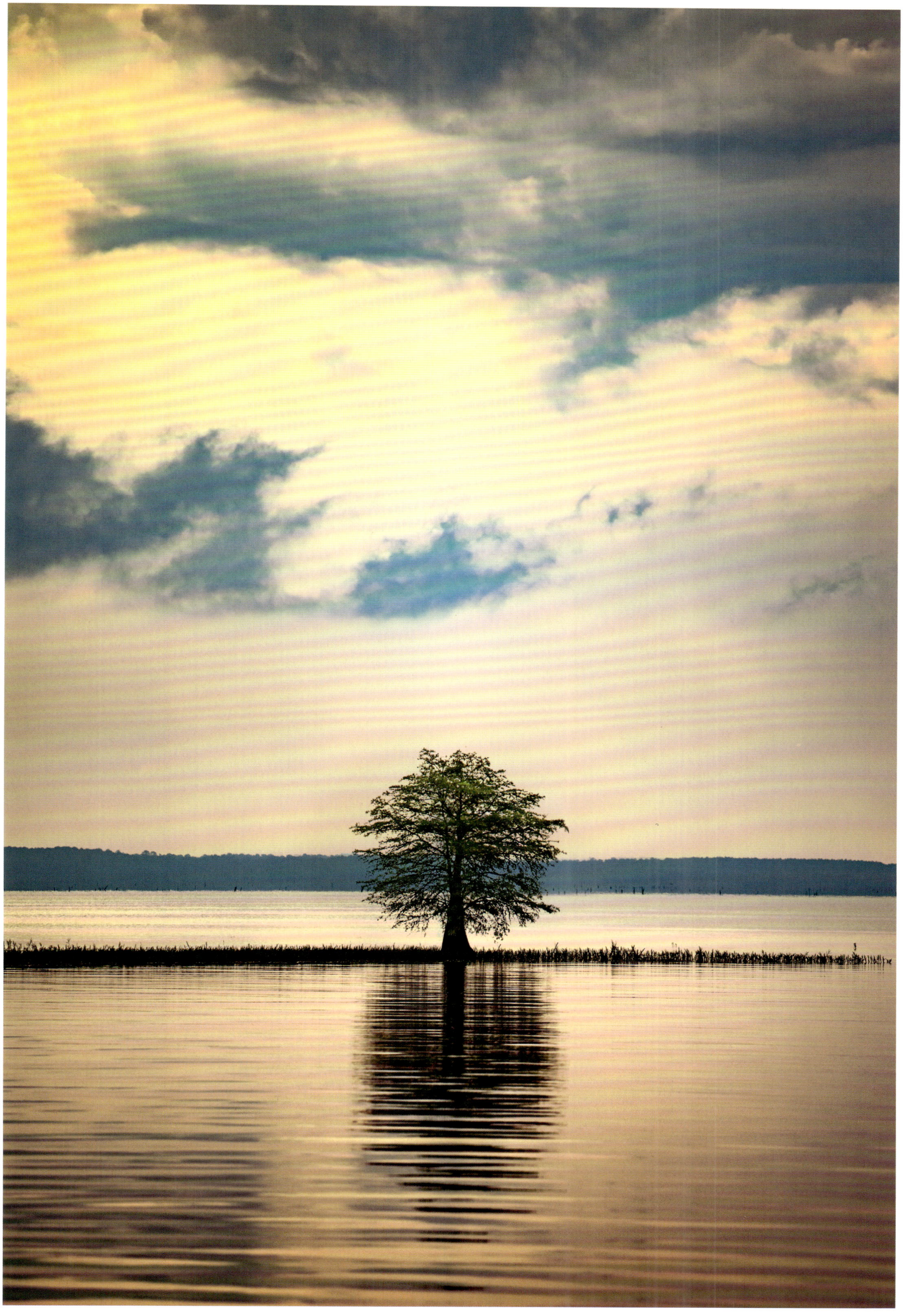

TOLEDO BEND Sabine National Forest, 2012

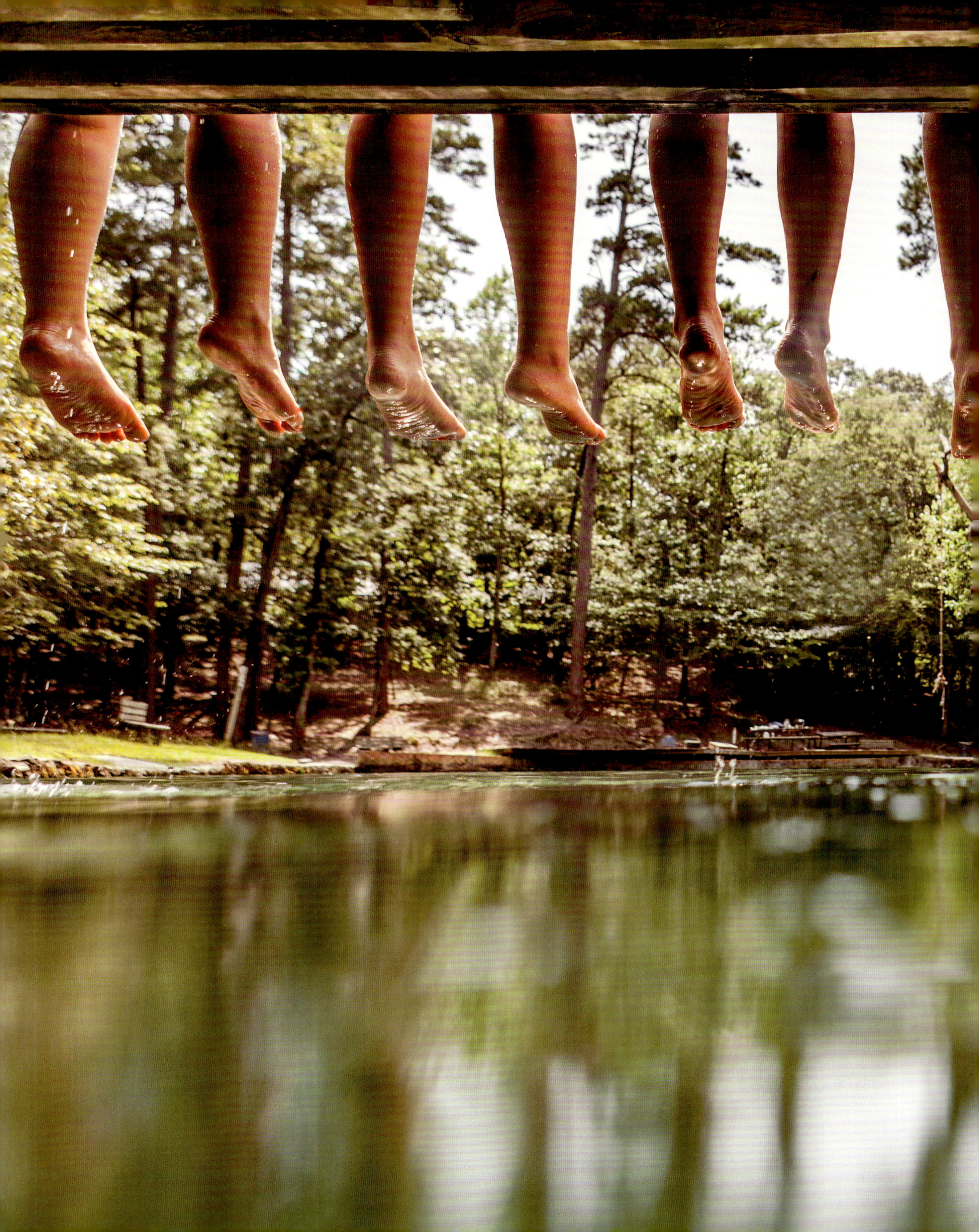

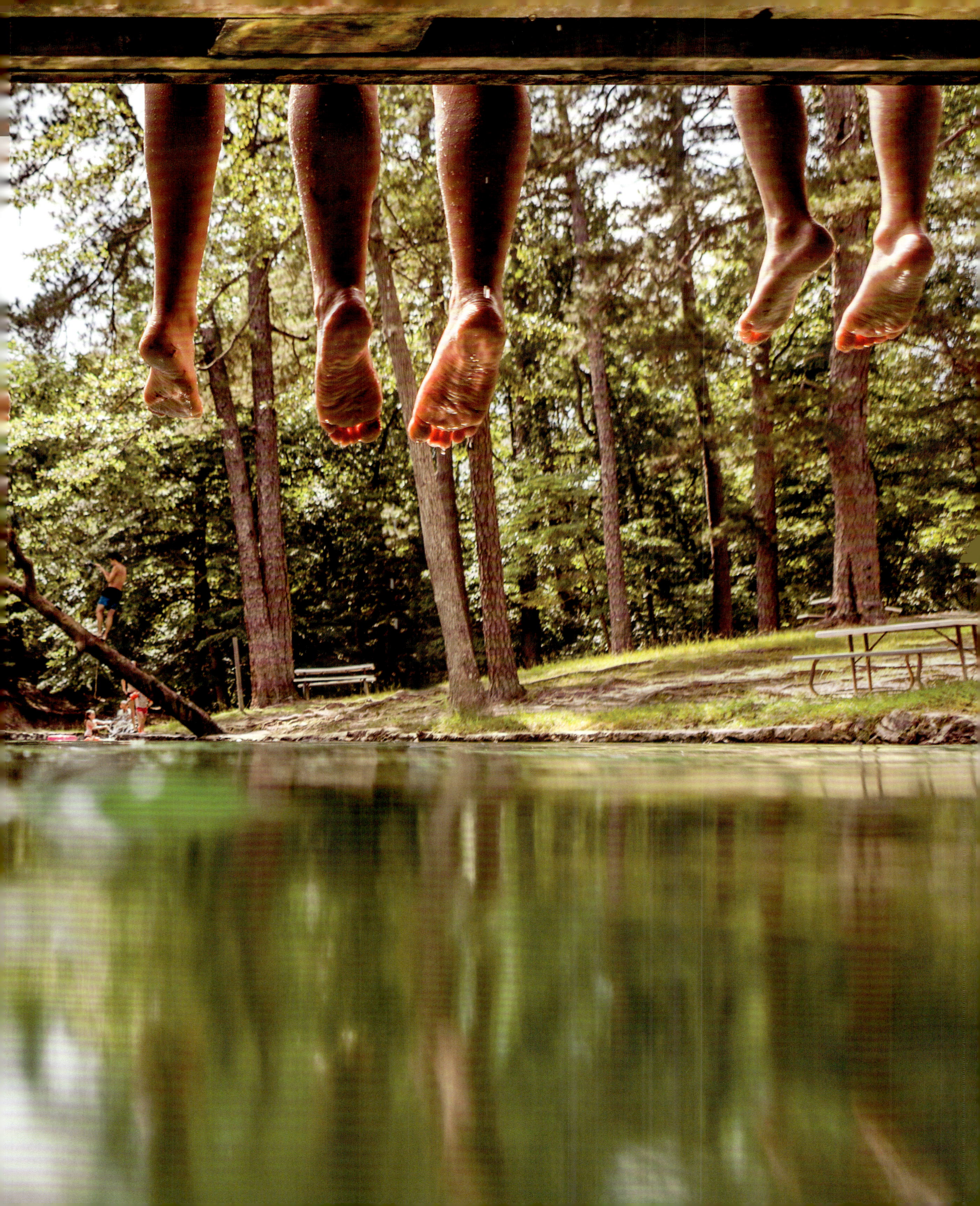

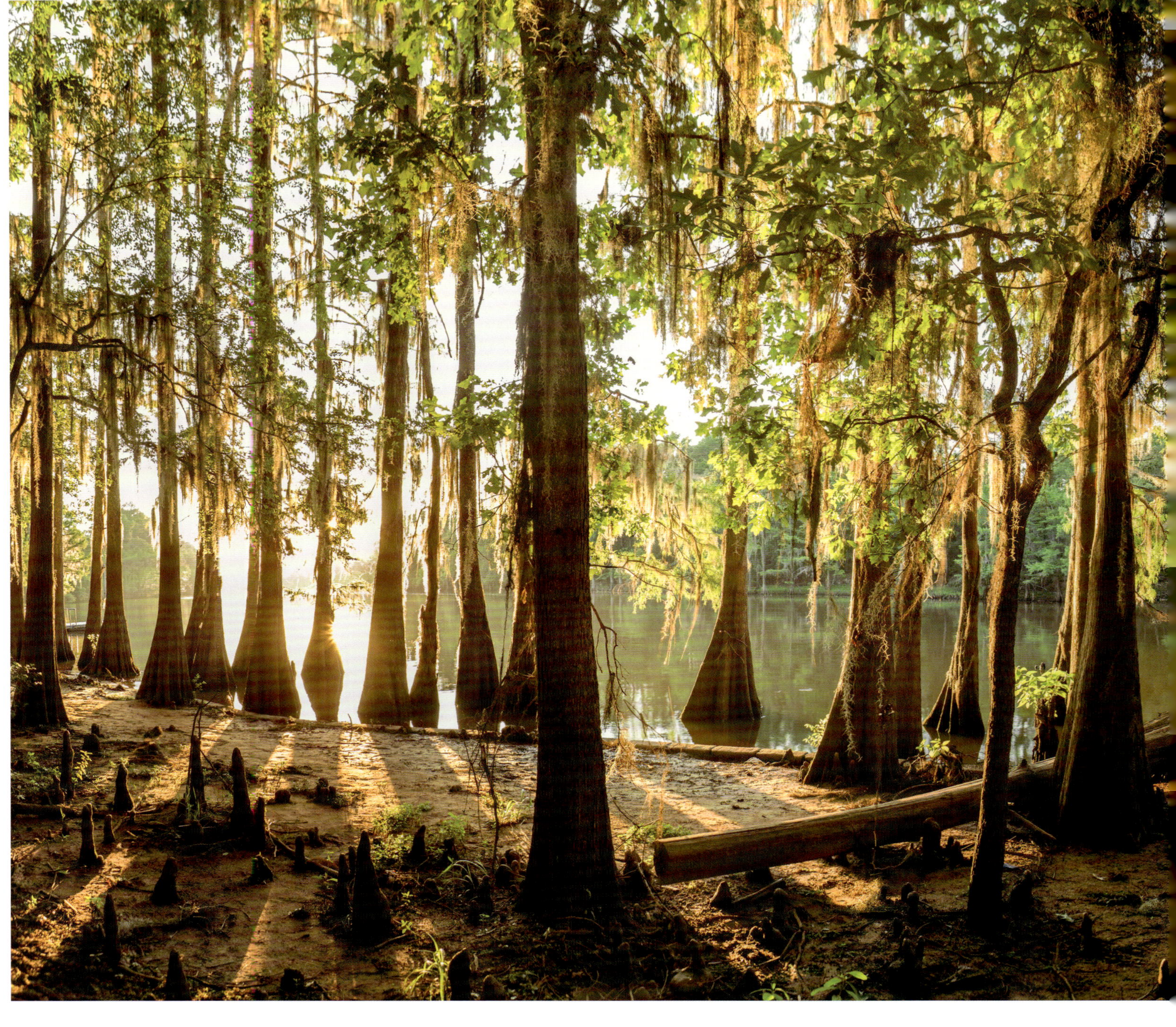

CYPRESS GROVE Caddo Lake State Park, Karnack, 2017

HIEROGLYPHICS Sabine River, near West Bluff, 2012 >

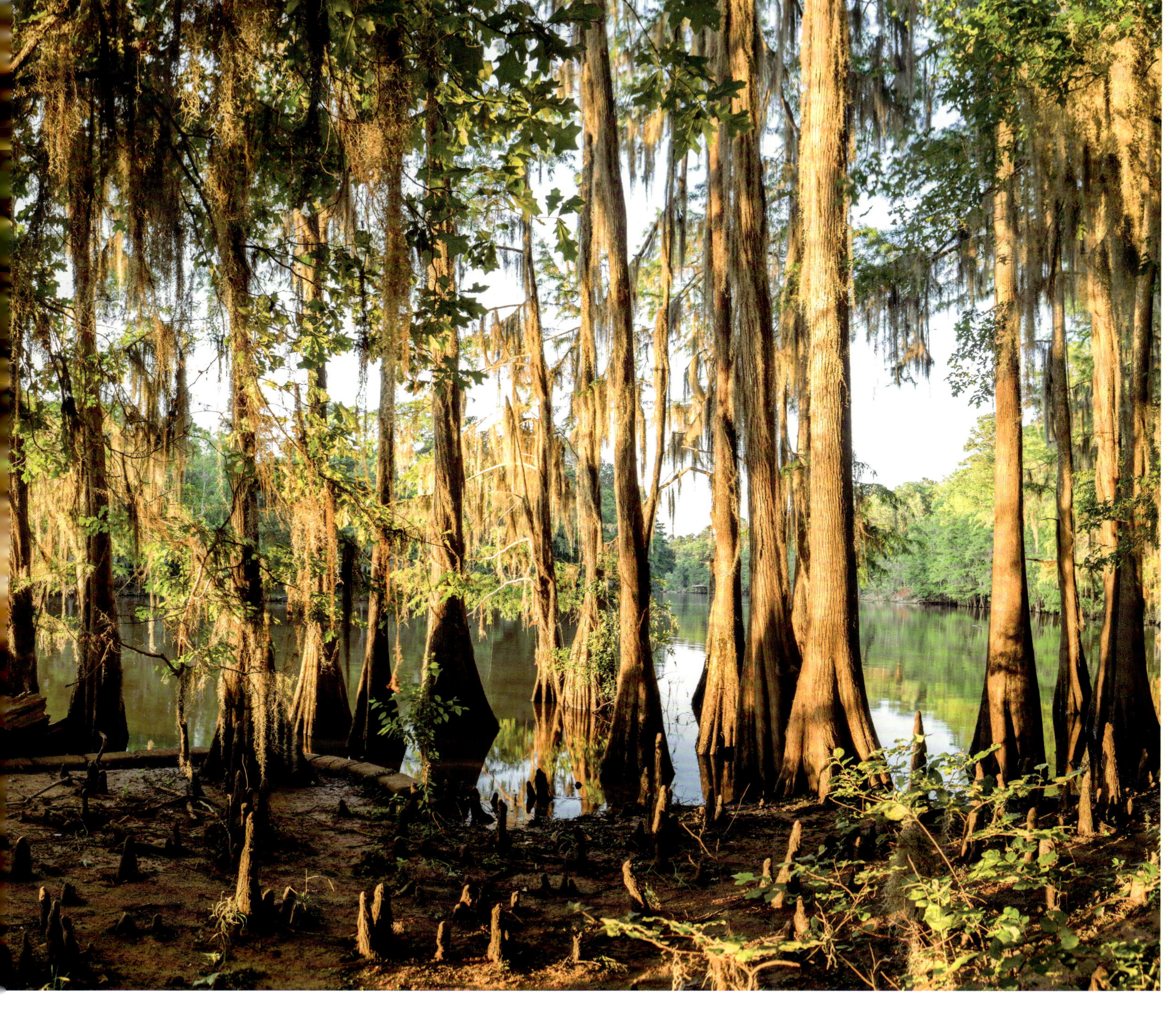

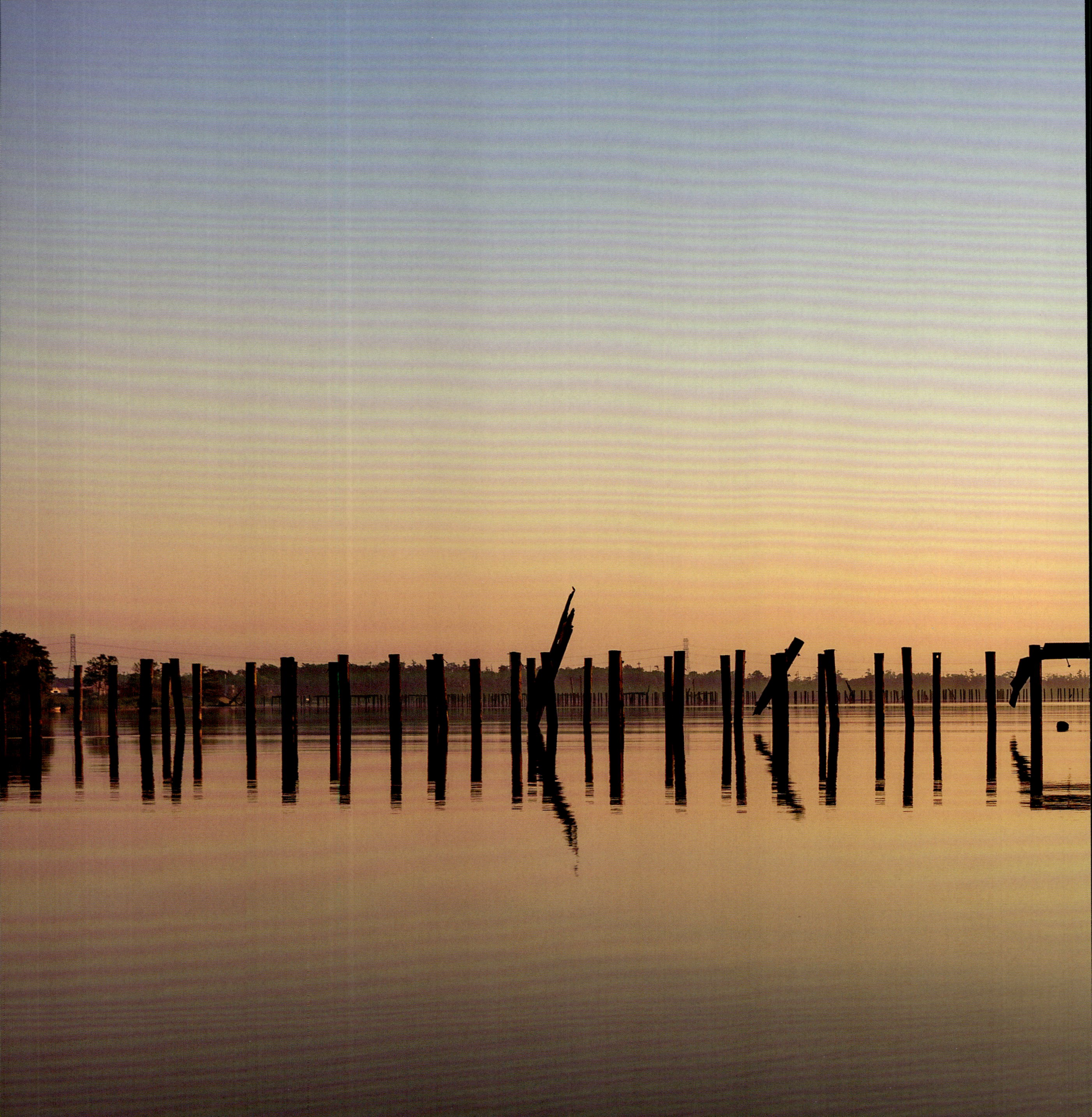

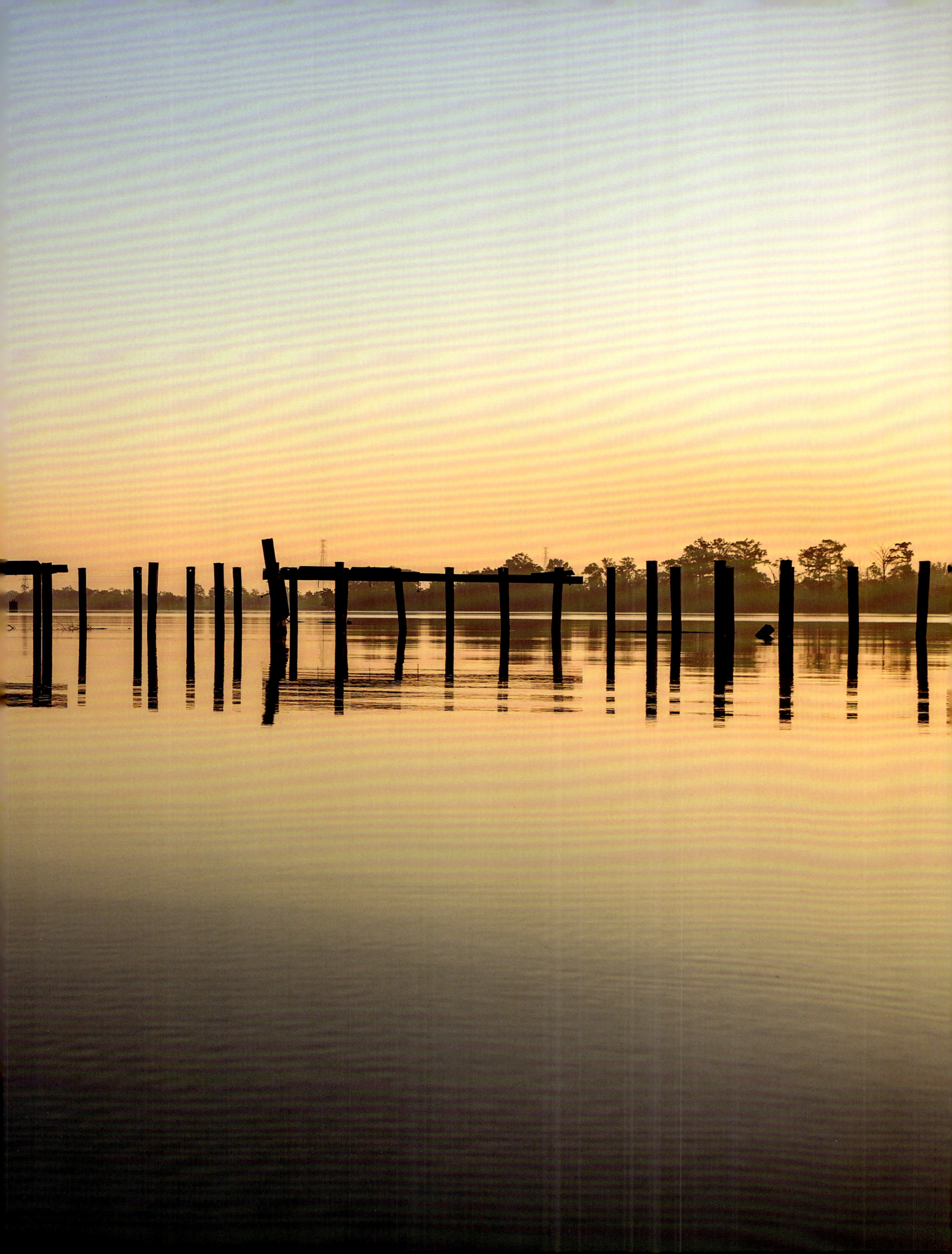

154

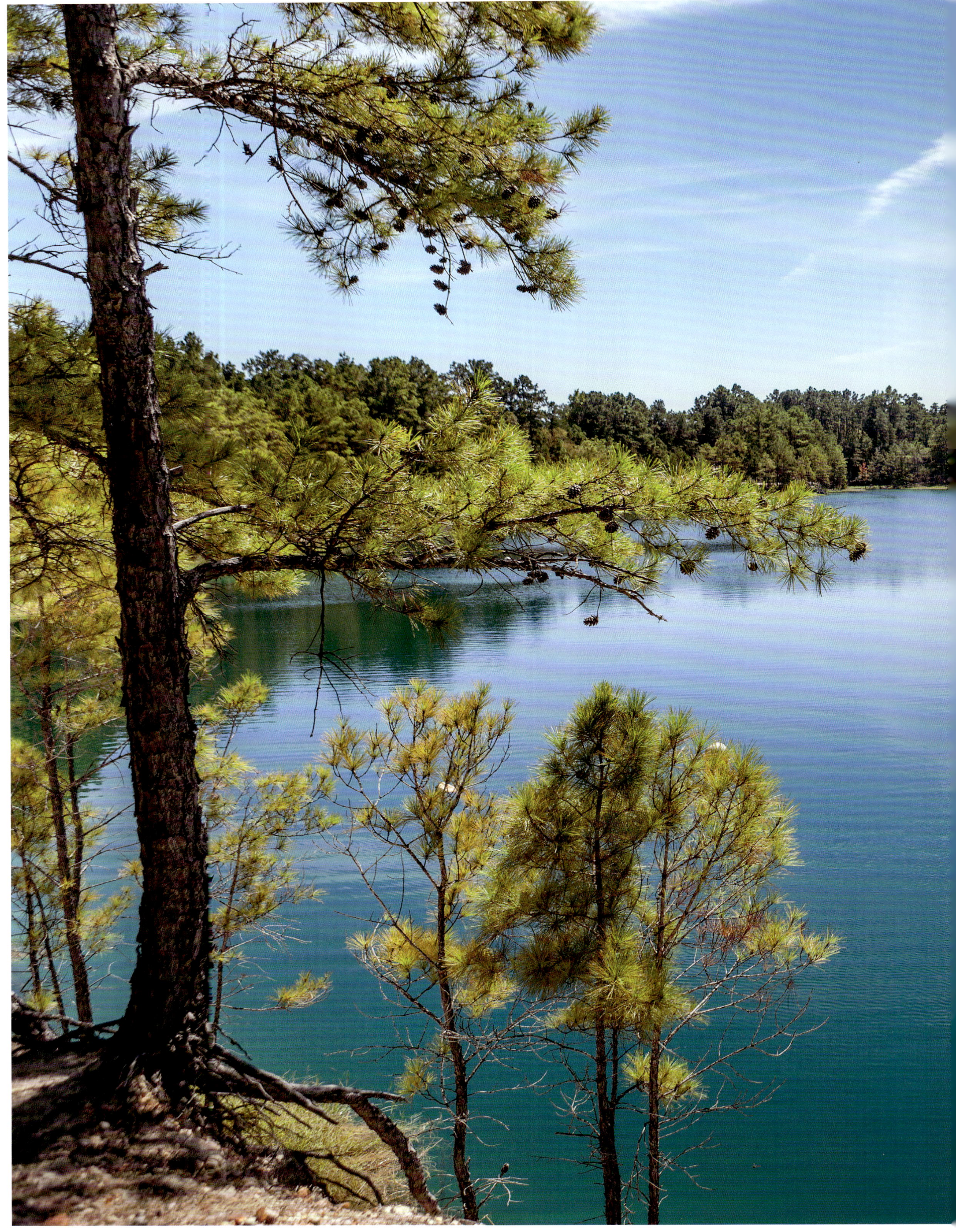

BLUE LAGOON LAKE near Huntsville, 2016

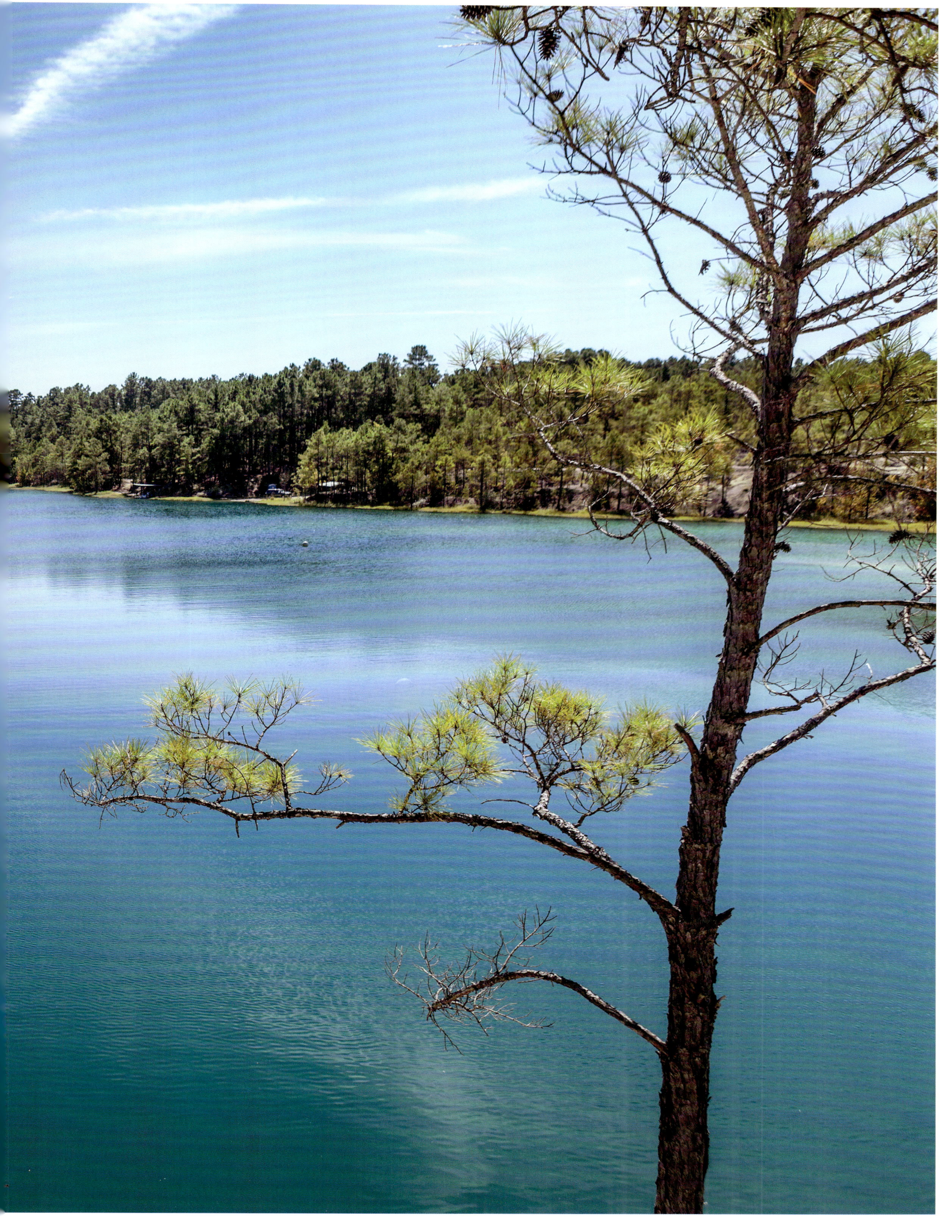

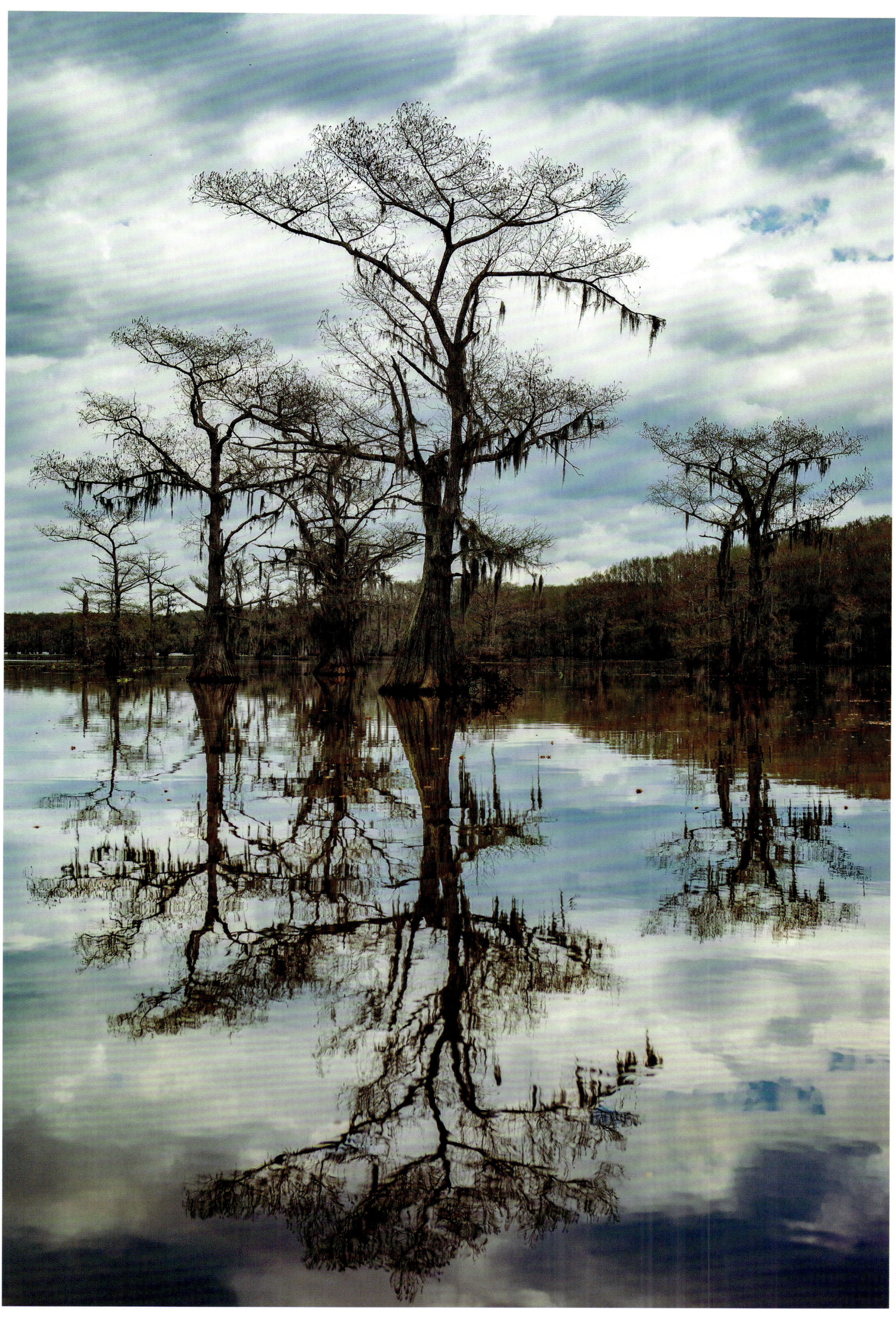

157

CYPRESS TREES Caddo Lake, near Uncertain, 2015

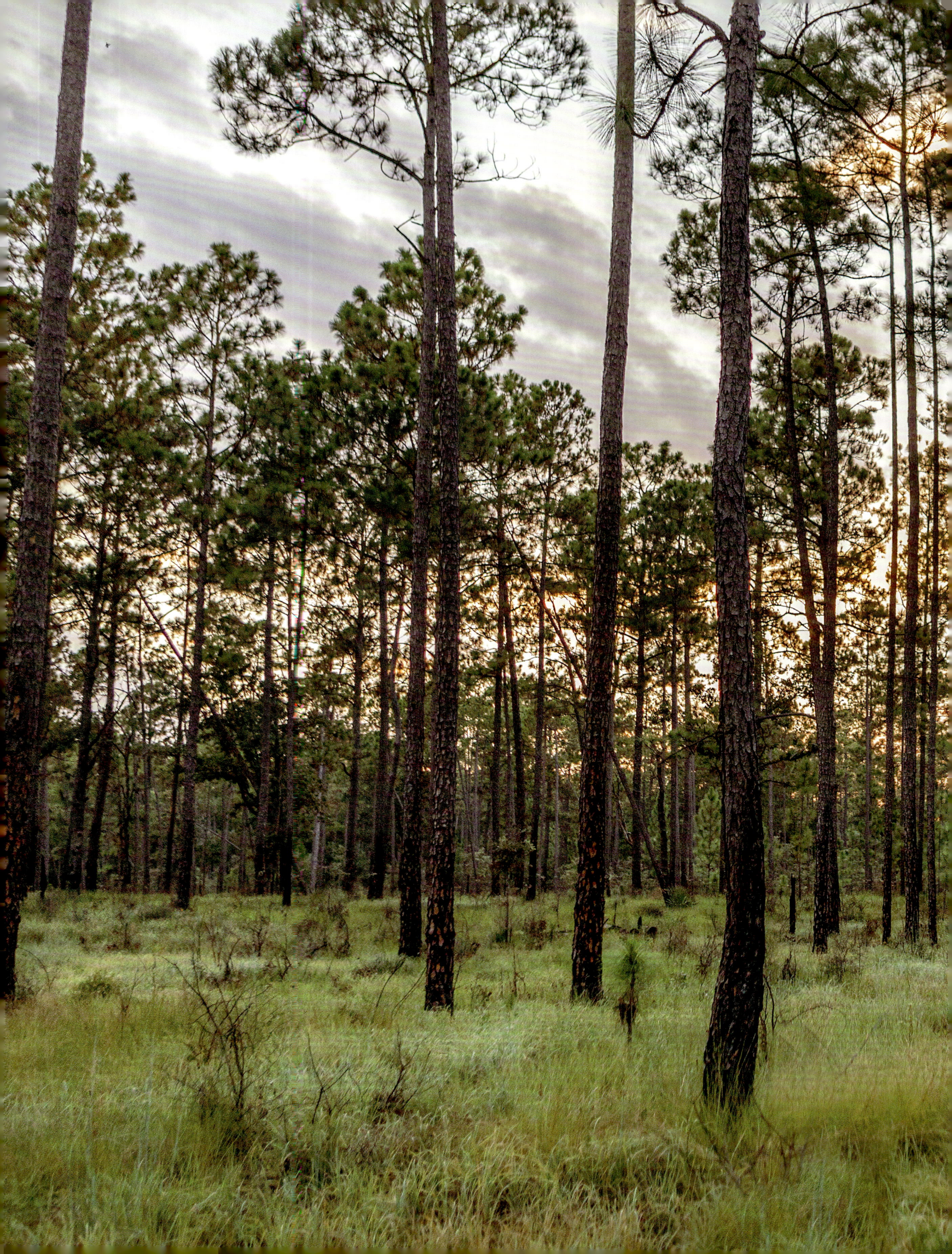

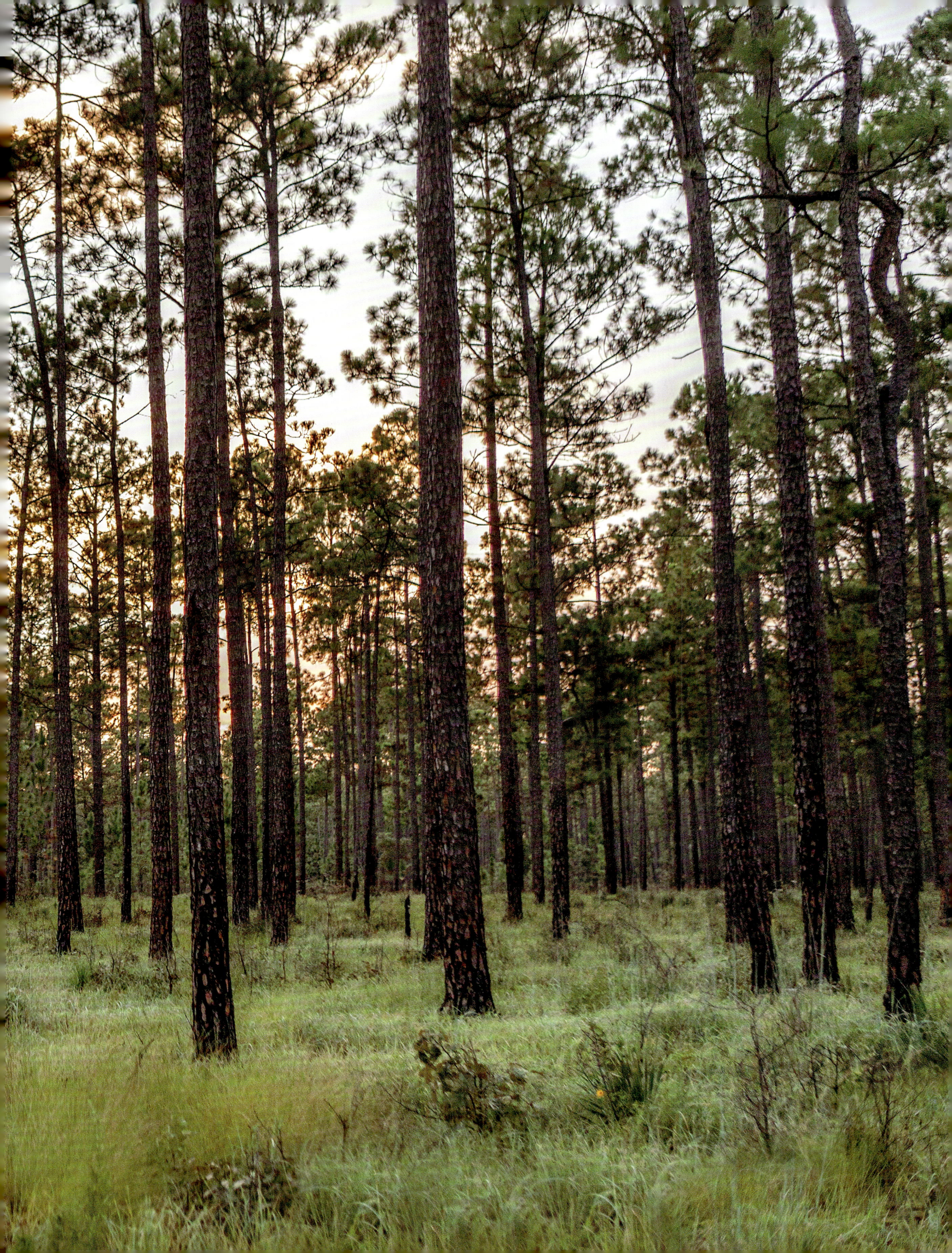

< **PINE FOREST** Roy E. Larsen Sandyland Sanctuary, near Silsbee, 2016

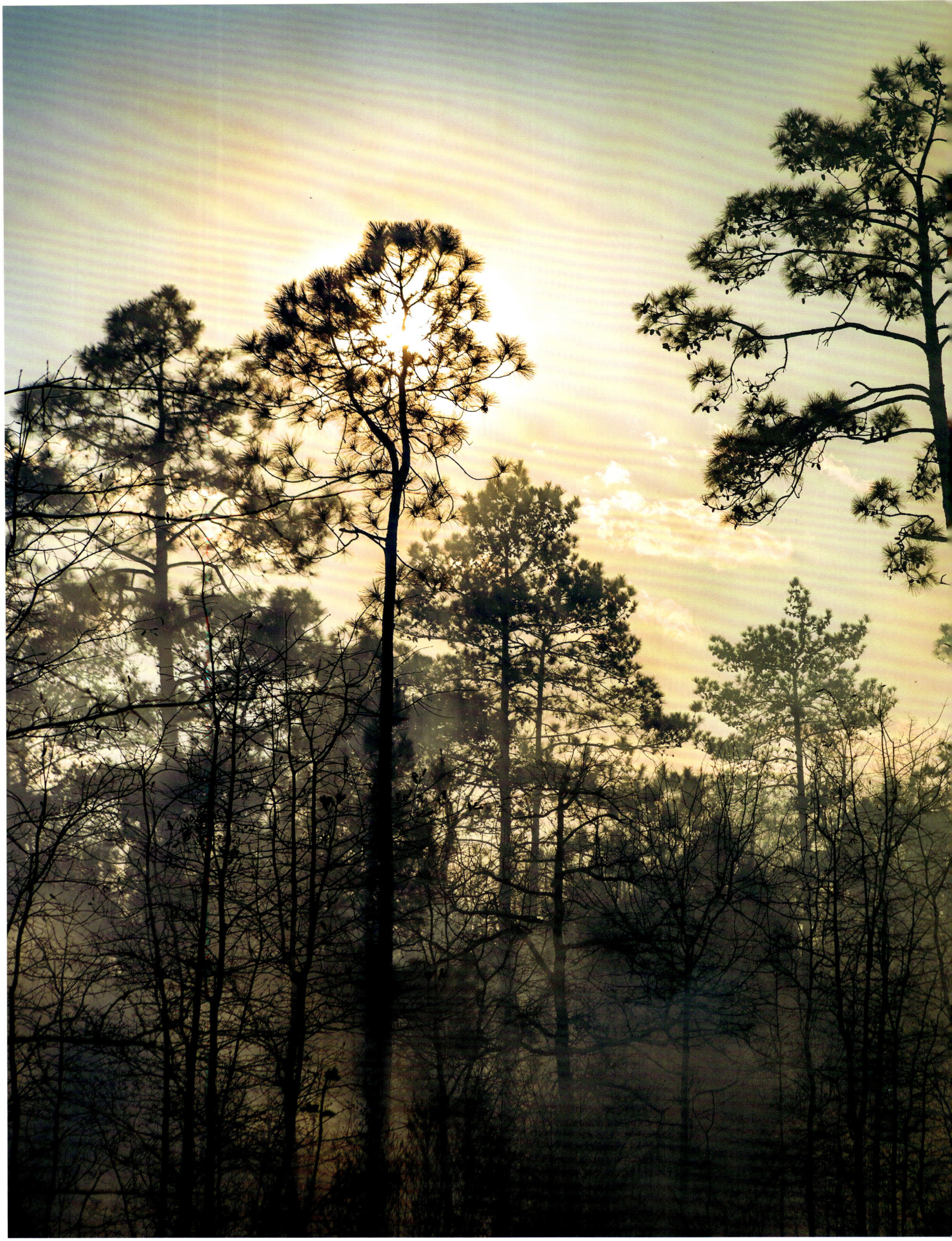

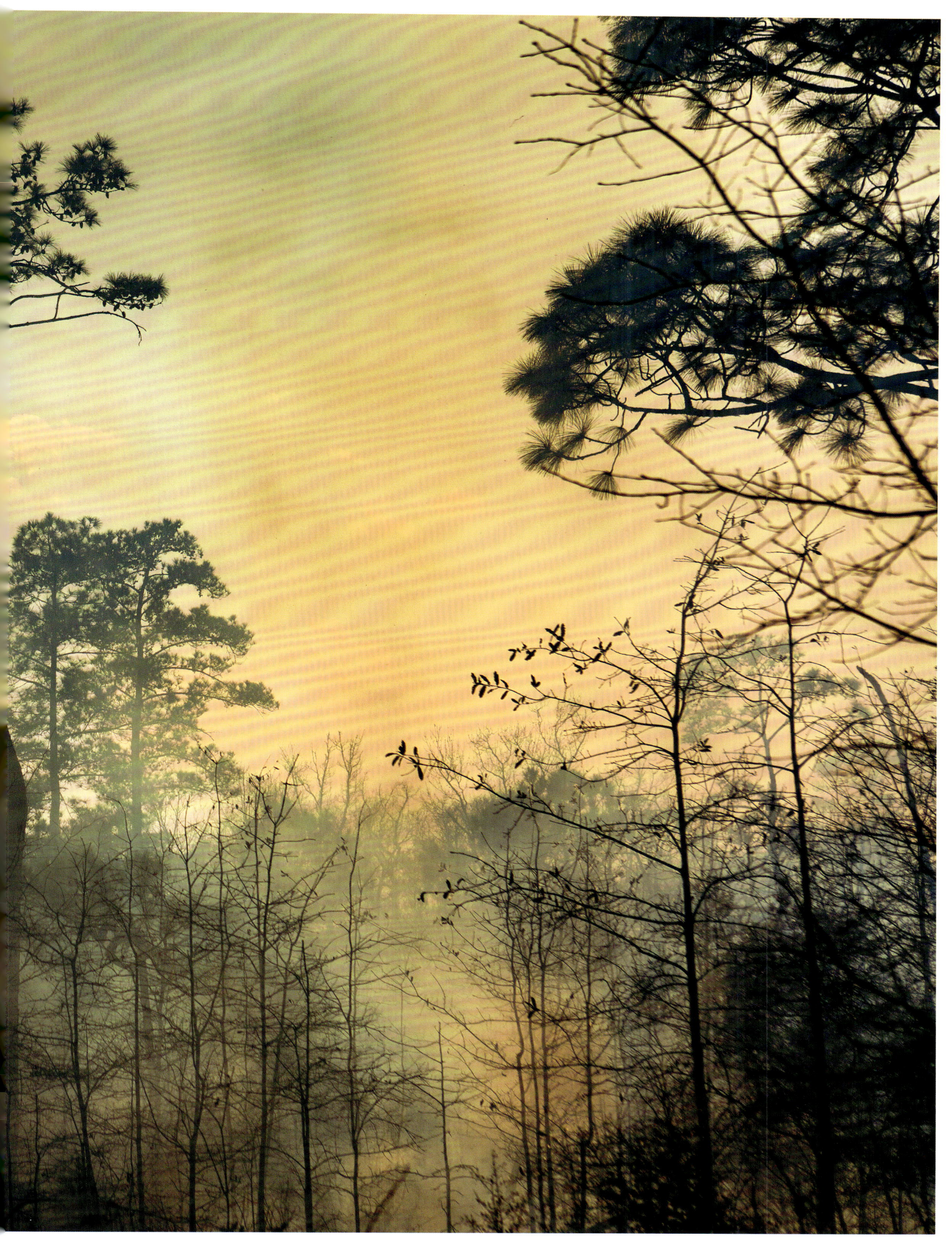

SMOKY PINES controlled burn at Roy E. Larsen Sandyland Sanctuary, near Silsbee, 2017

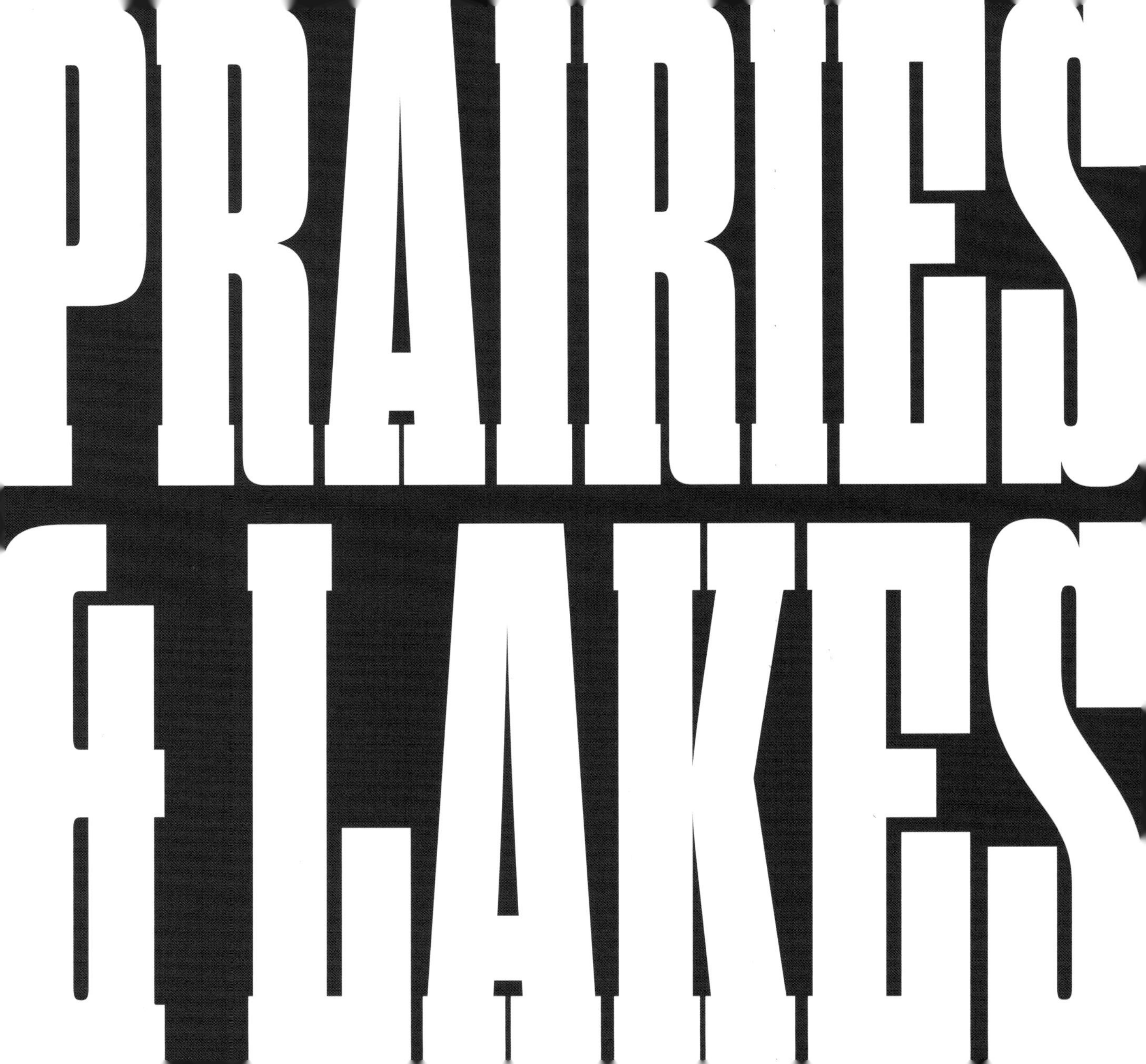
PRAIRIES
& LAKES

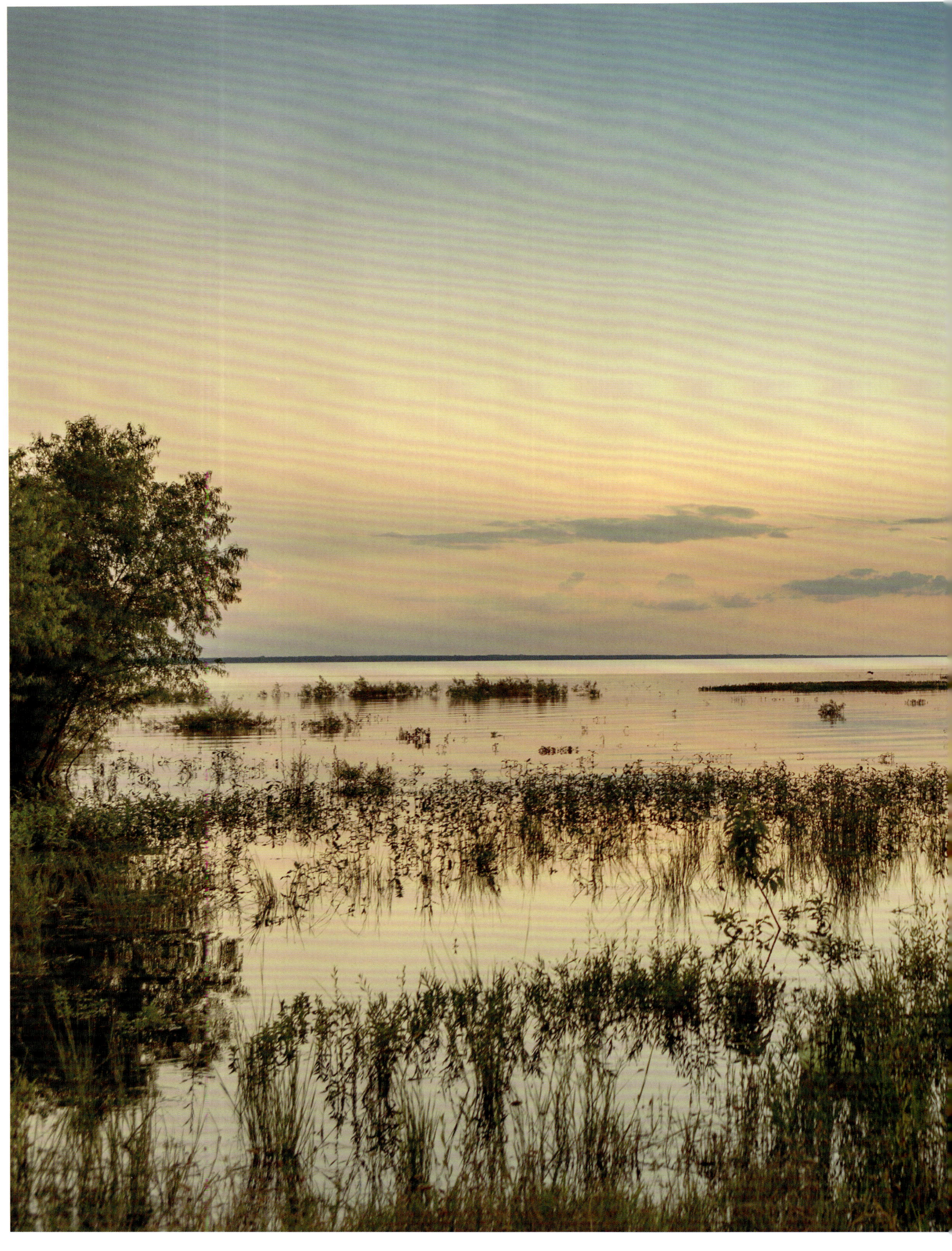

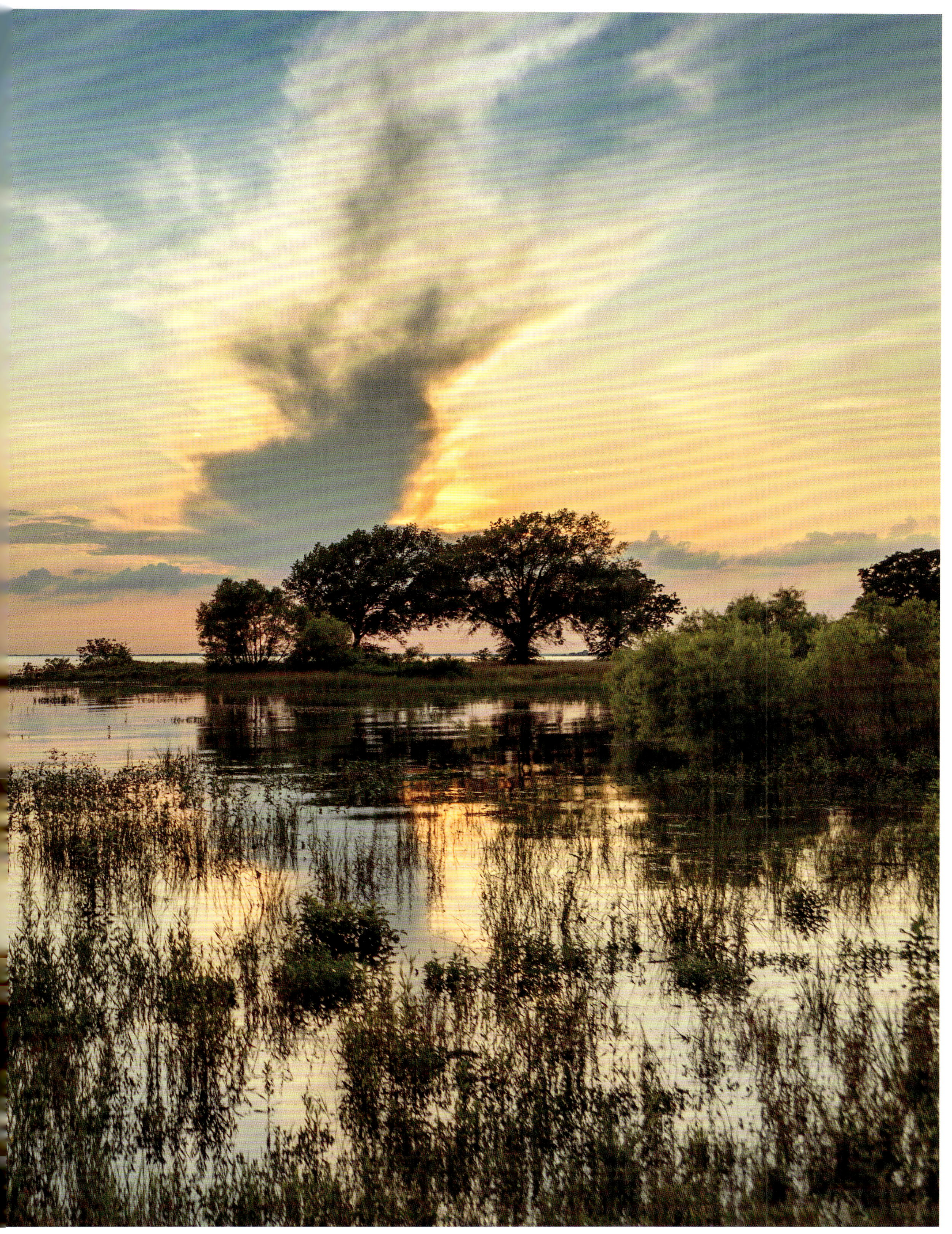

LAKE TAWAKONI near Emory, 2012

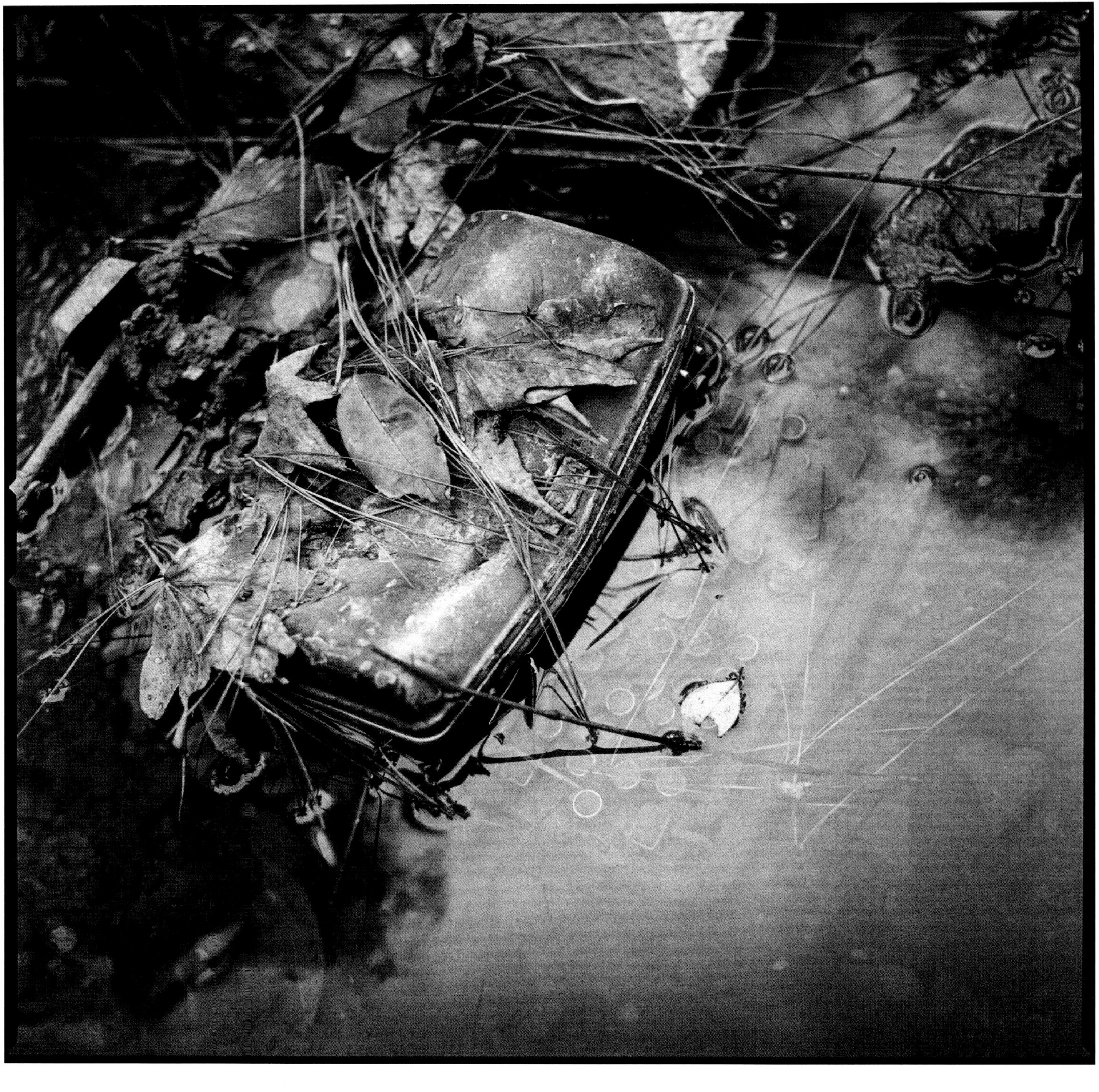

TYPEWRITER Brazos River, near Navasota, 1995

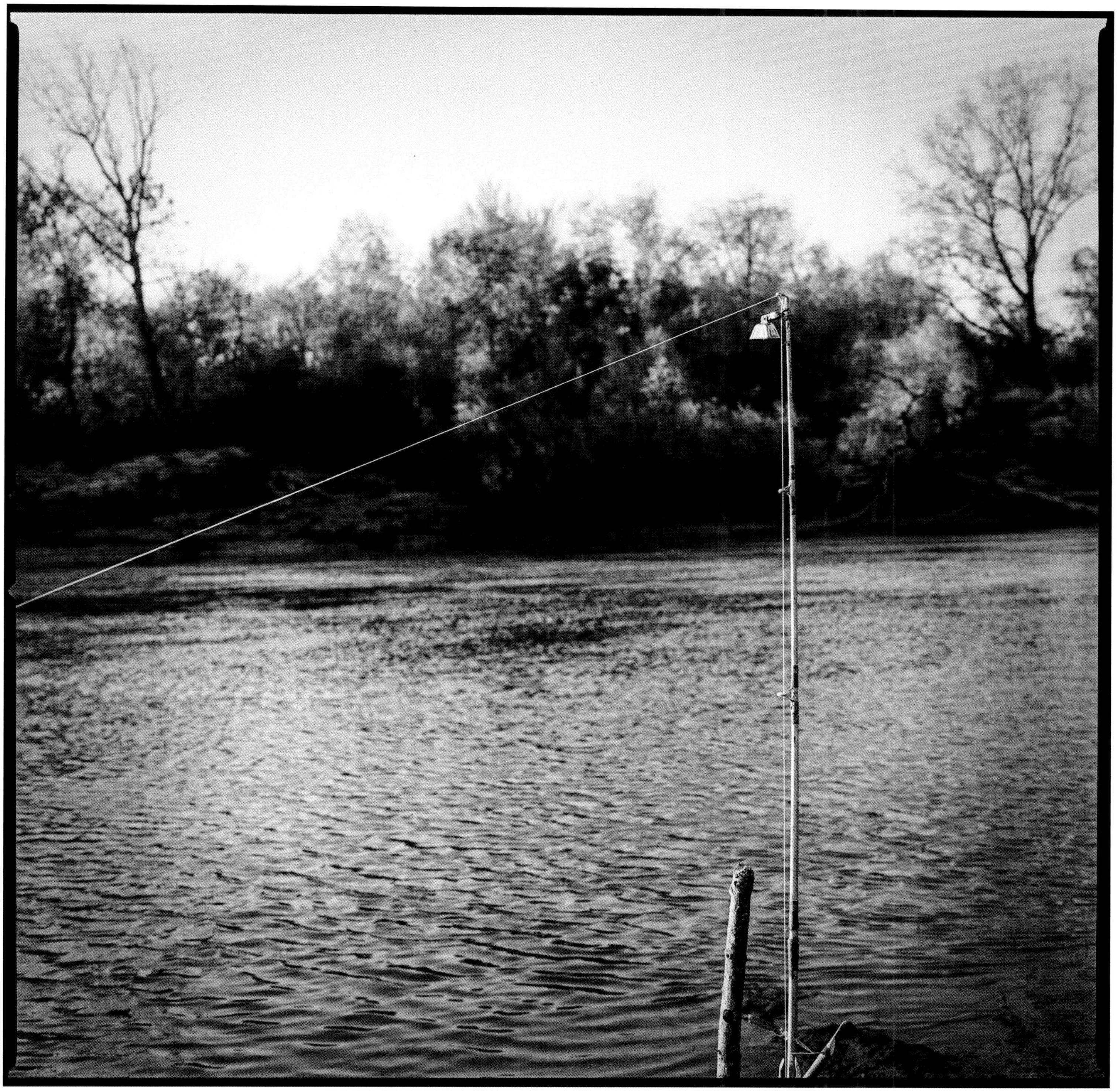

FISHING POLE Brazos River, near Navasota, 1995

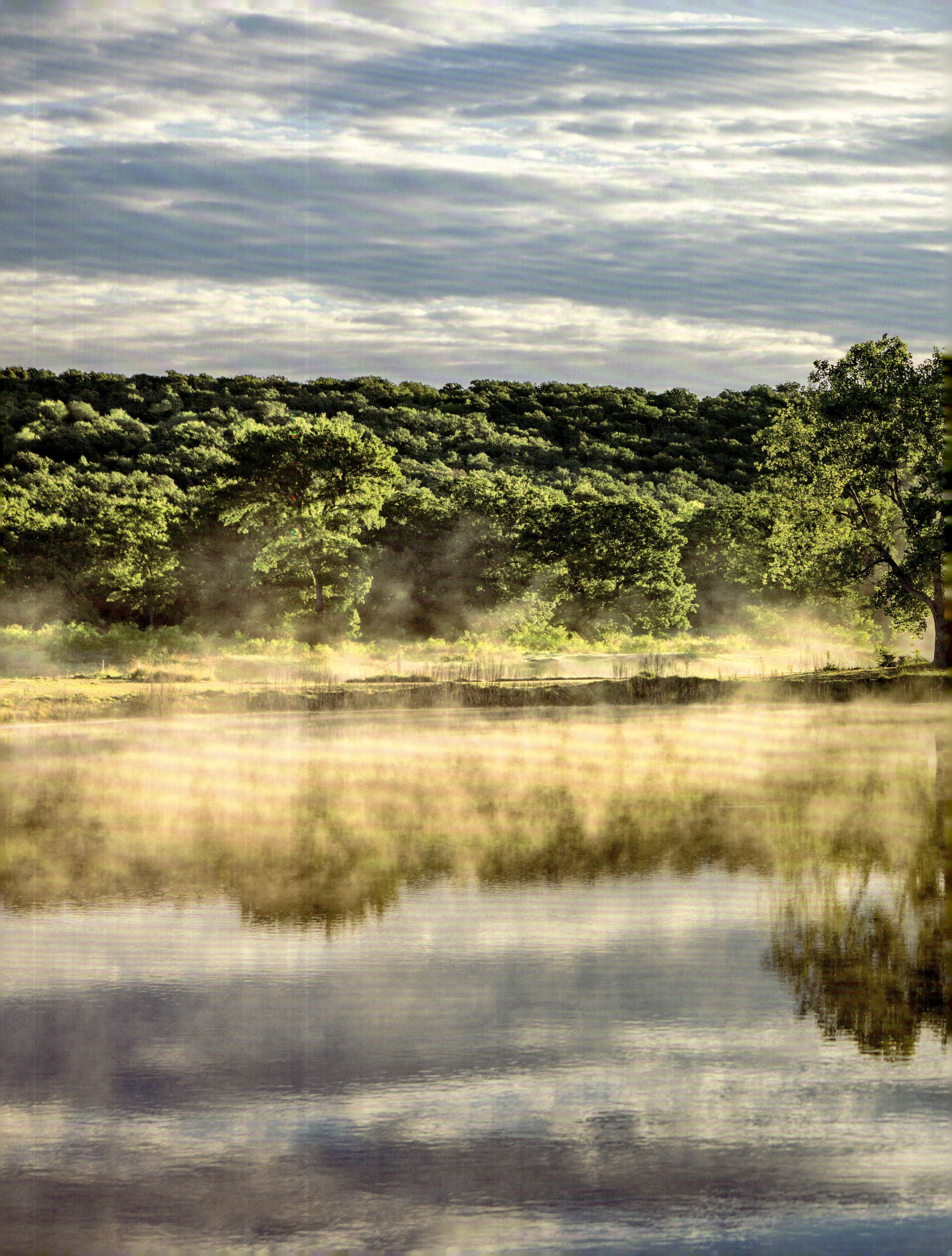

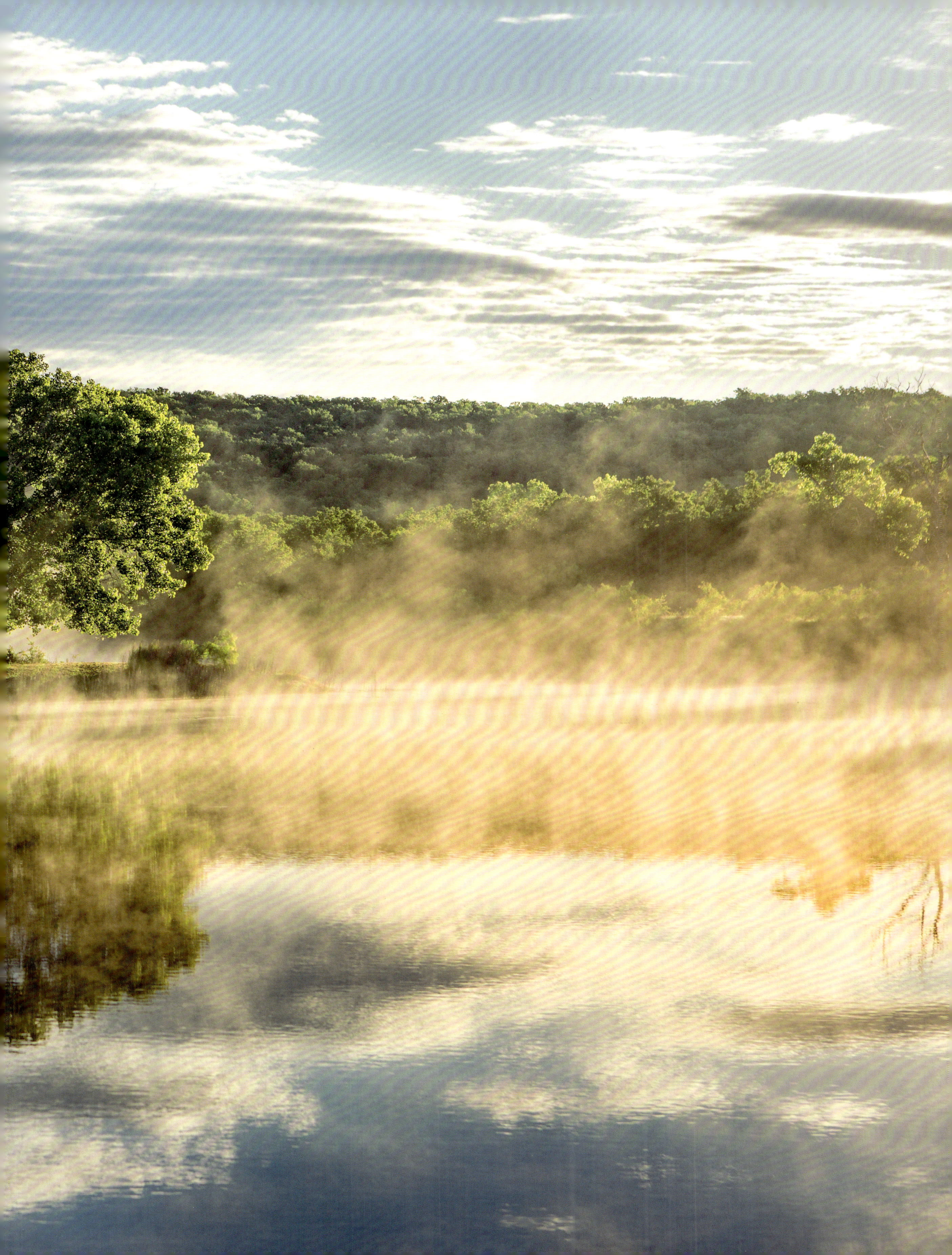

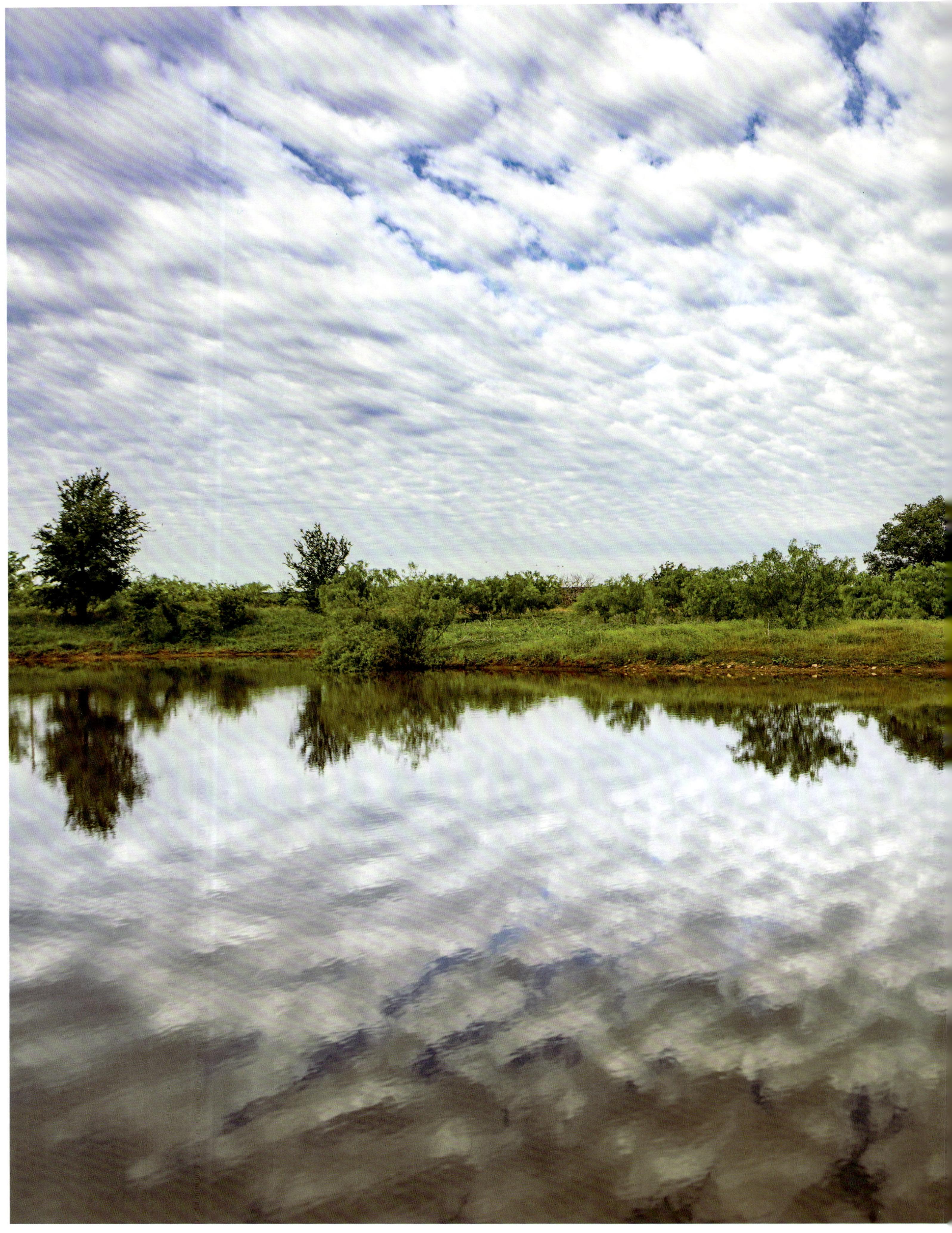

WILDCATTER RANCH near Graham, 2017

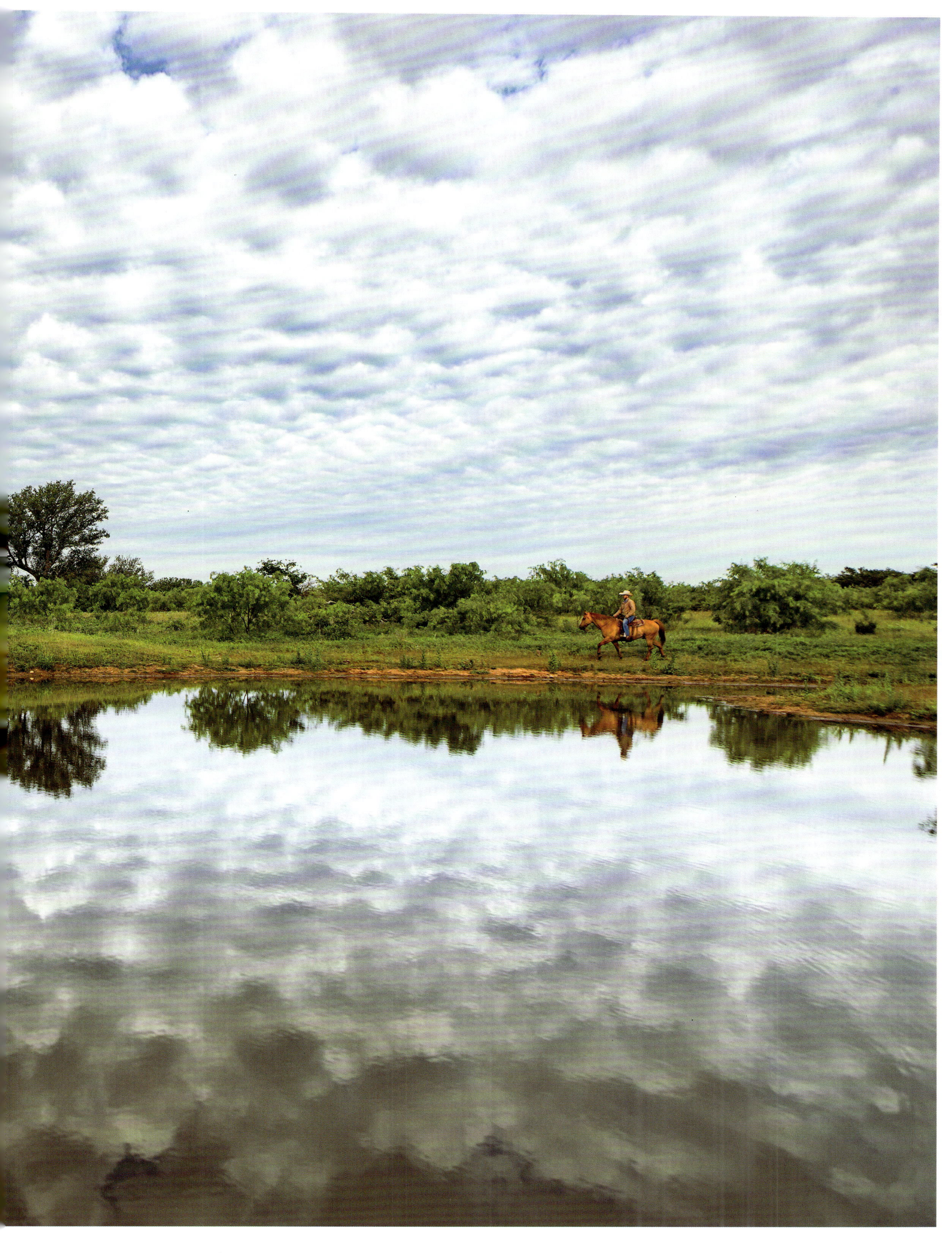

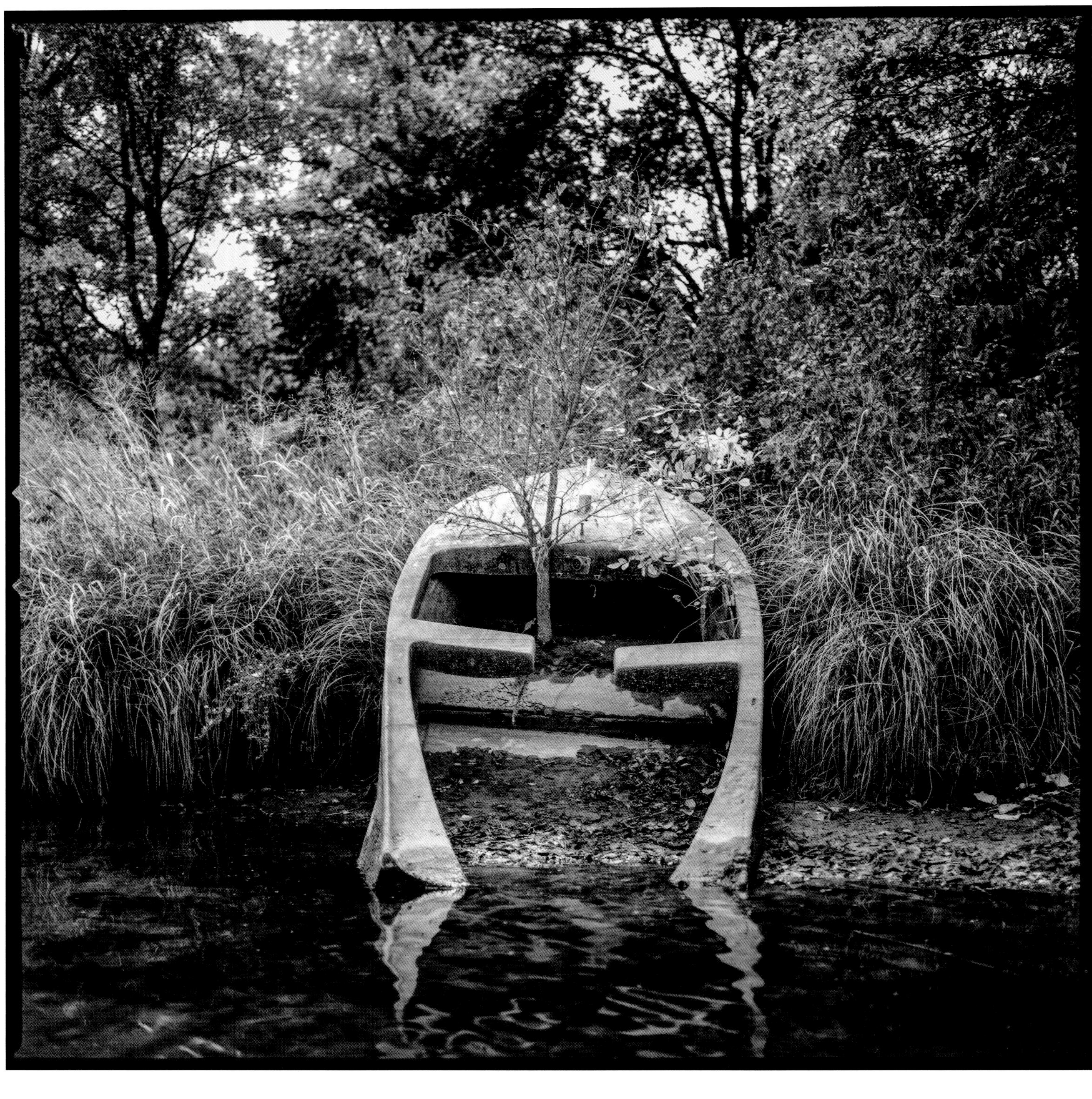

MAROONED Brazos River, near Graford, 2007

HELL'S GATE Possum Kingdom Lake, near Graford, 2010 >

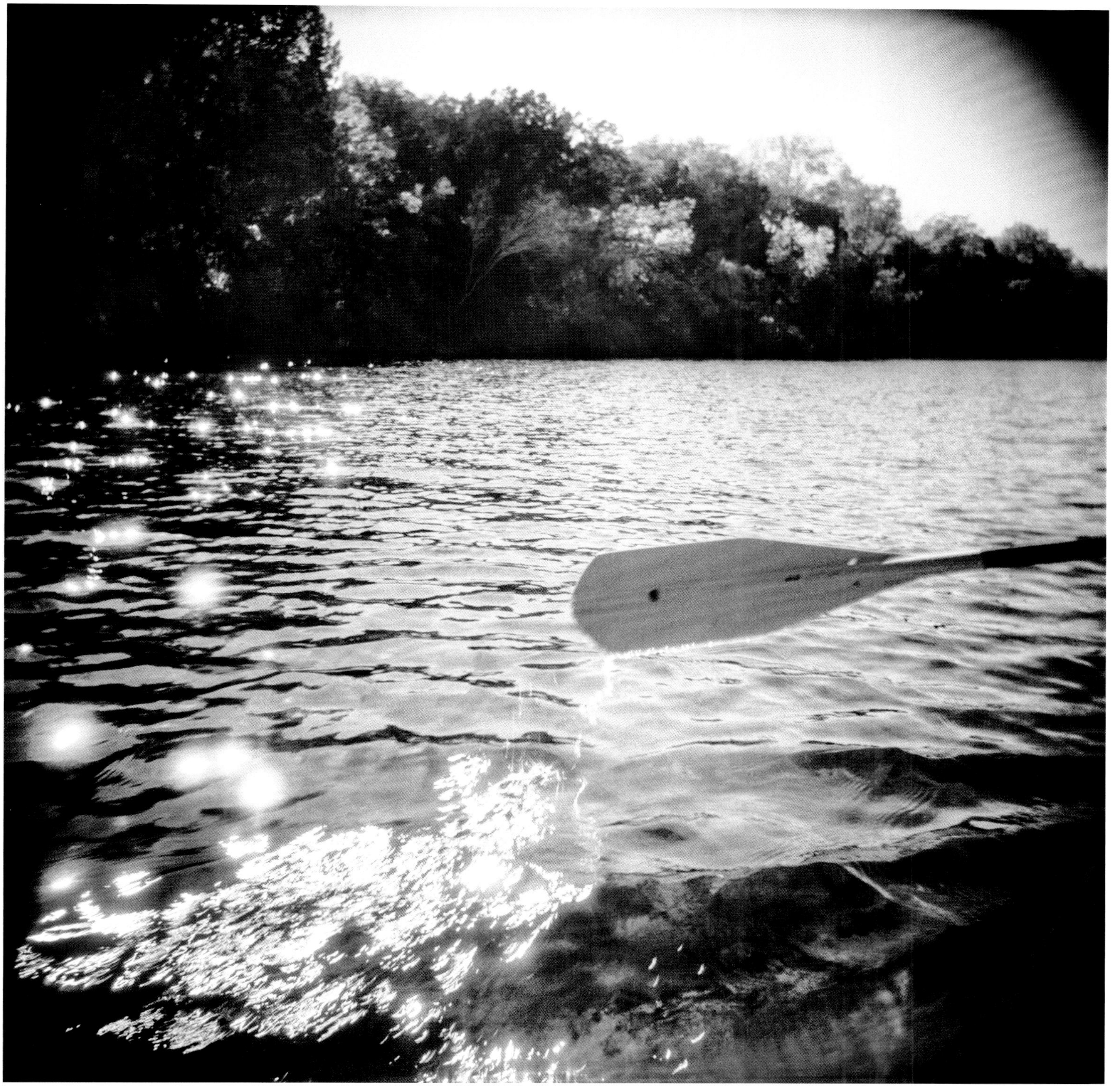

PADDLE Brazos River, near Graford, 2007

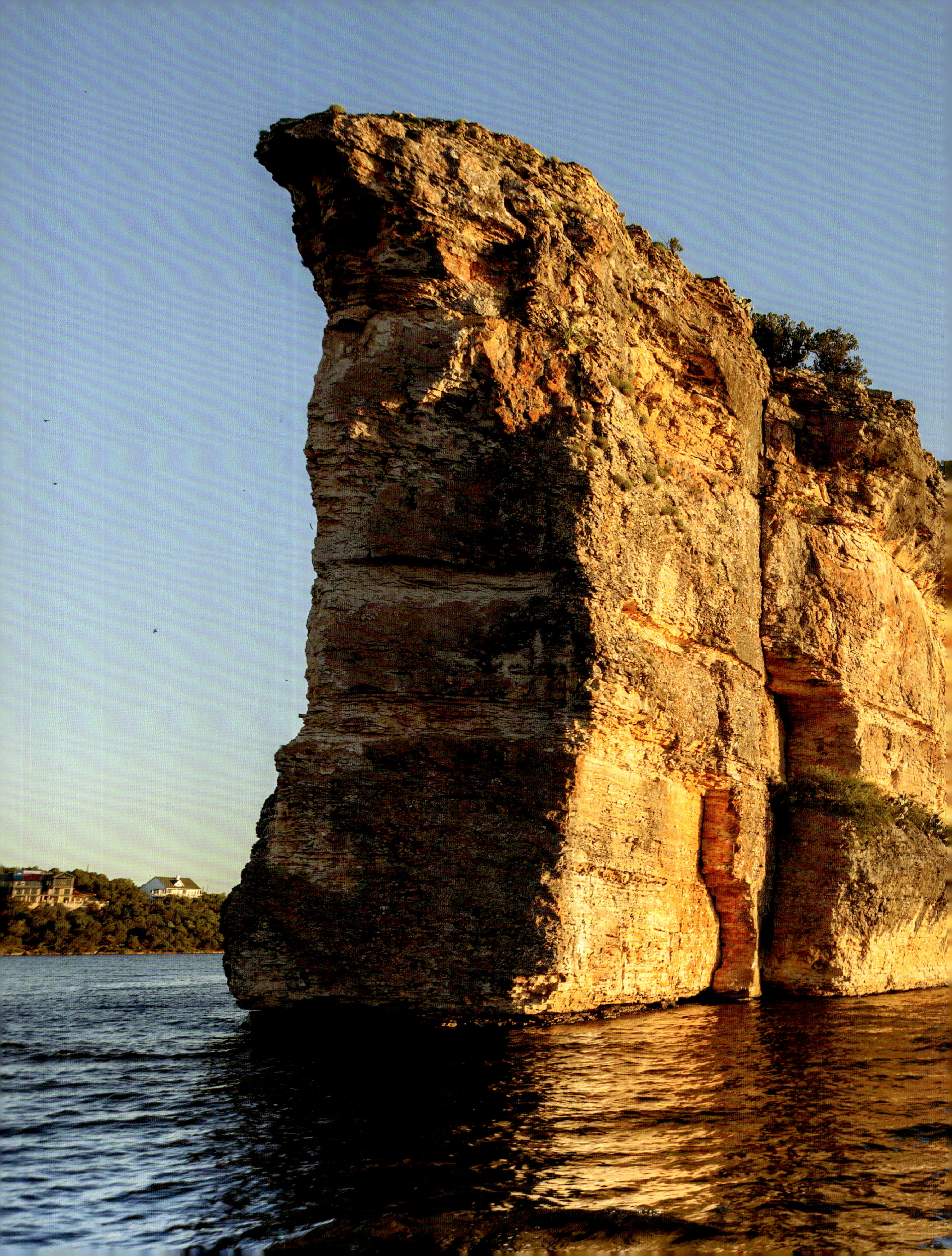

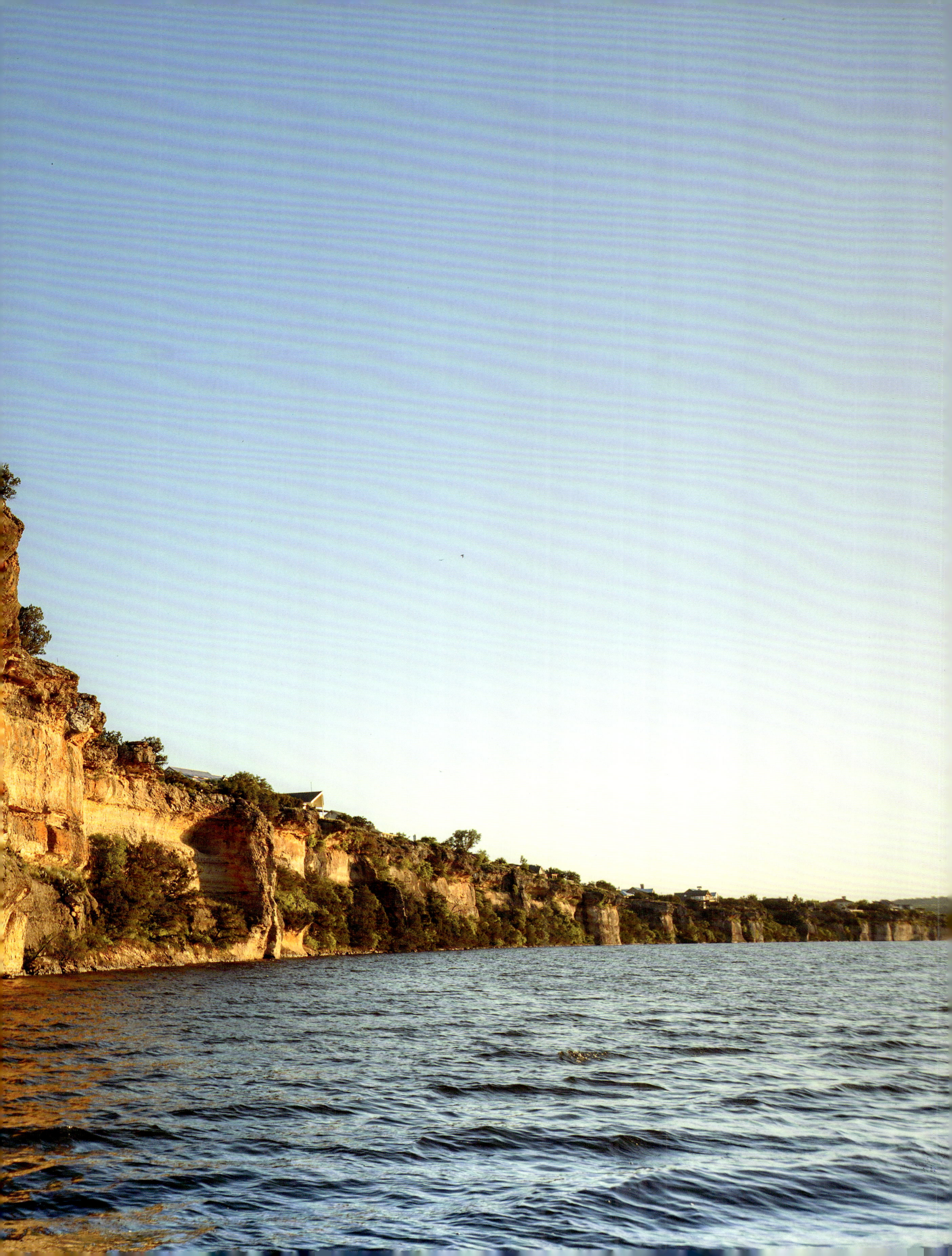

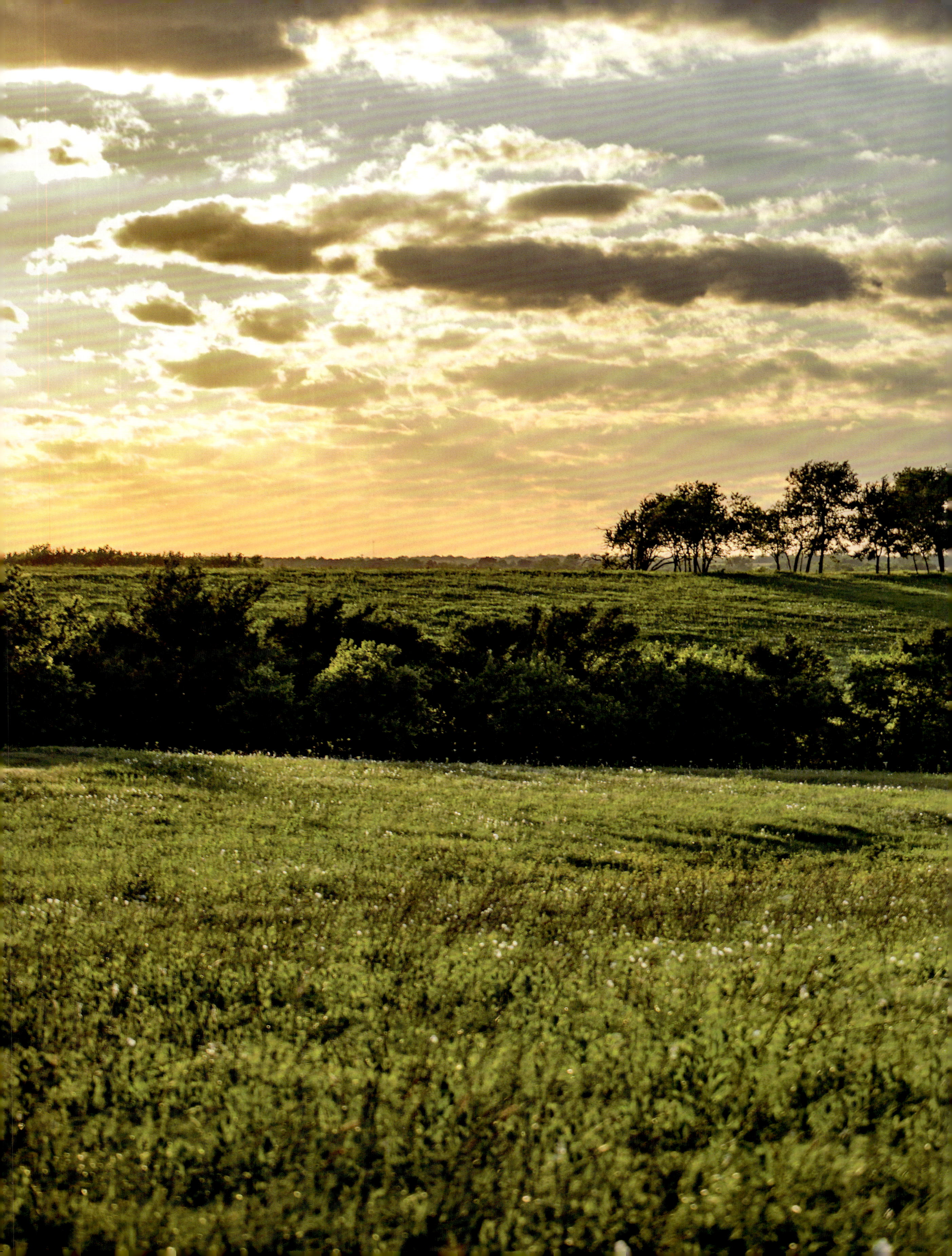

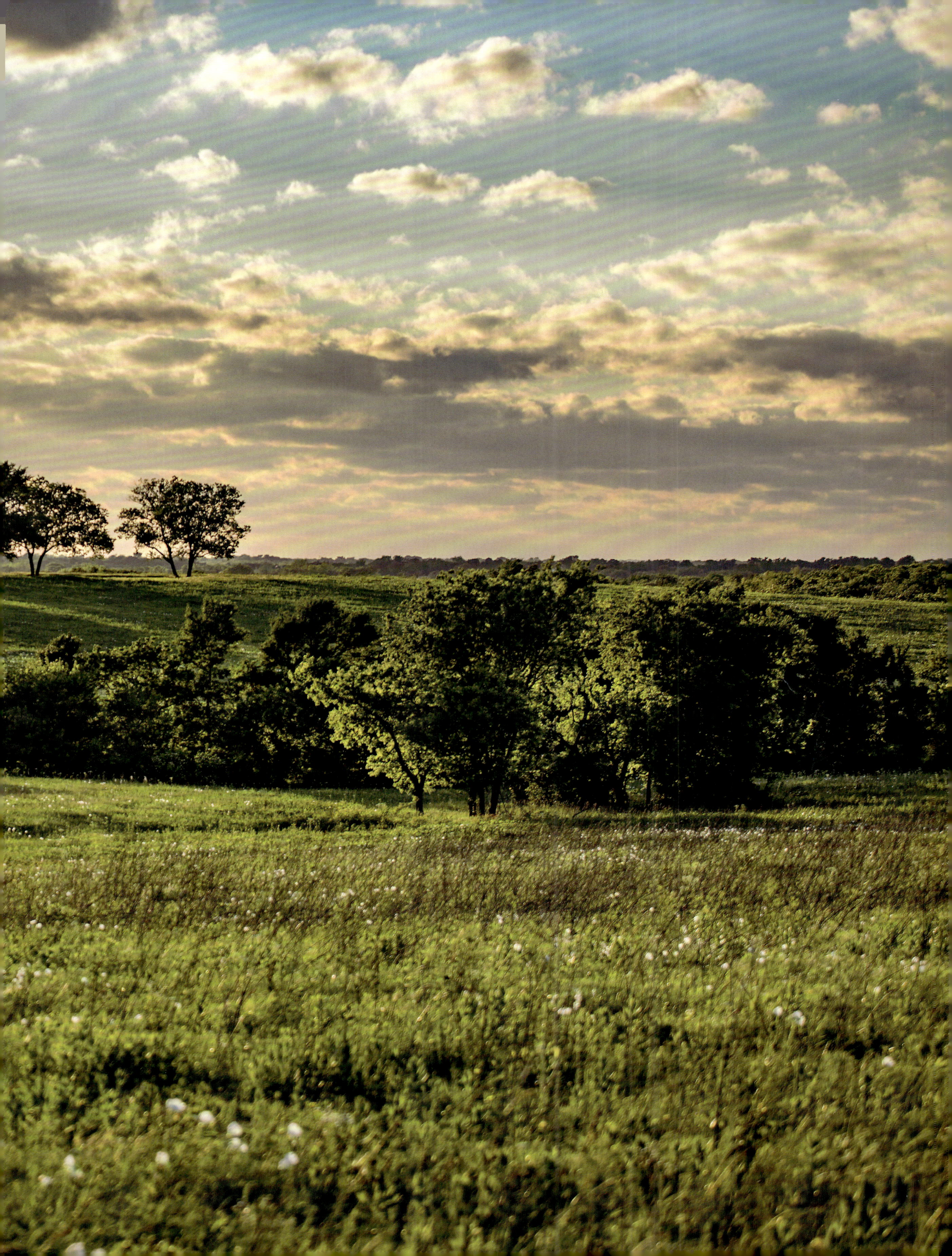

< **BLACKLAND PRAIRIE** Greenville, 2017

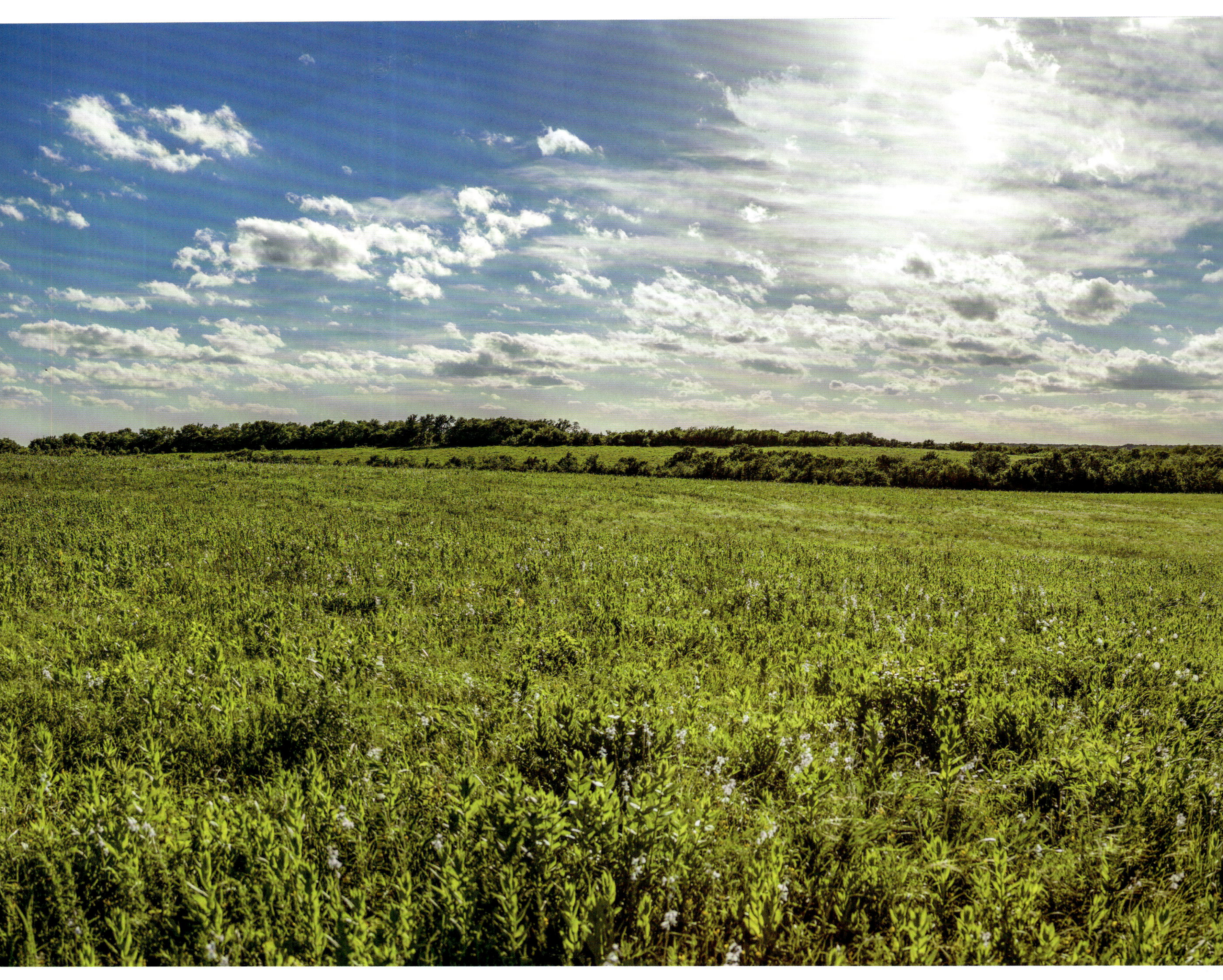

CLYMER MEADOW PRESERVE Texas tallgrass prairie, Greenville, 2017

QUEEN ANNE'S LACE Greenville, 2017 >

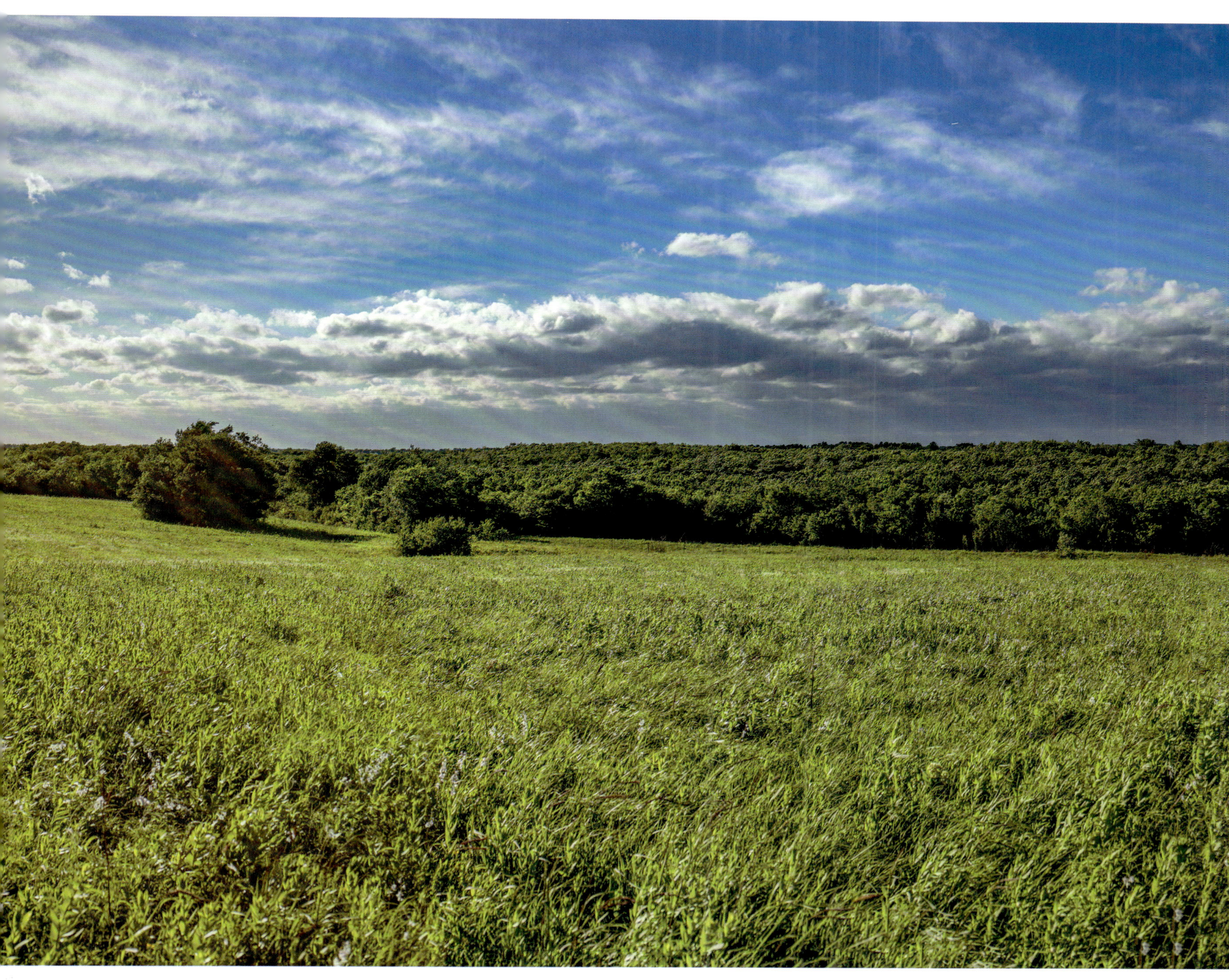

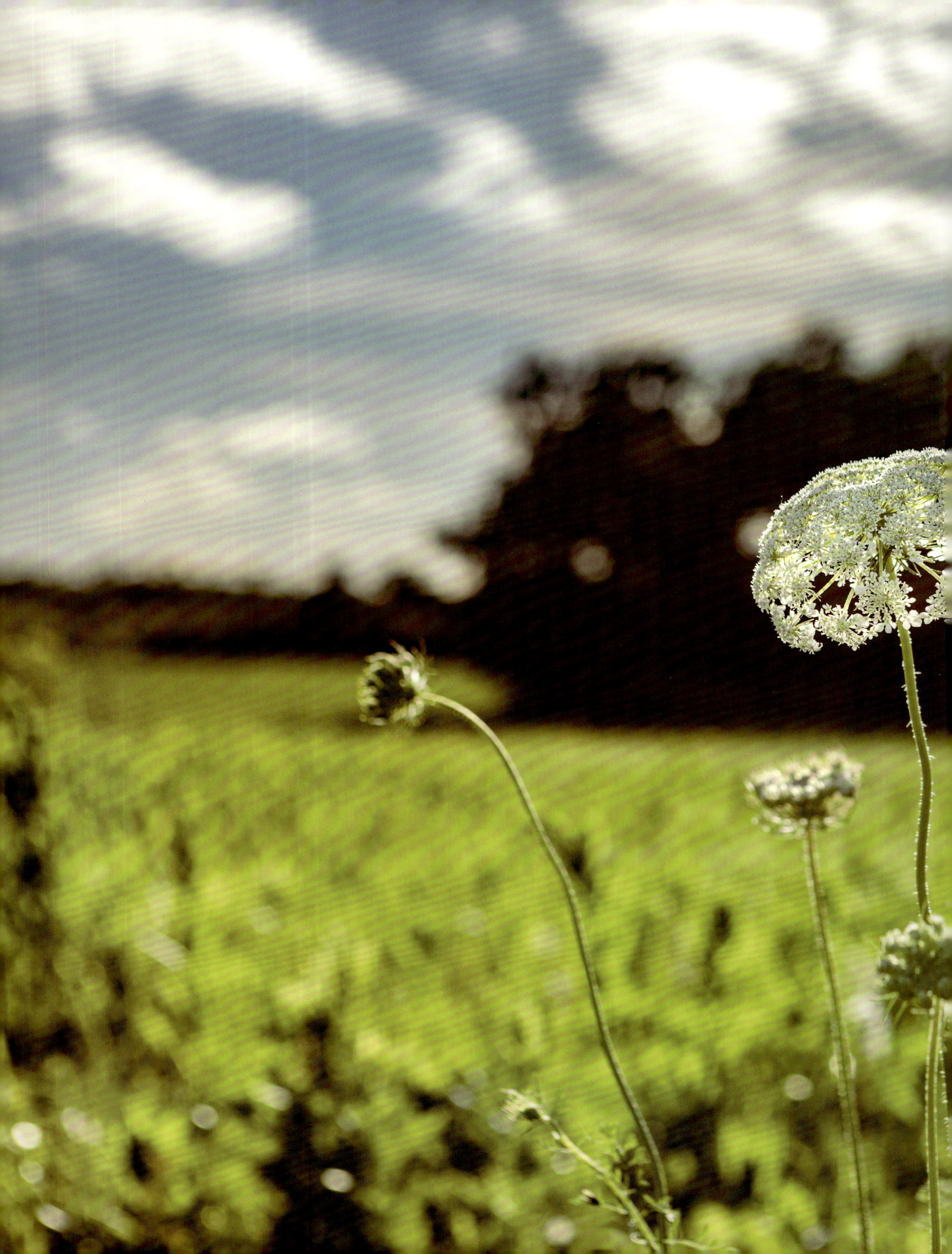

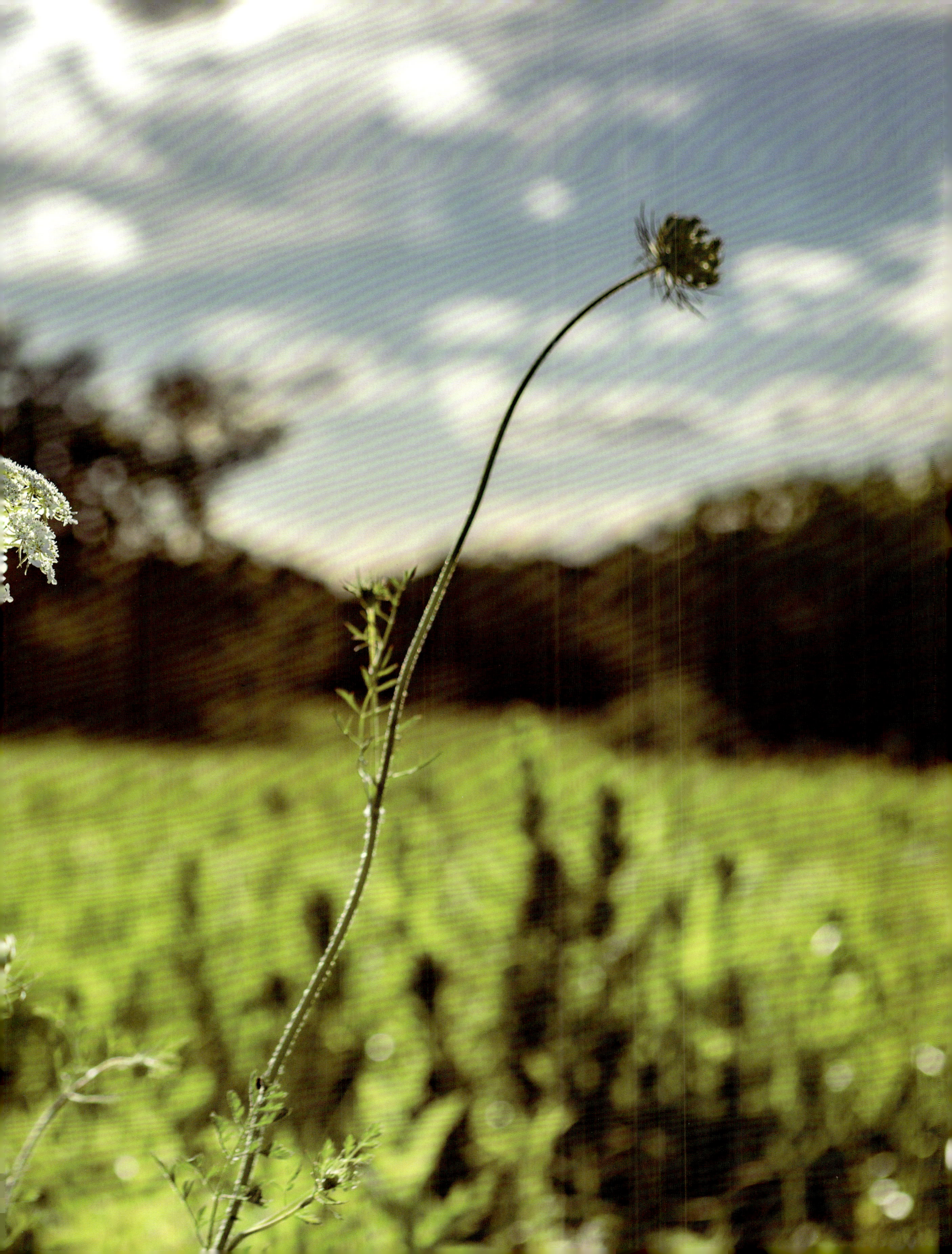

SOUTH

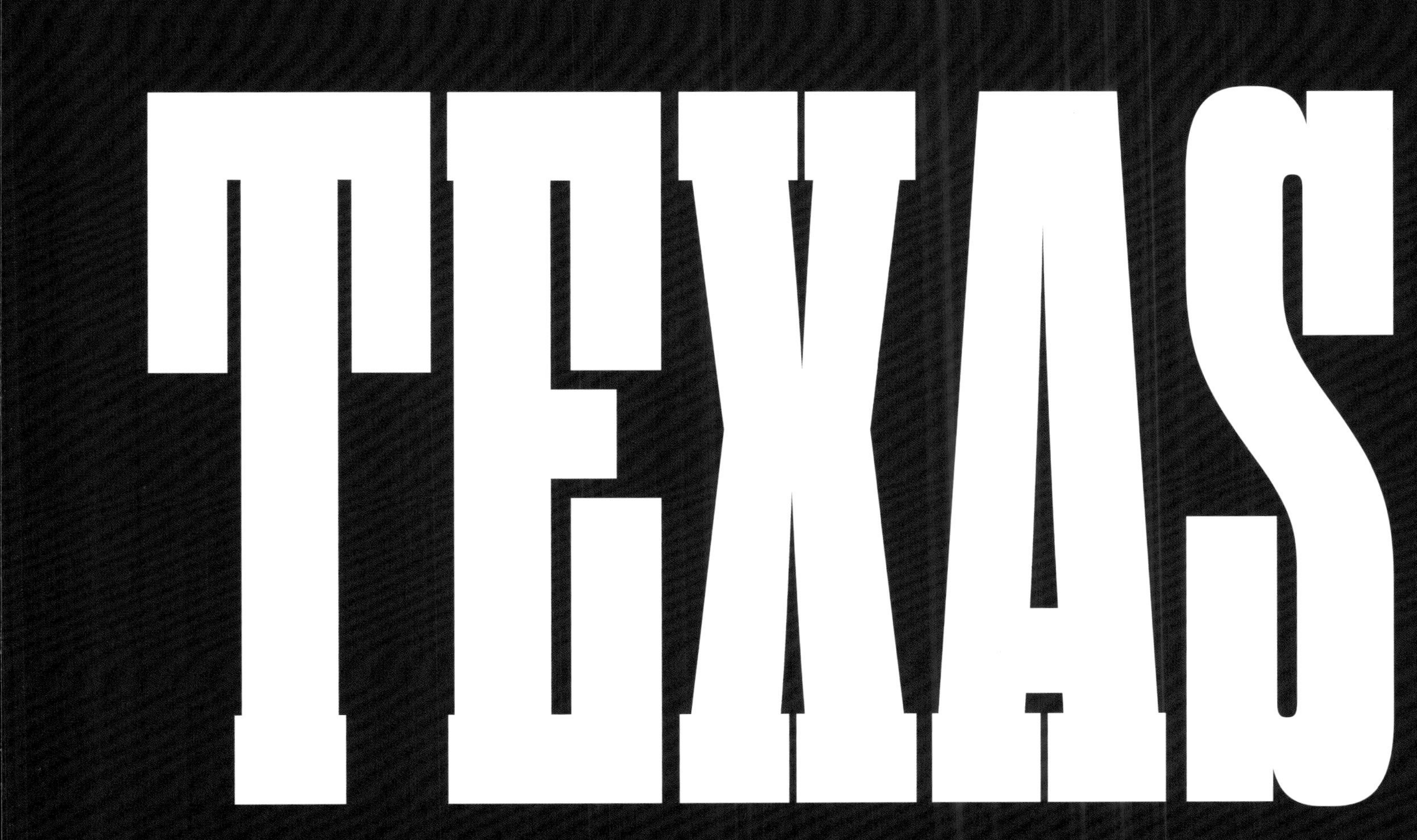
TEXAS

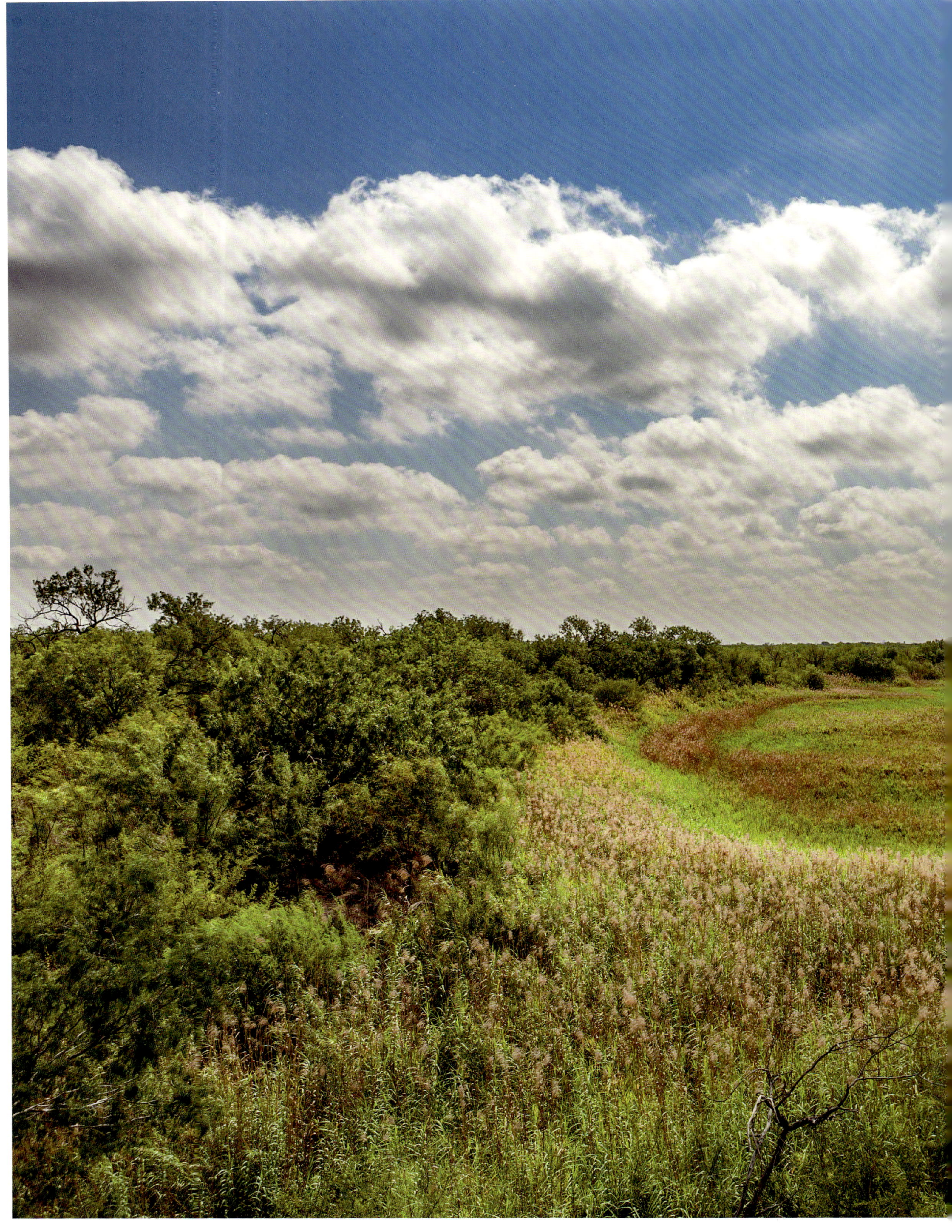

BENTSEN-RIO GRANDE VALLEY STATE PARK Mission, 2006

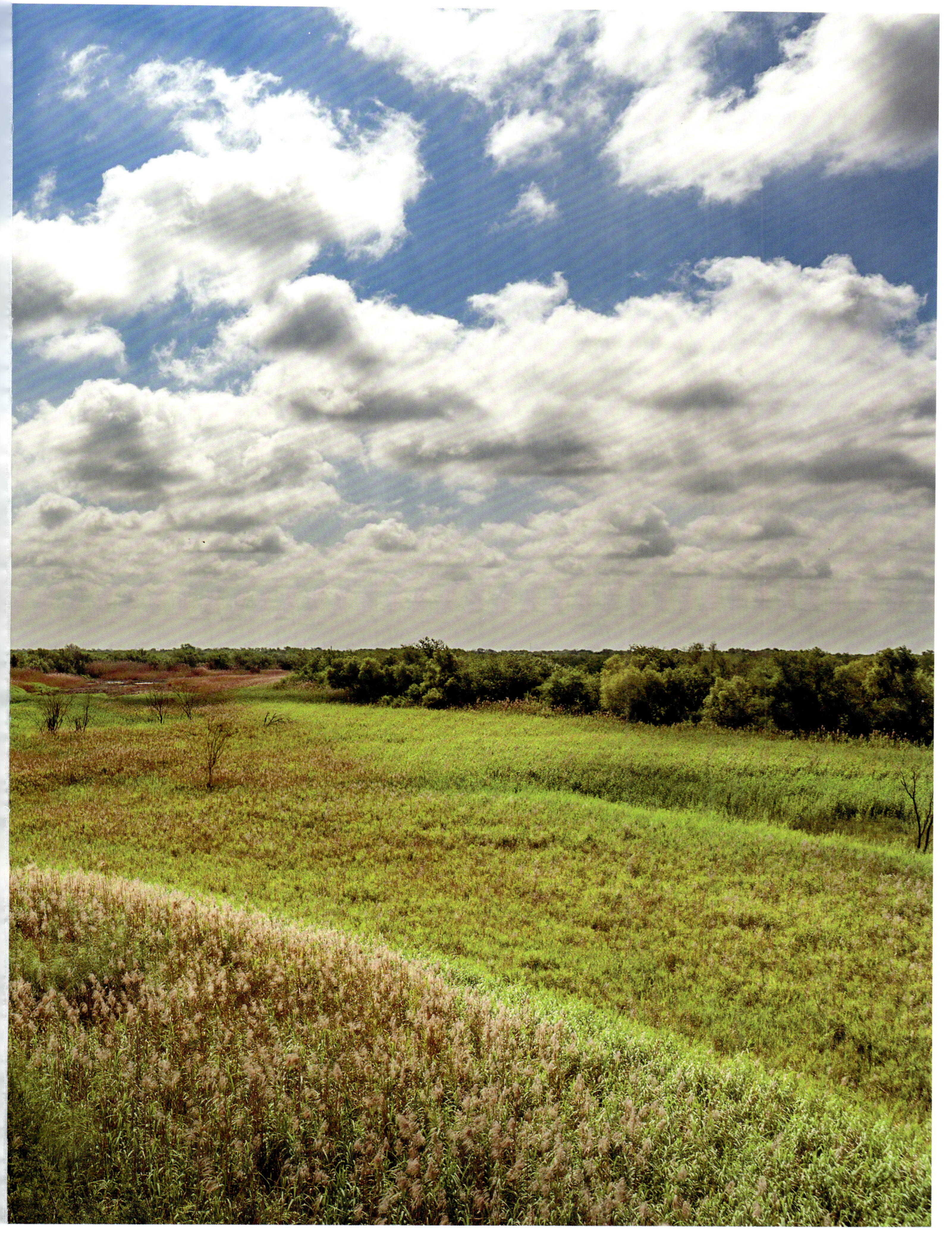

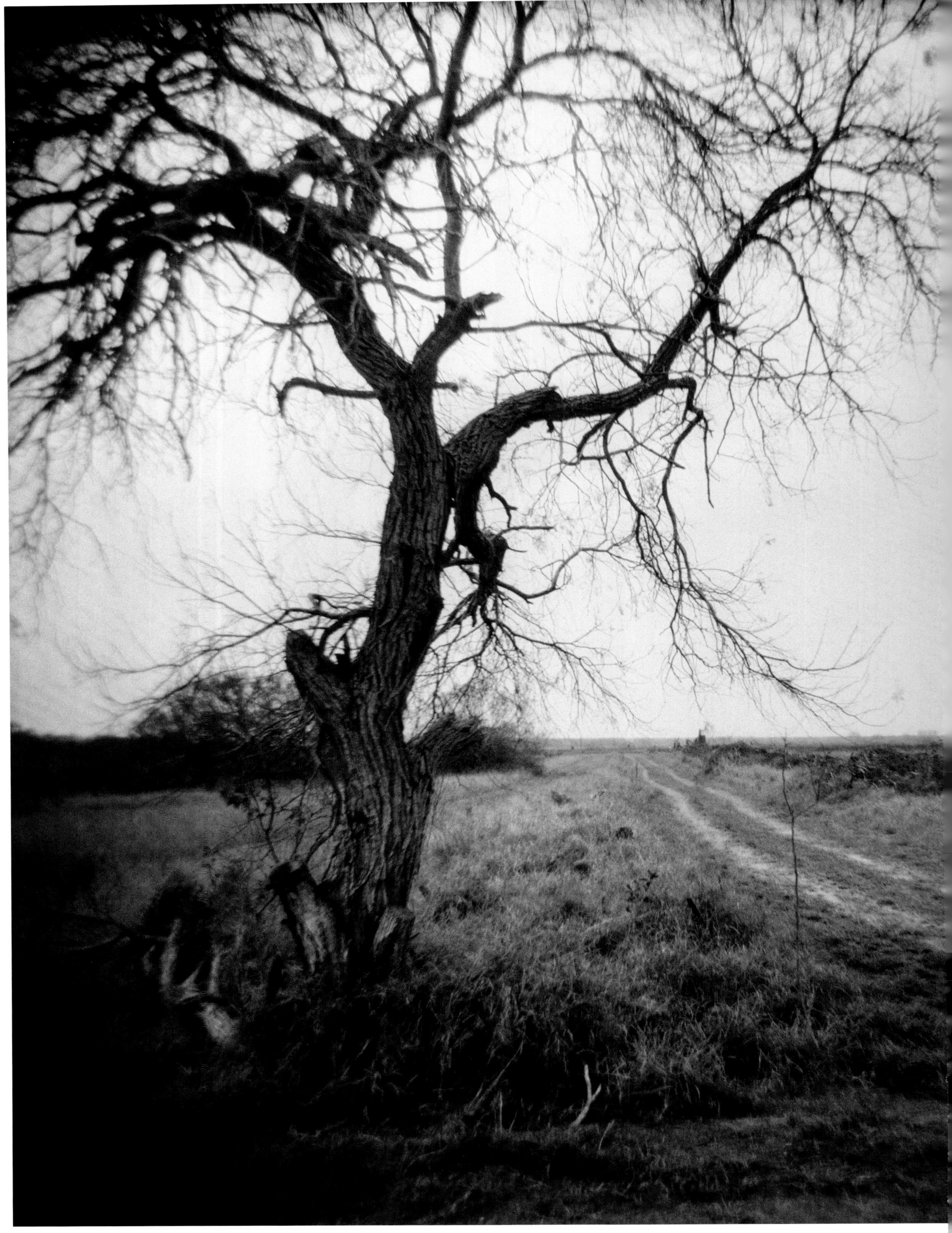

PALMITO RANCH BATTLEFIELD final battle site of the Civil War, near Brownsville, 2011

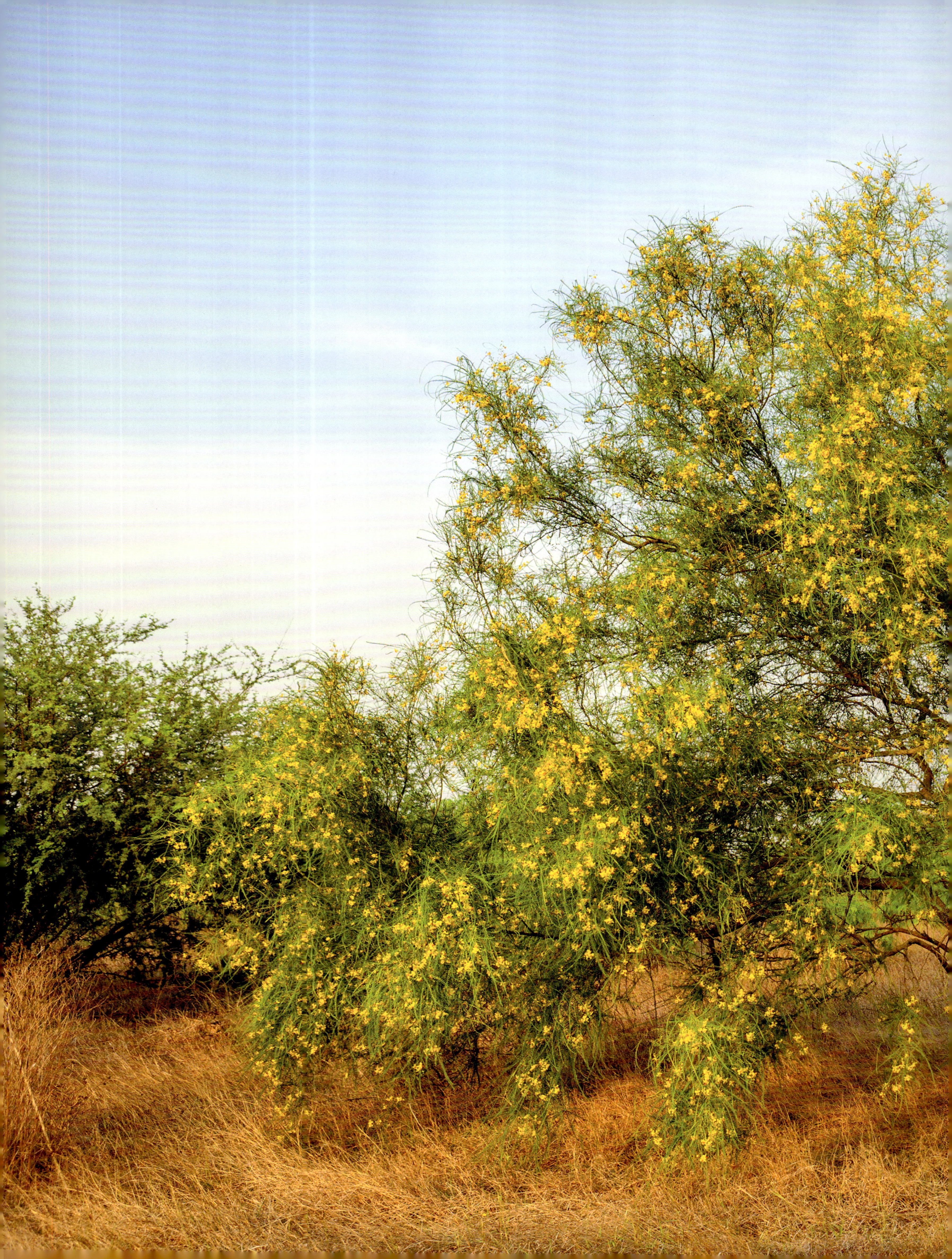

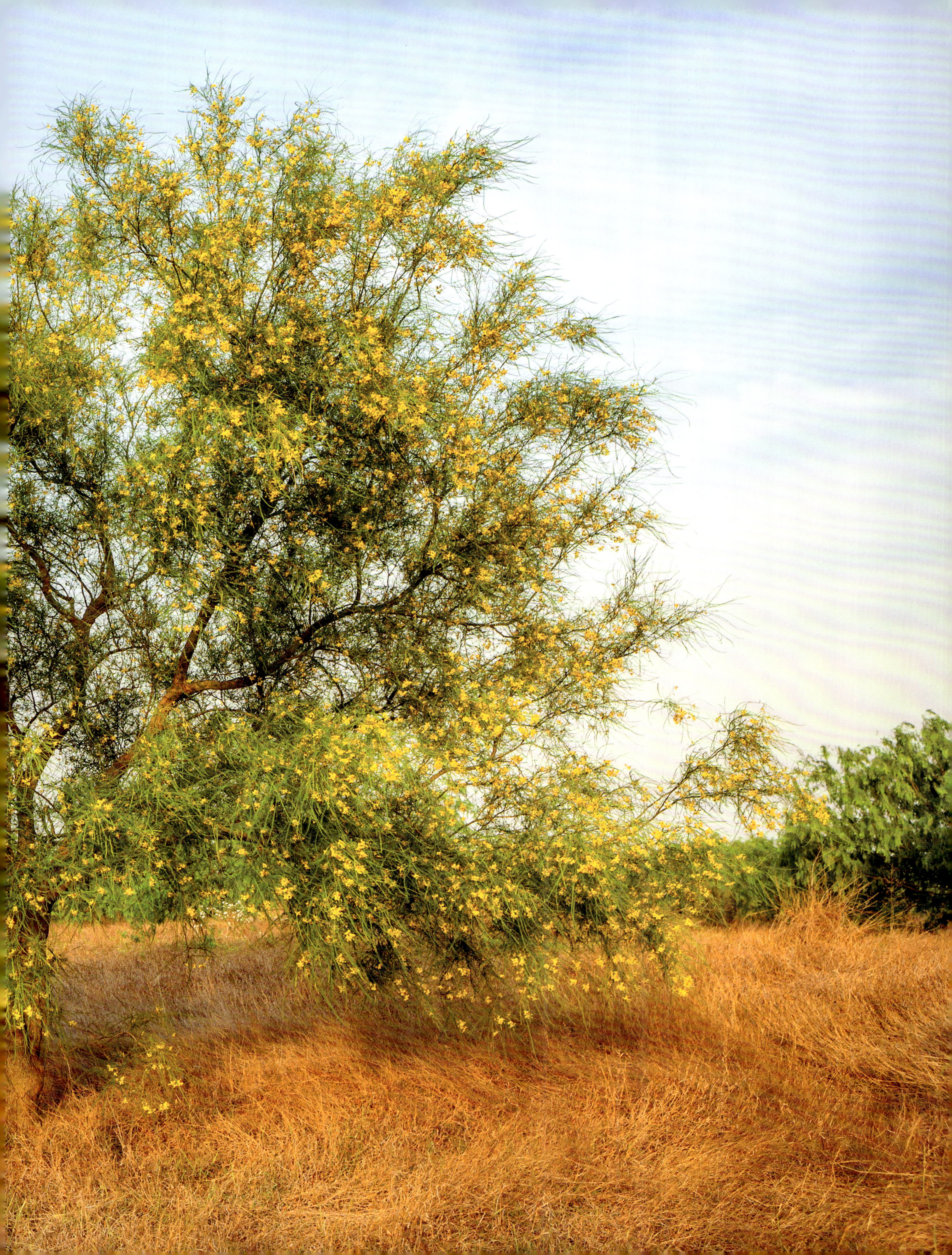

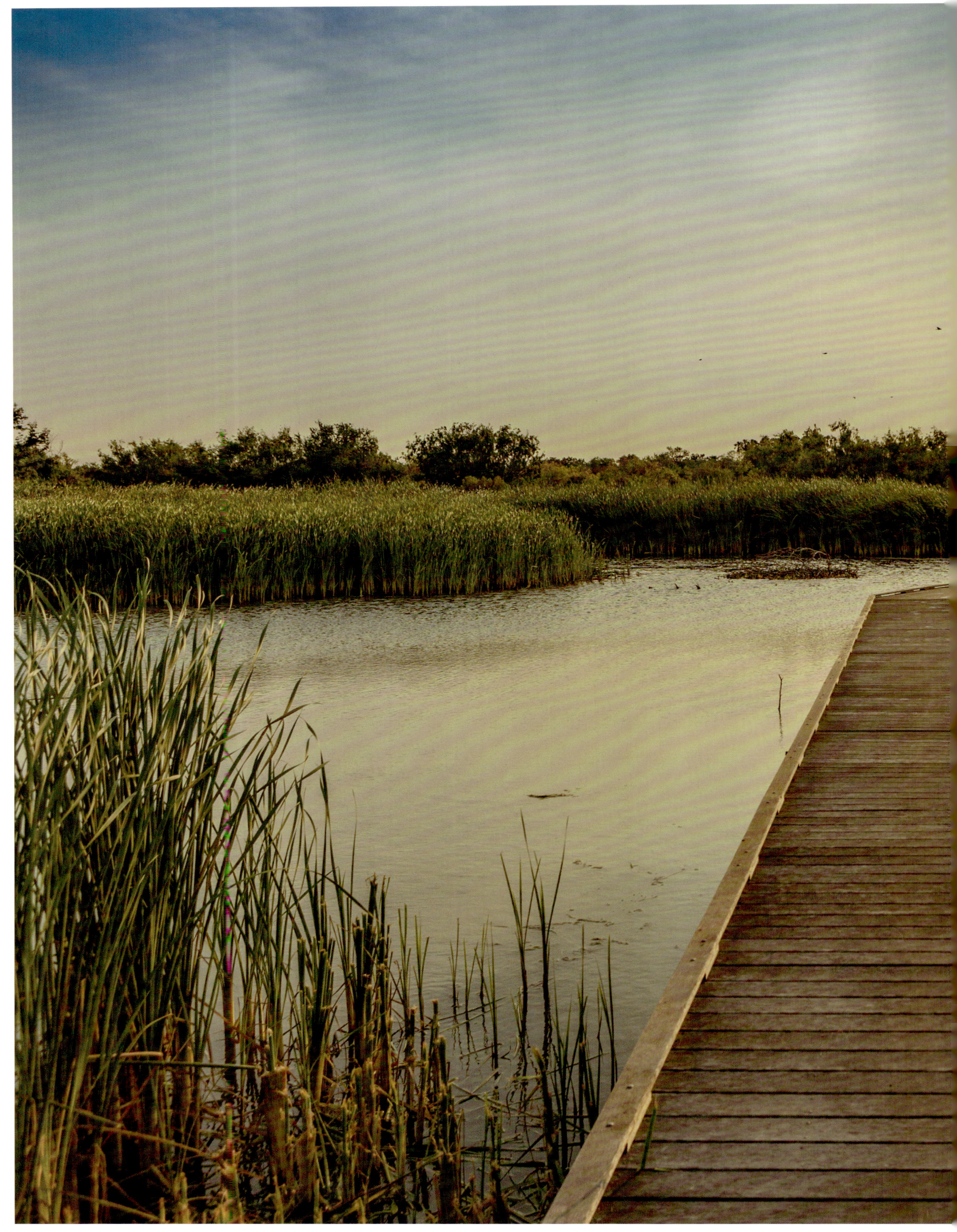

BOARDWALK Estero Llano Grande State Park, near Weslaco, 2011

IBIS POND Estero Llano Grande State Park, near Weslaco, 2011 >

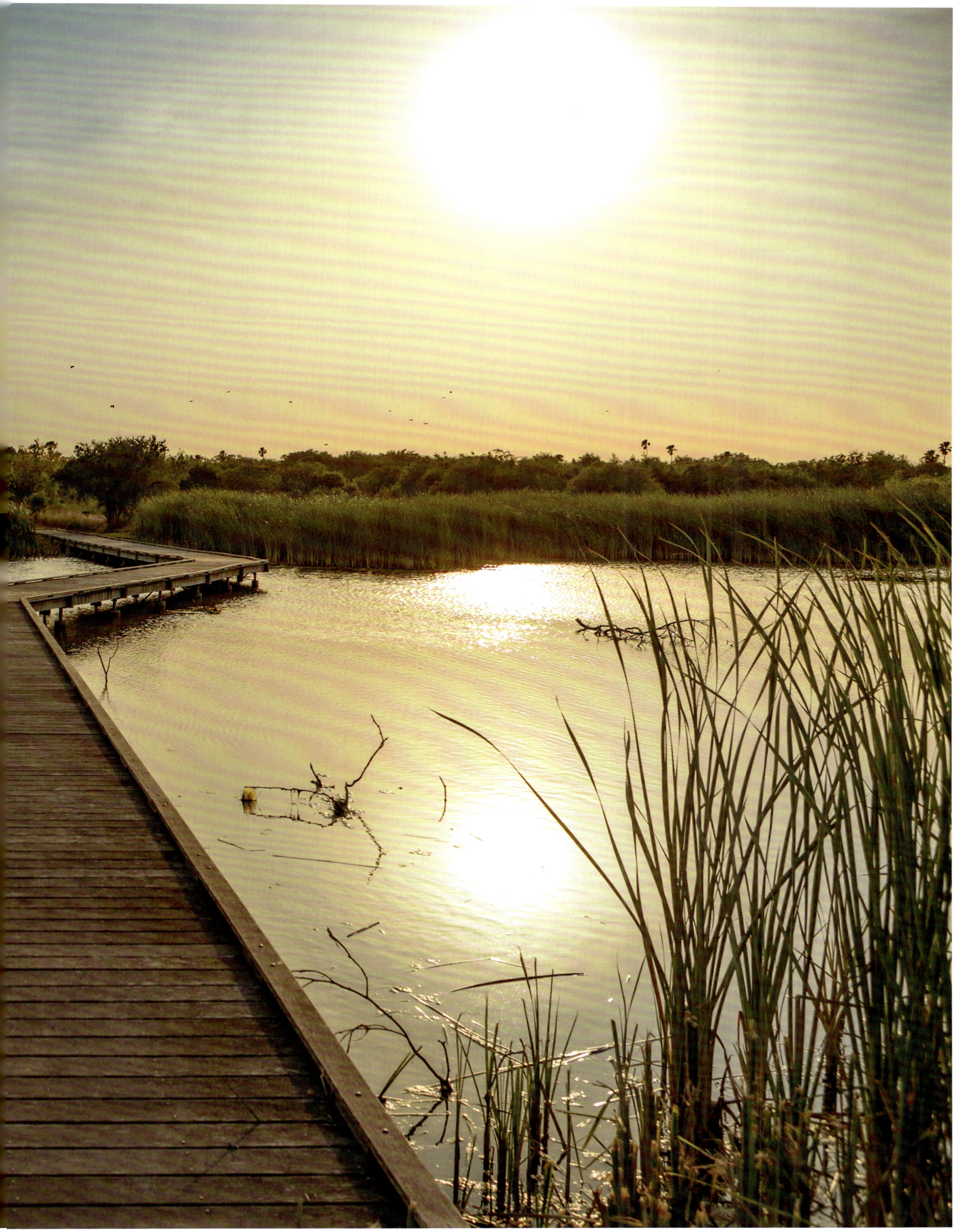

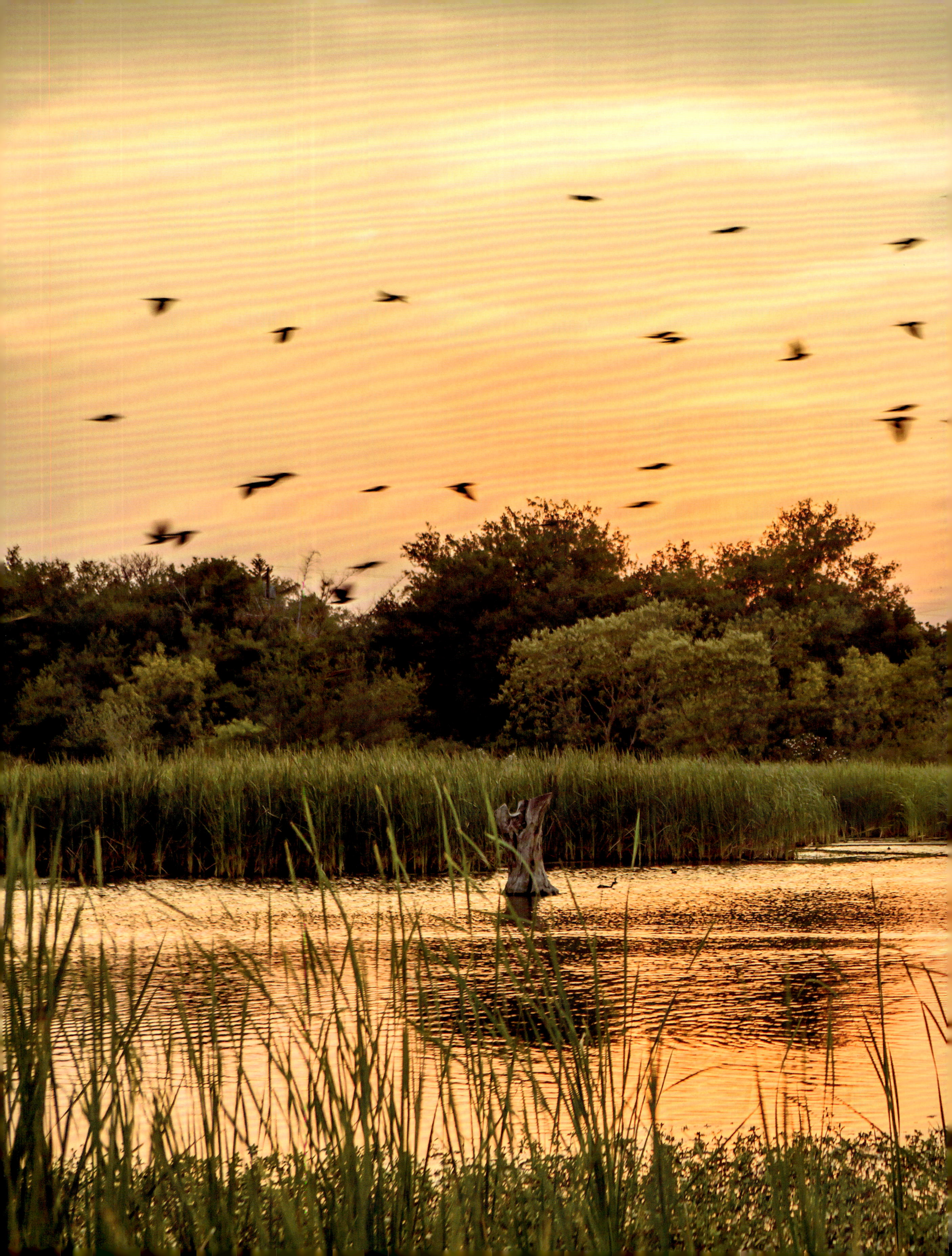

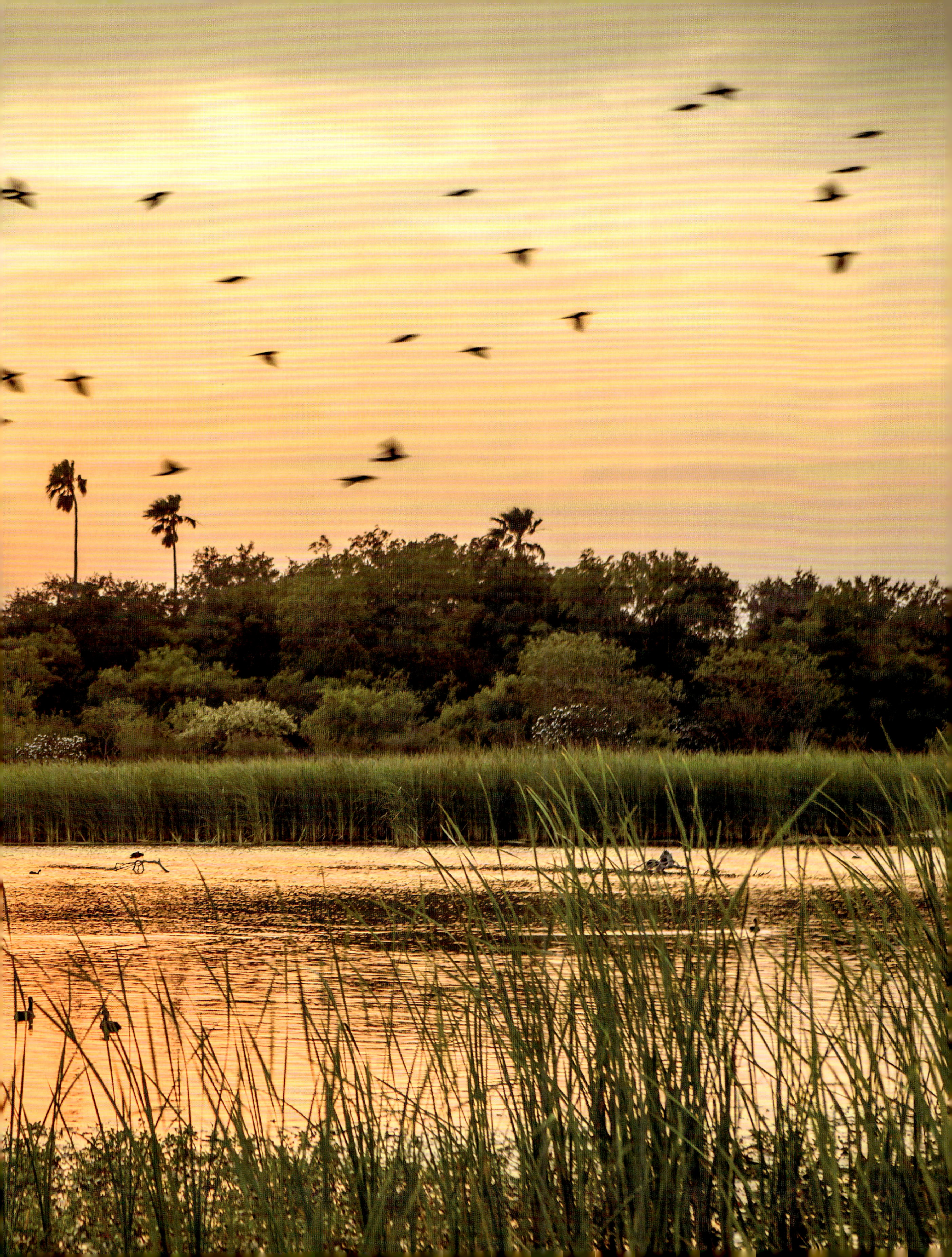

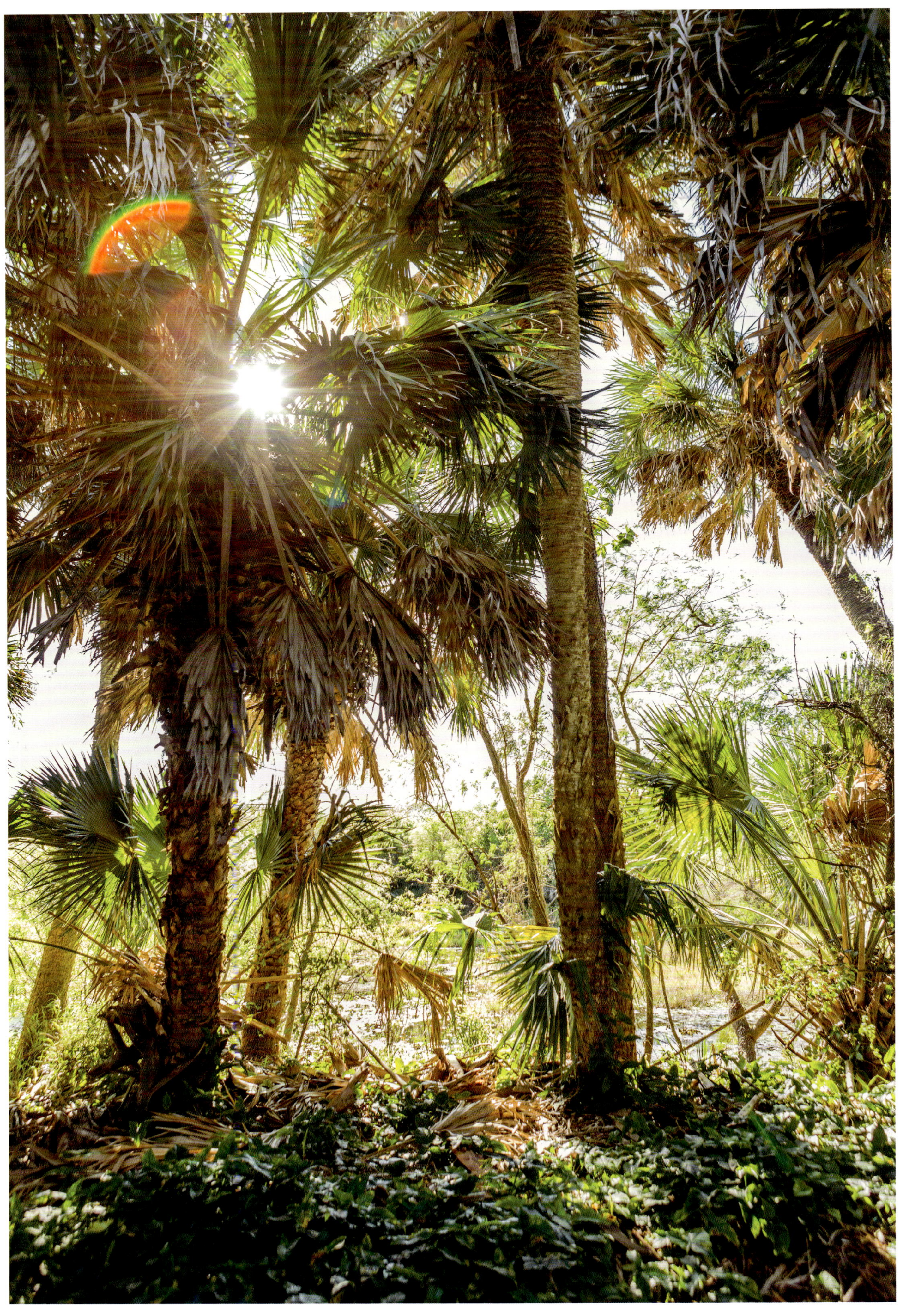

SABAL PALM SANCTUARY Brownsville, 2017

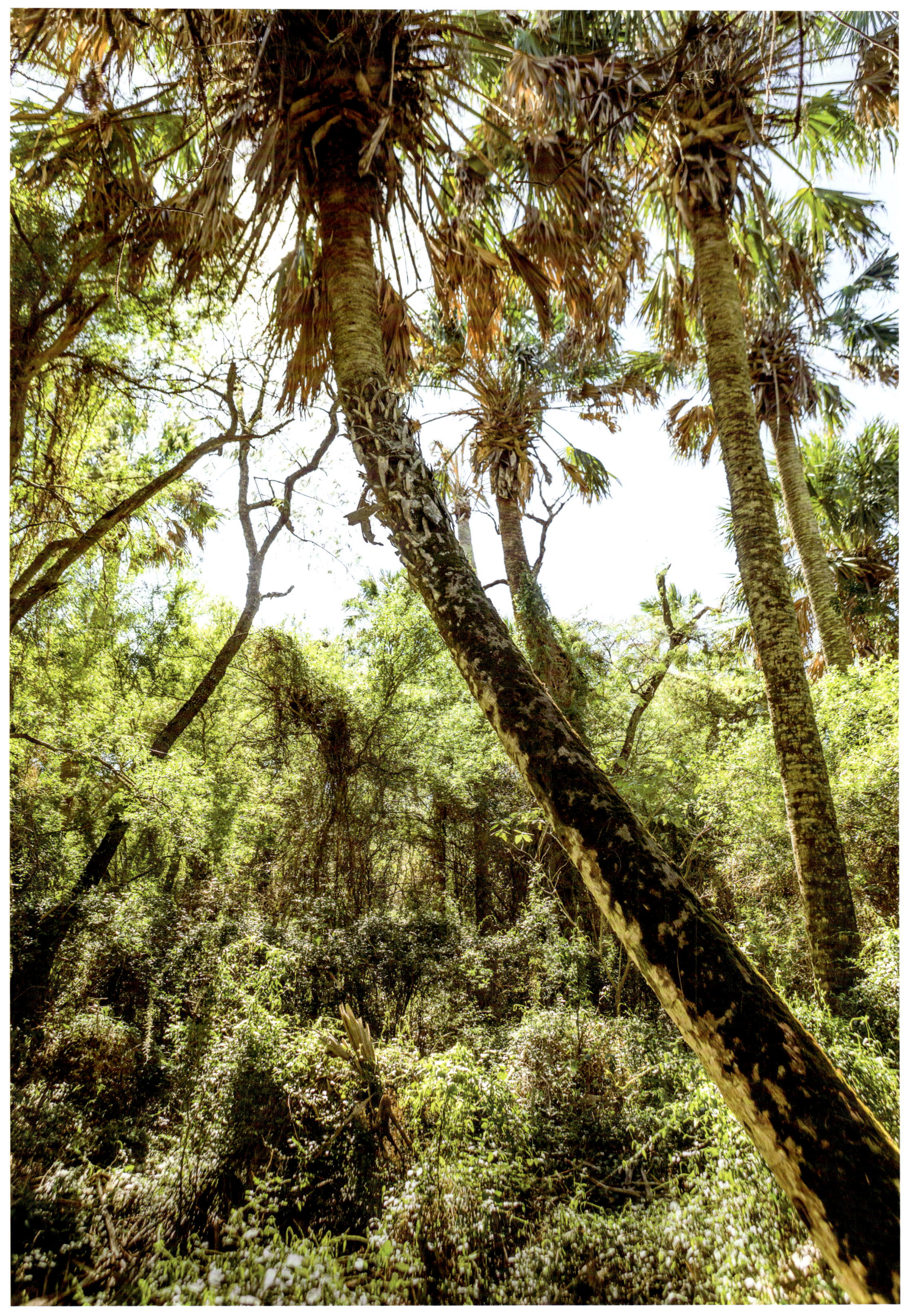

GRAPEFRUIT grapefruit grove, near Edinburg, 2017

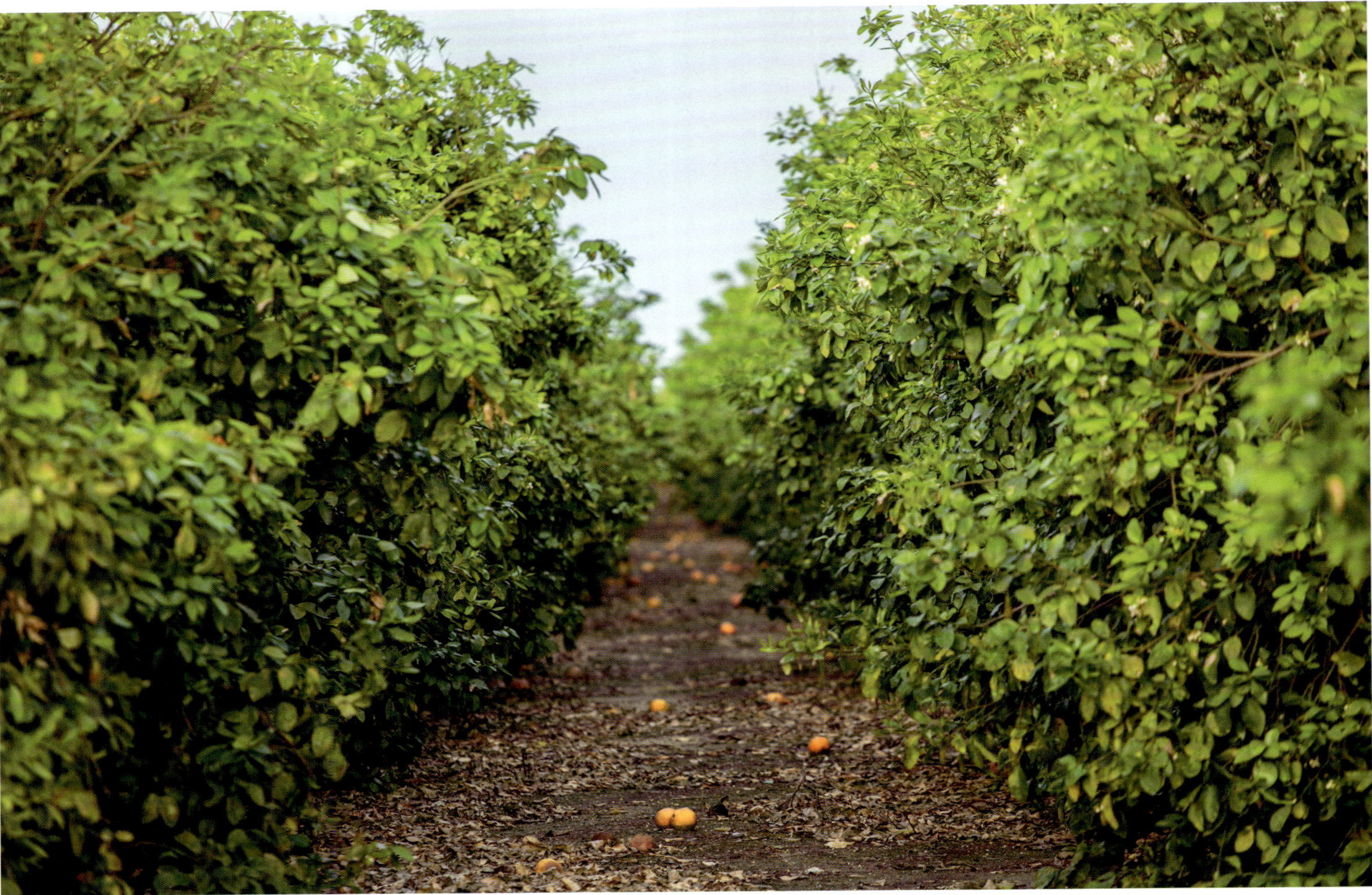

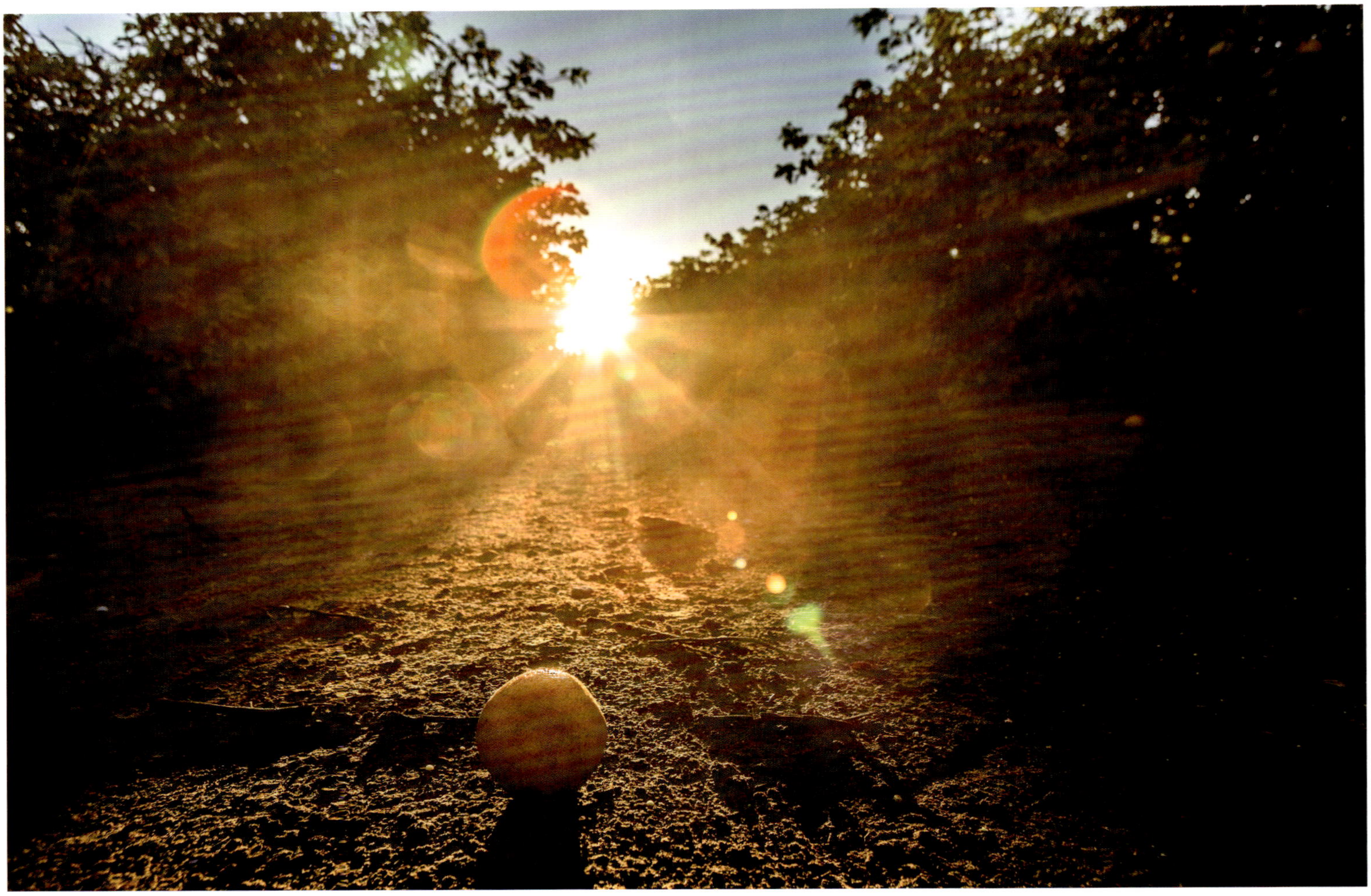

FALLEN FRUIT grapefruit grove, near Edinburg, 2017

RUBY REDS, grapefruit grove, near Edinburg, 2017

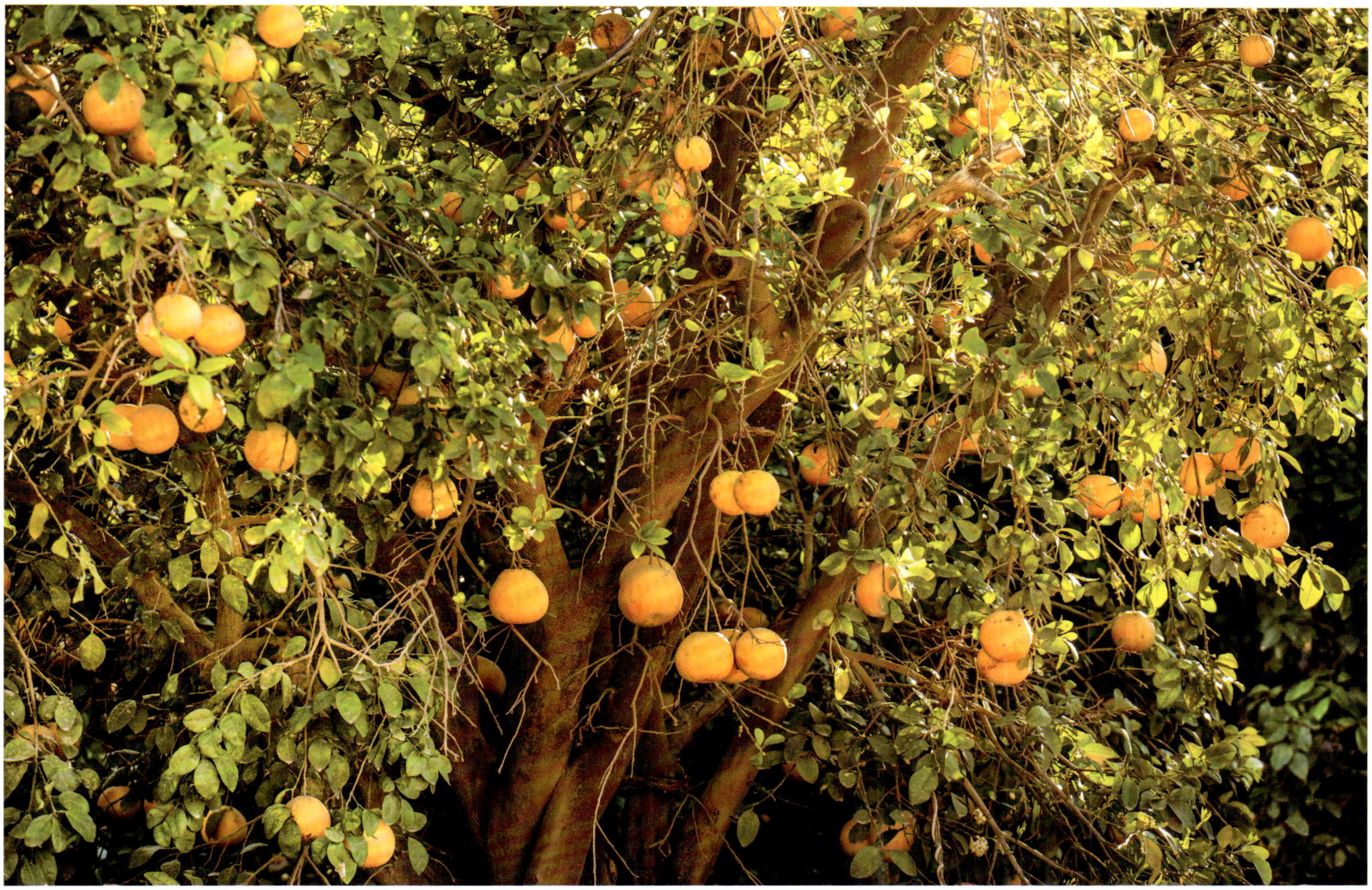

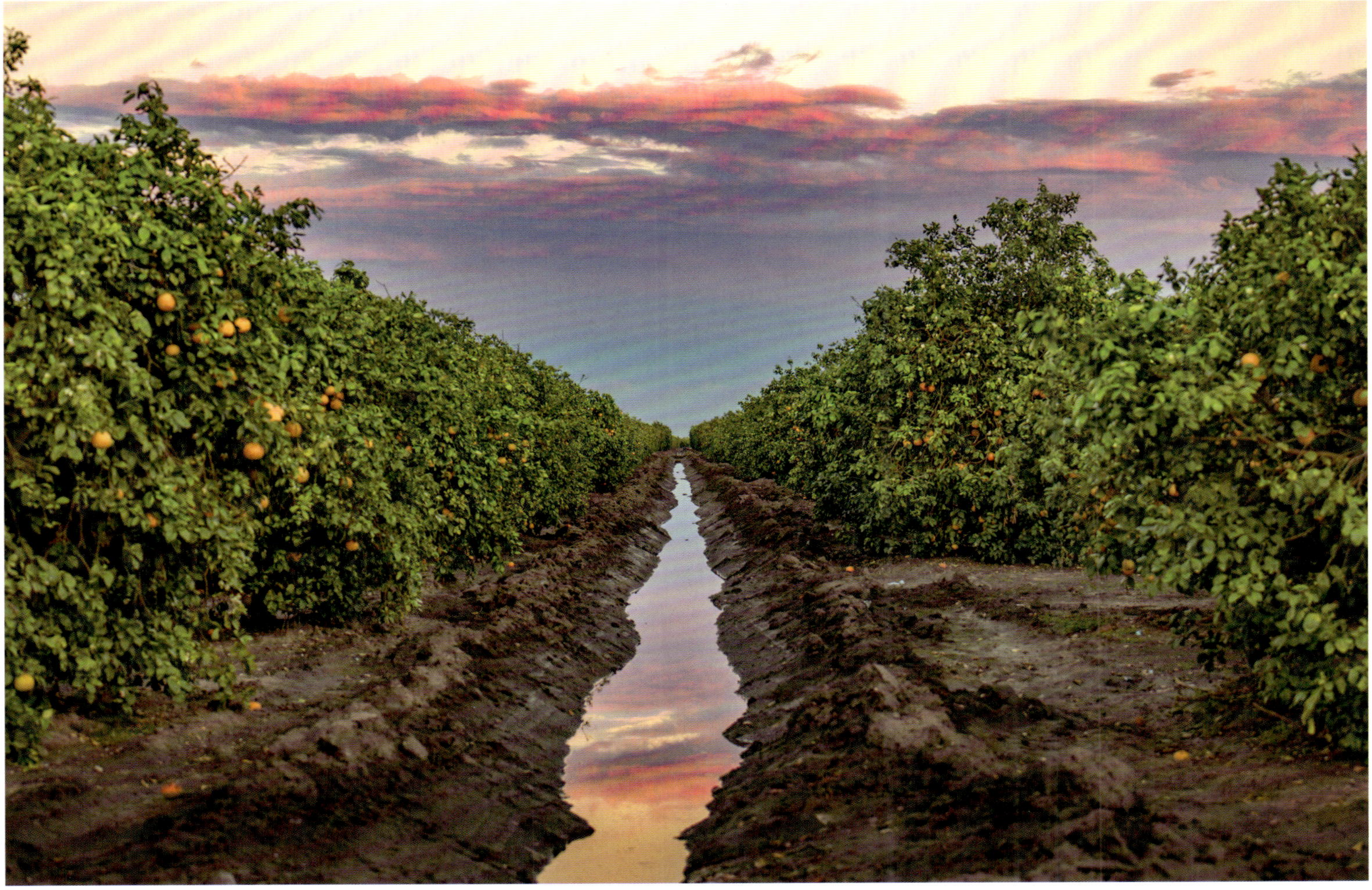

IRRIGATION CHANNEL grapefruit grove, near Edinburg, 2017

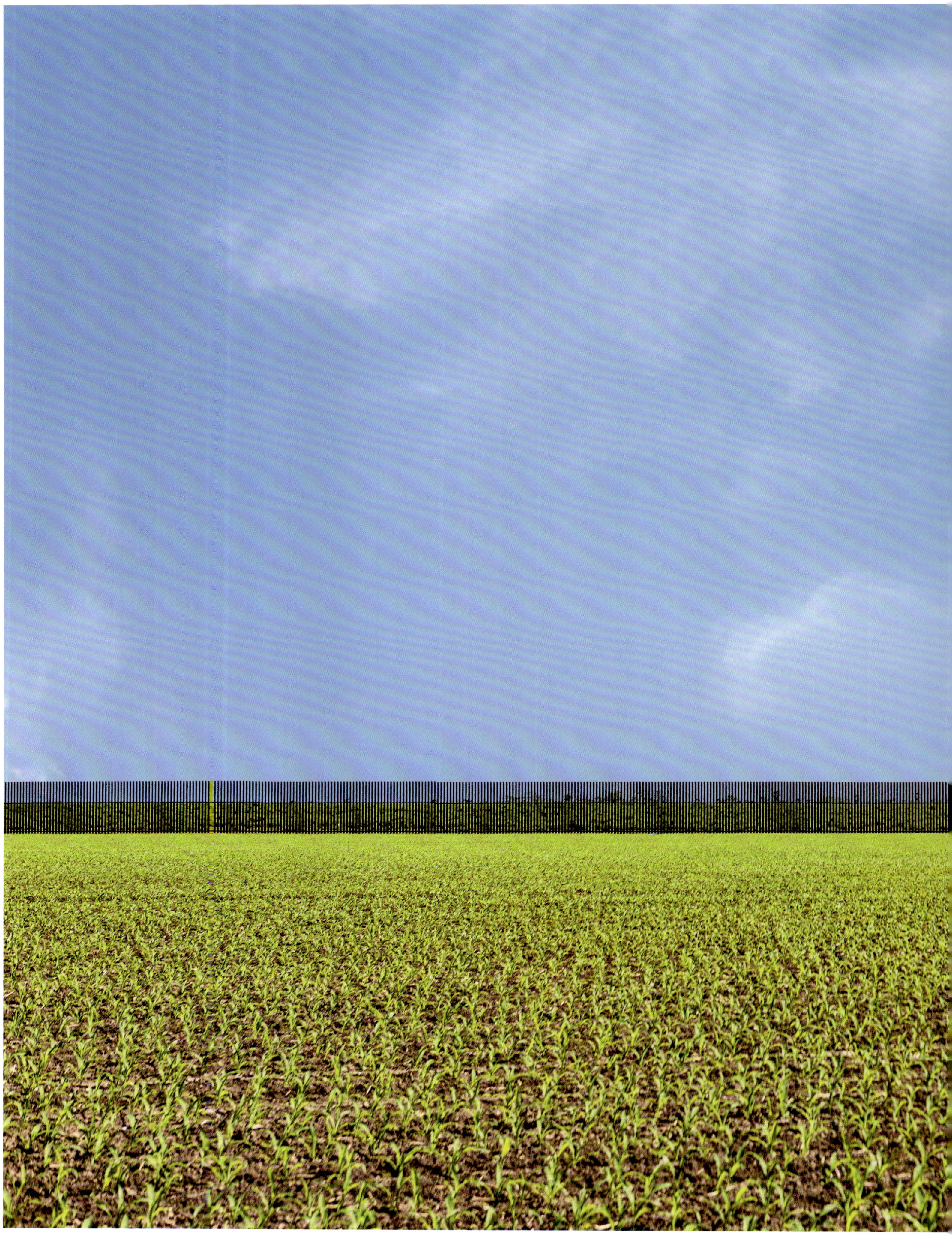

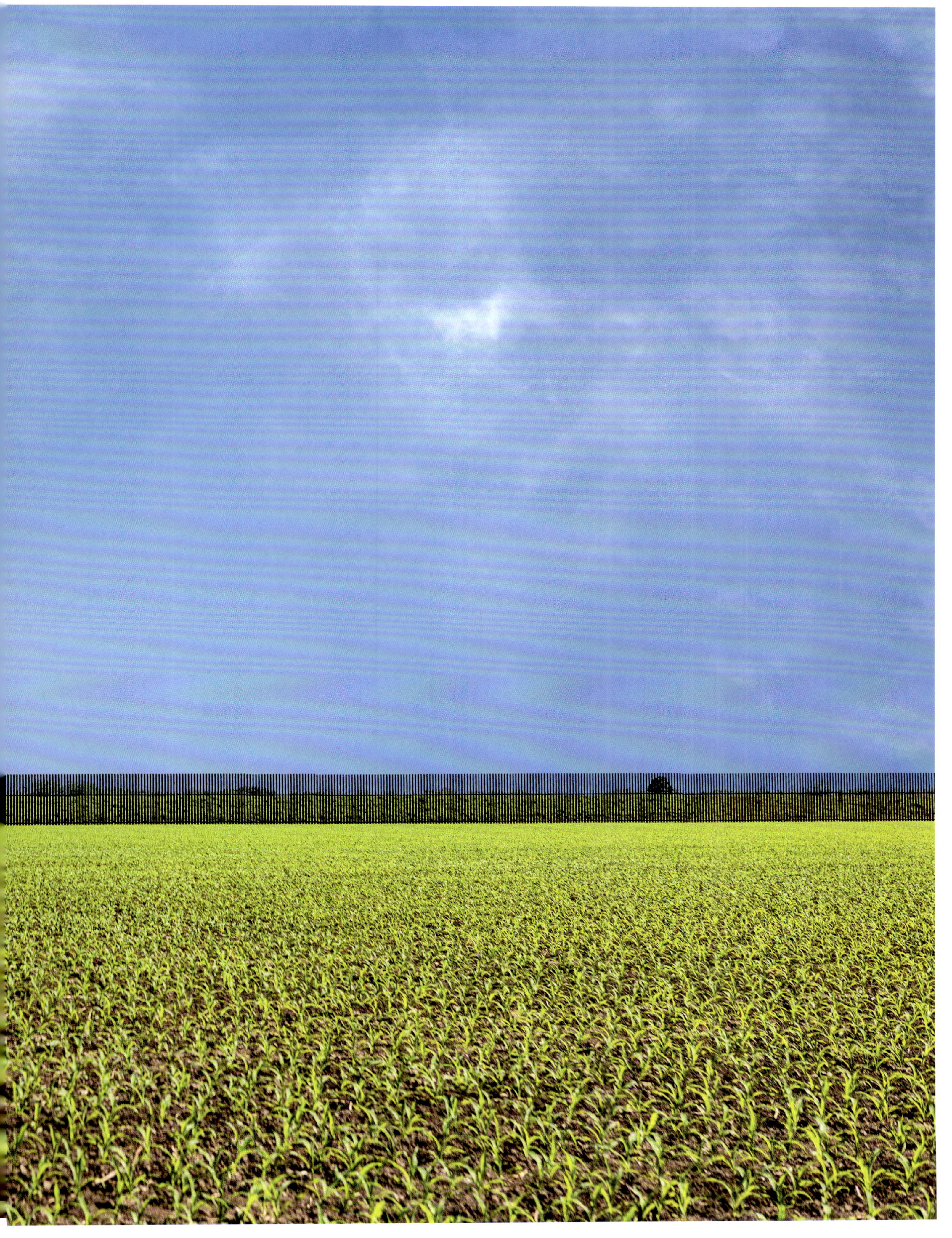

BORDER FENCE near Brownsville, 2017